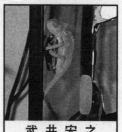

武井宏之
(This is my chameleon.)

We've made the 20-volume mark at last...
but I almost want to yell at myself because
the story's stuck here! Actually, we are
finally moving past the midpoint of the
story. I'm thinking about really spicing
things up after the "Epilogue" arc. Please
stick with me a little longer. Enjoy!

—Hiroyuki Takei

Unconventional author/artist Hiroyuki Takei began his
career by winning the coveted Hop Step Award (for new
manga artists) and the Osamu Tezuka Award (named after
the famous artist of the same name). After working as an
assistant to famed artist Nobuhiro Watsuki, Takei debuted
in **Weekly Shonen Jump** in 1997 with **Butsu Zone**, an
action series based on Buddhist mythology. His multi-
cultural adventure manga **Shaman King**, which debuted
in 1998, became a hit and was adapted into an anime TV
series. Takei lists Osamu Tezuka, American comics and
robot anime among his many influences.

SHAMAN KING VOL. 20
The SHONEN JUMP Manga Edition

STORY AND ART BY
HIROYUKI TAKEI

English Adaptation/Lance Caselman
Translation/Lillian Olsen
Touch-up Art & Lettering/John Hunt
Design/Nozomi Akashi
Editor/Carol Fox

Editor in Chief, Books/Alvin Lu
Editor in Chief, Magazines/Marc Weidenbaum
VP, Publishing Licensing/Rika Inouye
VP, Sales & Product Marketing/Gonzalo Ferreyra
VP, Creative/Linda Espinosa
Publisher/Hyoe Narita

Printed in the U.S.A.

Published by VIZ Media, LLC
P.O. Box 77010
San Francisco, CA 94107

SHONEN JUMP Manga Edition
10 9 8 7 6 5 4 3 2 1
First printing, January 2009

T 252534

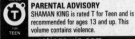

PARENTAL ADVISORY
SHAMAN KING is rated T for Teen and is
recommended for ages 13 and up. This
volume contains violence.
ratings.viz.com

THE WORLD'S
MOST POPULAR MANGA

www.viz.com

www.shonenjump.com

SHONEN JUMP MANGA

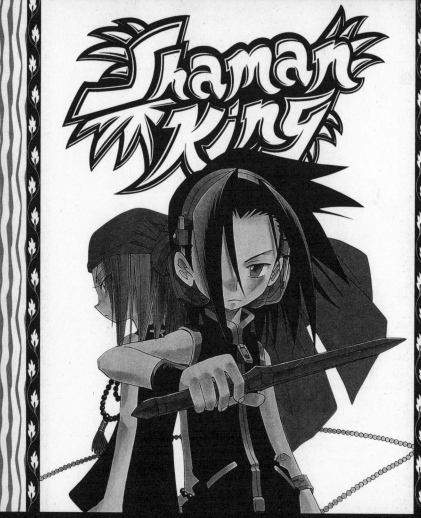

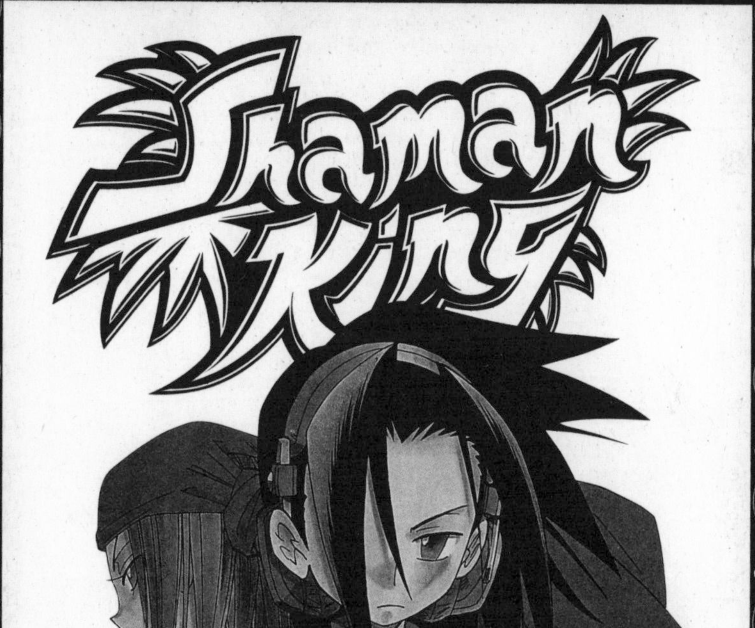
Shaman King

VOL. 20

EPILOGUE

STORY AND ART BY

HIROYUKI TAKEI

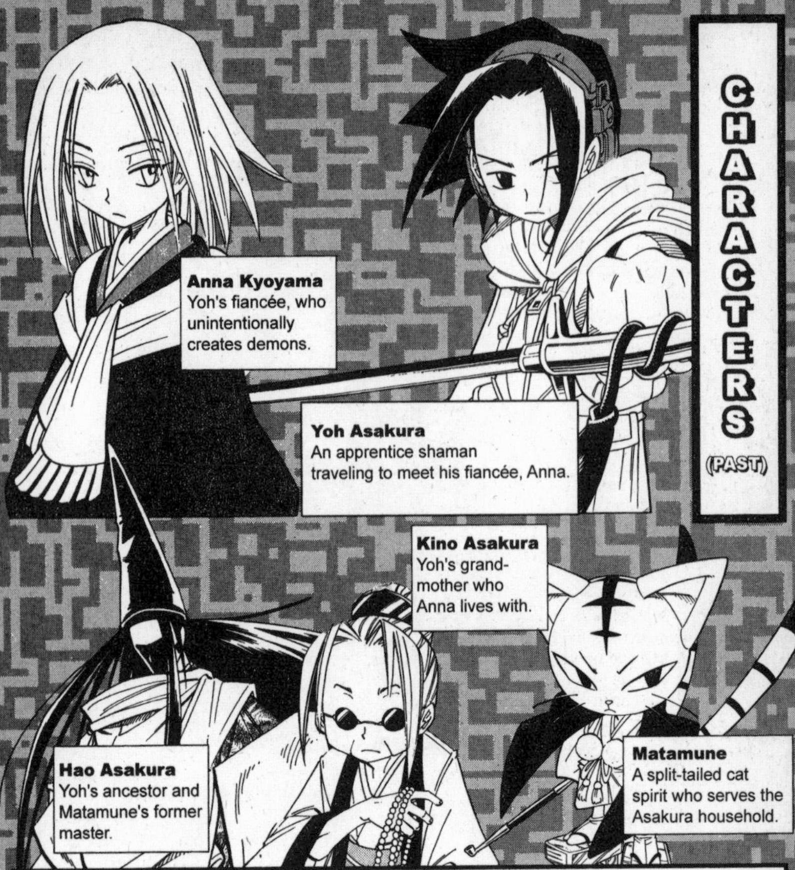
CHARACTERS
(PAST)
Anna Kyoyama
Yoh's fiancée, who unintentionally creates demons.
Yoh Asakura
An apprentice shaman traveling to meet his fiancée, Anna.
Kino Asakura
Yoh's grand-mother who Anna lives with.
Matamune
A split-tailed cat spirit who serves the Asakura household.
Hao Asakura
Yoh's ancestor and Matamune's former master.

THE STORY THUS FAR

Yoh Asakura not only sees dead people, he talks and fights with them, too. That's because Yoh is a shaman, a traditional holy man able to interact with the spirit world. Yoh is now a competitor in the Shaman Fight, a tournament held every 500 years to decide who will become the Shaman King and shape humanity's future.

When Ren is fatally wounded, Yoh promises Lady Jeanne he will withdraw from the Shaman Fight if she will save Ren's life. When Anna finds out, she thinks back to when she and Yoh first met. Yoh had come to visit her with his first spirit ally, a thousand-year-old cat named Matamune. But soon Yoh and Matamune found themselves facing menacing demons of Anna's own creation...

PRESENT

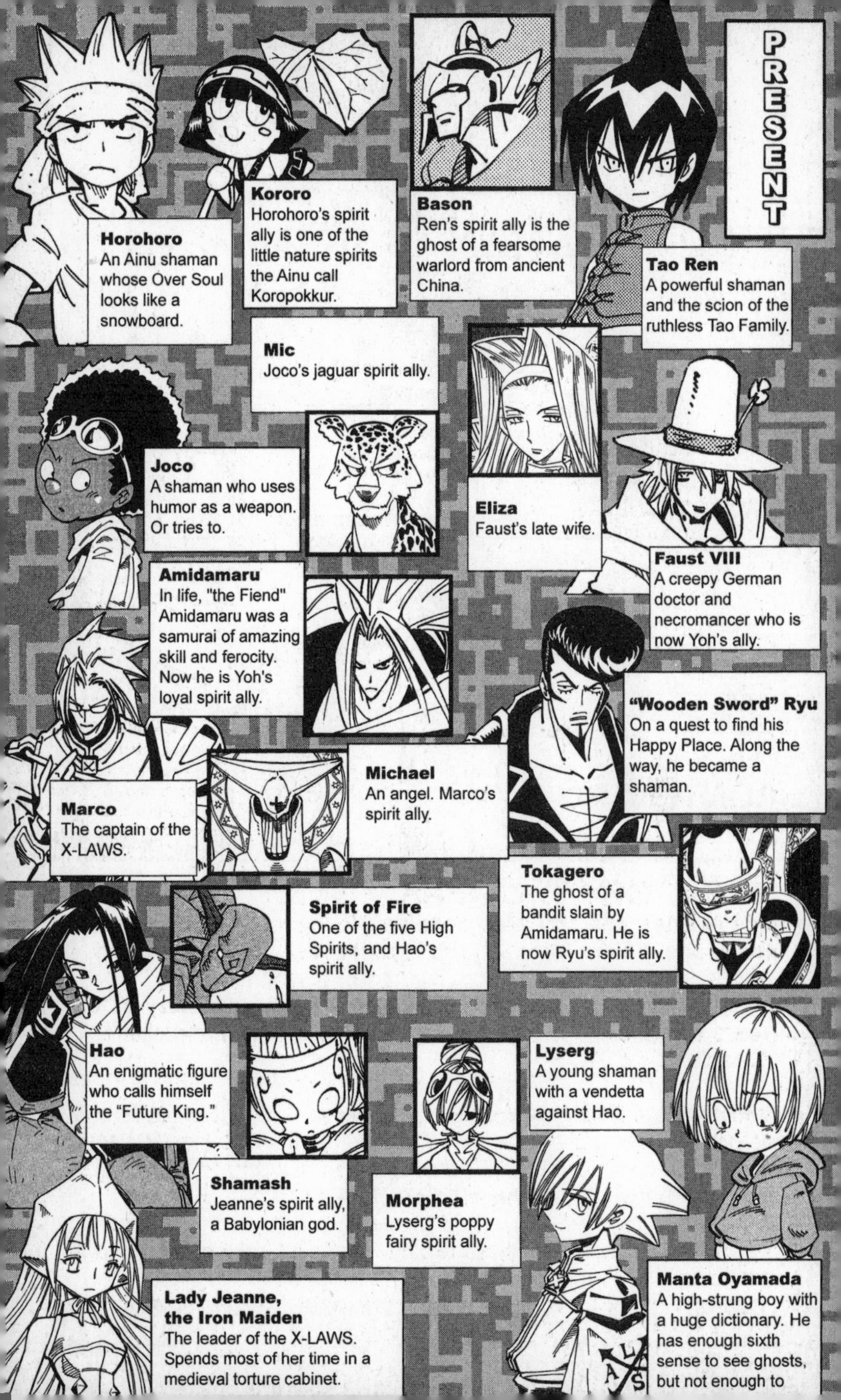

Horohoro
An Ainu shaman whose Over Soul looks like a snowboard.

Kororo
Horohoro's spirit ally is one of the little nature spirits the Ainu call Koropokkur.

Bason
Ren's spirit ally is the ghost of a fearsome warlord from ancient China.

Tao Ren
A powerful shaman and the scion of the ruthless Tao Family.

Mic
Joco's jaguar spirit ally.

Joco
A shaman who uses humor as a weapon. Or tries to.

Eliza
Faust's late wife.

Faust VIII
A creepy German doctor and necromancer who is now Yoh's ally.

Amidamaru
In life, "the Fiend" Amidamaru was a samurai of amazing skill and ferocity. Now he is Yoh's loyal spirit ally.

"Wooden Sword" Ryu
On a quest to find his Happy Place. Along the way, he became a shaman.

Marco
The captain of the X-LAWS.

Michael
An angel. Marco's spirit ally.

Spirit of Fire
One of the five High Spirits, and Hao's spirit ally.

Tokagero
The ghost of a bandit slain by Amidamaru. He is now Ryu's spirit ally.

Hao
An enigmatic figure who calls himself the "Future King."

Lyserg
A young shaman with a vendetta against Hao.

Shamash
Jeanne's spirit ally, a Babylonian god.

Morphea
Lyserg's poppy fairy spirit ally.

Lady Jeanne, the Iron Maiden
The leader of the X-LAWS. Spends most of her time in a medieval torture cabinet.

Manta Oyamada
A high-strung boy with a huge dictionary. He has enough sixth sense to see ghosts, but not enough to

SHAMAN KING 20
エピローグ
目 次

VOL. 20
EPILOGUE

CONTENTS

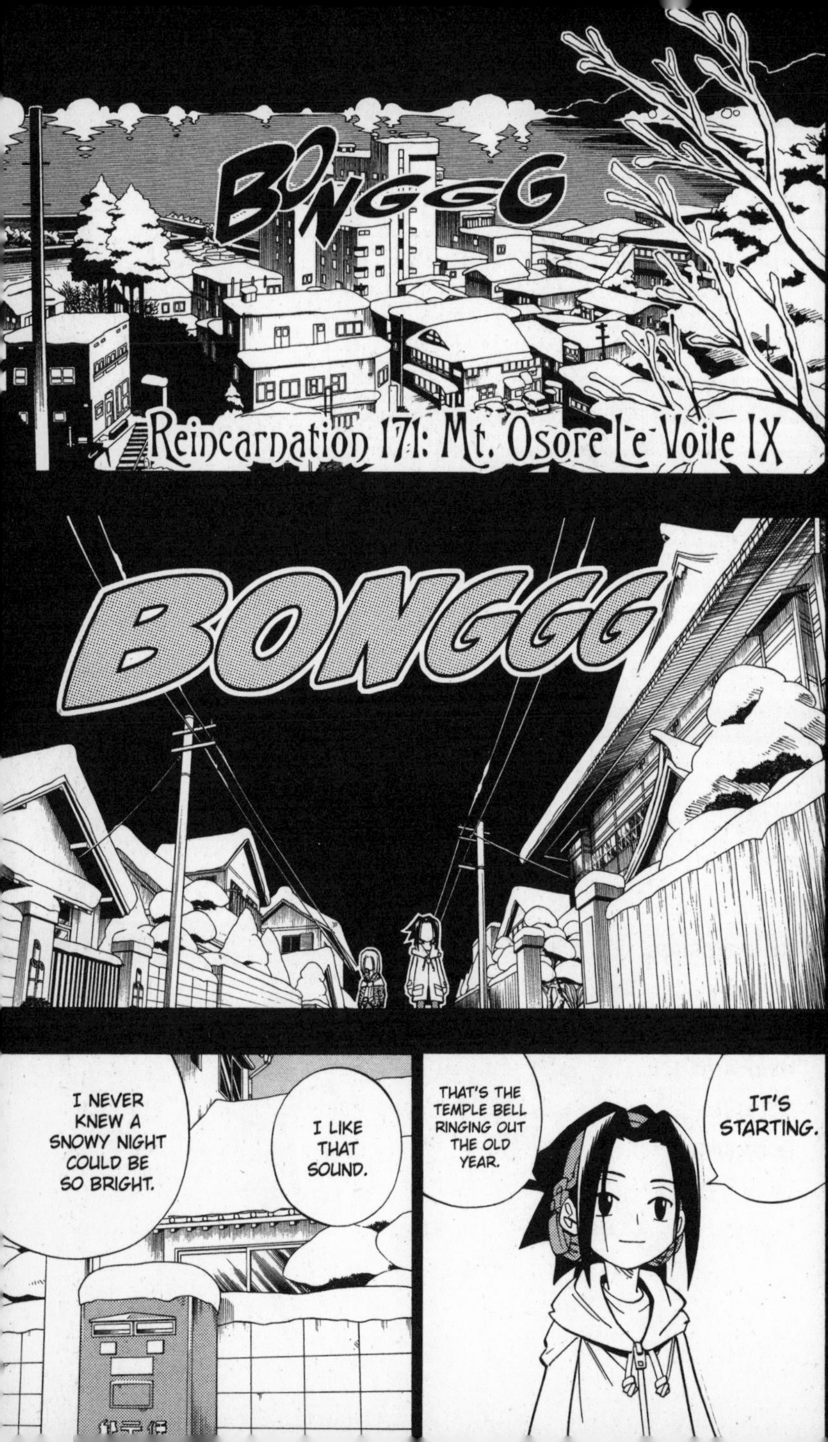
BONGGG
Reincarnation 171: Mt. Osore Le Voile IX
BONGGG
IT'S STARTING.
THAT'S THE TEMPLE BELL RINGING OUT THE OLD YEAR.
I LIKE THAT SOUND.
I NEVER KNEW A SNOWY NIGHT COULD BE SO BRIGHT.

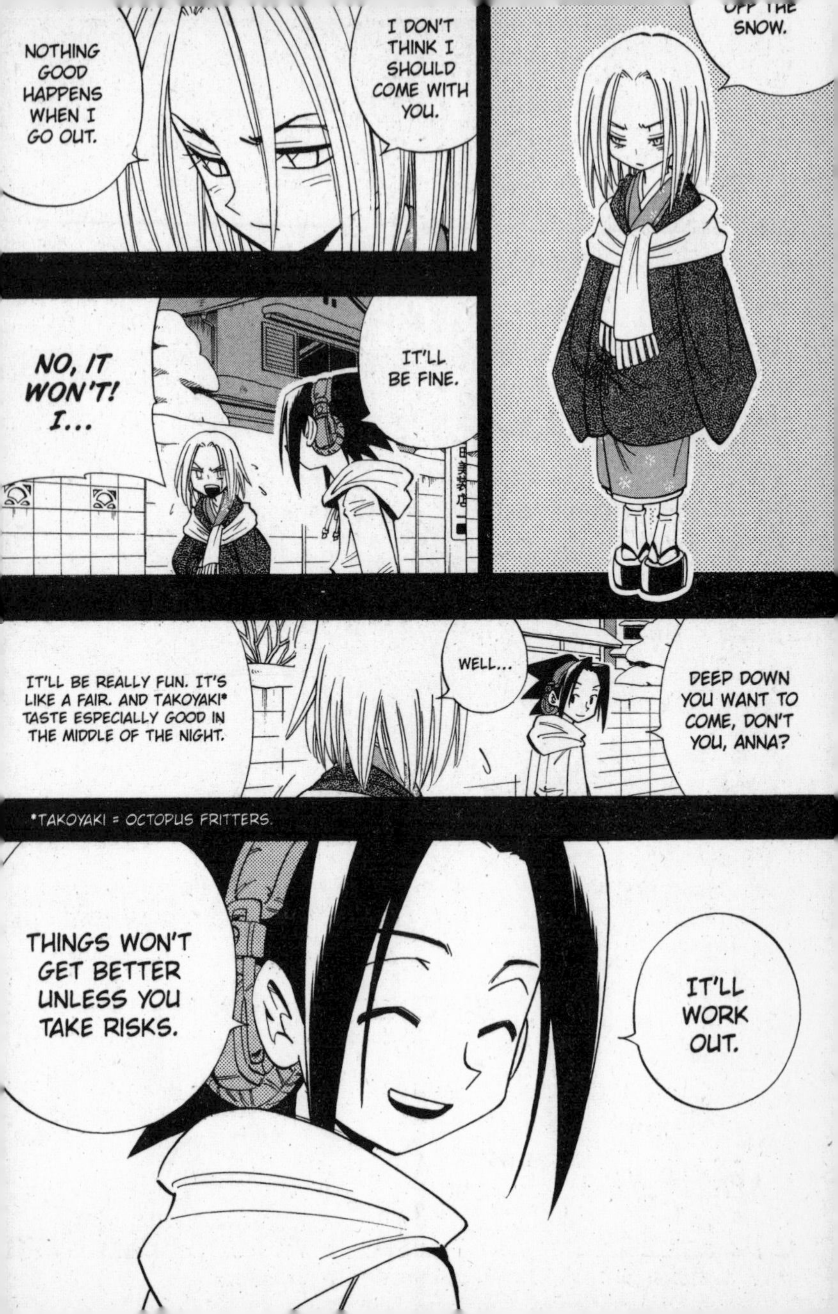
OFF THE SNOW.
I DON'T THINK I SHOULD COME WITH YOU.
NOTHING GOOD HAPPENS WHEN I GO OUT.
IT'LL BE FINE.
NO, IT WON'T! I...
DEEP DOWN YOU WANT TO COME, DON'T YOU, ANNA?
WELL...
IT'LL BE REALLY FUN. IT'S LIKE A FAIR. AND TAKOYAKI* TASTE ESPECIALLY GOOD IN THE MIDDLE OF THE NIGHT.
*TAKOYAKI = OCTOPUS FRITTERS.
IT'LL WORK OUT.
THINGS WON'T GET BETTER UNLESS YOU TAKE RISKS.

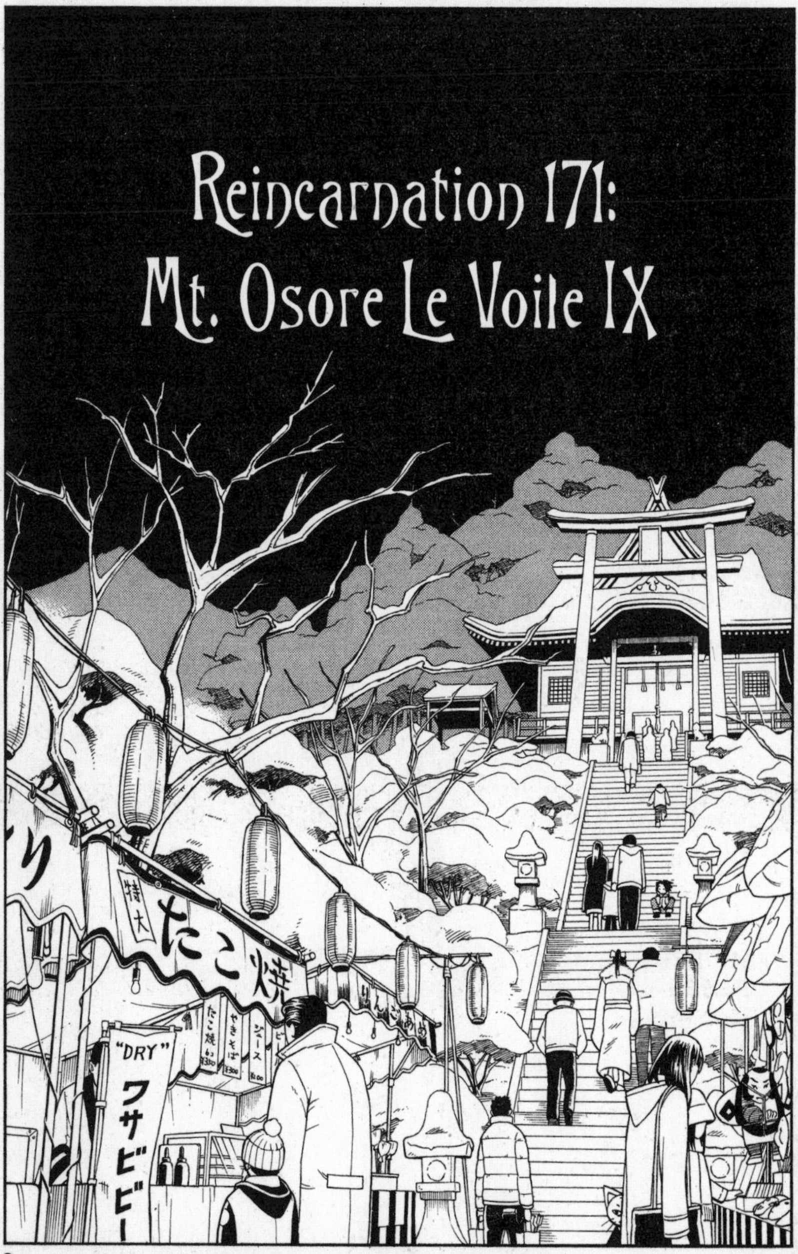
Reincarnation 171:
Mt. Osore Le Voile IX
特大
たこ焼
りんごあめ
たこ焼
やきそば
ジュース
"DRY"
ワサビビー

SIGNS: CANDY APPLES; TAKOYAKI; BEER; JUICE, YAKISOBA

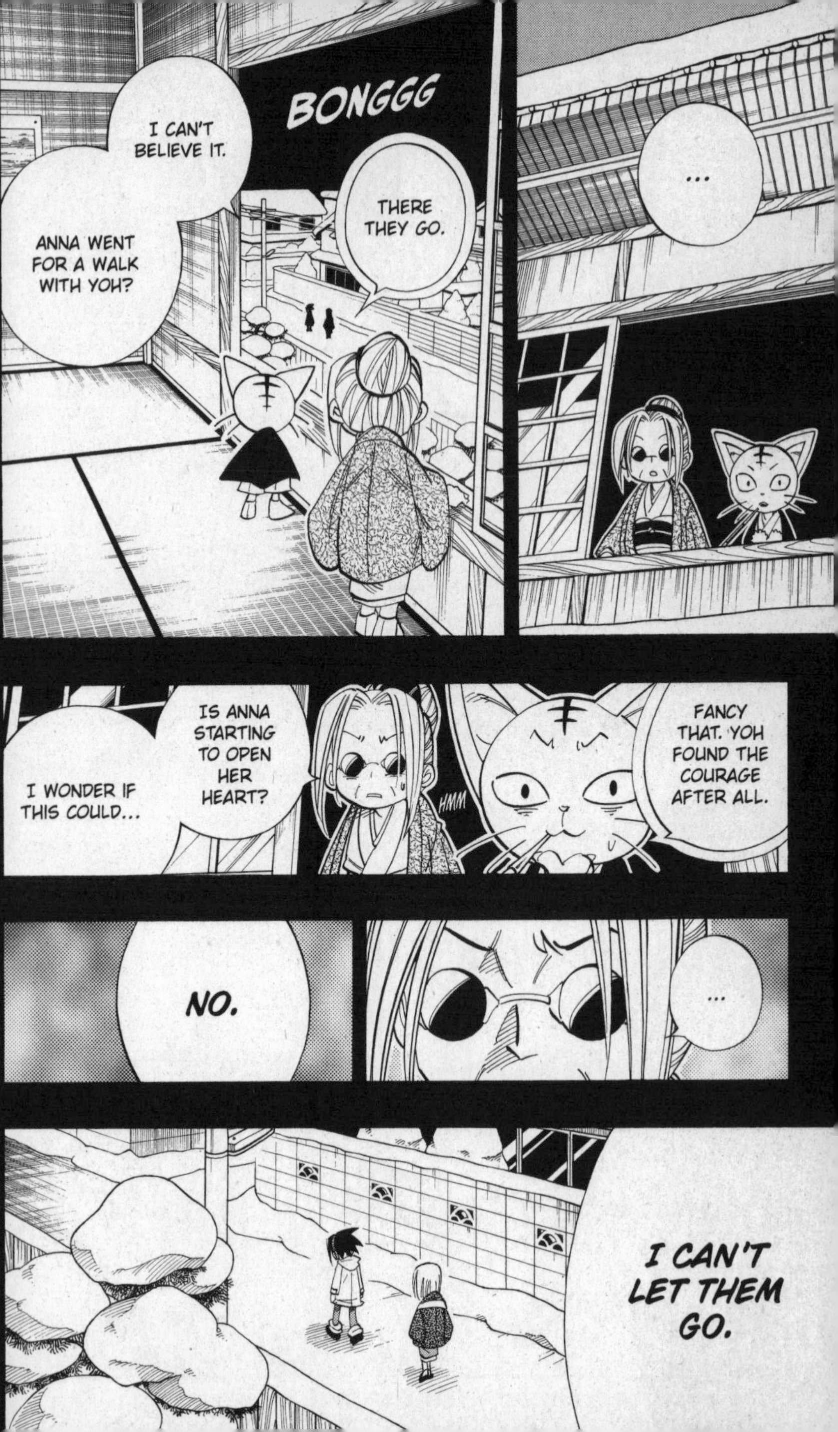
...
BONGGG
THERE THEY GO.
I CAN'T BELIEVE IT.
ANNA WENT FOR A WALK WITH YOH?
FANCY THAT. YOH FOUND THE COURAGE AFTER ALL.
HMM
IS ANNA STARTING TO OPEN HER HEART?
I WONDER IF THIS COULD...
...
NO.
I CAN'T LET THEM GO.

READ THIS WAY

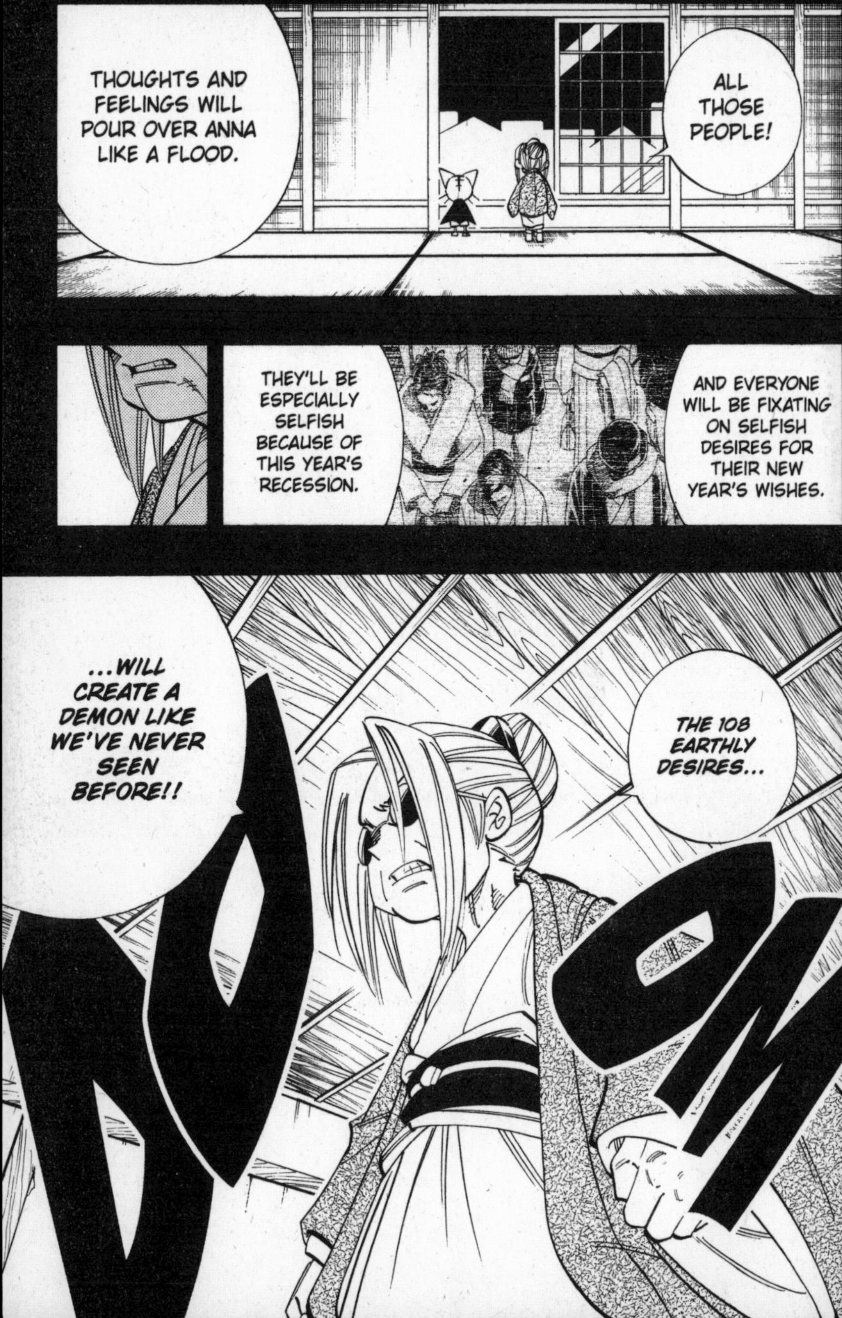
ALL THOSE PEOPLE!
THOUGHTS AND FEELINGS WILL POUR OVER ANNA LIKE A FLOOD.
AND EVERYONE WILL BE FIXATING ON SELFISH DESIRES FOR THEIR NEW YEAR'S WISHES.
THEY'LL BE ESPECIALLY SELFISH BECAUSE OF THIS YEAR'S RECESSION.
THE 108 EARTHLY DESIRES...
...WILL CREATE A DEMON LIKE WE'VE NEVER SEEN BEFORE!!

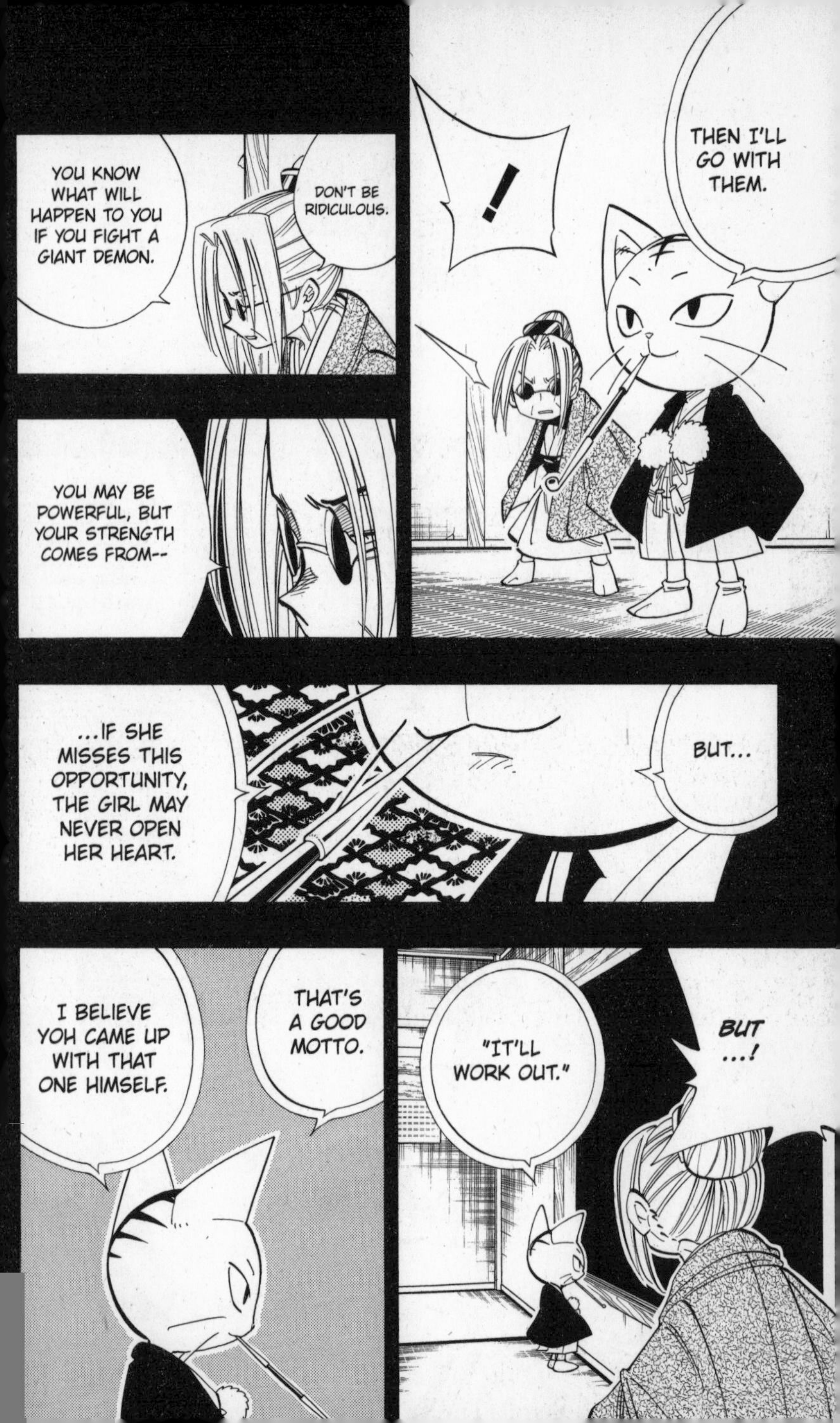
THEN I'LL GO WITH THEM.
!
DON'T BE RIDICULOUS.
YOU KNOW WHAT WILL HAPPEN TO YOU IF YOU FIGHT A GIANT DEMON.
YOU MAY BE POWERFUL, BUT YOUR STRENGTH COMES FROM--
BUT...
...IF SHE MISSES THIS OPPORTUNITY, THE GIRL MAY NEVER OPEN HER HEART.
BUT ...!
"IT'LL WORK OUT."
THAT'S A GOOD MOTTO.
I BELIEVE YOH CAME UP WITH THAT ONE HIMSELF.

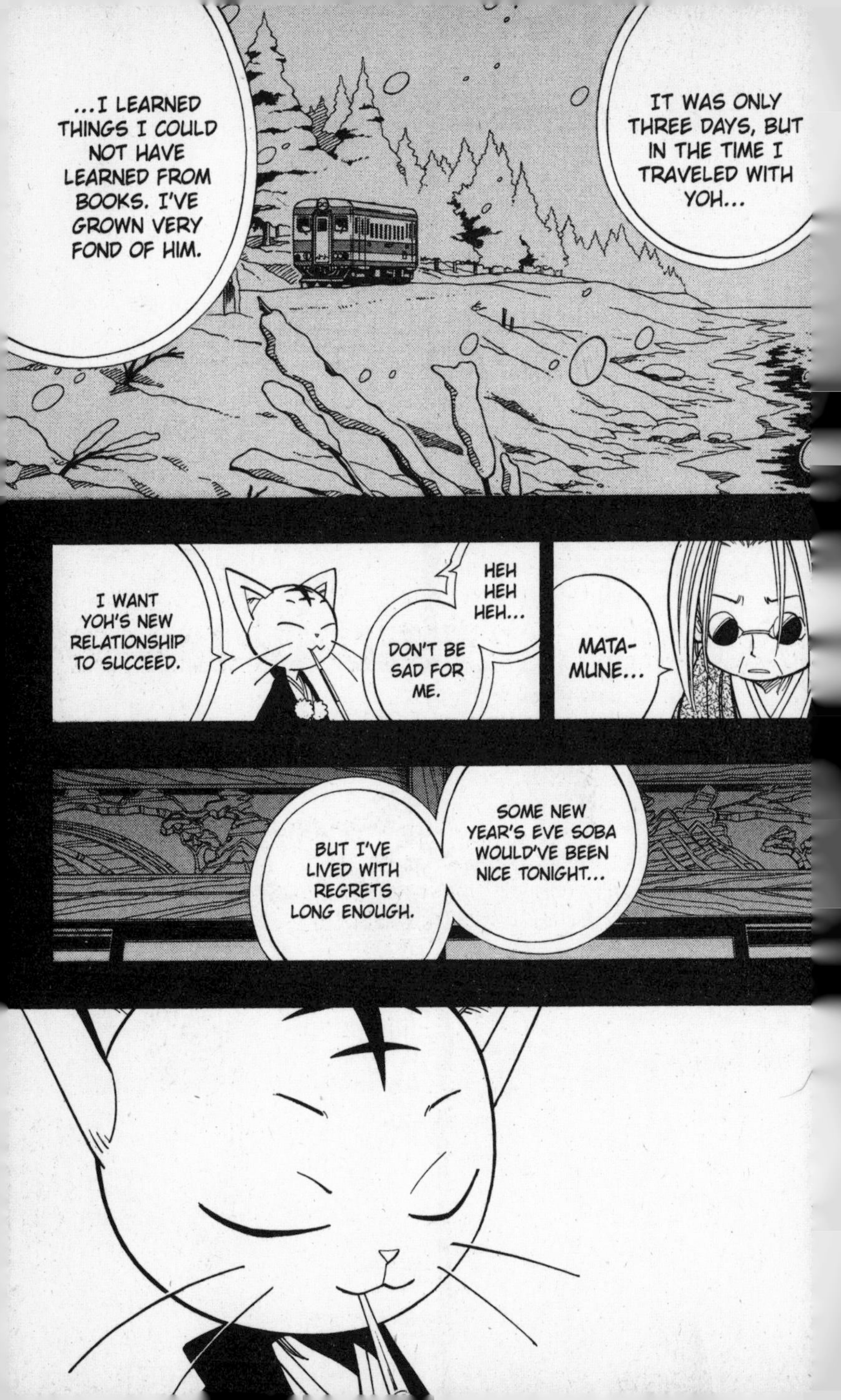
IT WAS ONLY THREE DAYS, BUT IN THE TIME I TRAVELED WITH YOH...
...I LEARNED THINGS I COULD NOT HAVE LEARNED FROM BOOKS. I'VE GROWN VERY FOND OF HIM.
MATA-MUNE...
HEH HEH HEH...
DON'T BE SAD FOR ME.
I WANT YOH'S NEW RELATIONSHIP TO SUCCEED.
SOME NEW YEAR'S EVE SOBA WOULD'VE BEEN NICE TONIGHT...
BUT I'VE LIVED WITH REGRETS LONG ENOUGH.

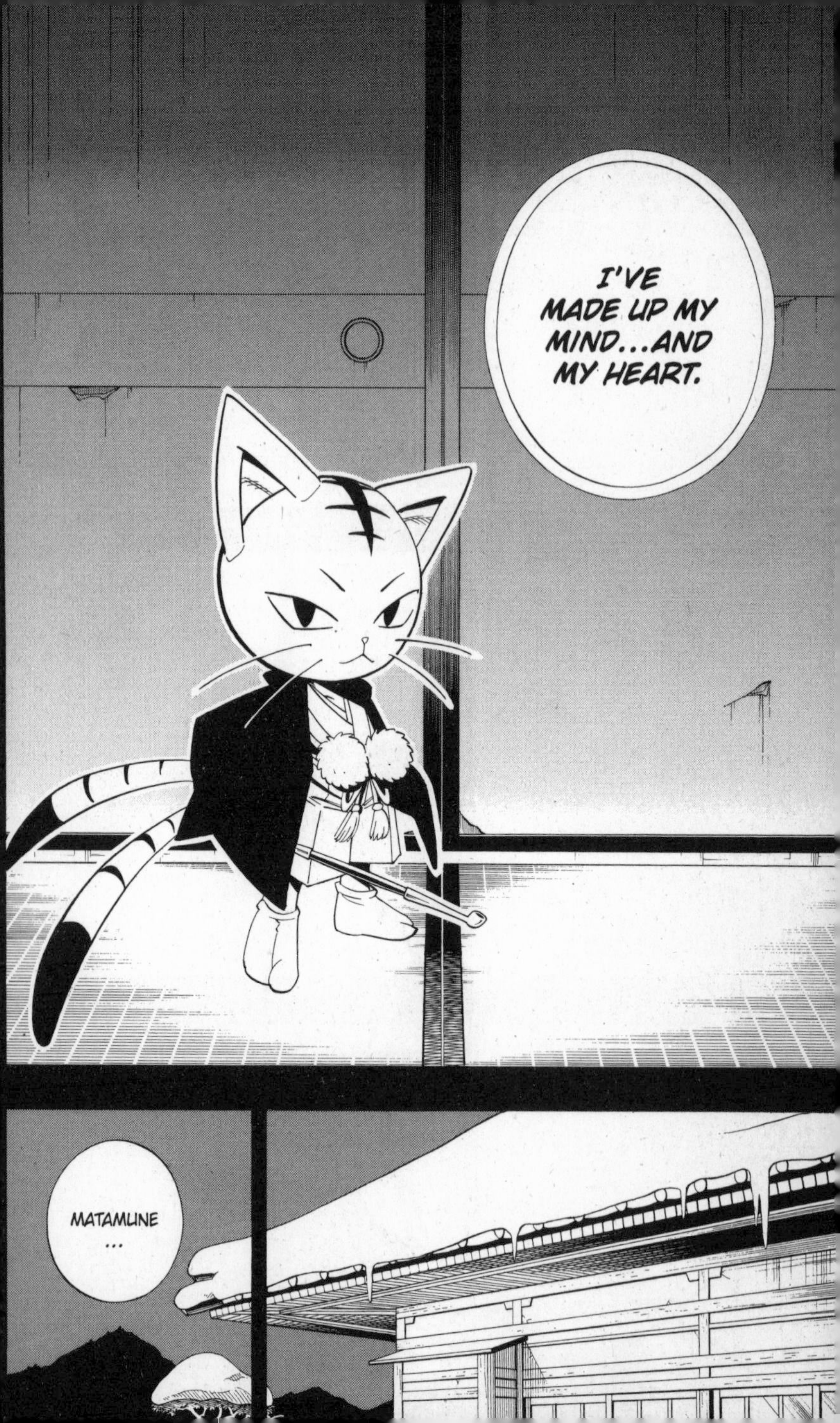
I'VE MADE UP MY MIND...AND MY HEART.
MATAMUNE ...

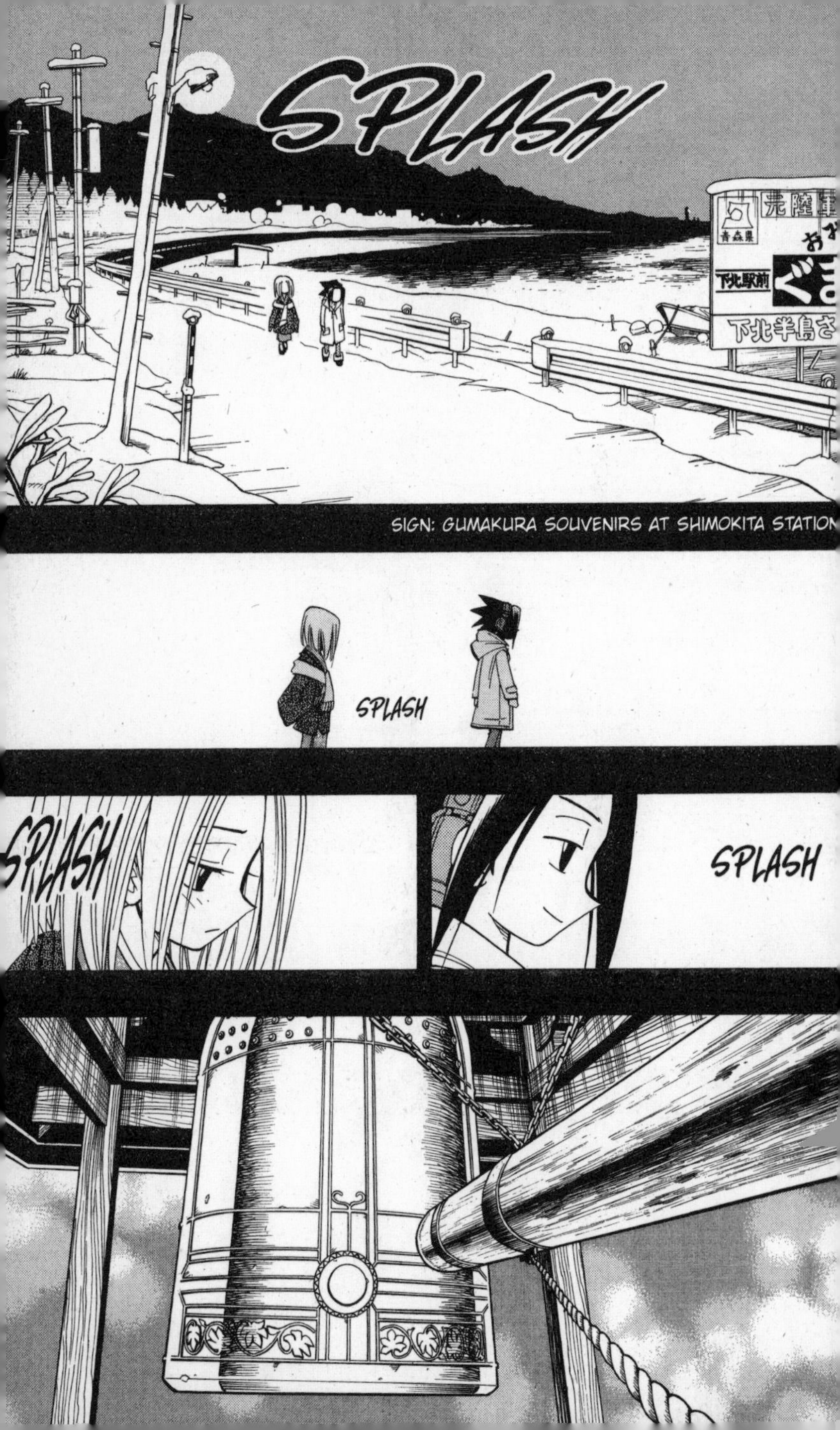
SPLASH
青森県
下北駅前
SIGN: GUMAKURA SOUVENIRS AT SHIMOKITA STATION
SPLASH
SPLASH
SPLASH

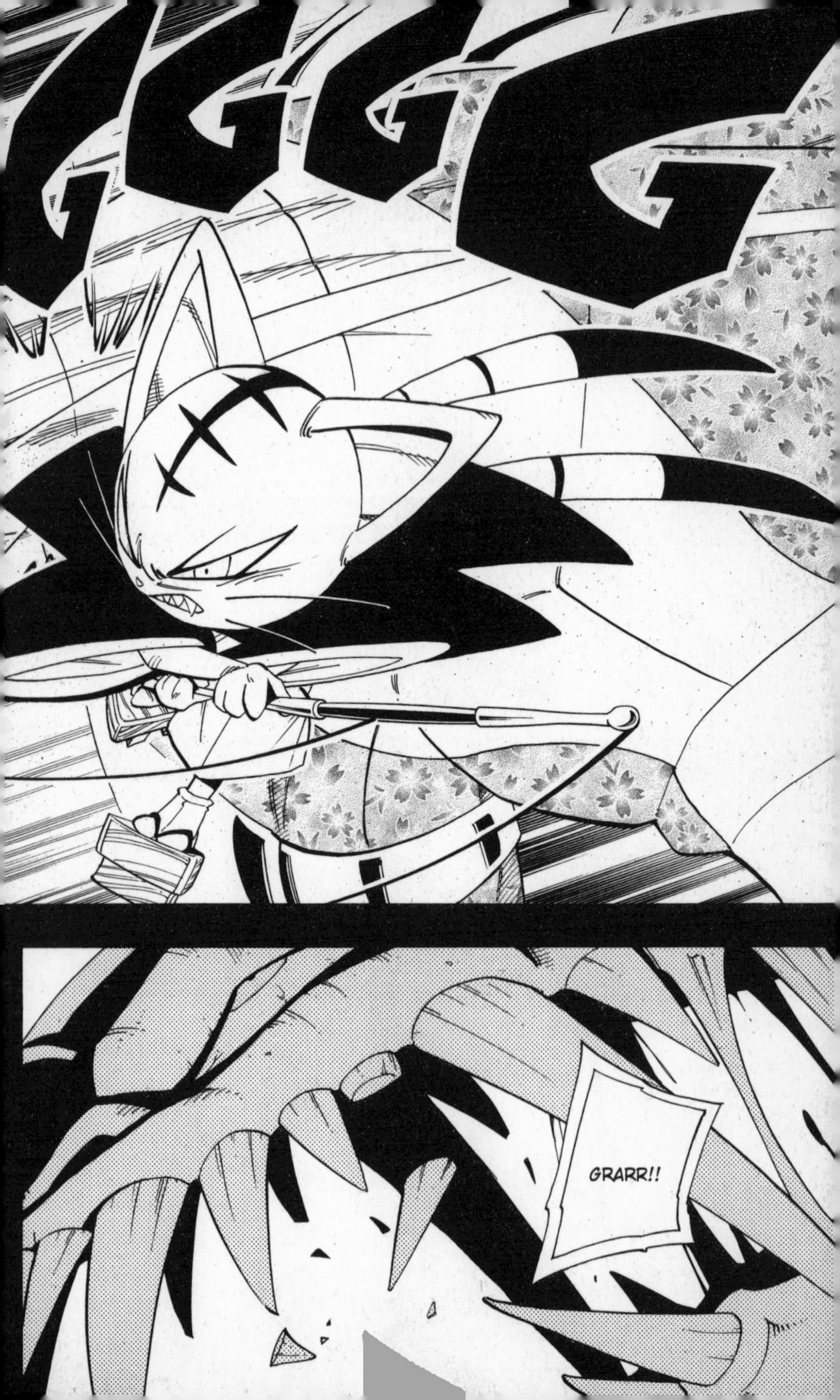
GRARR!!

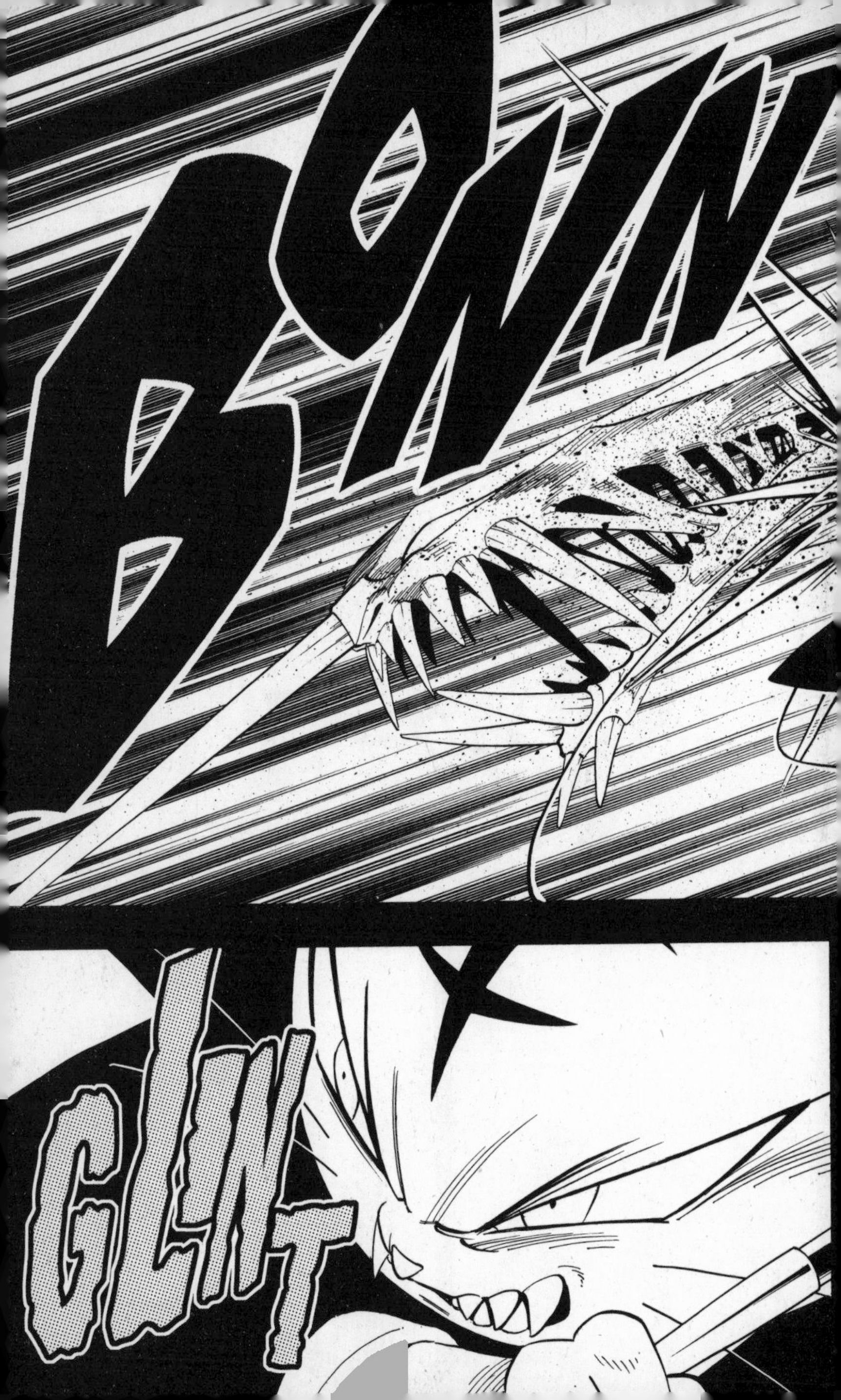
GLINT

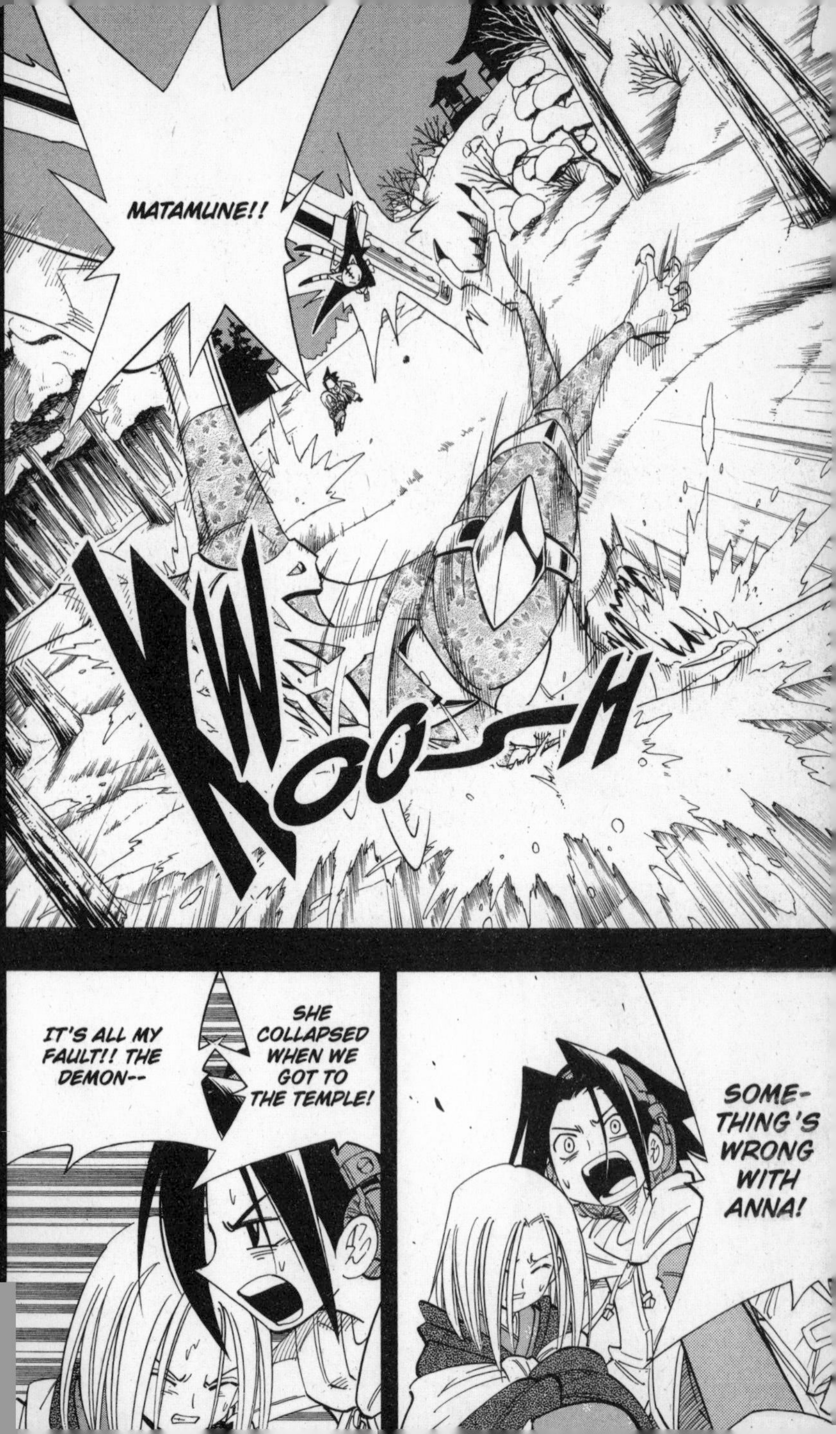
MATAMUNE!!
WHOOSH
SOME-THING'S WRONG WITH ANNA!
SHE COLLAPSED WHEN WE GOT TO THE TEMPLE!
IT'S ALL MY FAULT!! THE DEMON--

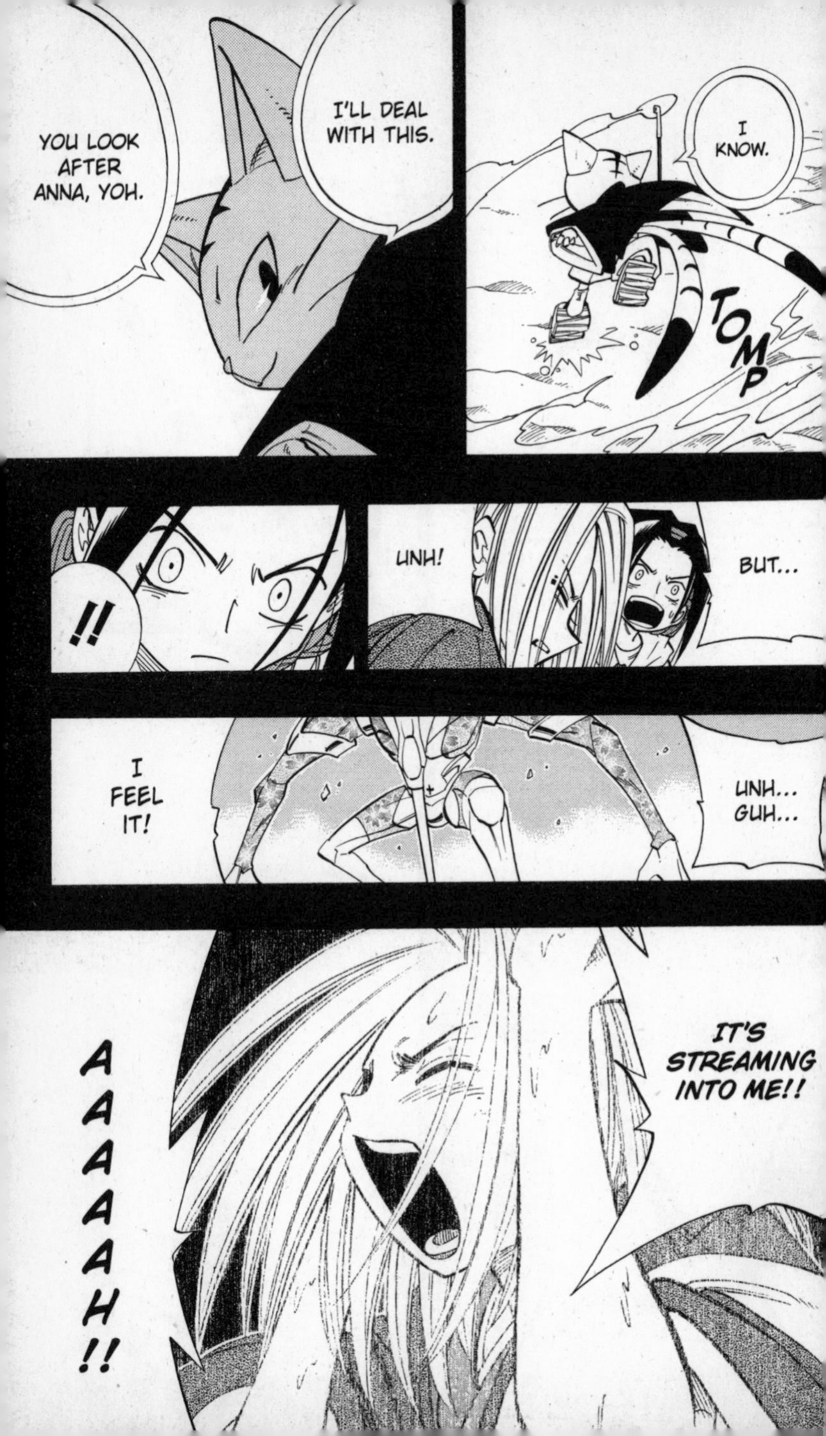
I KNOW.
TOMP
I'LL DEAL WITH THIS.
YOU LOOK AFTER ANNA, YOH.
BUT...
UNH!
!!
UNH... GUH...
I FEEL IT!
IT'S STREAMING INTO ME!!
AAAAAAH!!

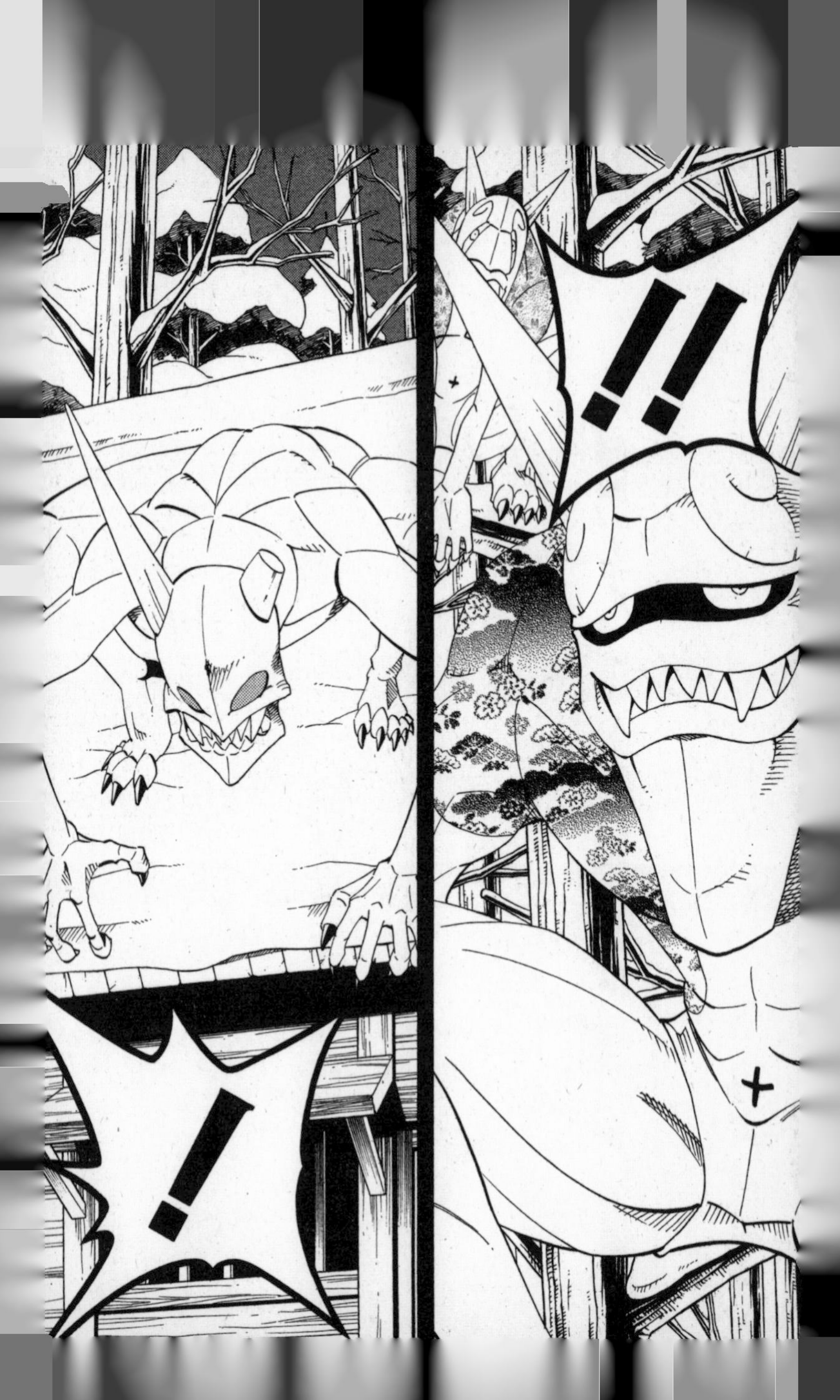
!!
!

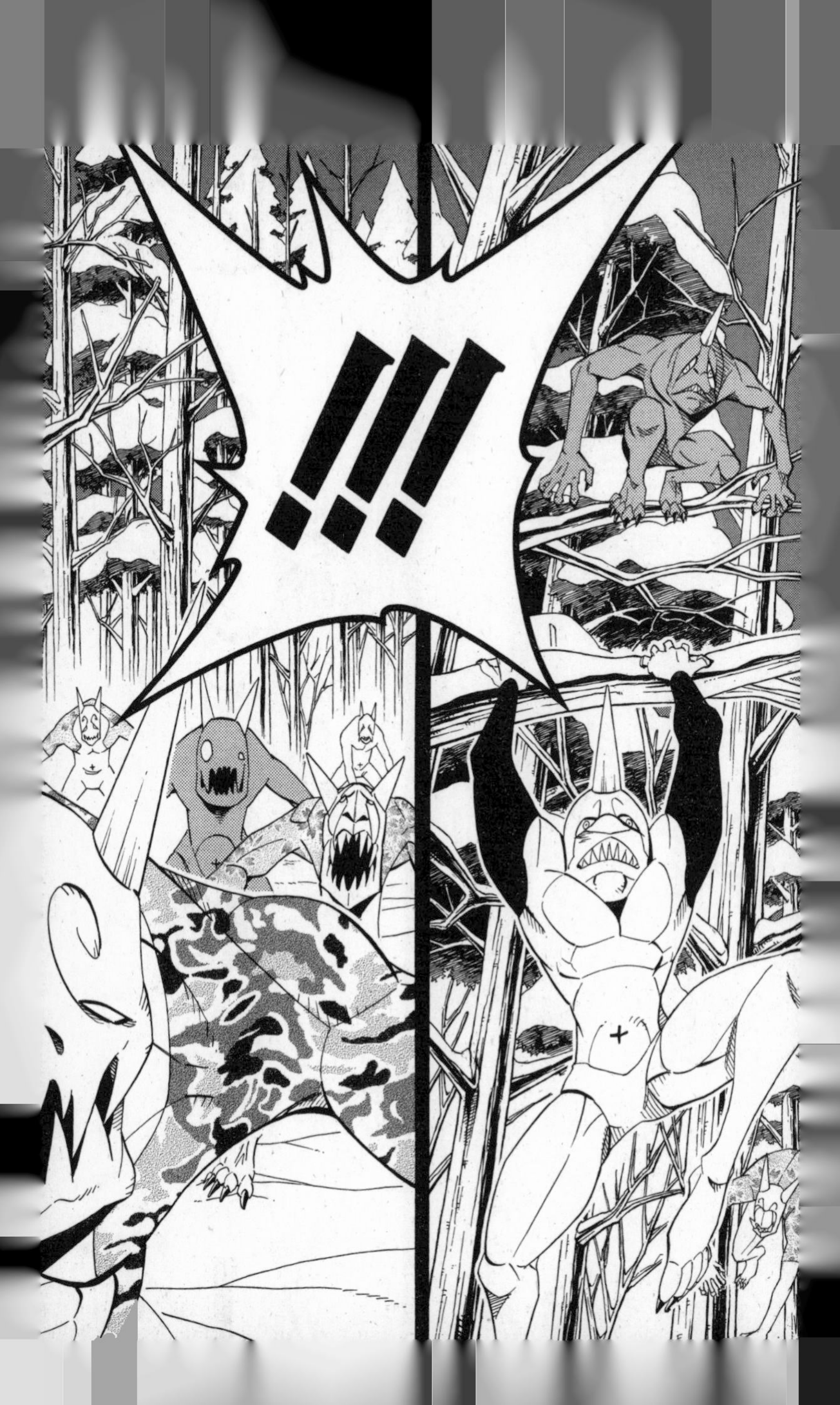
!!!

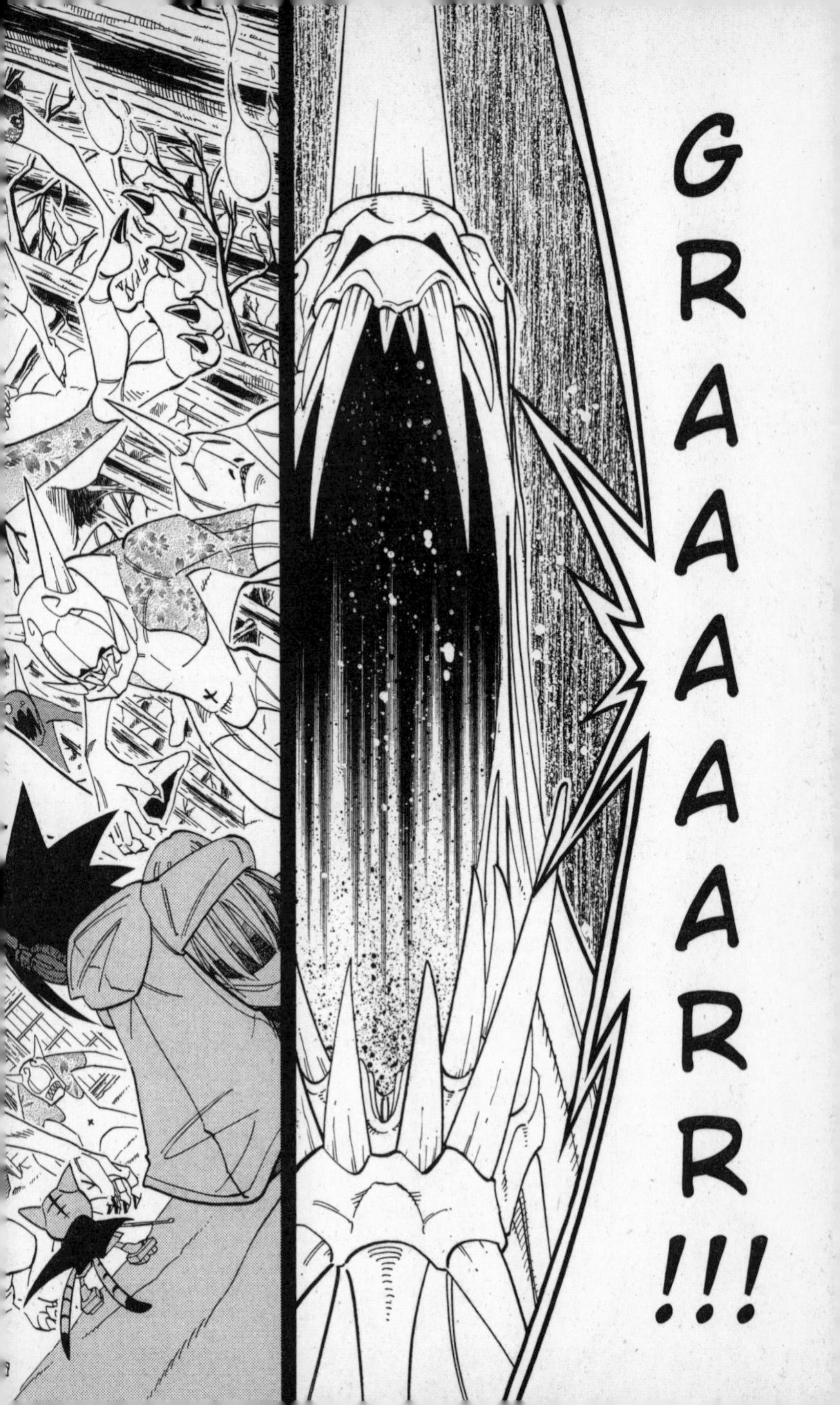
GRAAAARR!!!

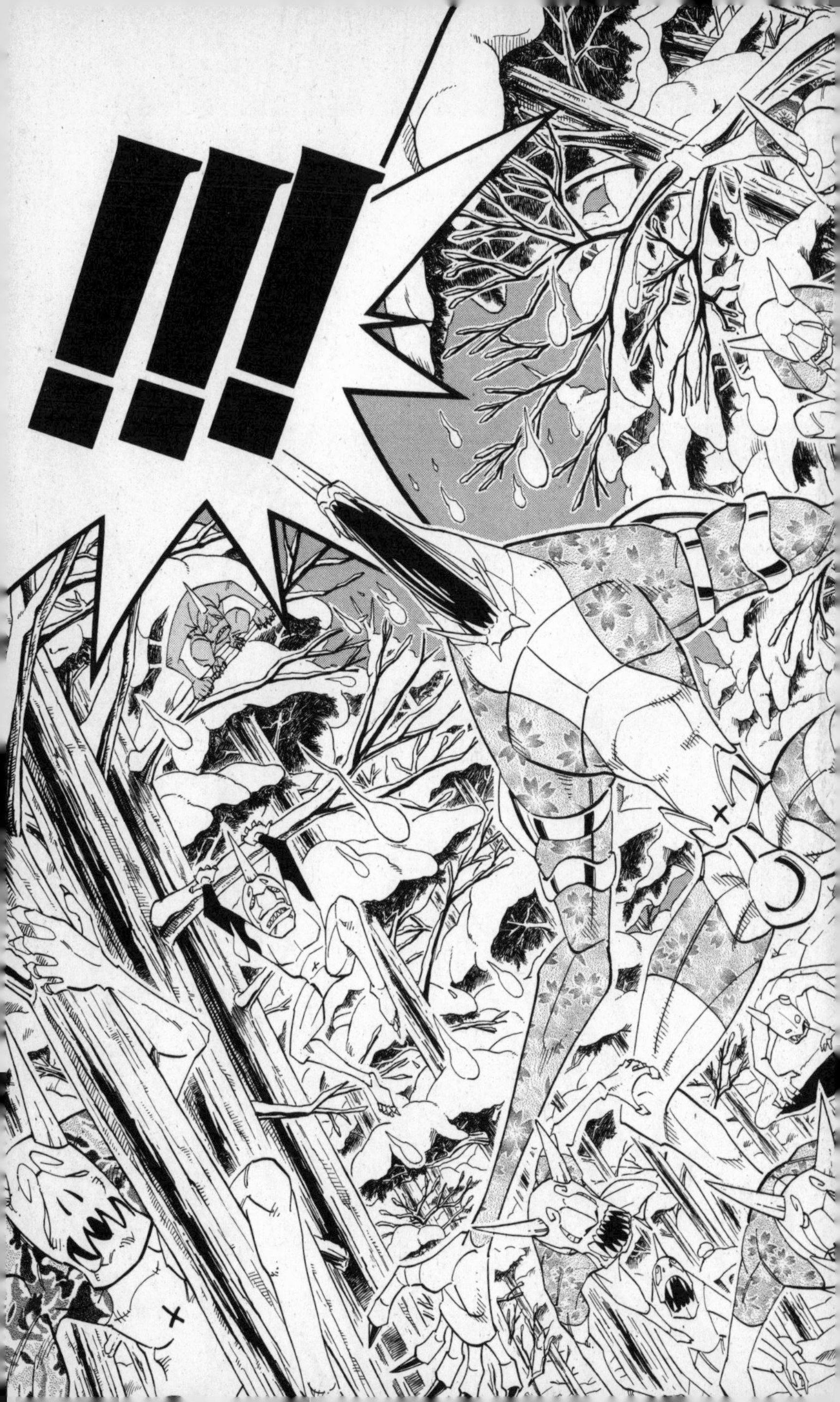
!!!

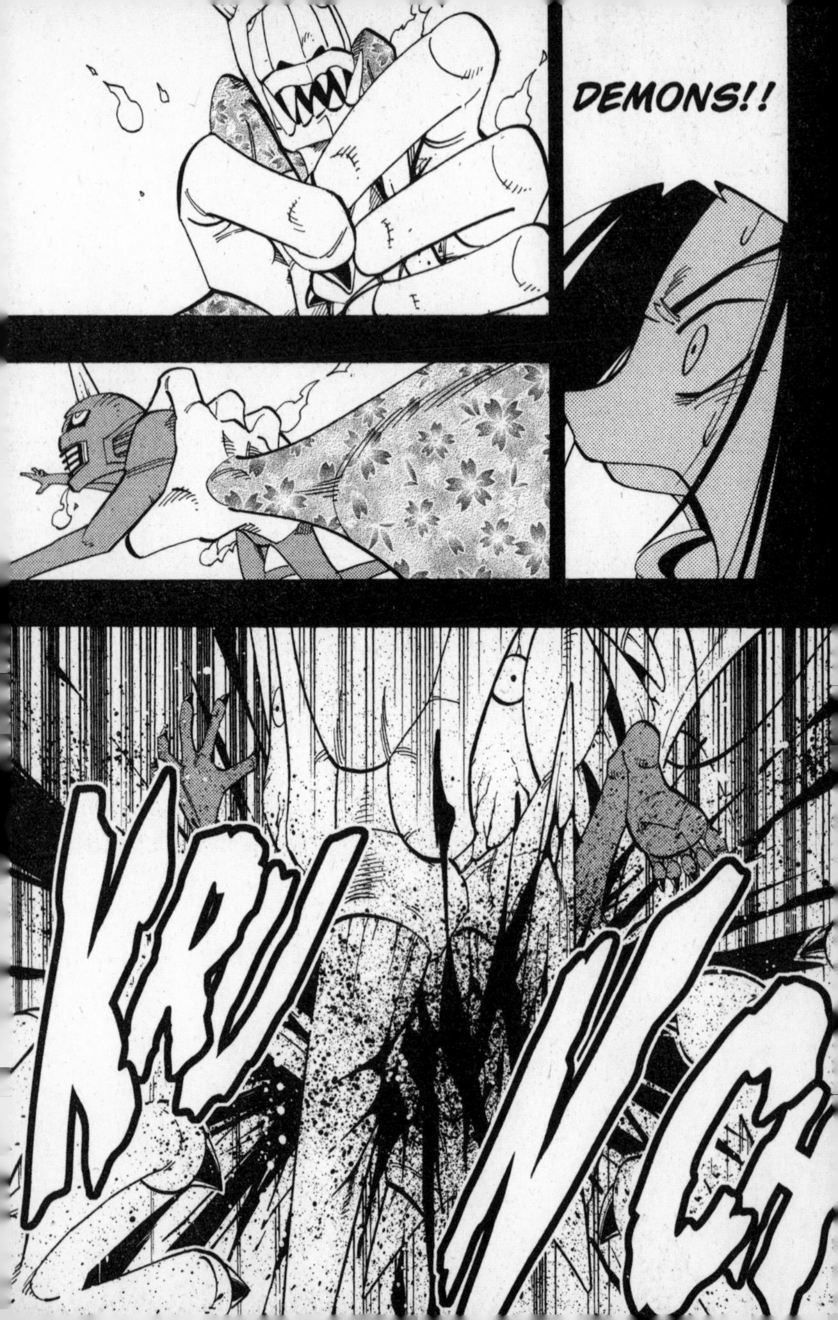
DEMONS!!
KRUNC

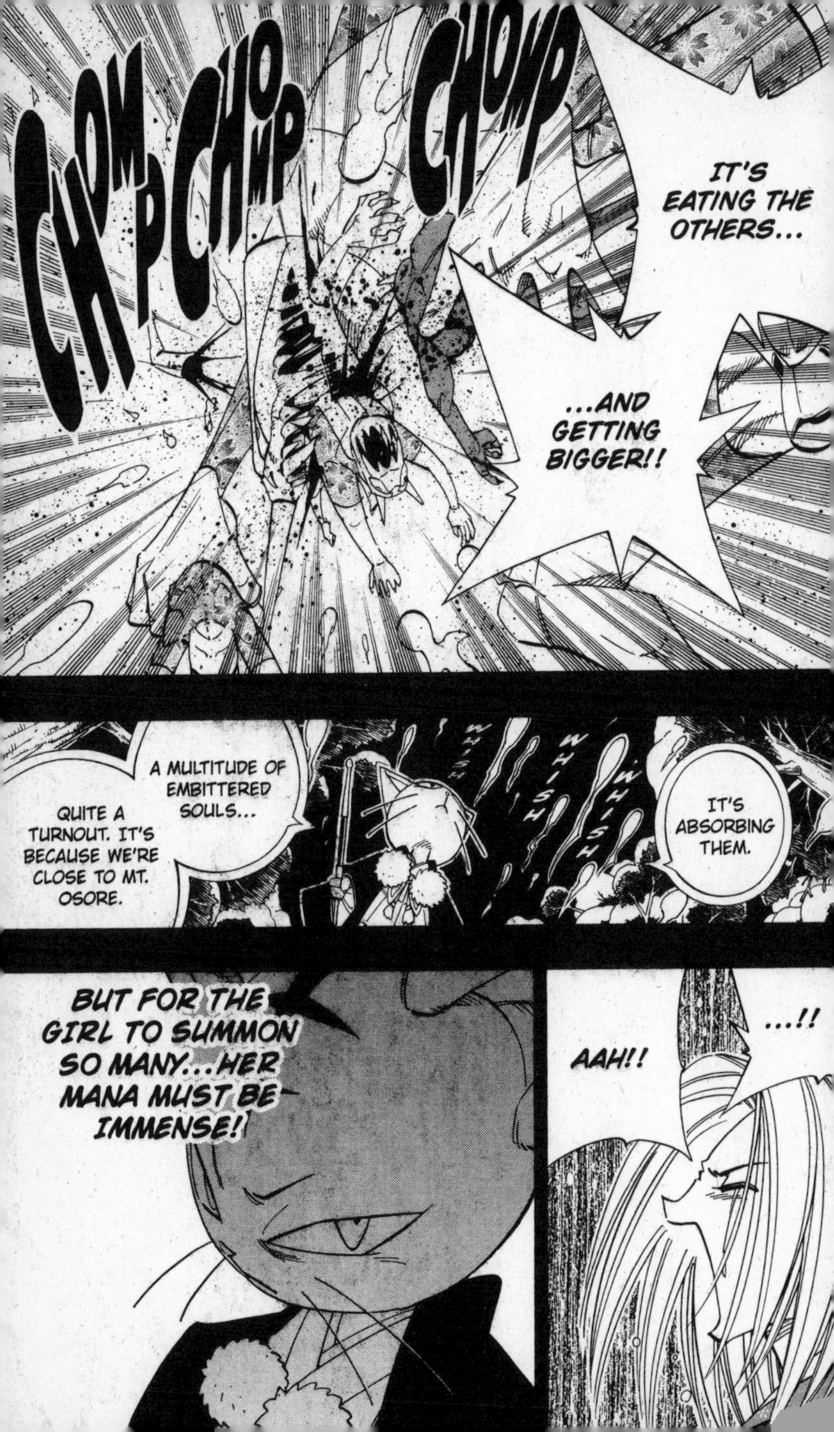

IT'S EATING THE OTHERS...
CHOMP
CHOMP
CHOMP
...AND GETTING BIGGER!!
IT'S ABSORBING THEM.
WHISH
WHISH
WHISH
A MULTITUDE OF EMBITTERED SOULS...
QUITE A TURNOUT. IT'S BECAUSE WE'RE CLOSE TO MT. OSORE.
...!!
AAH!!
BUT FOR THE GIRL TO SUMMON SO MANY...HER MANA MUST BE IMMENSE!

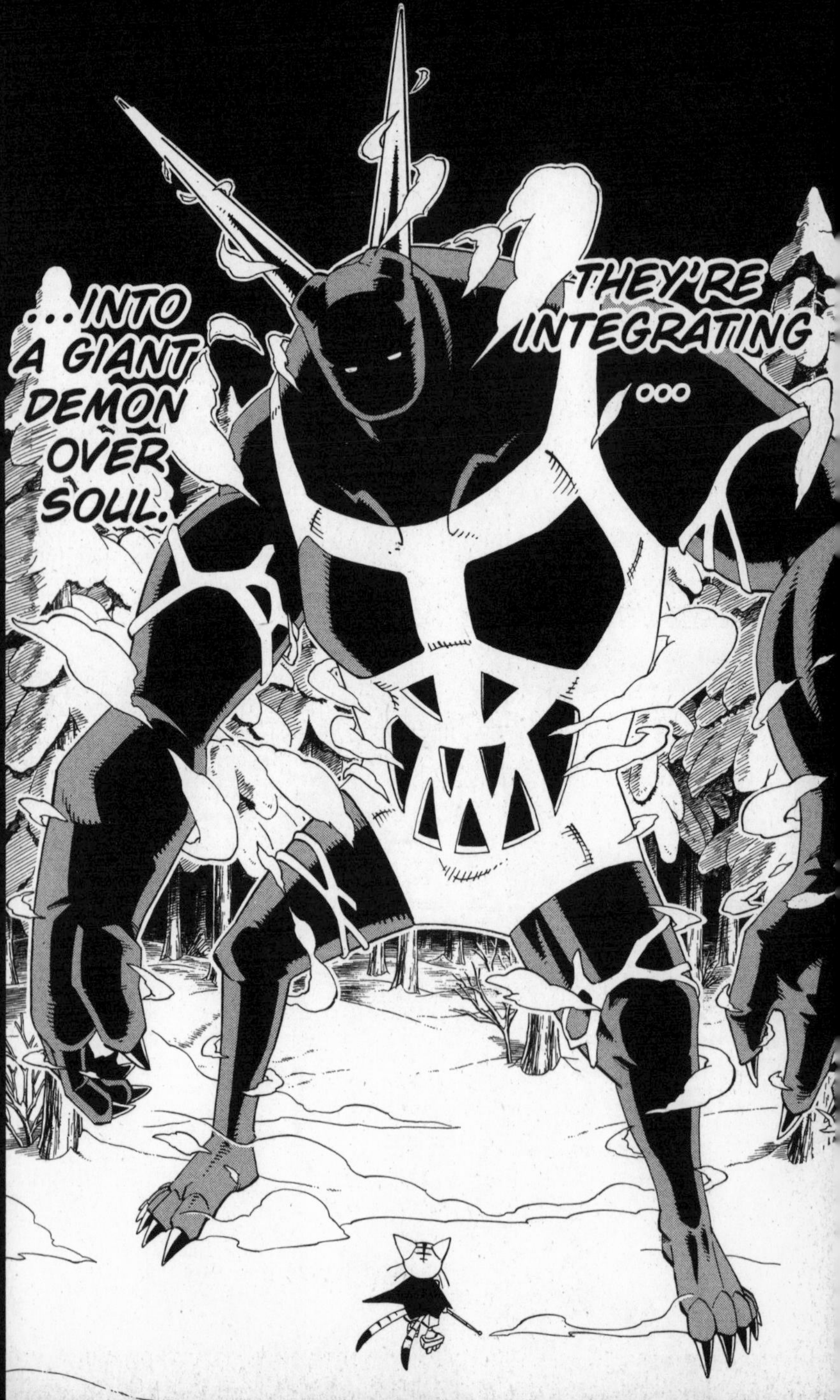
THEY'RE INTEGRATING...
...INTO A GIANT DEMON OVER SOUL.

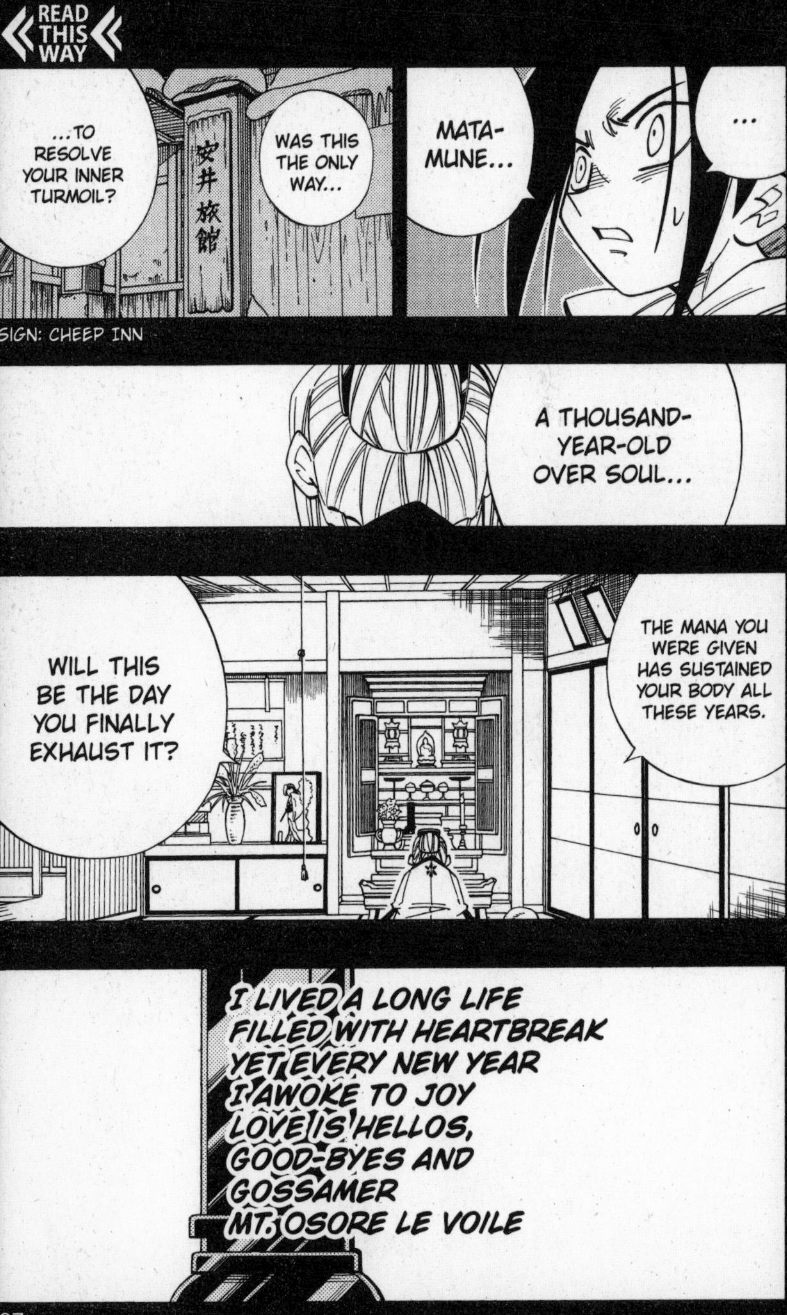
READ THIS WAY
...
MATA-MUNE...
WAS THIS THE ONLY WAY...
...TO RESOLVE YOUR INNER TURMOIL?
安井旅館
SIGN: CHEEP INN
A THOUSAND-YEAR-OLD OVER SOUL...
THE MANA YOU WERE GIVEN HAS SUSTAINED YOUR BODY ALL THESE YEARS.
WILL THIS BE THE DAY YOU FINALLY EXHAUST IT?
I LIVED A LONG LIFE
FILLED WITH HEARTBREAK
YET EVERY NEW YEAR
I AWOKE TO JOY
LOVE IS HELLOS,
GOOD-BYES AND
GOSSAMER
MT. OSORE LE VOILE

SHAMAN KING CHARACTER FILE No.104

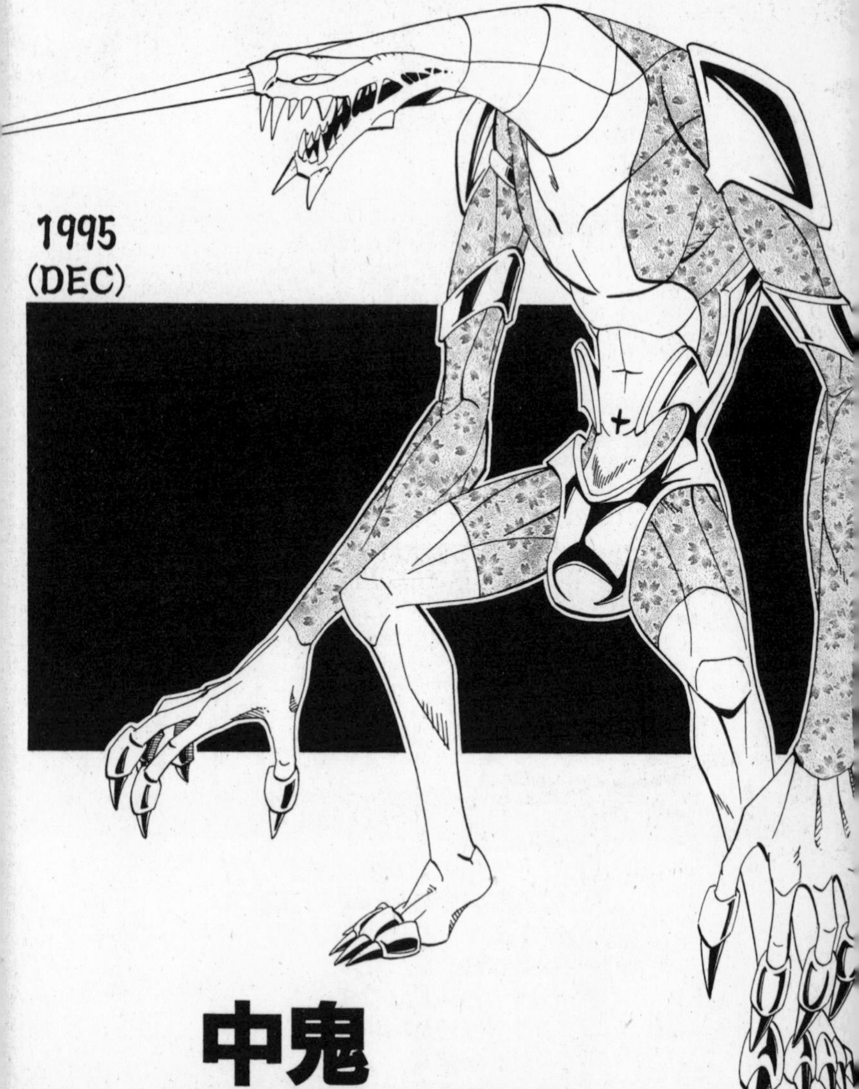
1995
(DEC)

中鬼

MEDIUM-SIZED DEMON

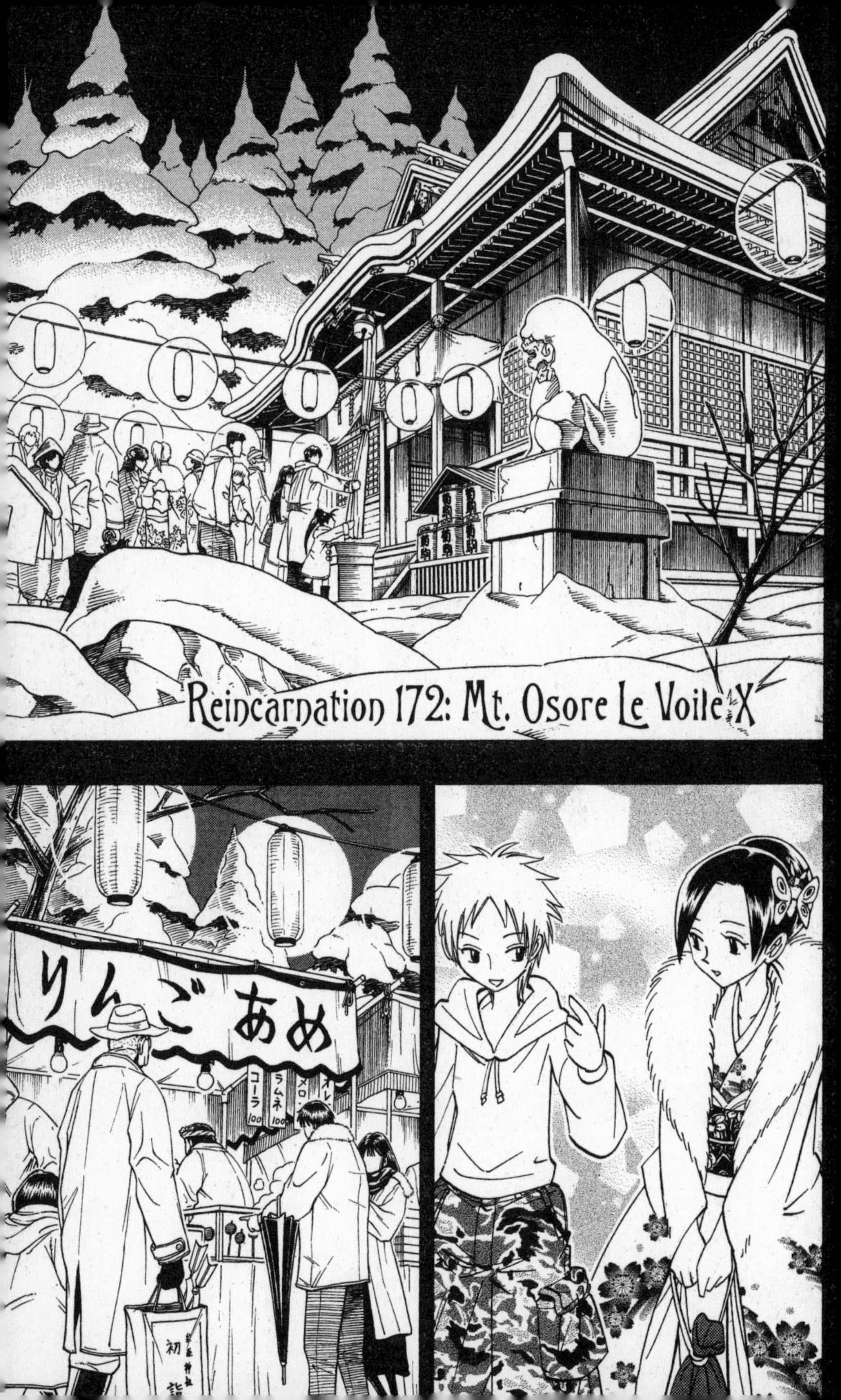
Reincarnation 172: Mt. Osore Le Voile X
りんごあめ
コーラ 100
ラムネ 100
メロ
オレ

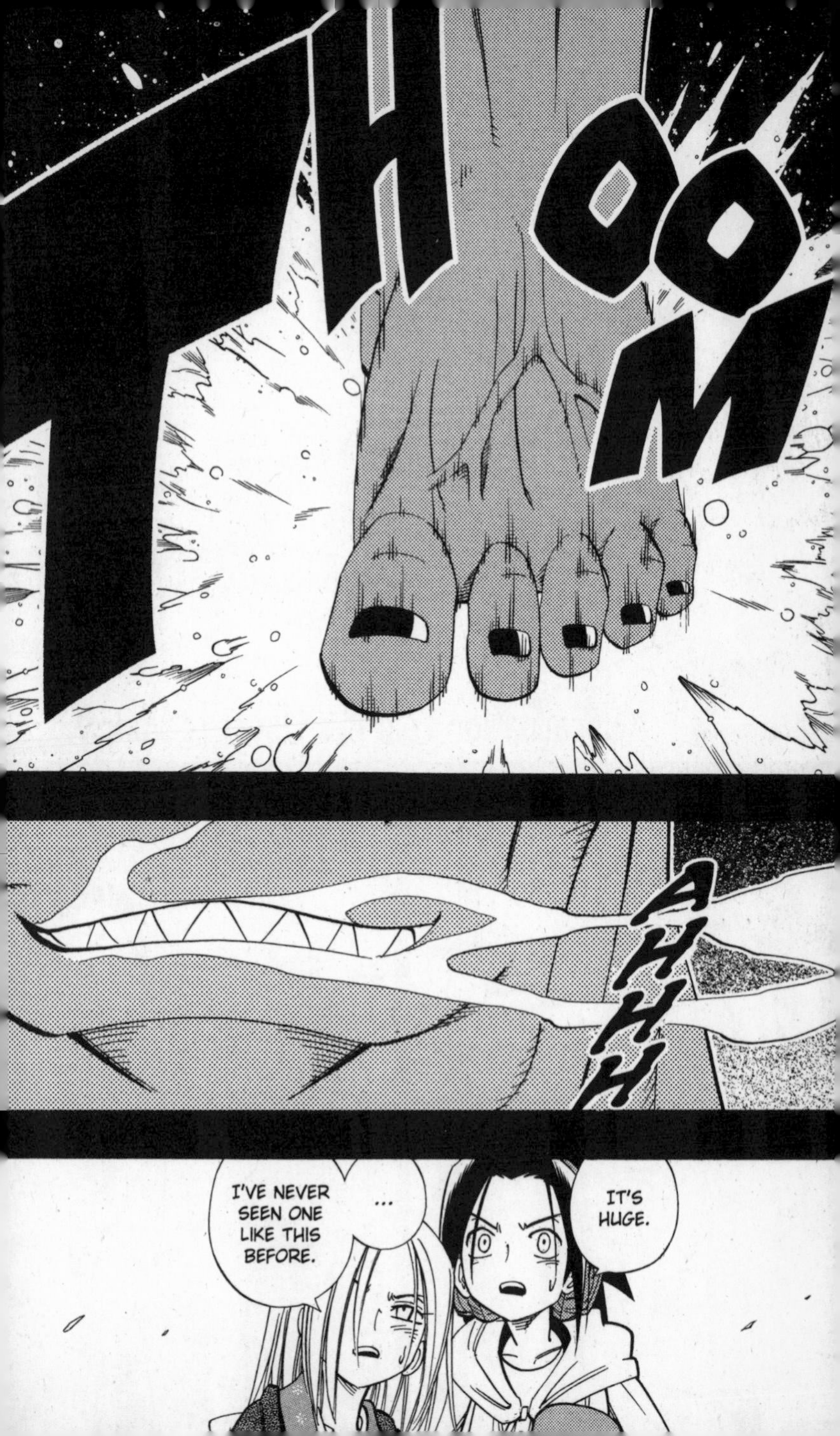
THOOM!
AHHHH
IT'S HUGE.
...
I'VE NEVER SEEN ONE LIKE THIS BEFORE.

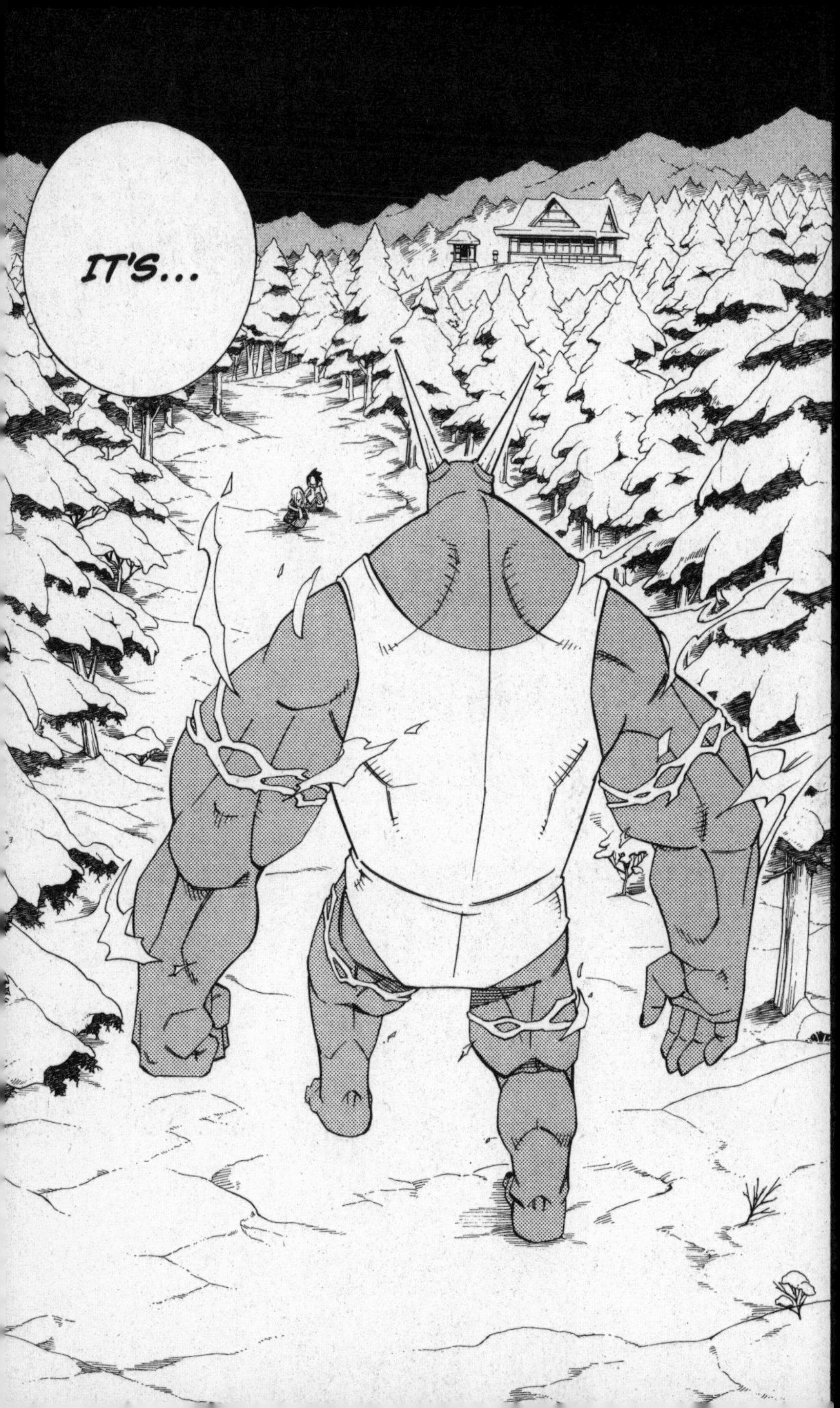
IT'S...

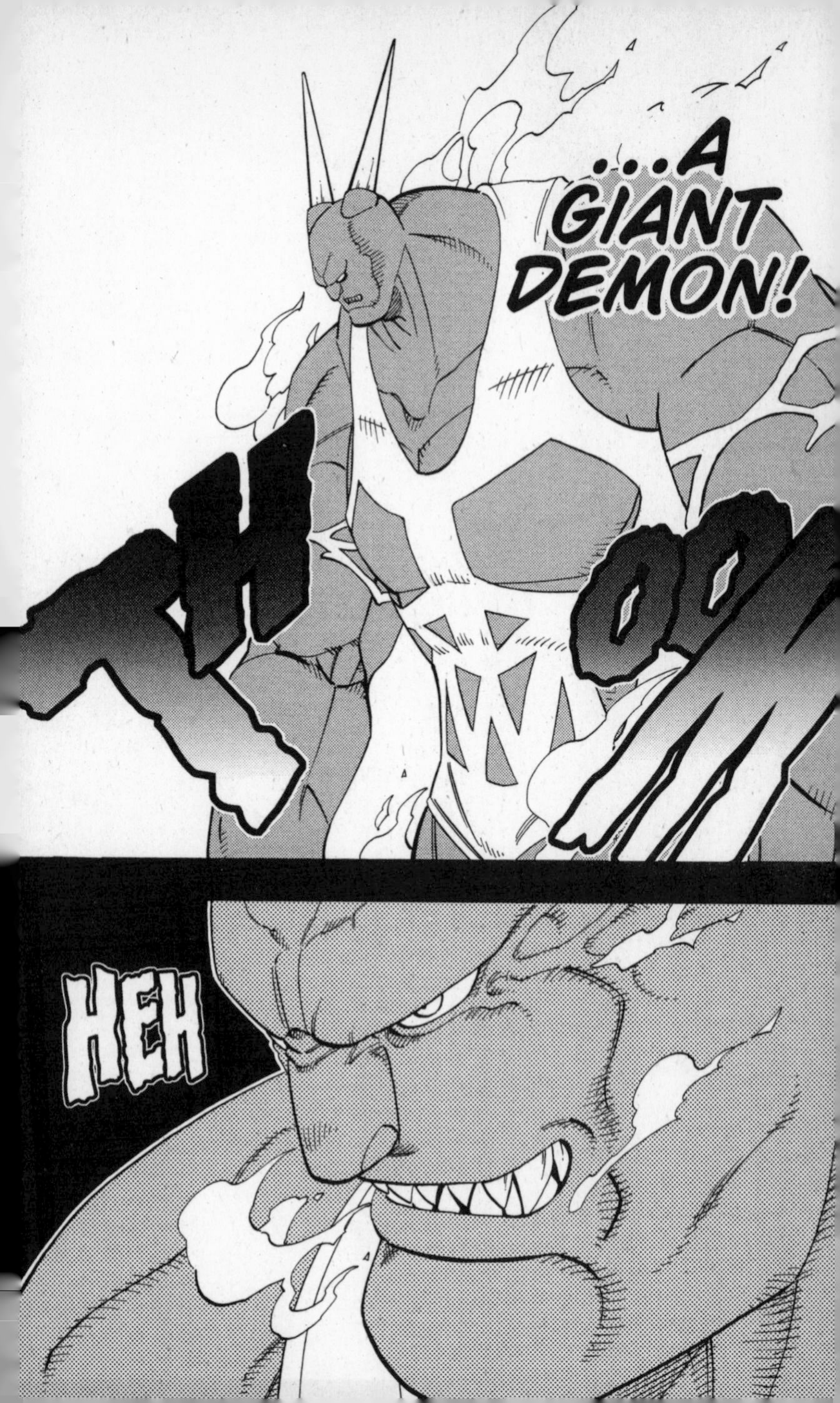
...A GIANT DEMON!
TH
OO
HEH

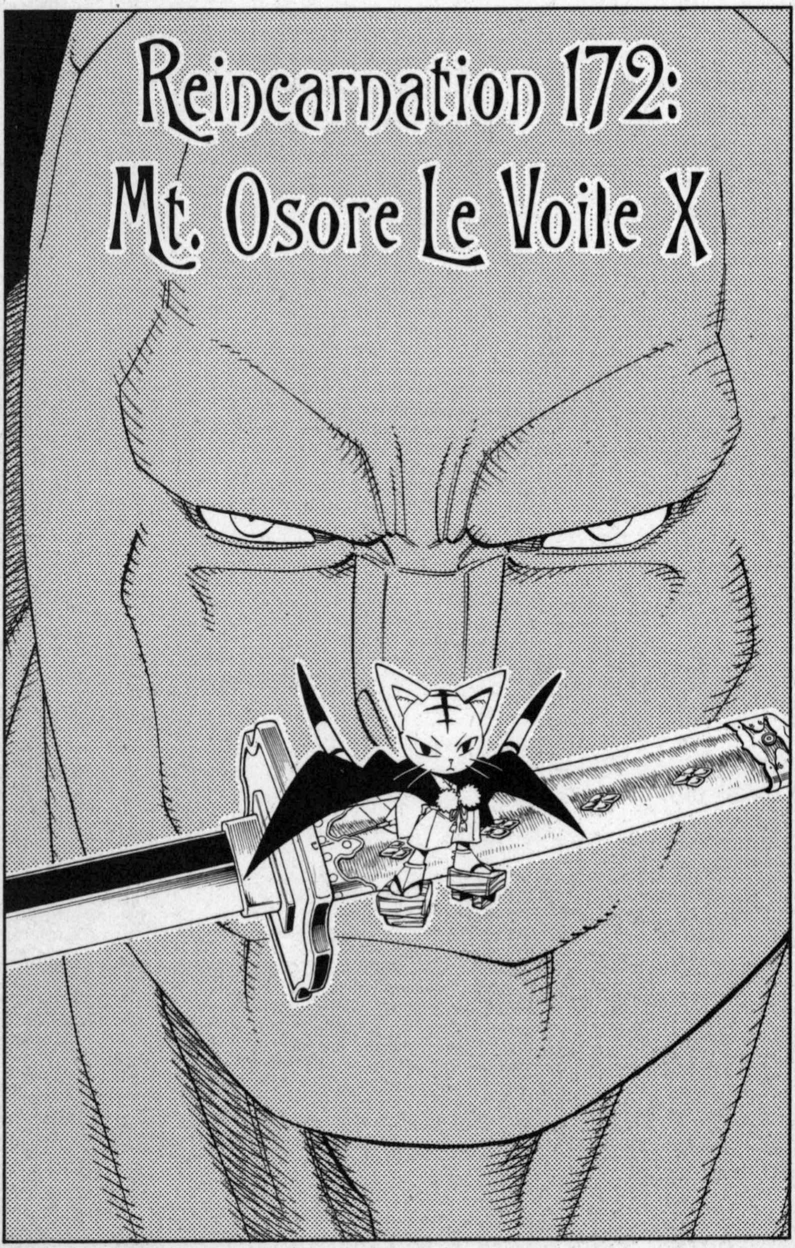
Reincarnation 172:
Mt. Osore Le Voile X

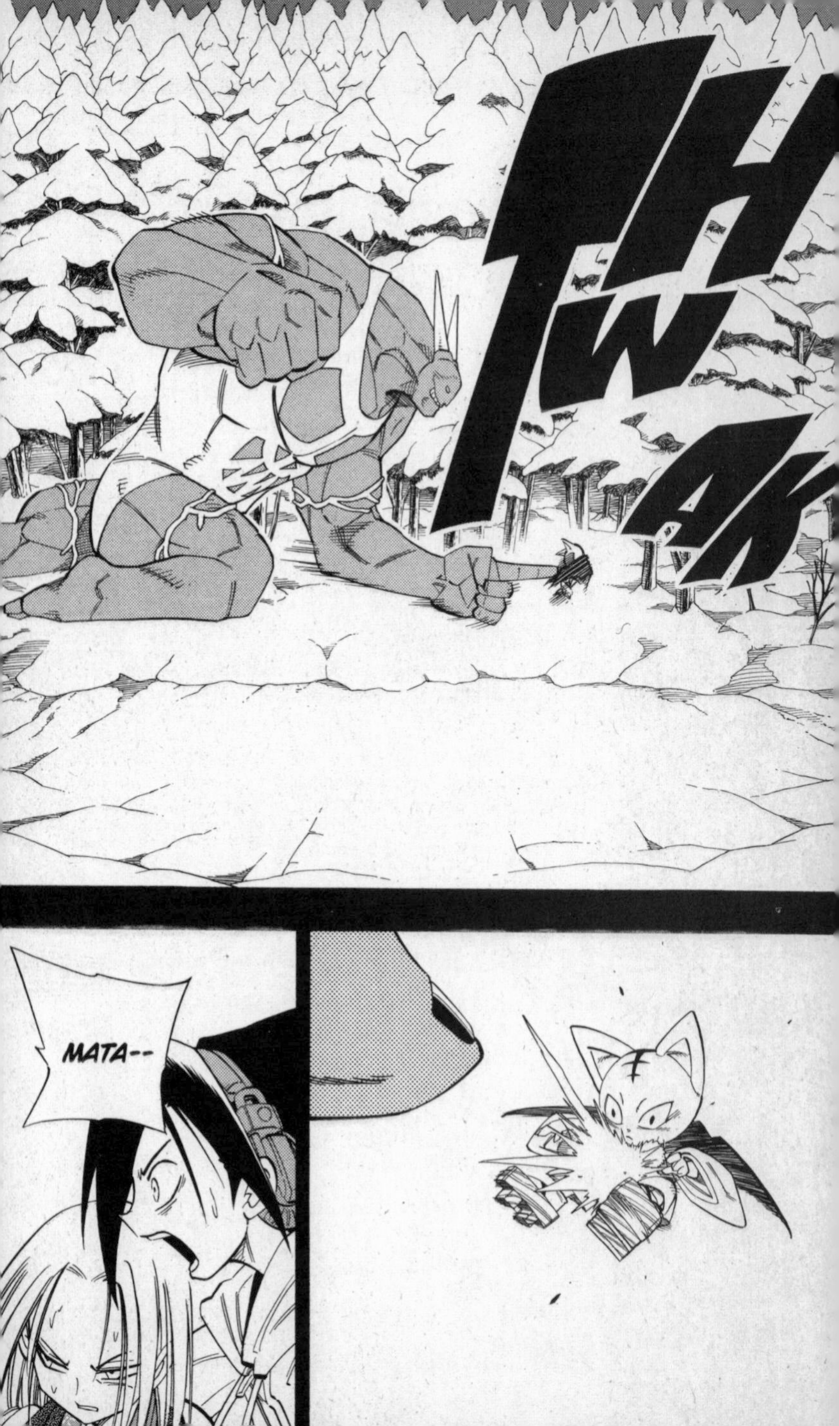
THWAK
MATA--

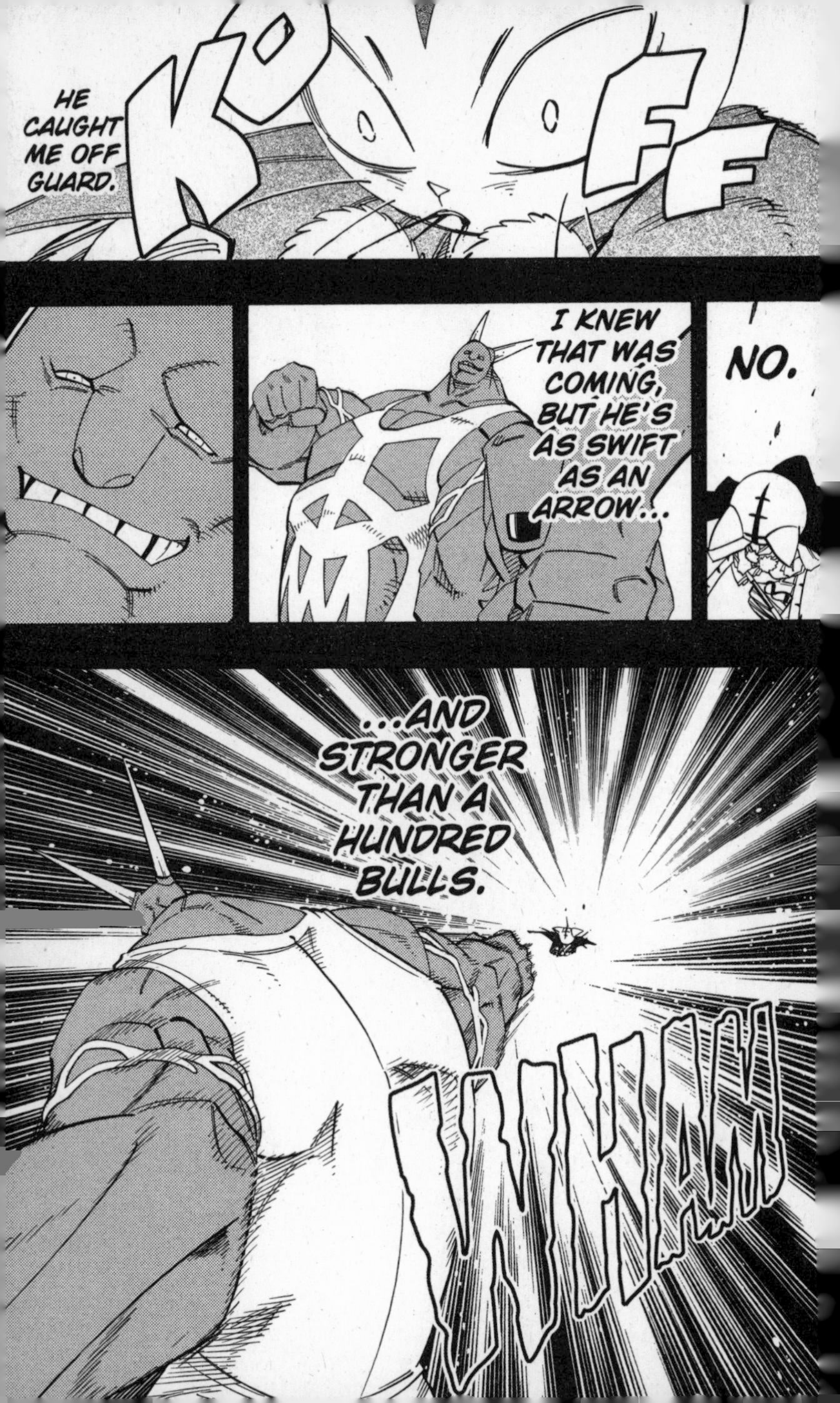
HE CAUGHT ME OFF GUARD.
NO.
I KNEW THAT WAS COMING, BUT HE'S AS SWIFT AS AN ARROW...
...AND STRONGER THAN A HUNDRED BULLS.

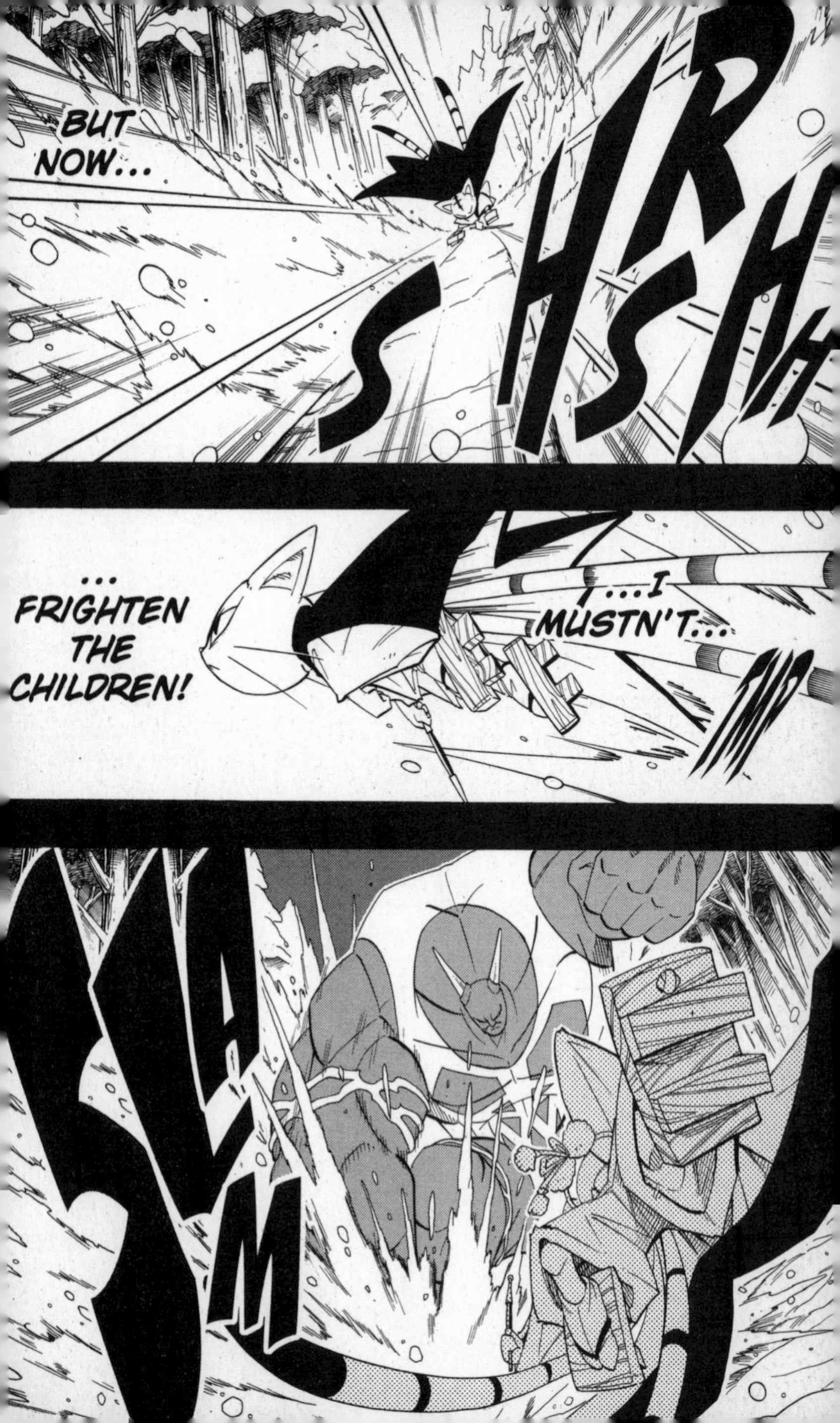
BUT NOW...
...I MUSTN'T...
... FRIGHTEN THE CHILDREN!

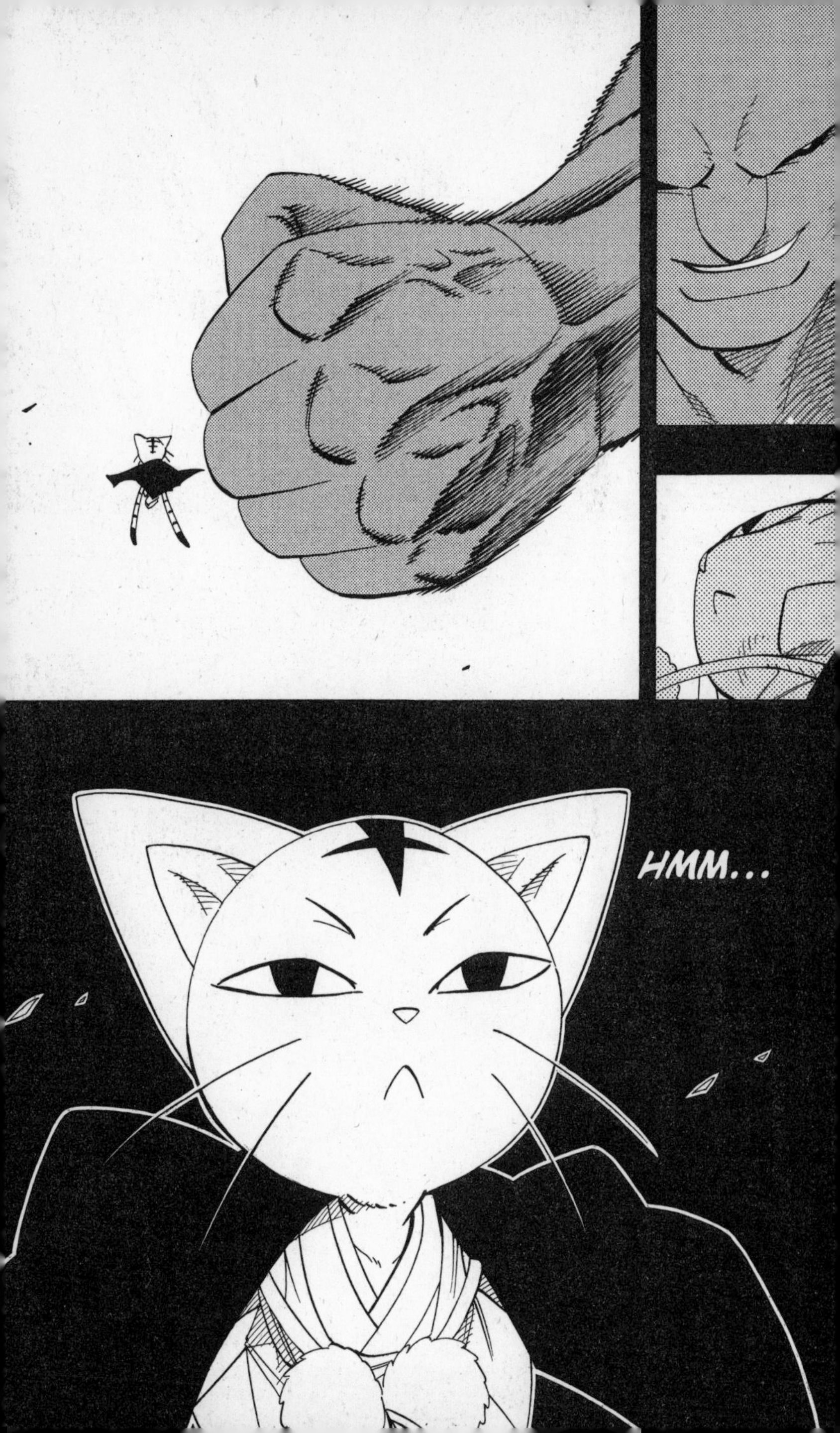
HMM...

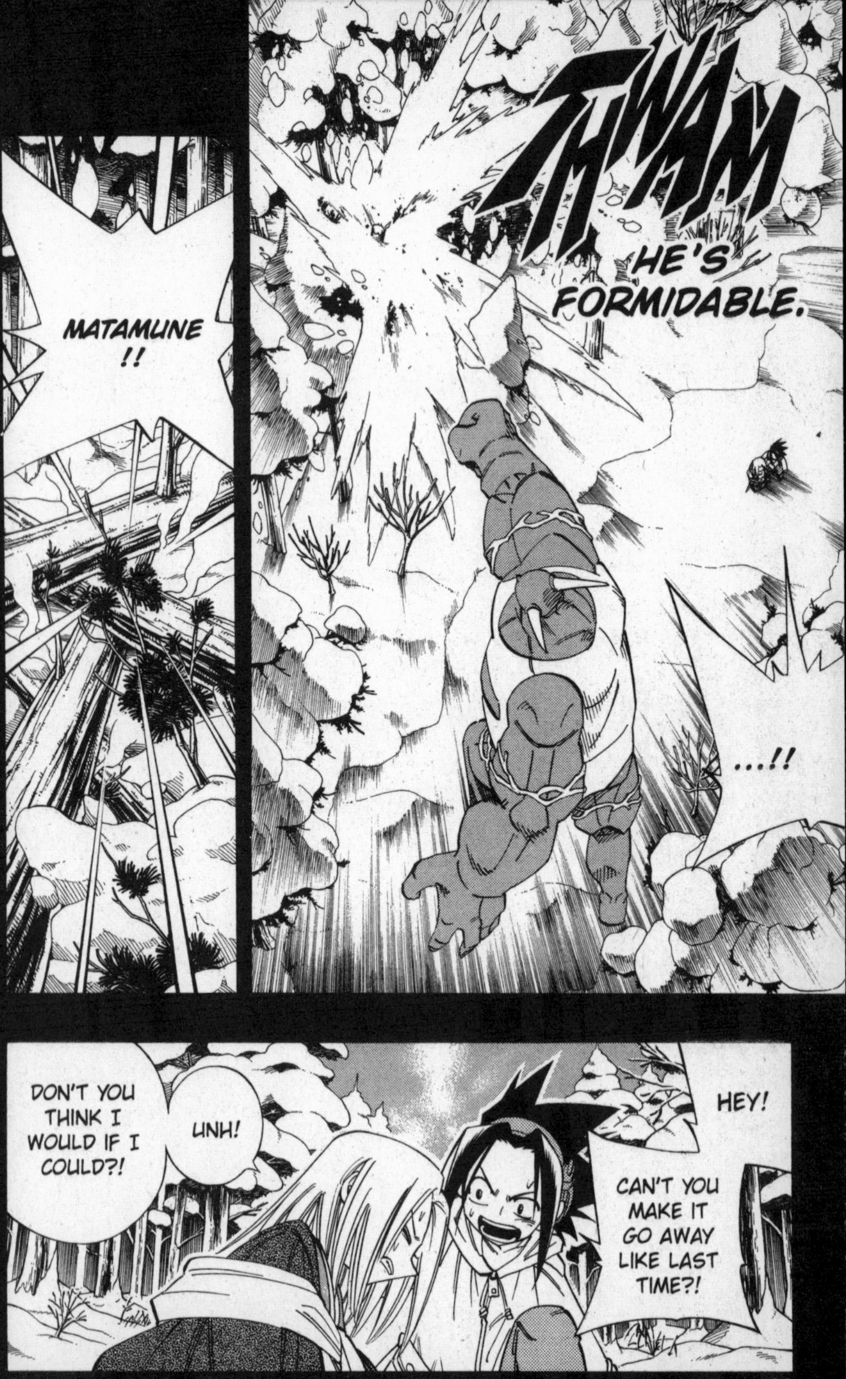
THWAM
HE'S FORMIDABLE.
...!!
MATAMUNE !!
HEY!
CAN'T YOU MAKE IT GO AWAY LIKE LAST TIME?!
UNH!
DON'T YOU THINK I WOULD IF I COULD?!

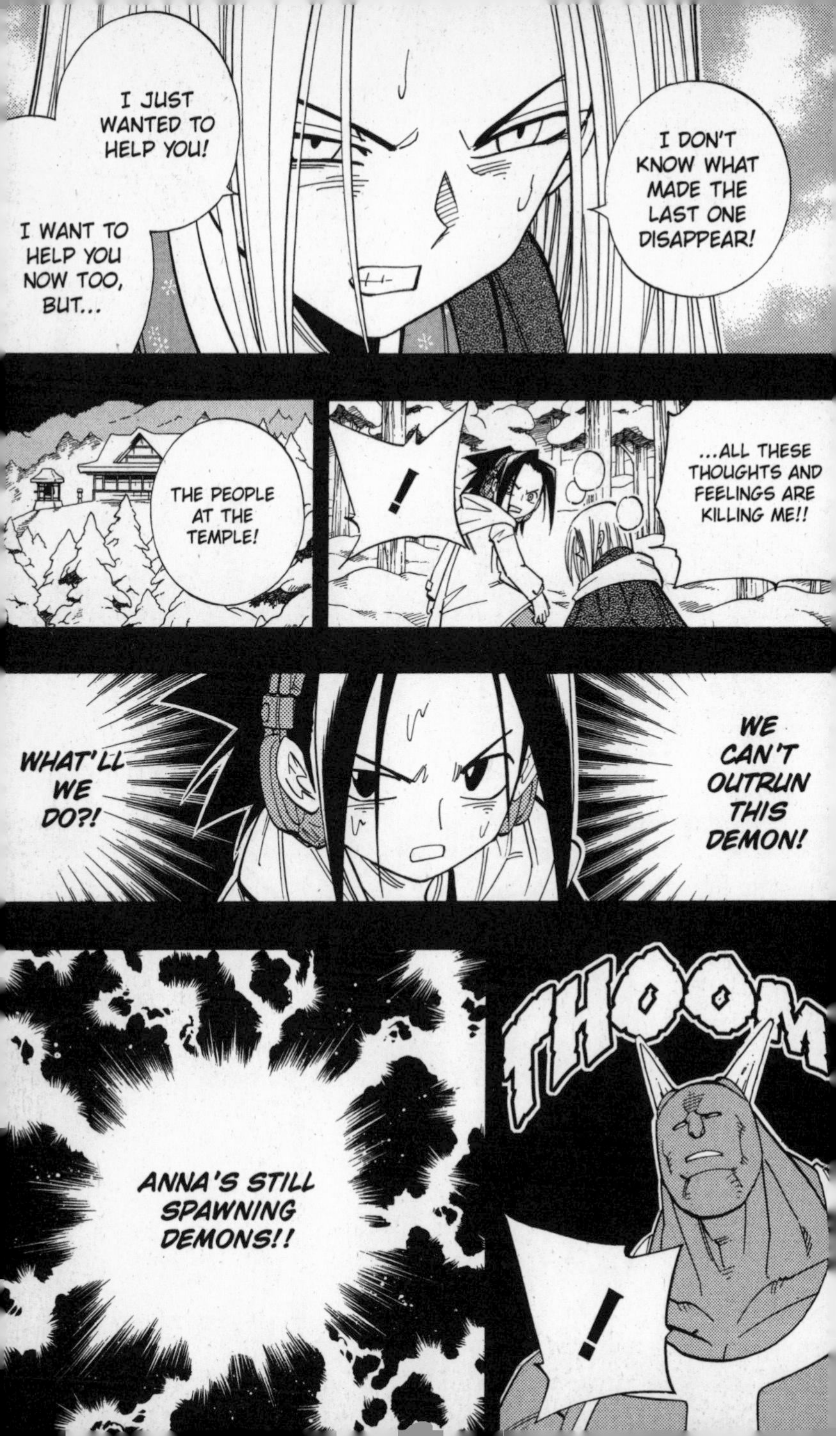
I DON'T KNOW WHAT MADE THE LAST ONE DISAPPEAR!
I JUST WANTED TO HELP YOU!
I WANT TO HELP YOU NOW TOO, BUT...
...ALL THESE THOUGHTS AND FEELINGS ARE KILLING ME!!
!
THE PEOPLE AT THE TEMPLE!
WE CAN'T OUTRUN THIS DEMON!
WHAT'LL WE DO?!
THOOM
!
ANNA'S STILL SPAWNING DEMONS!!

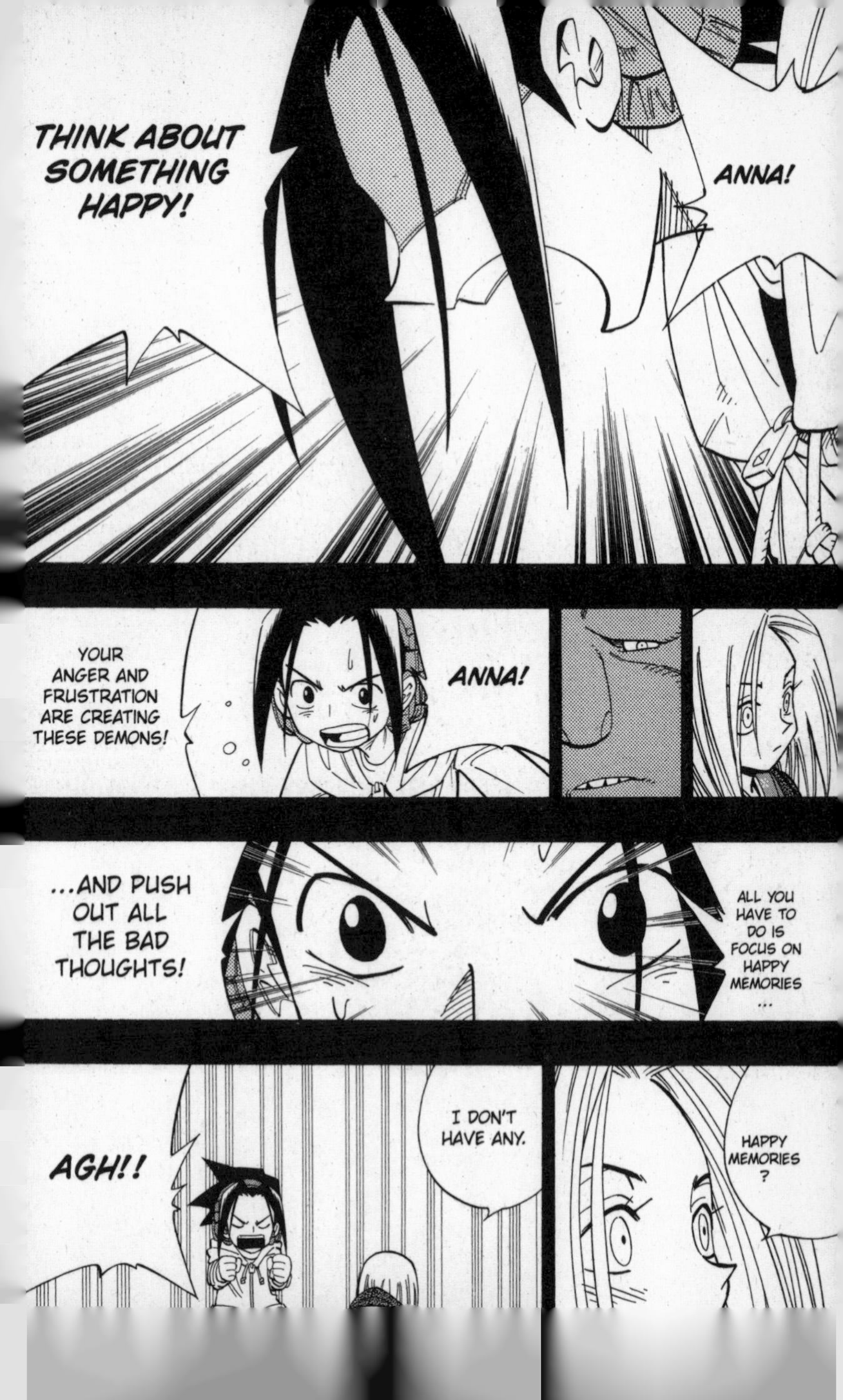
ANNA!
THINK ABOUT SOMETHING HAPPY!
ANNA!
YOUR ANGER AND FRUSTRATION ARE CREATING THESE DEMONS!
ALL YOU HAVE TO DO IS FOCUS ON HAPPY MEMORIES ...
...AND PUSH OUT ALL THE BAD THOUGHTS!
HAPPY MEMORIES ?
I DON'T HAVE ANY.
AGH!!

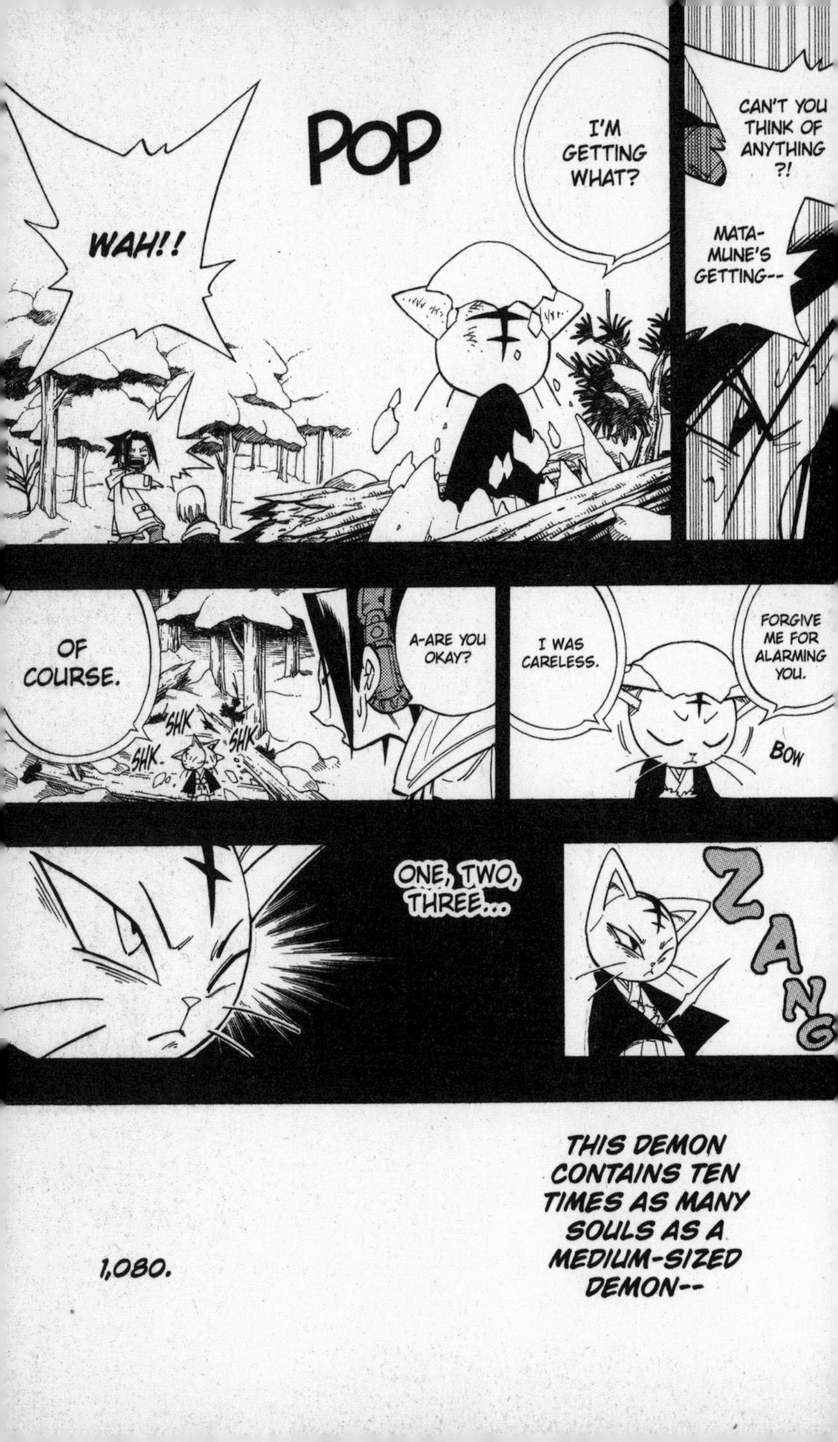
CAN'T YOU THINK OF ANYTHING ?!
MATA-MUNE'S GETTING--
I'M GETTING WHAT?
POP
WAH!!
FORGIVE ME FOR ALARMING YOU.
I WAS CARELESS.
BOW
A-ARE YOU OKAY?
OF COURSE.
SHK
SHK
SHK.
ZANG
ONE, TWO, THREE...
THIS DEMON CONTAINS TEN TIMES AS MANY SOULS AS A MEDIUM-SIZED DEMON--
1,080.

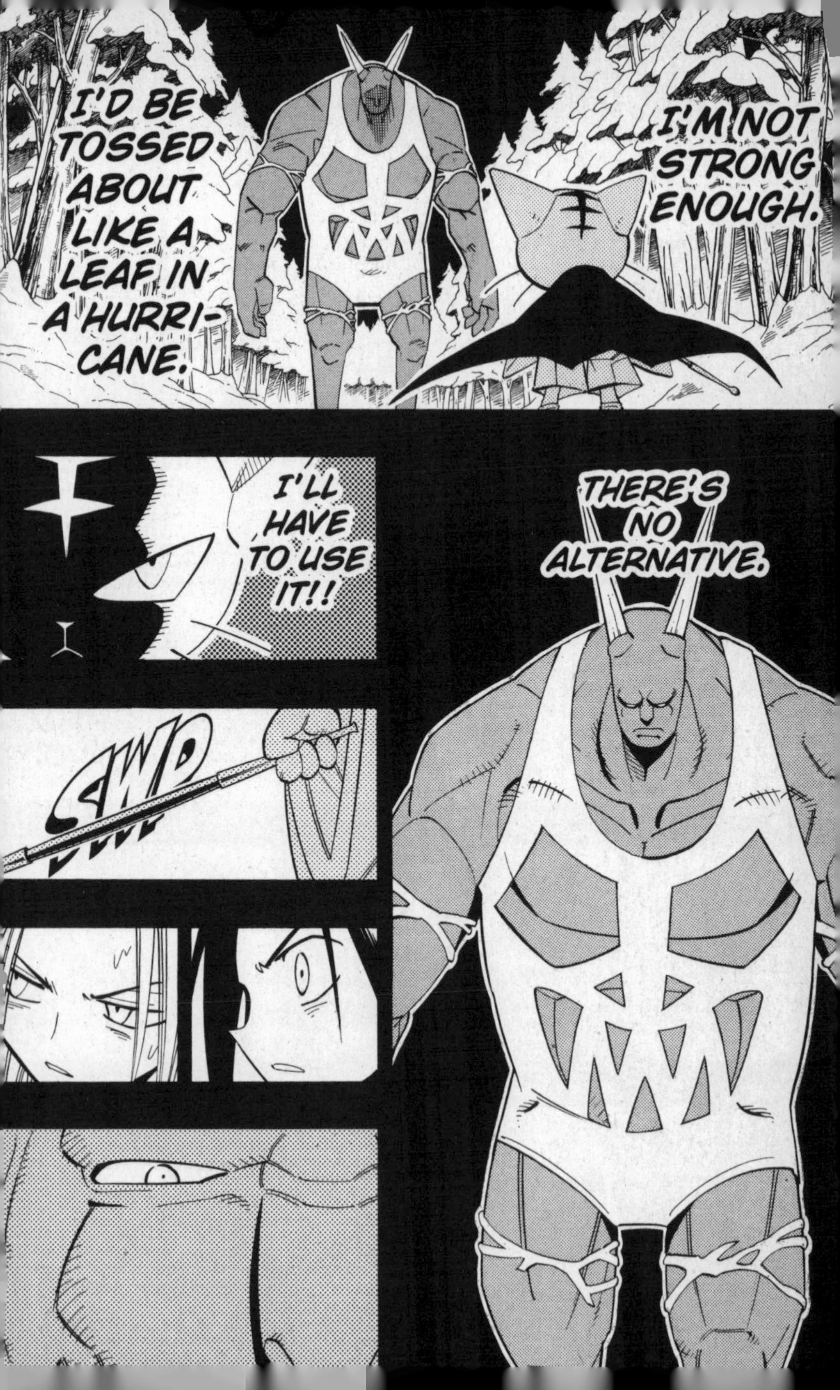
I'M NOT STRONG ENOUGH.
I'D BE TOSSED ABOUT LIKE A LEAF IN A HURRI-CANE.
THERE'S NO ALTERNATIVE.
I'LL HAVE TO USE IT!!
SWIP

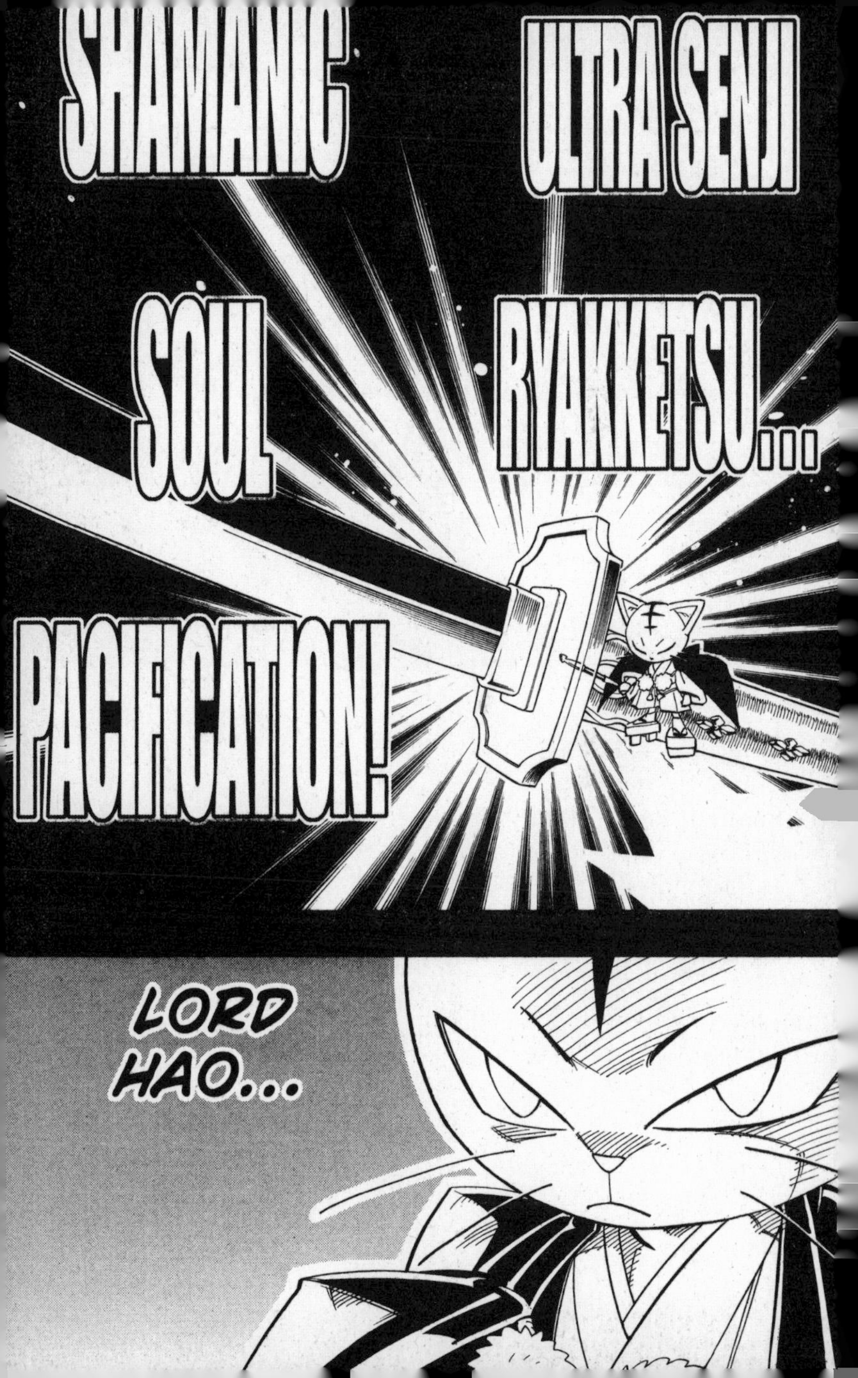
ULTRA SENJI RYAKKETSU...
SHAMANIC SOUL PACIFICATION!
LORD HAO...

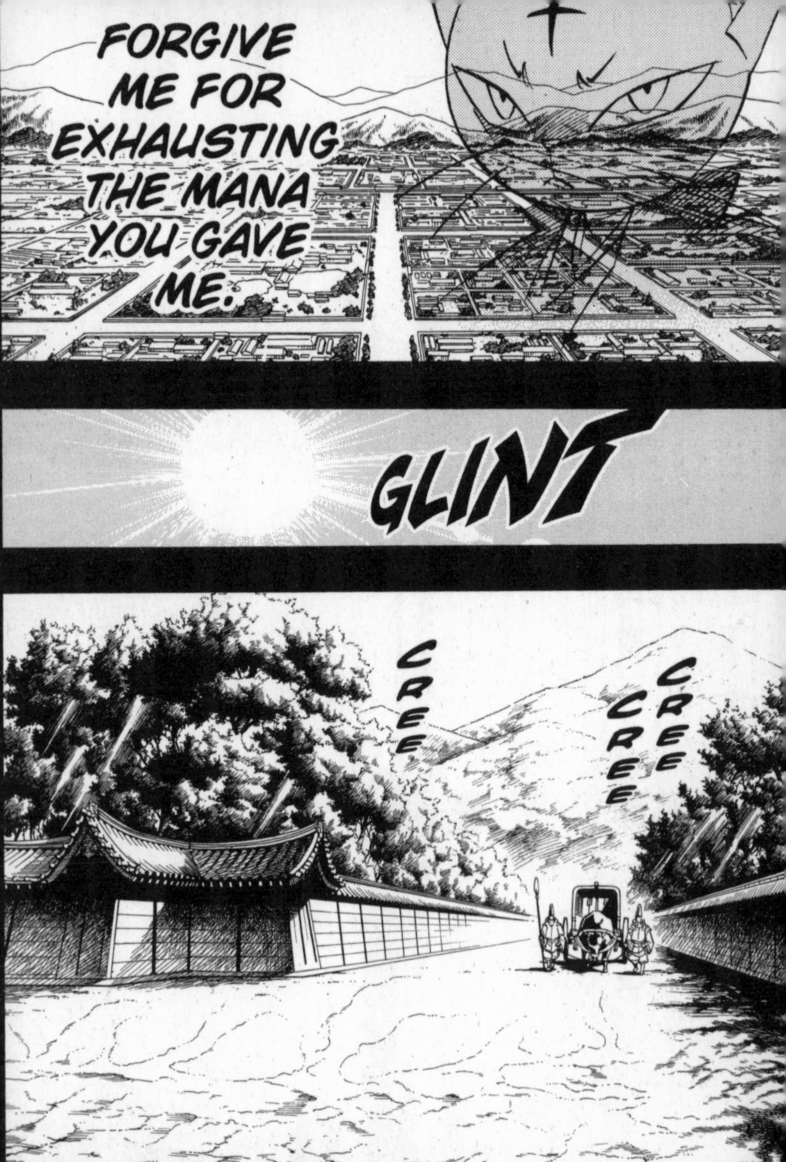
FORGIVE ME FOR EXHAUSTING THE MANA YOU GAVE ME.
GLINT
CREE
CREE
CREE

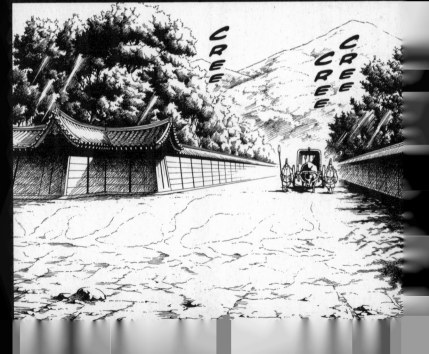

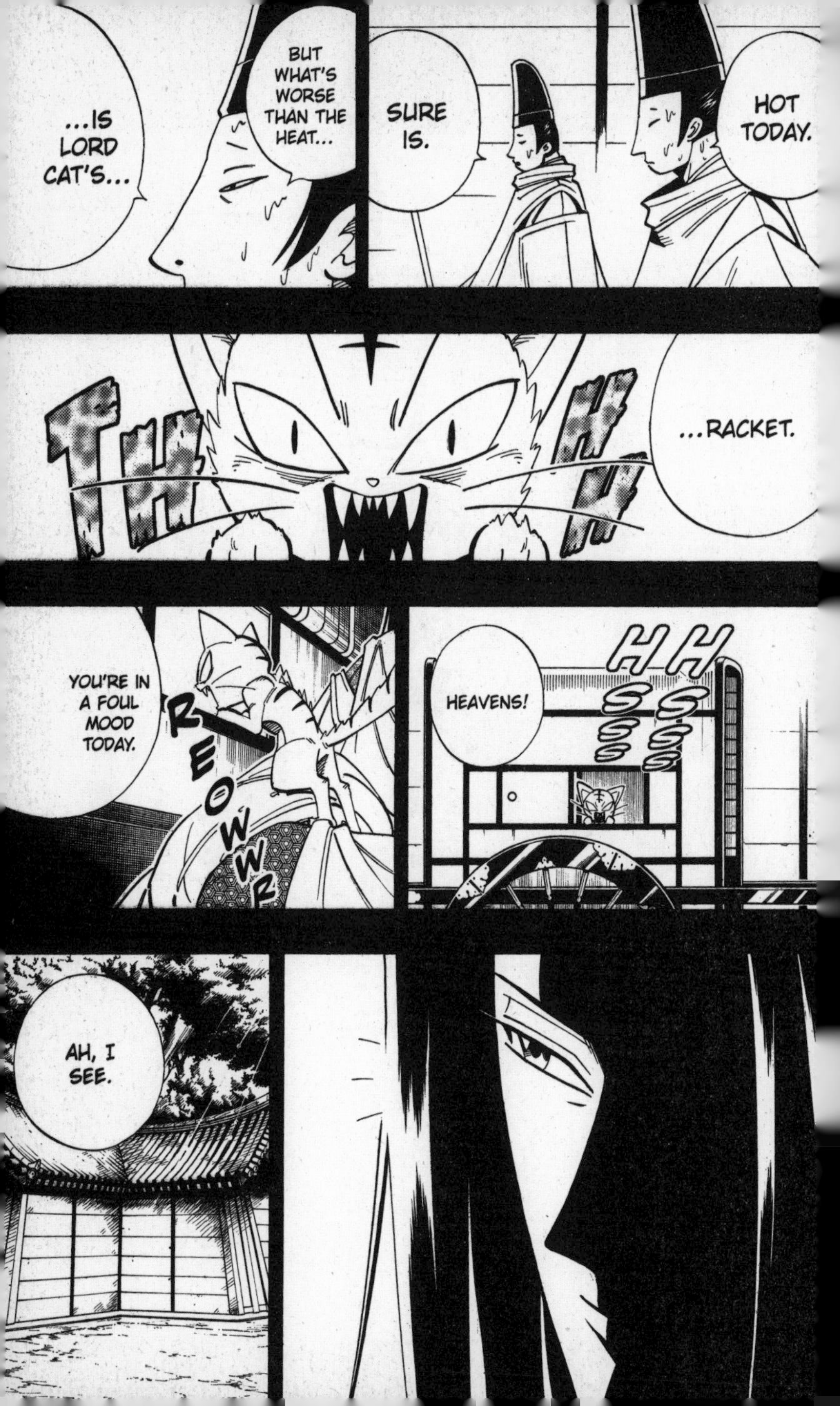
HOT TODAY.
SURE IS.
BUT WHAT'S WORSE THAN THE HEAT...
...IS LORD CAT'S...
...RACKET.
THHH
HEAVENS!
HHSSSS
YOU'RE IN A FOUL MOOD TODAY.
REOWWR
AH, I SEE.

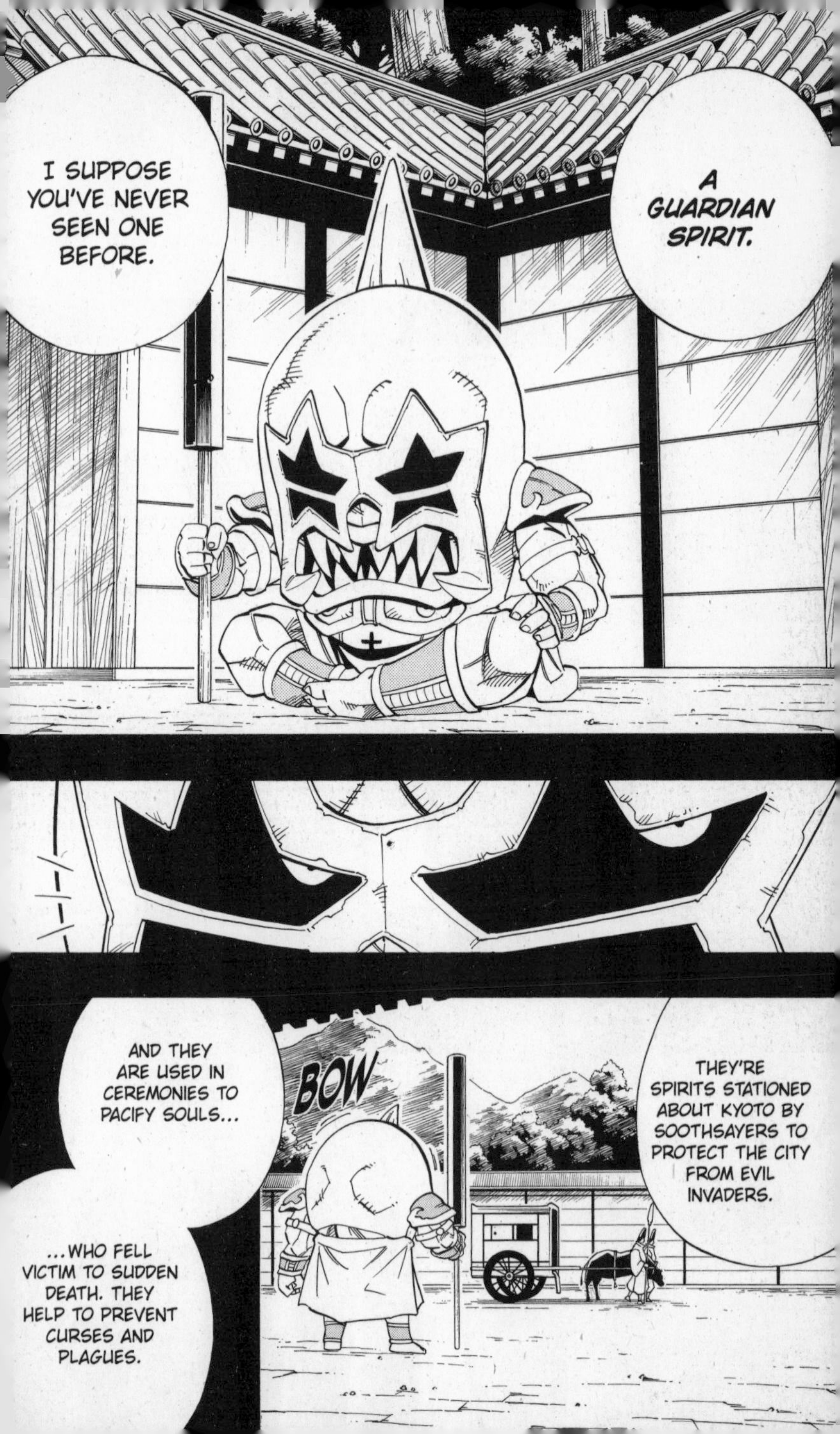
A GUARDIAN SPIRIT.
I SUPPOSE YOU'VE NEVER SEEN ONE BEFORE.
THEY'RE SPIRITS STATIONED ABOUT KYOTO BY SOOTHSAYERS TO PROTECT THE CITY FROM EVIL INVADERS.
BOW
AND THEY ARE USED IN CEREMONIES TO PACIFY SOULS...
...WHO FELL VICTIM TO SUDDEN DEATH. THEY HELP TO PREVENT CURSES AND PLAGUES.

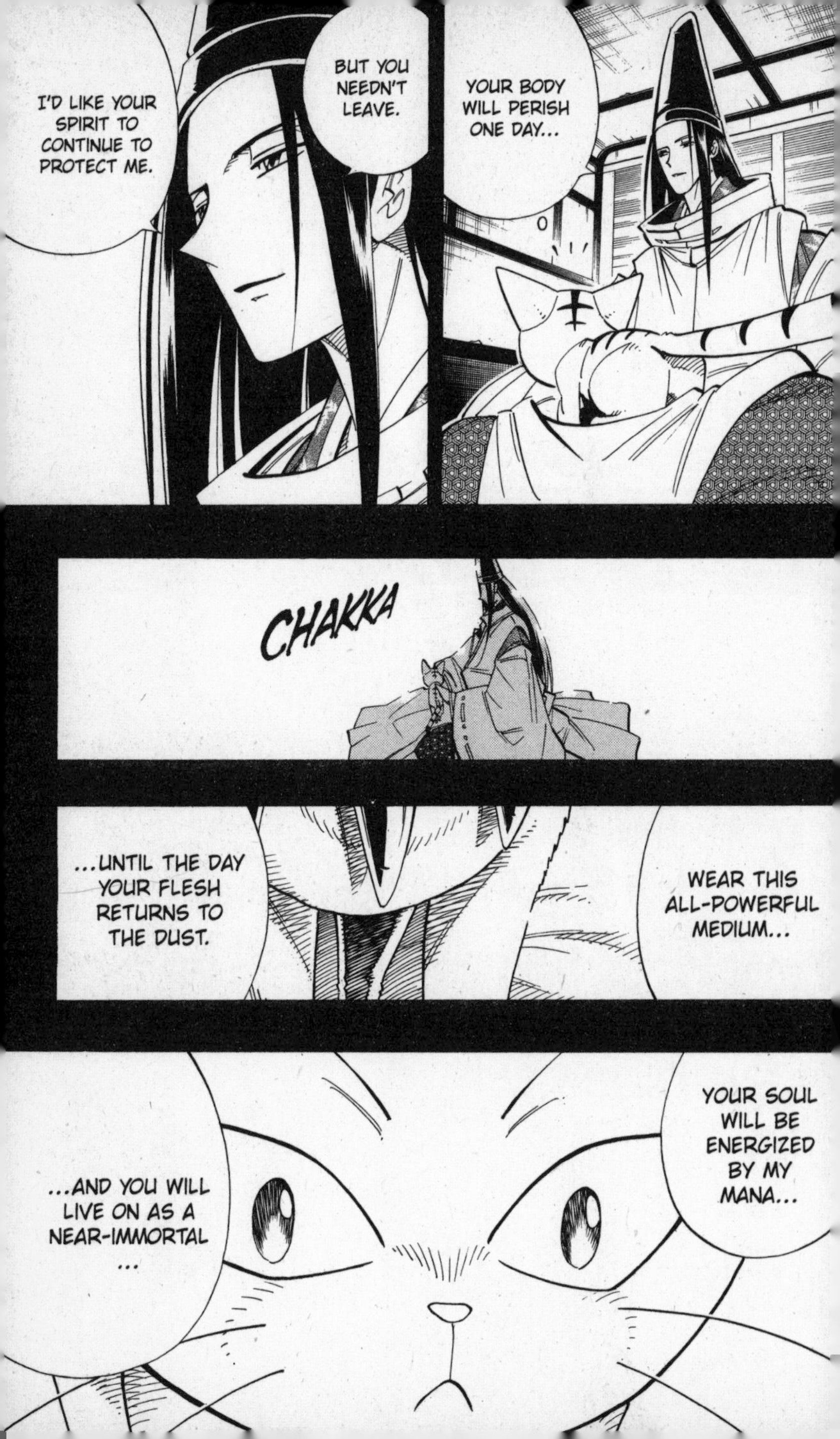
YOUR BODY WILL PERISH ONE DAY...
BUT YOU NEEDN'T LEAVE.
I'D LIKE YOUR SPIRIT TO CONTINUE TO PROTECT ME.
CHAKKA
WEAR THIS ALL-POWERFUL MEDIUM...
...UNTIL THE DAY YOUR FLESH RETURNS TO THE DUST.
YOUR SOUL WILL BE ENERGIZED BY MY MANA...
...AND YOU WILL LIVE ON AS A NEAR-IMMORTAL ...

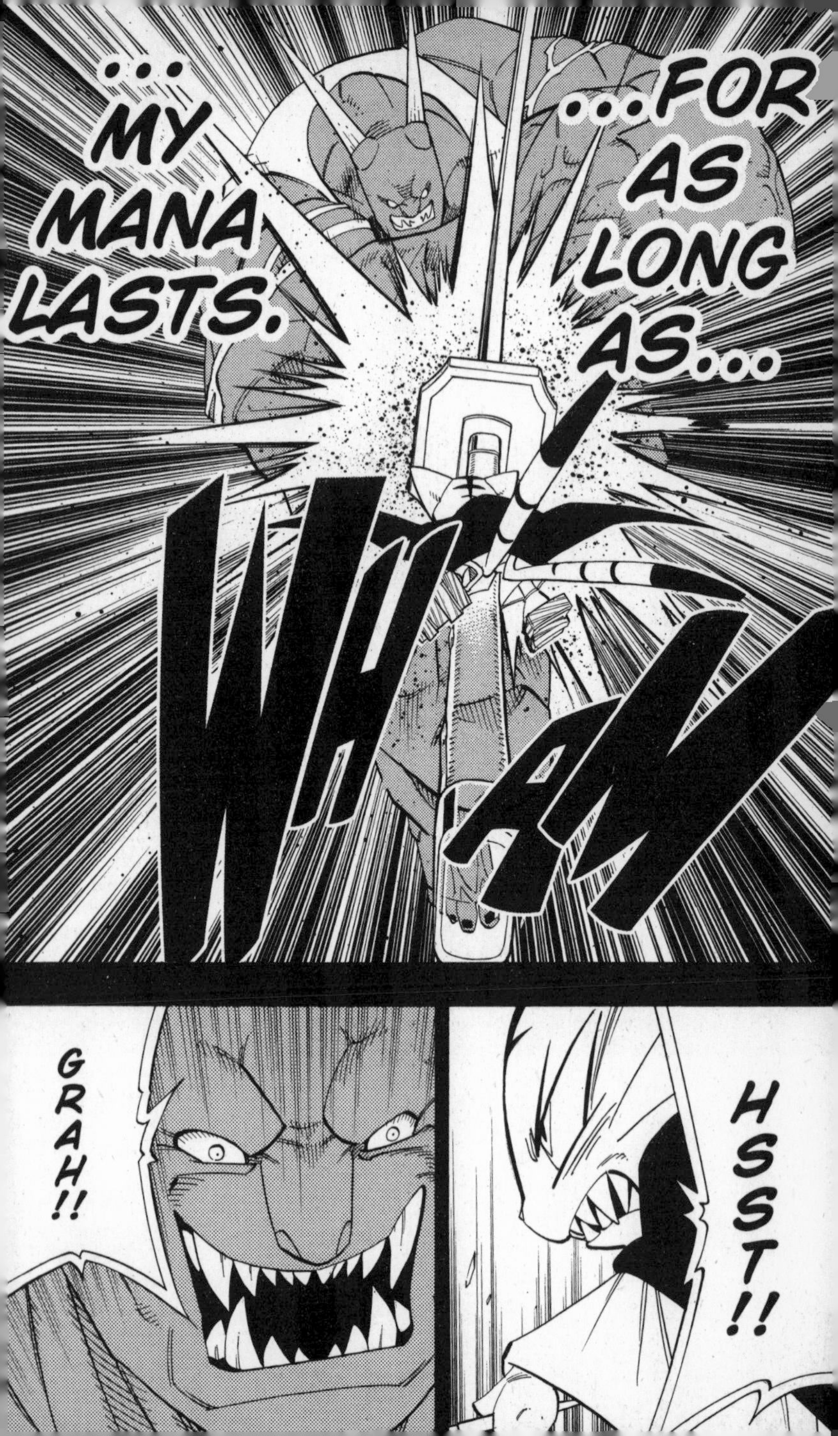
...FOR AS LONG AS...
...MY MANA LASTS.
WHAM
HSST!!
GRAH!!

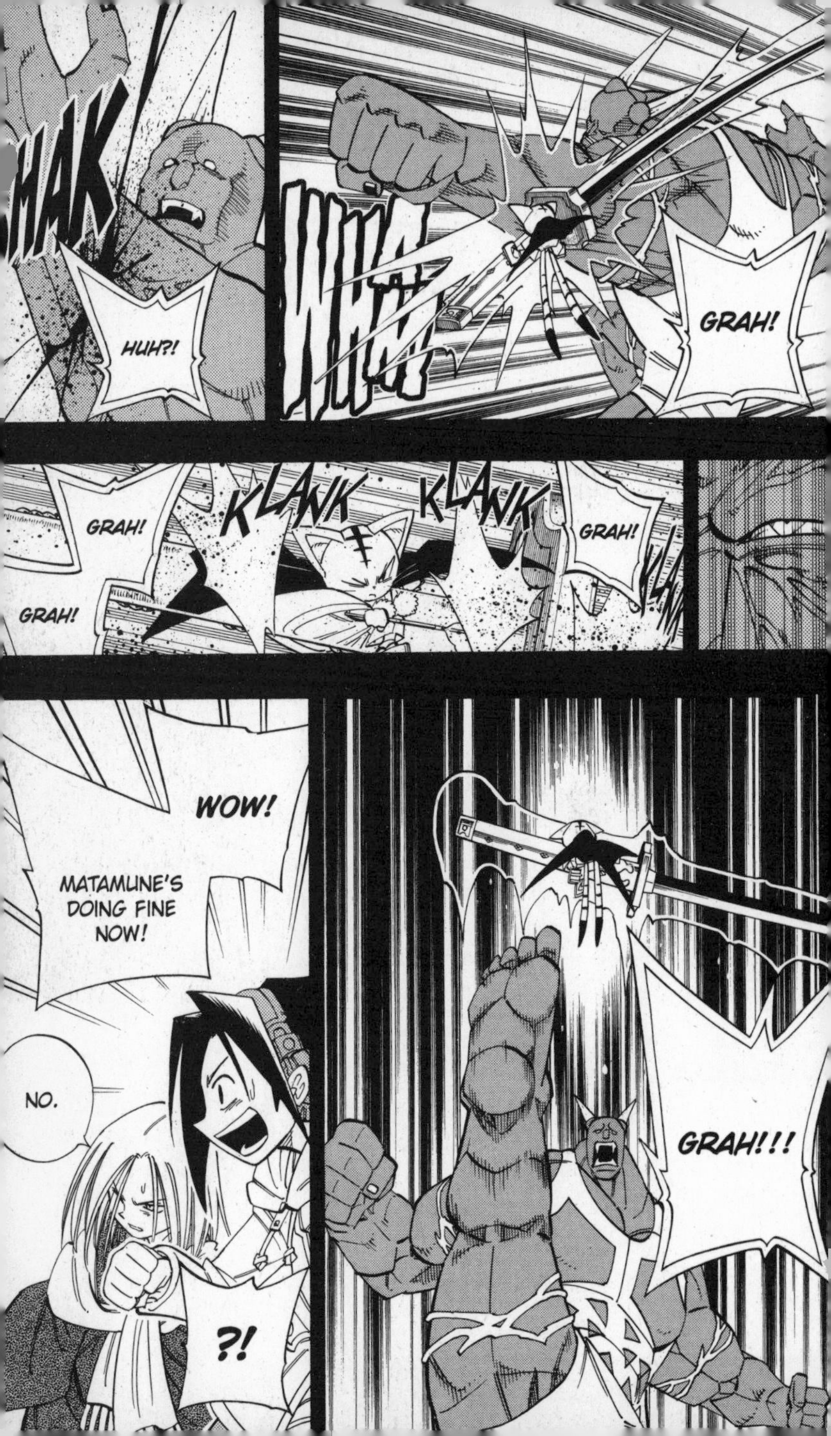
GRAH!
HUH?!
GRAH!
KLANK
KLANK
GRAH!
GRAH!
GRAH!!!
WOW!
MATAMUNE'S DOING FINE NOW!
NO.
?!

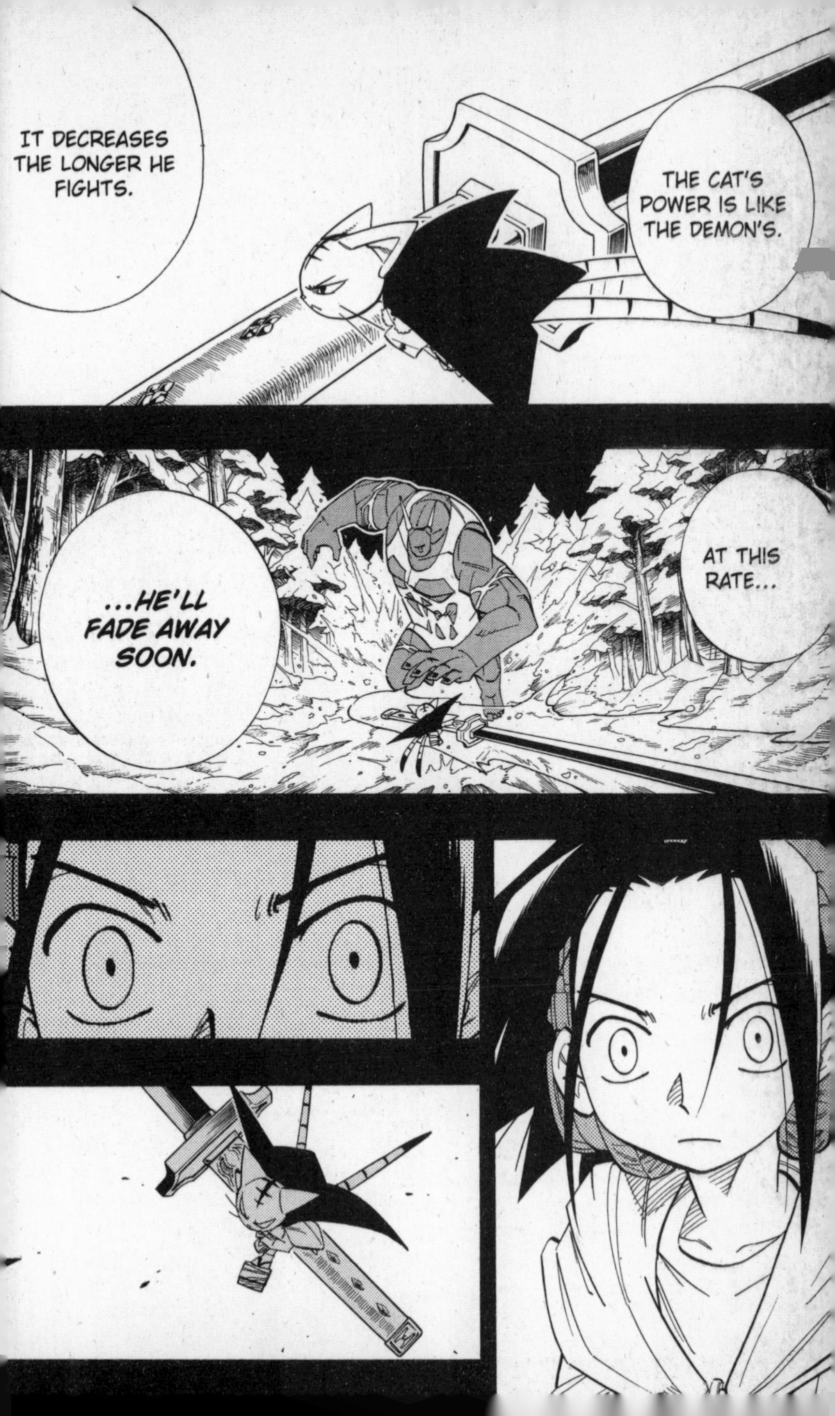
THE CAT'S POWER IS LIKE THE DEMON'S.
IT DECREASES THE LONGER HE FIGHTS.
AT THIS RATE...
...HE'LL FADE AWAY SOON.

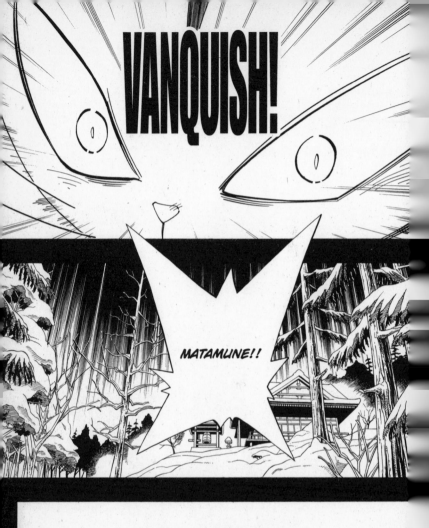

THOUGH I AM UNDESERVING
I HAVE FELT THE GREATEST OF JOYS
LIFE IS EVER-CHANGING
THOUGH IT IS OFTEN CRUEL
I DO NOT MIND
PLEASE, JUST GIVE ME A SMILE

SHAMAN KING CHARACTER FILE No.105

御霊神

GUARDIAN SPIRITS

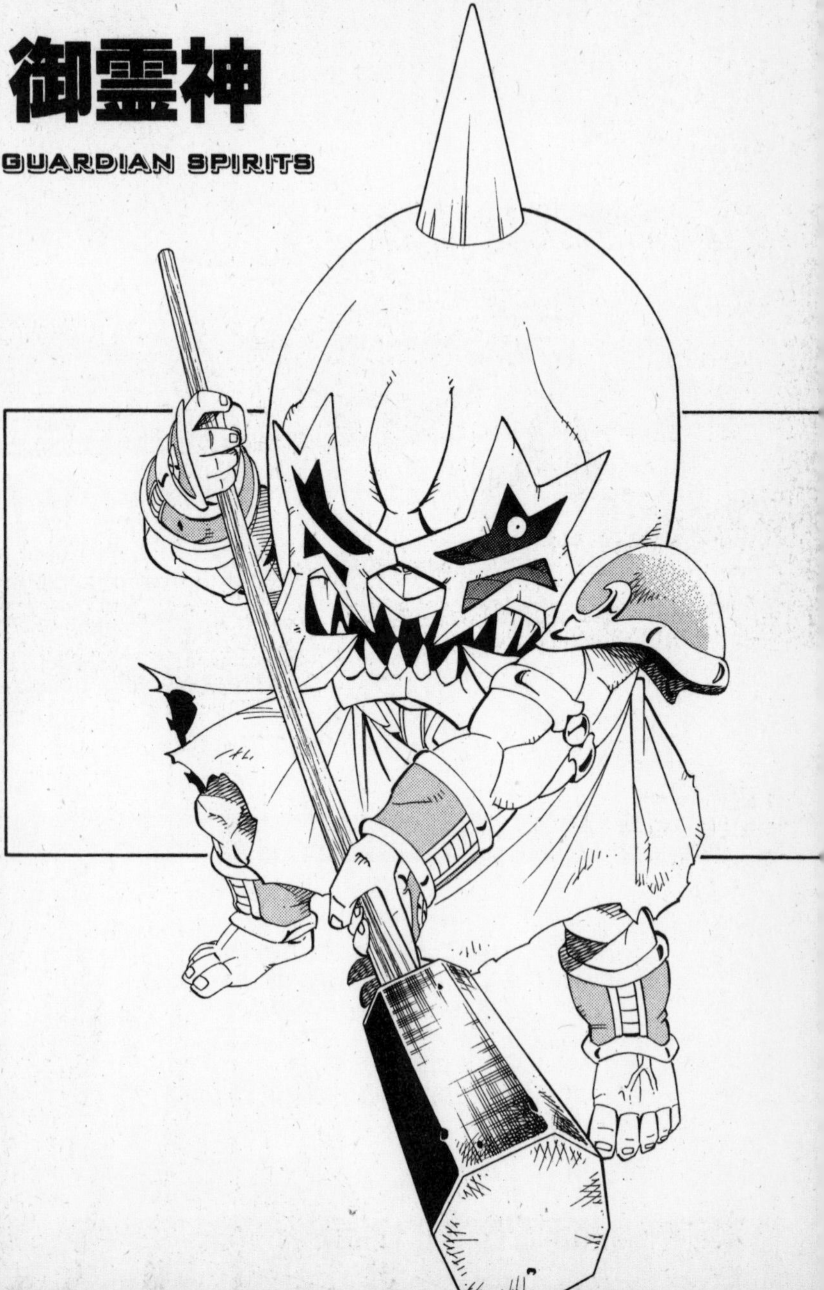

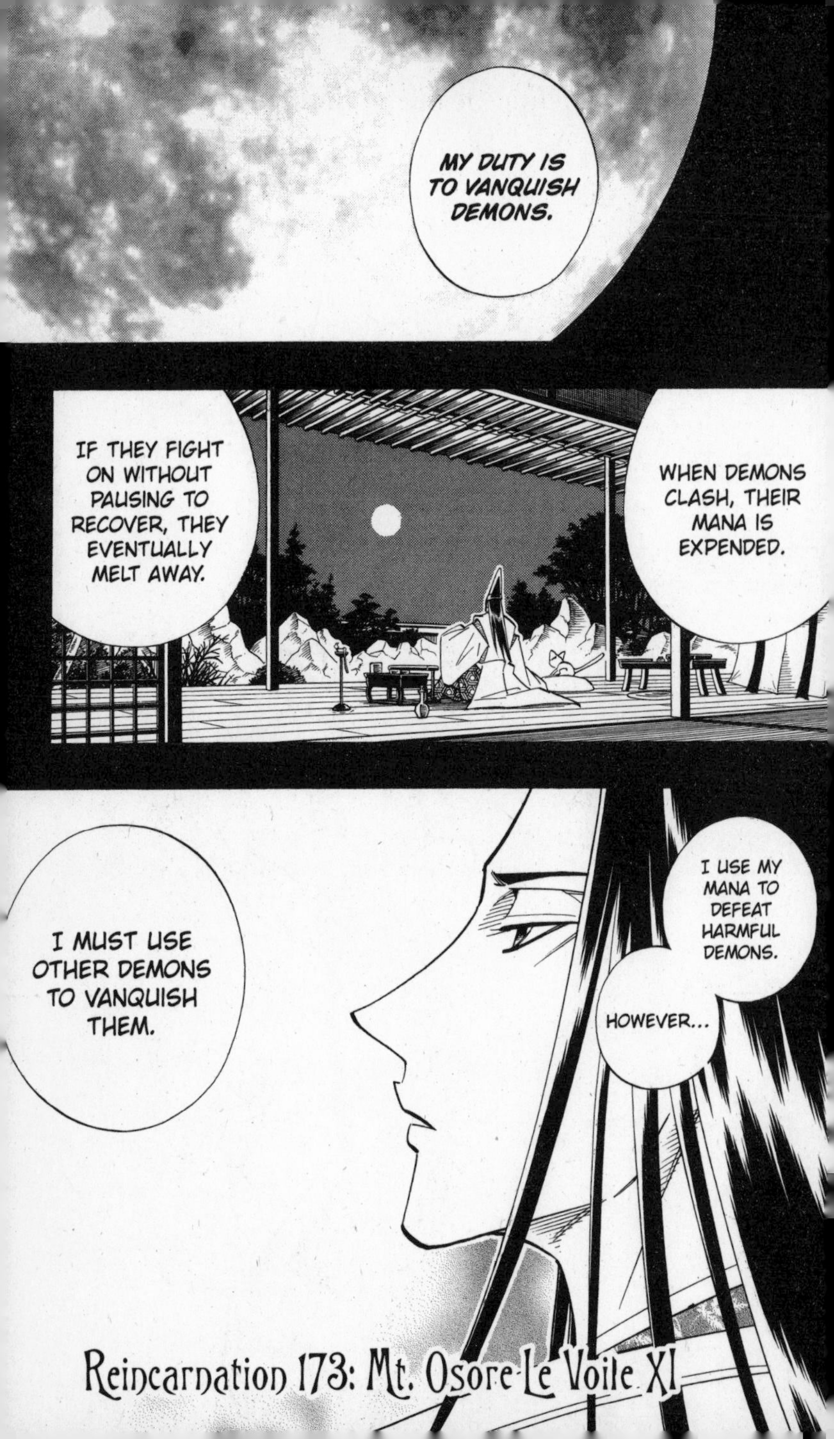
MY DUTY IS TO VANQUISH DEMONS.
WHEN DEMONS CLASH, THEIR MANA IS EXPENDED.
IF THEY FIGHT ON WITHOUT PAUSING TO RECOVER, THEY EVENTUALLY MELT AWAY.
I USE MY MANA TO DEFEAT HARMFUL DEMONS.
HOWEVER...
I MUST USE OTHER DEMONS TO VANQUISH THEM.
Reincarnation 173: Mt. Osore-Le Voile XI

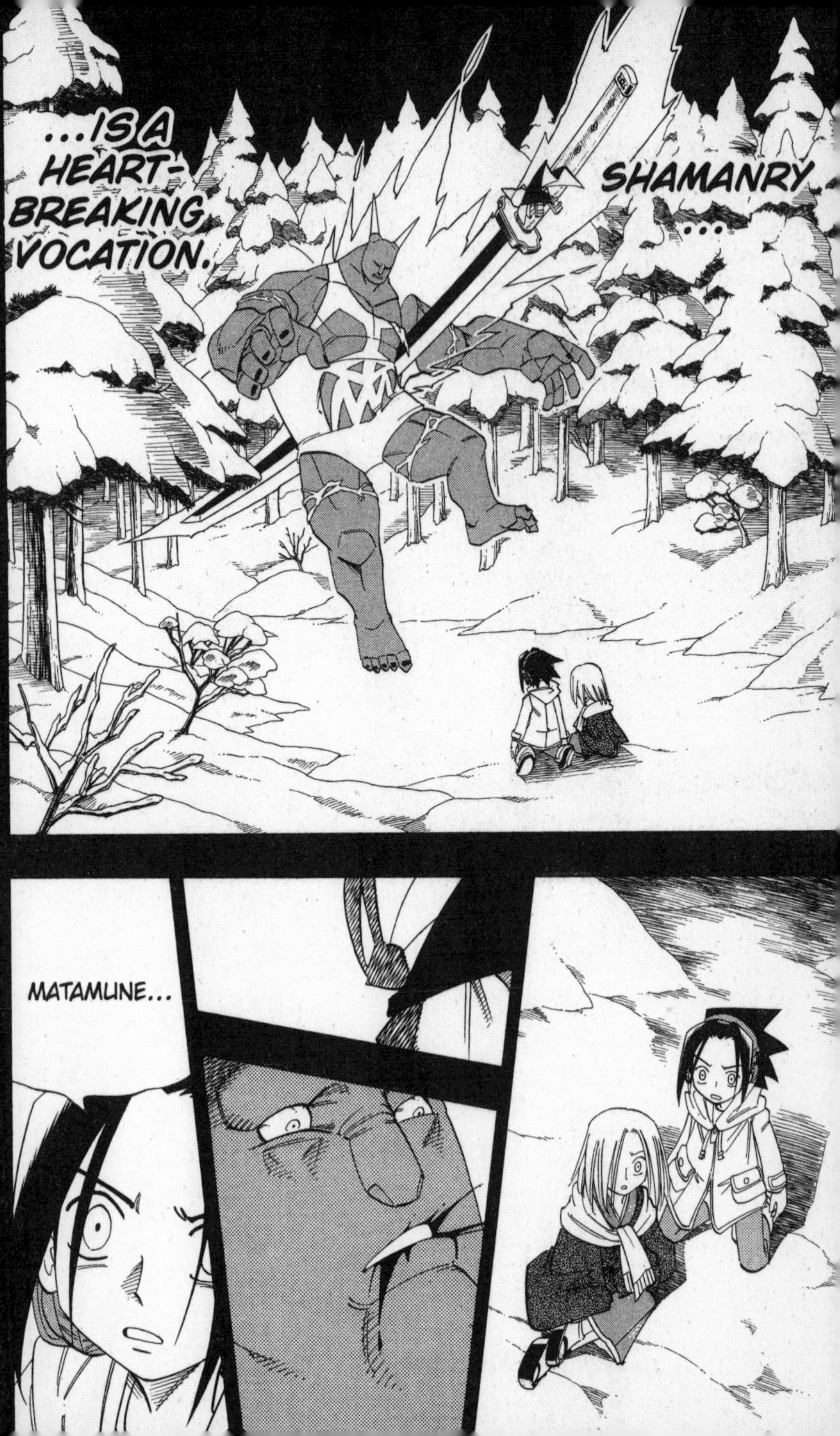
SHAMANRY...
...IS A HEART-BREAKING VOCATION.
MATAMUNE...

Reincarnation 173:
Mt. Osore Le Voile XI

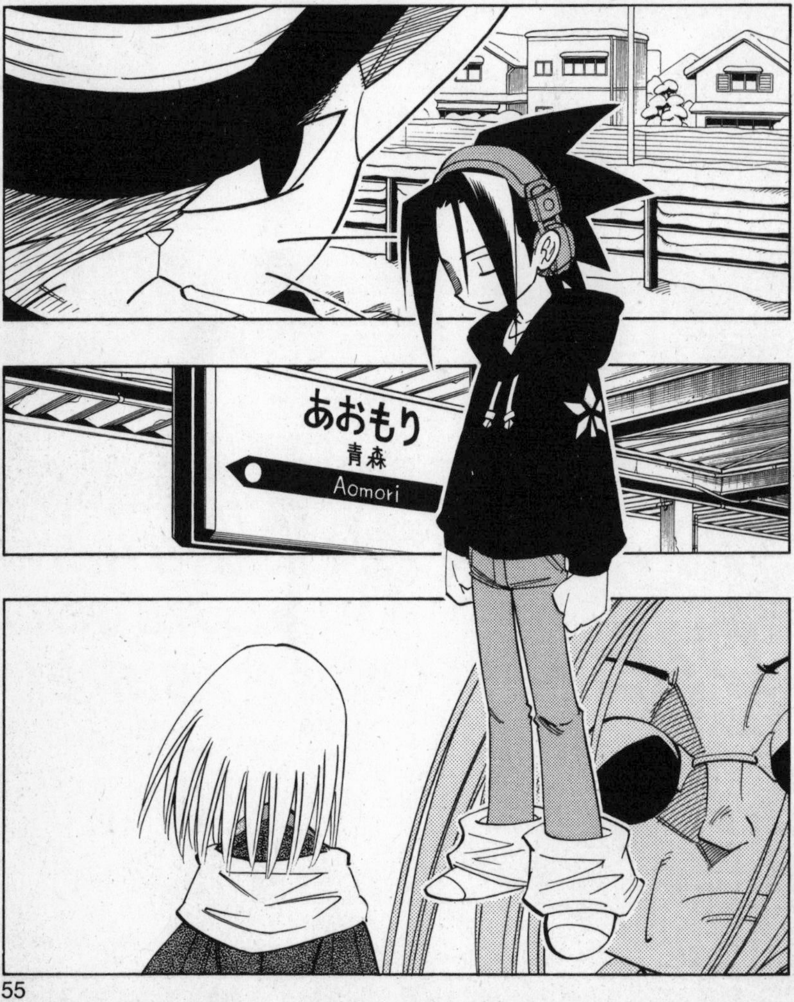
あおもり
青森
Aomori

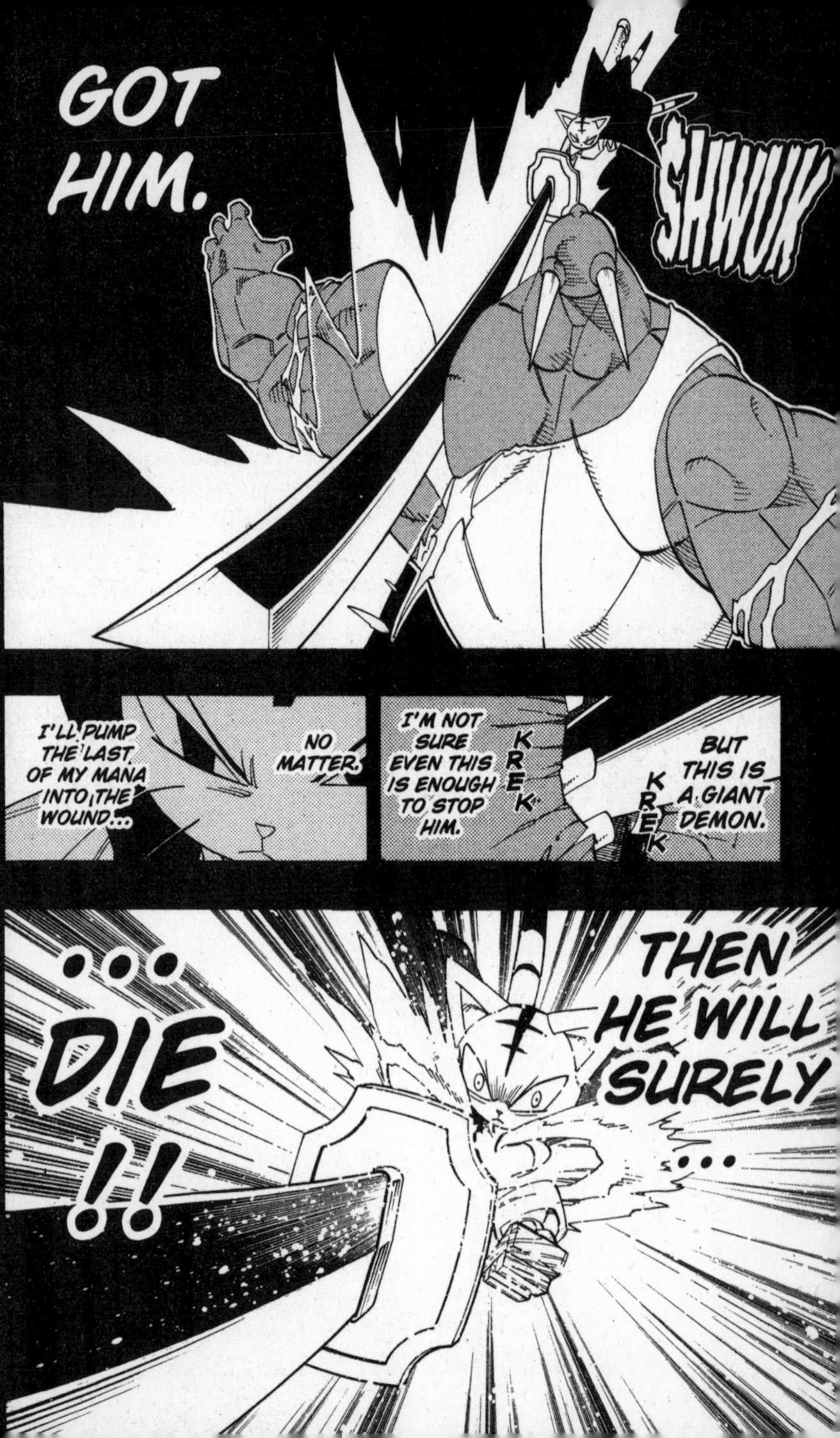
SHWUK
GOT HIM.
BUT THIS IS A GIANT DEMON.
KREK
KREK
I'M NOT SURE EVEN THIS IS ENOUGH TO STOP HIM.
NO MATTER.
I'LL PUMP THE LAST OF MY MANA INTO THE WOUND...
THEN HE WILL SURELY...
...DIE!!

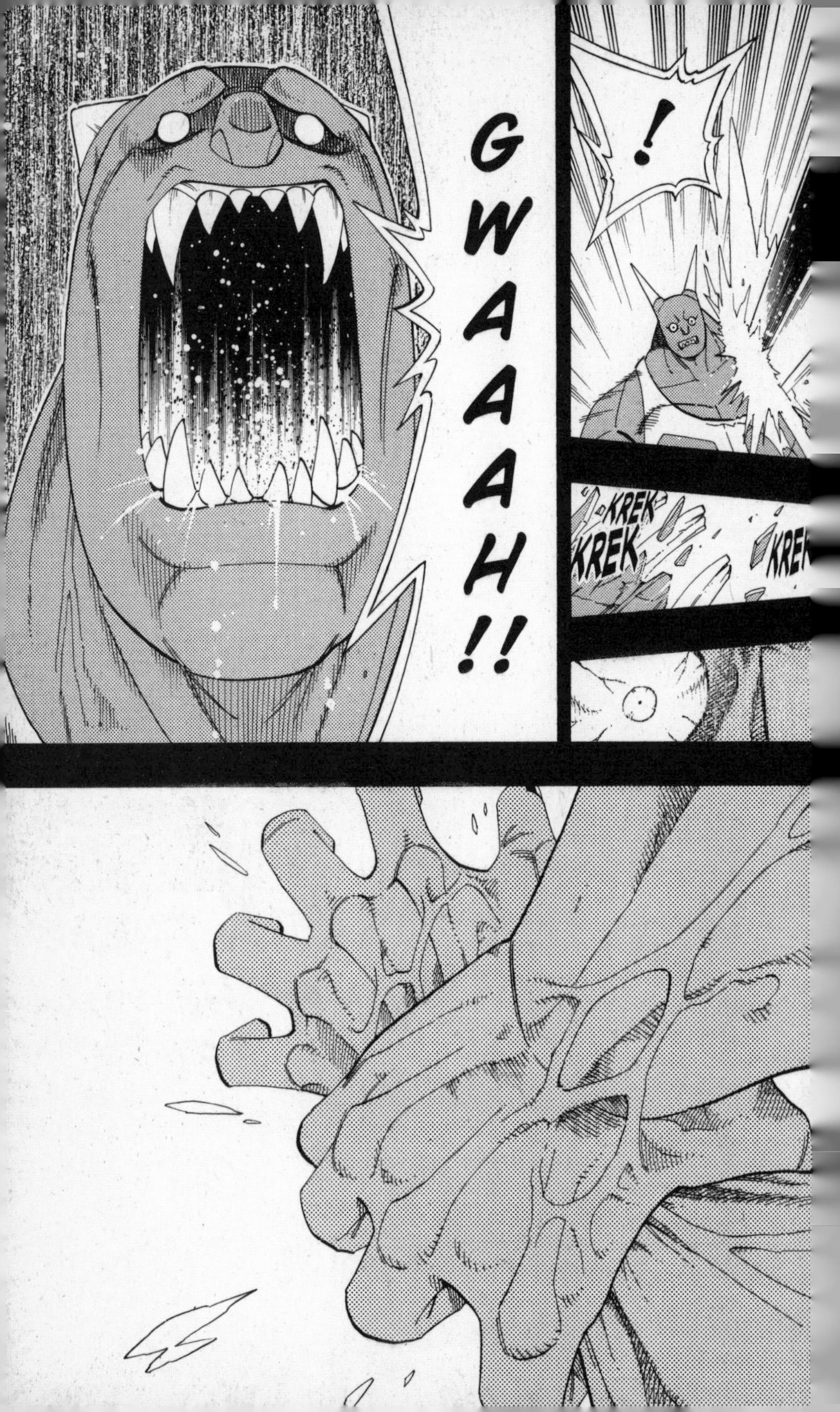
!
KREK
KREK
KREK
GWAAAH!!

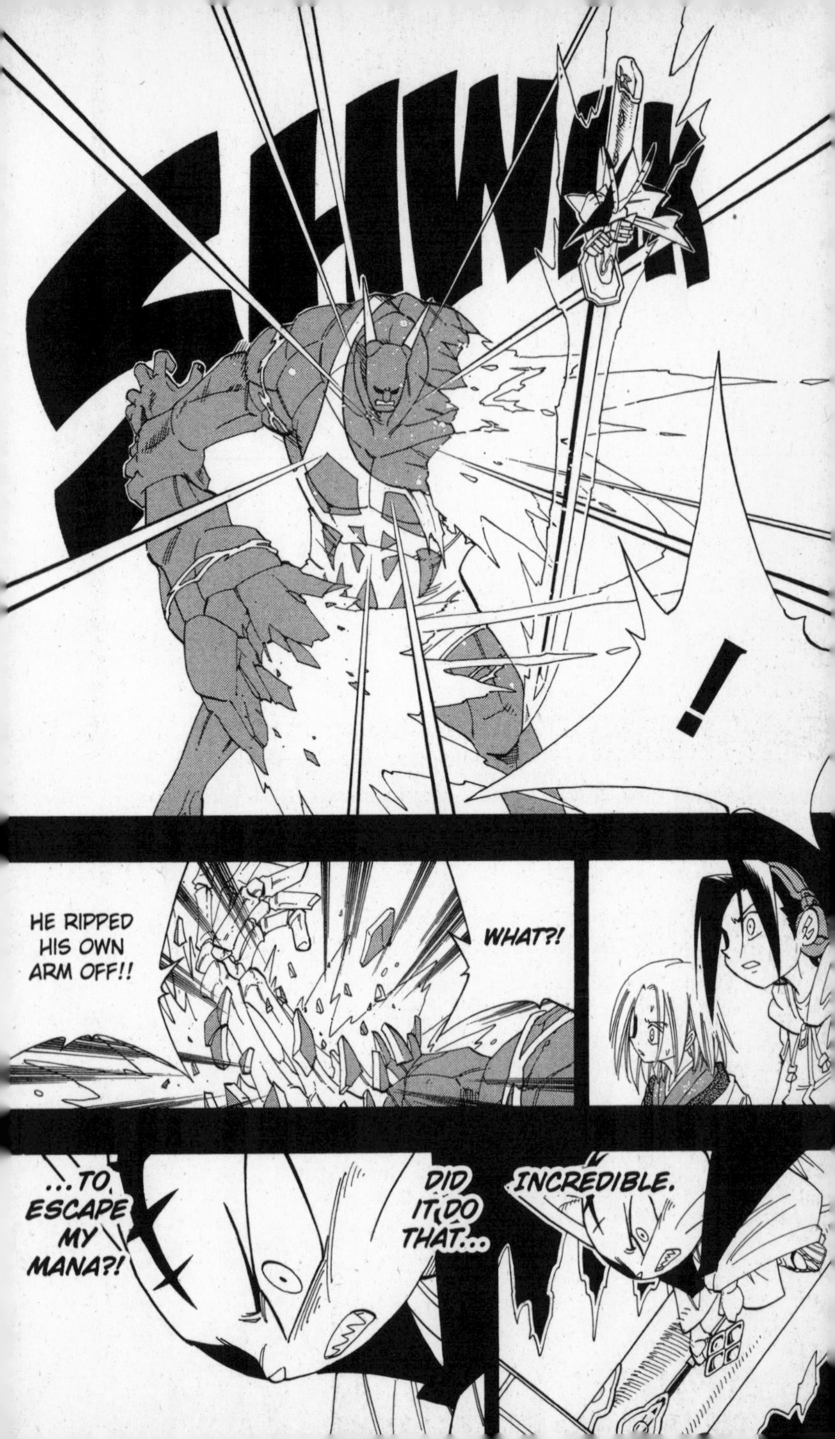
!
WHAT?!
HE RIPPED HIS OWN ARM OFF!!
INCREDIBLE.
DID IT DO THAT...
...TO ESCAPE MY MANA?!

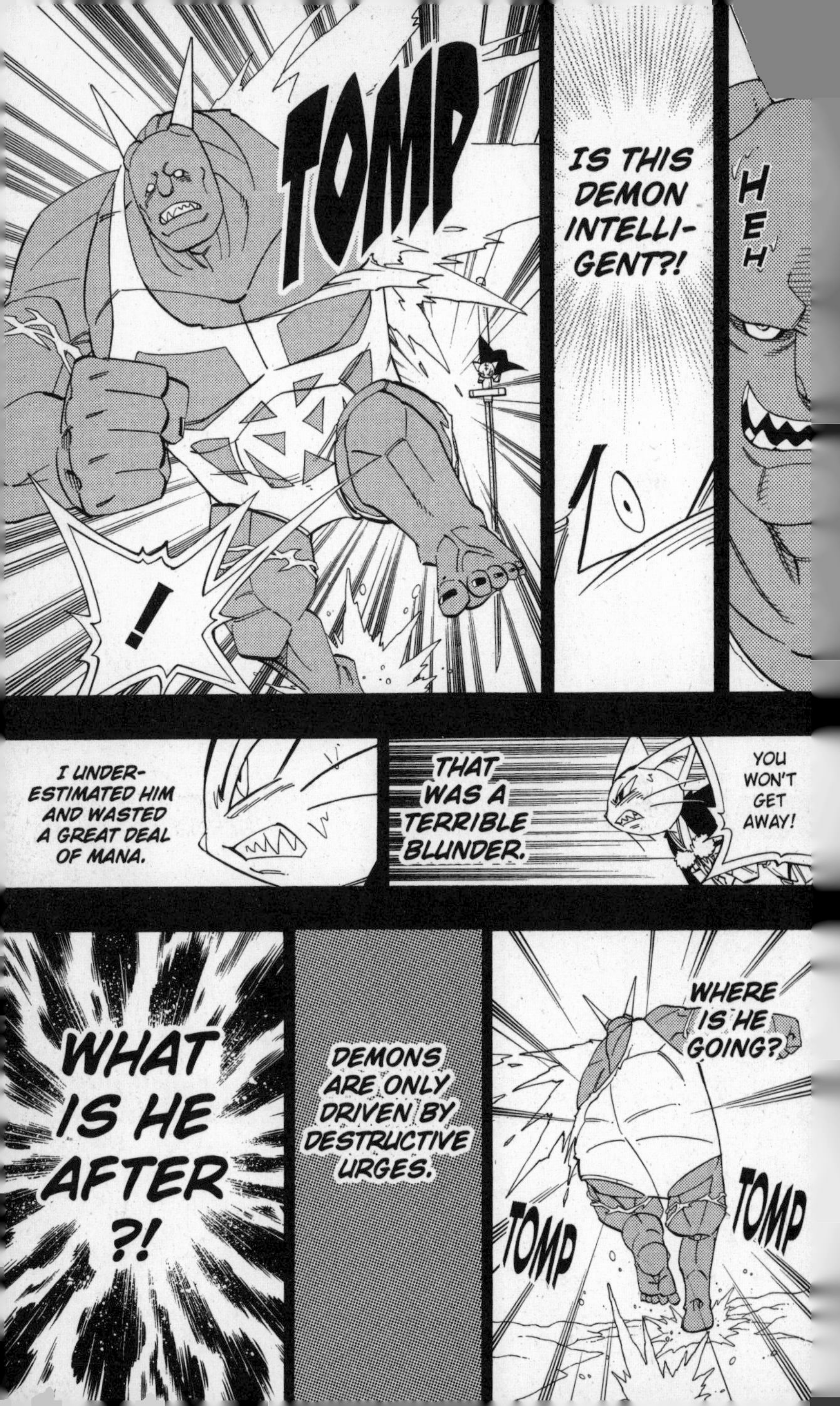

HEH
IS THIS DEMON INTELLI-GENT?!
TOMP
!
YOU WON'T GET AWAY!
THAT WAS A TERRIBLE BLUNDER.
I UNDER-ESTIMATED HIM AND WASTED A GREAT DEAL OF MANA.
WHERE IS HE GOING?
TOMP
TOMP
DEMONS ARE ONLY DRIVEN BY DESTRUCTIVE URGES.
WHAT IS HE AFTER ?!

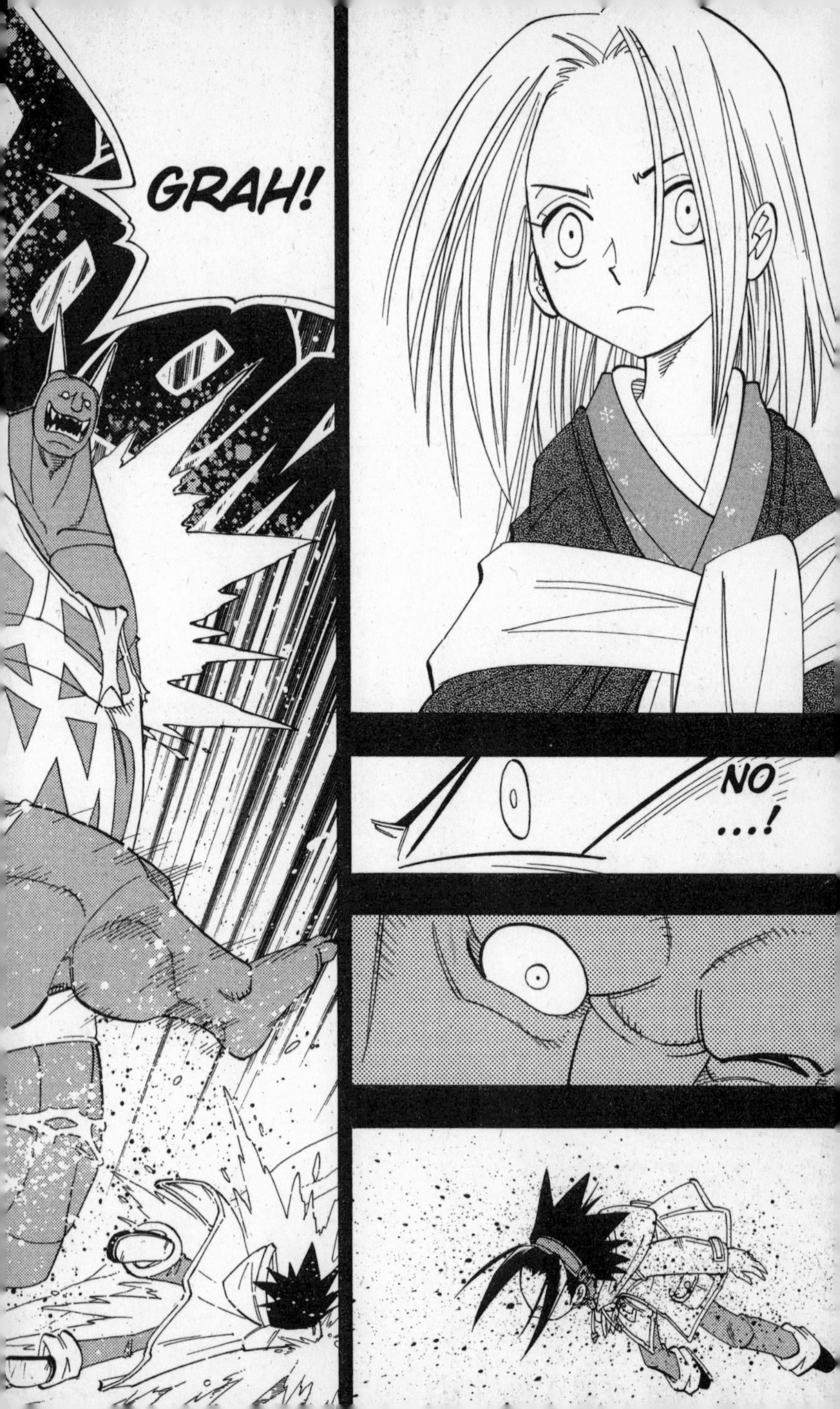
NO
...!
GRAH!

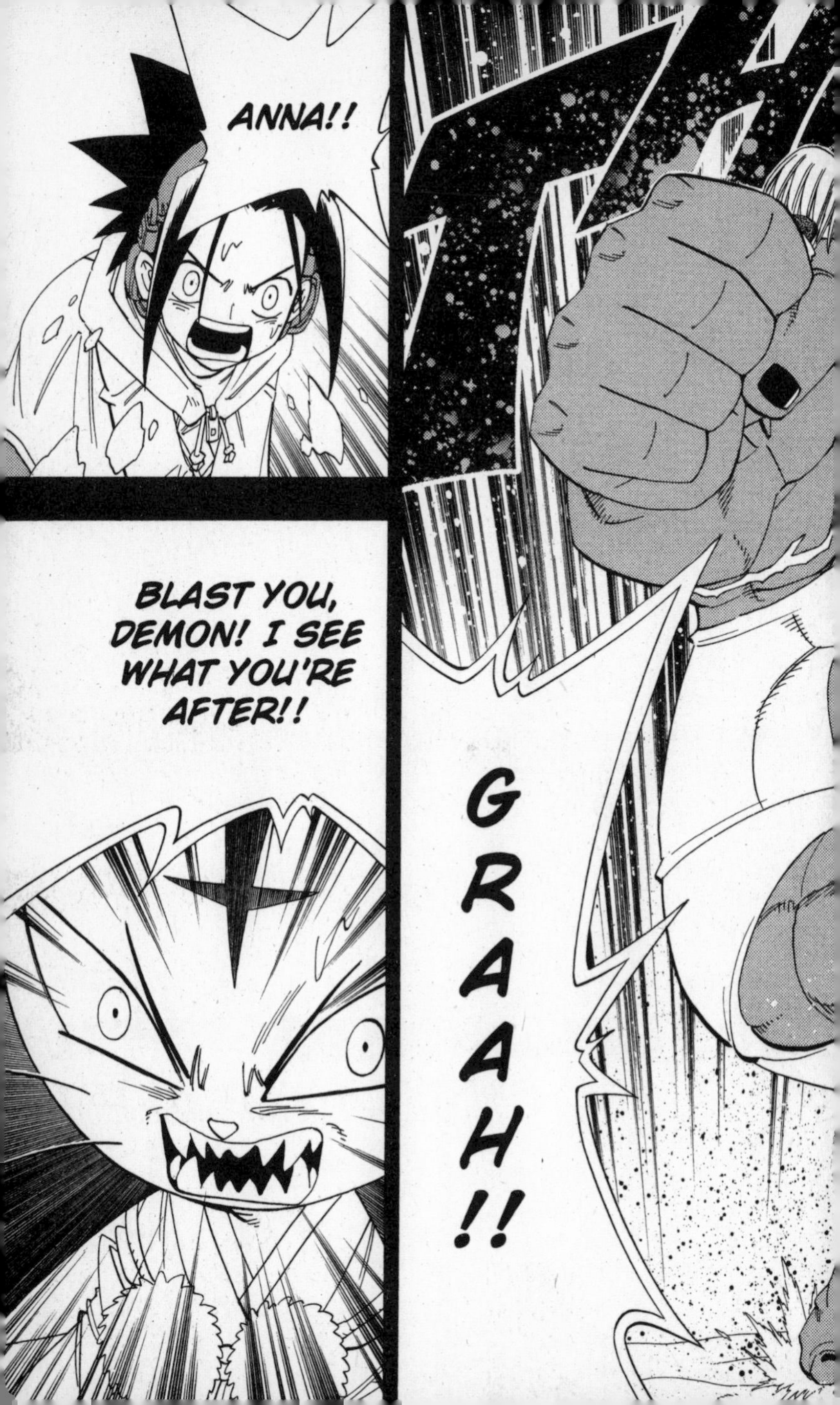

GRAAH!!
ANNA!!
BLAST YOU, DEMON! I SEE WHAT YOU'RE AFTER!!

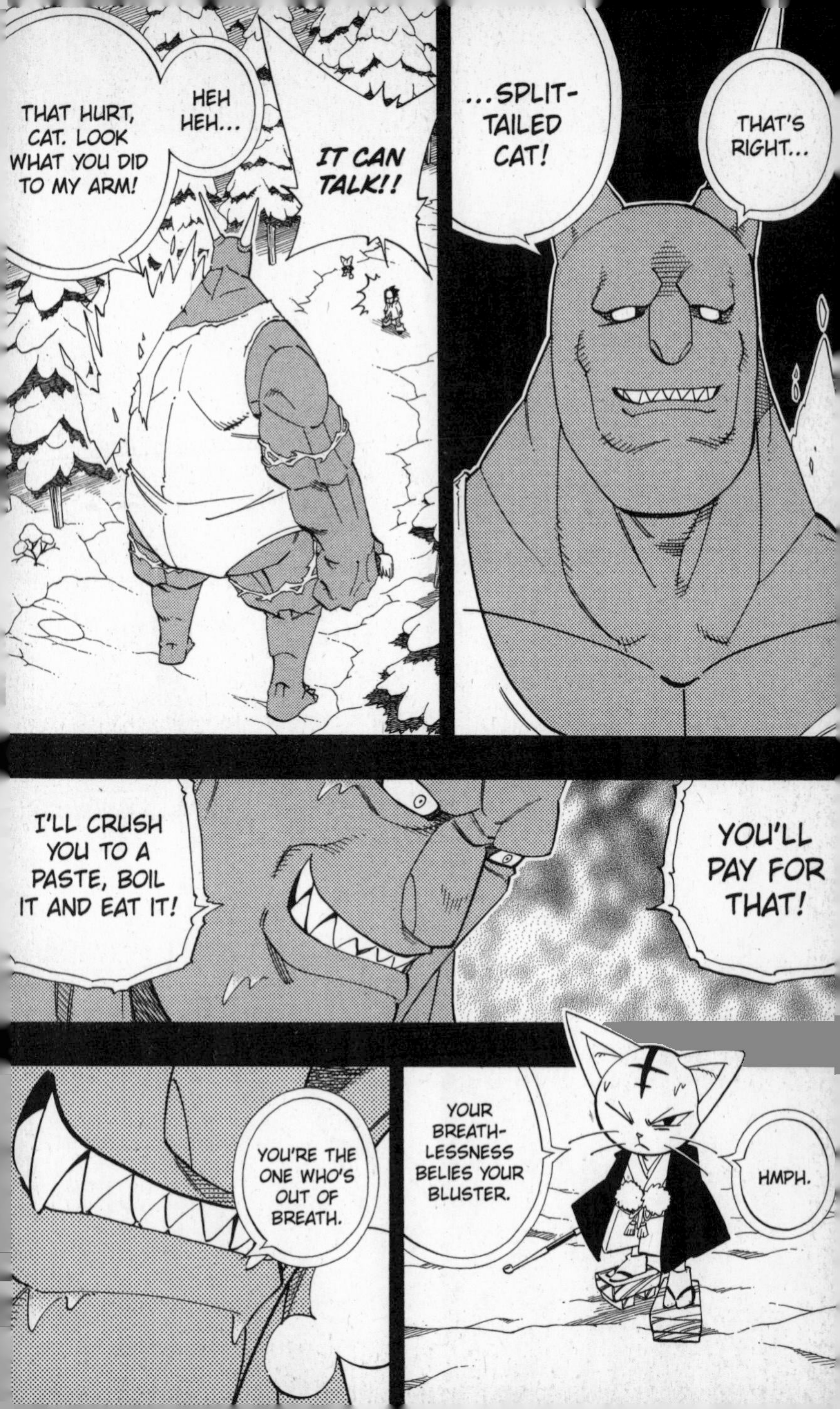
...SPLIT-TAILED CAT!
THAT'S RIGHT...
IT CAN TALK!!
HEH HEH...
THAT HURT, CAT. LOOK WHAT YOU DID TO MY ARM!
YOU'LL PAY FOR THAT!
I'LL CRUSH YOU TO A PASTE, BOIL IT AND EAT IT!
HMPH.
YOUR BREATHLESSNESS BELIES YOUR BLUSTER.
YOU'RE THE ONE WHO'S OUT OF BREATH.

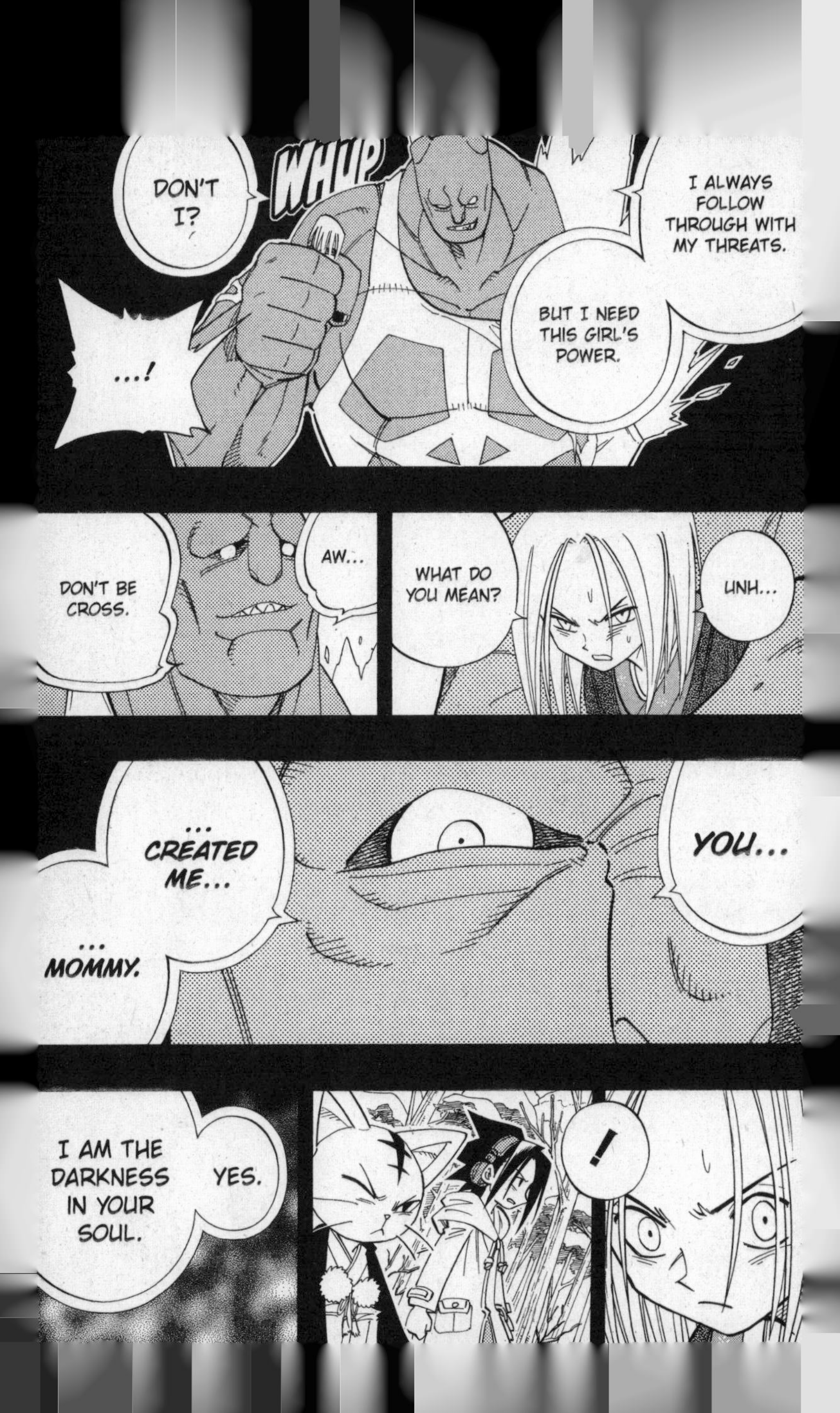

I ALWAYS FOLLOW THROUGH WITH MY THREATS.
BUT I NEED THIS GIRL'S POWER.
WHUP
DON'T I?
...!
UNH...
WHAT DO YOU MEAN?
AW...
DON'T BE CROSS.
YOU...
...CREATED ME...
...MOMMY.
!
YES.
I AM THE DARKNESS IN YOUR SOUL.

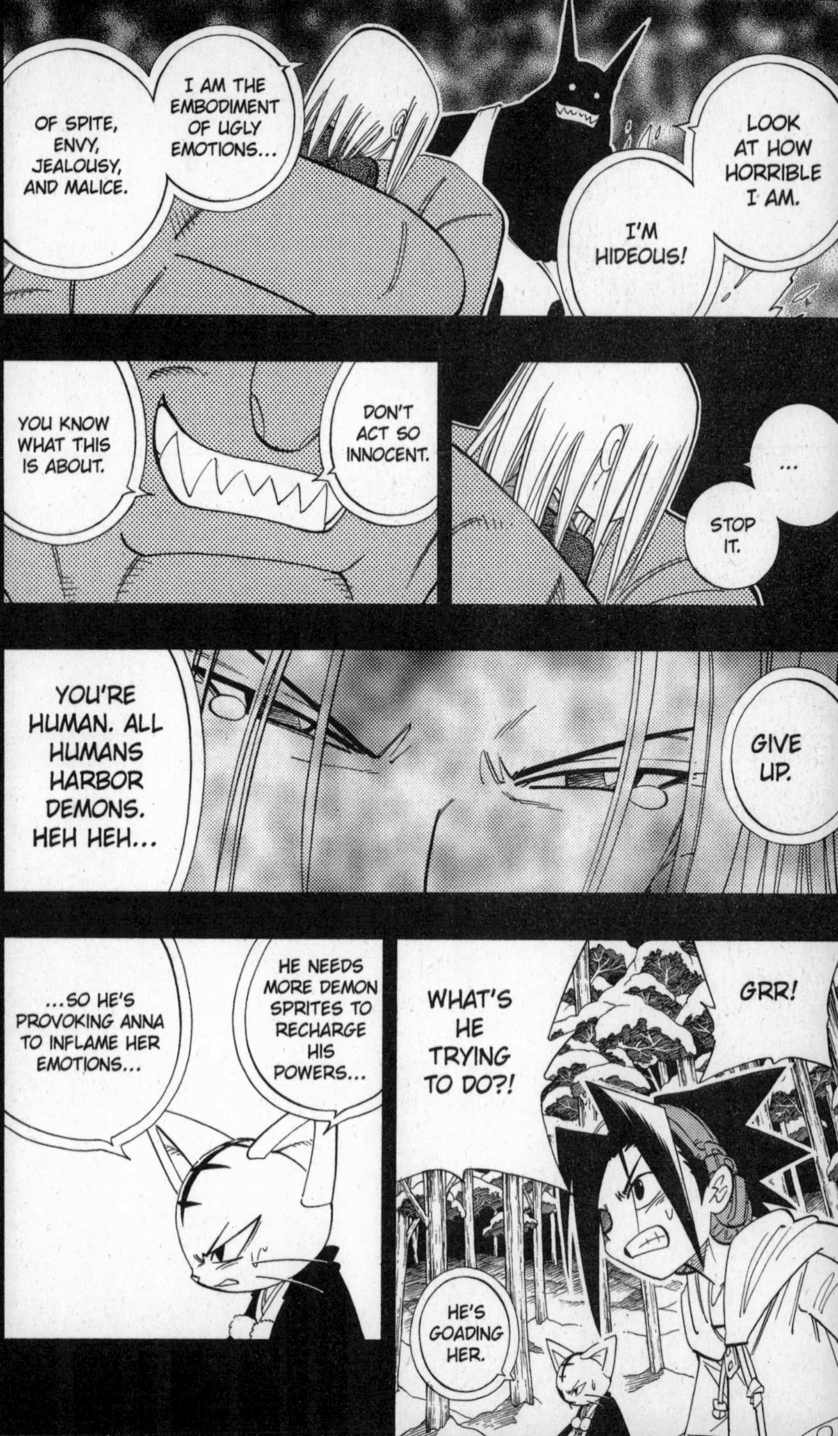
LOOK AT HOW HORRIBLE I AM.
I'M HIDEOUS!
I AM THE EMBODIMENT OF UGLY EMOTIONS...
OF SPITE, ENVY, JEALOUSY, AND MALICE.
...
STOP IT.
DON'T ACT SO INNOCENT.
YOU KNOW WHAT THIS IS ABOUT.
GIVE UP.
YOU'RE HUMAN. ALL HUMANS HARBOR DEMONS. HEH HEH...
GRR!
WHAT'S HE TRYING TO DO?!
HE'S GOADING HER.
HE NEEDS MORE DEMON SPRITES TO RECHARGE HIS POWERS...
...SO HE'S PROVOKING ANNA TO INFLAME HER EMOTIONS...

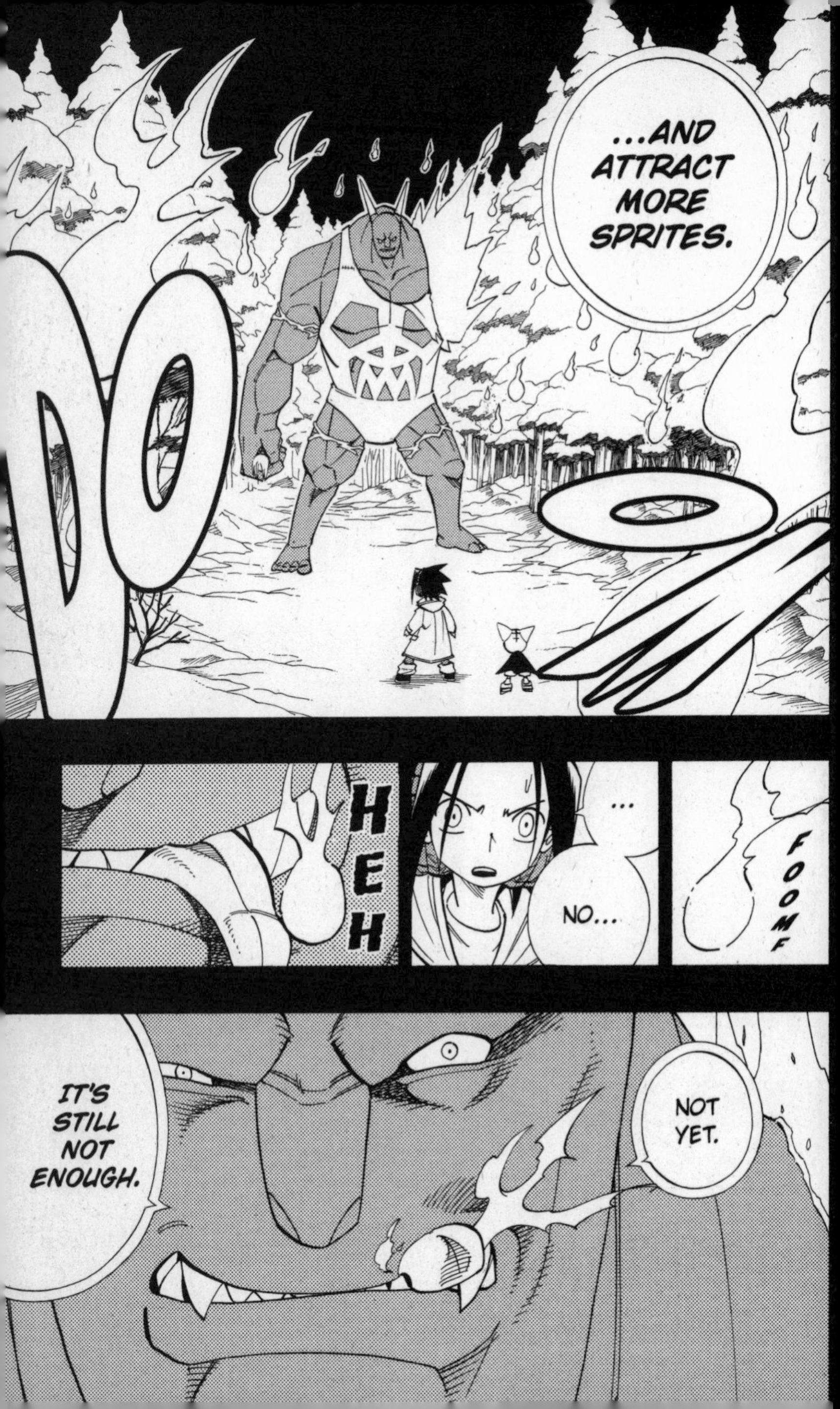
...AND ATTRACT MORE SPRITES.
DO
FOOMF
...
NO...
HEH
NOT YET.
IT'S STILL NOT ENOUGH.

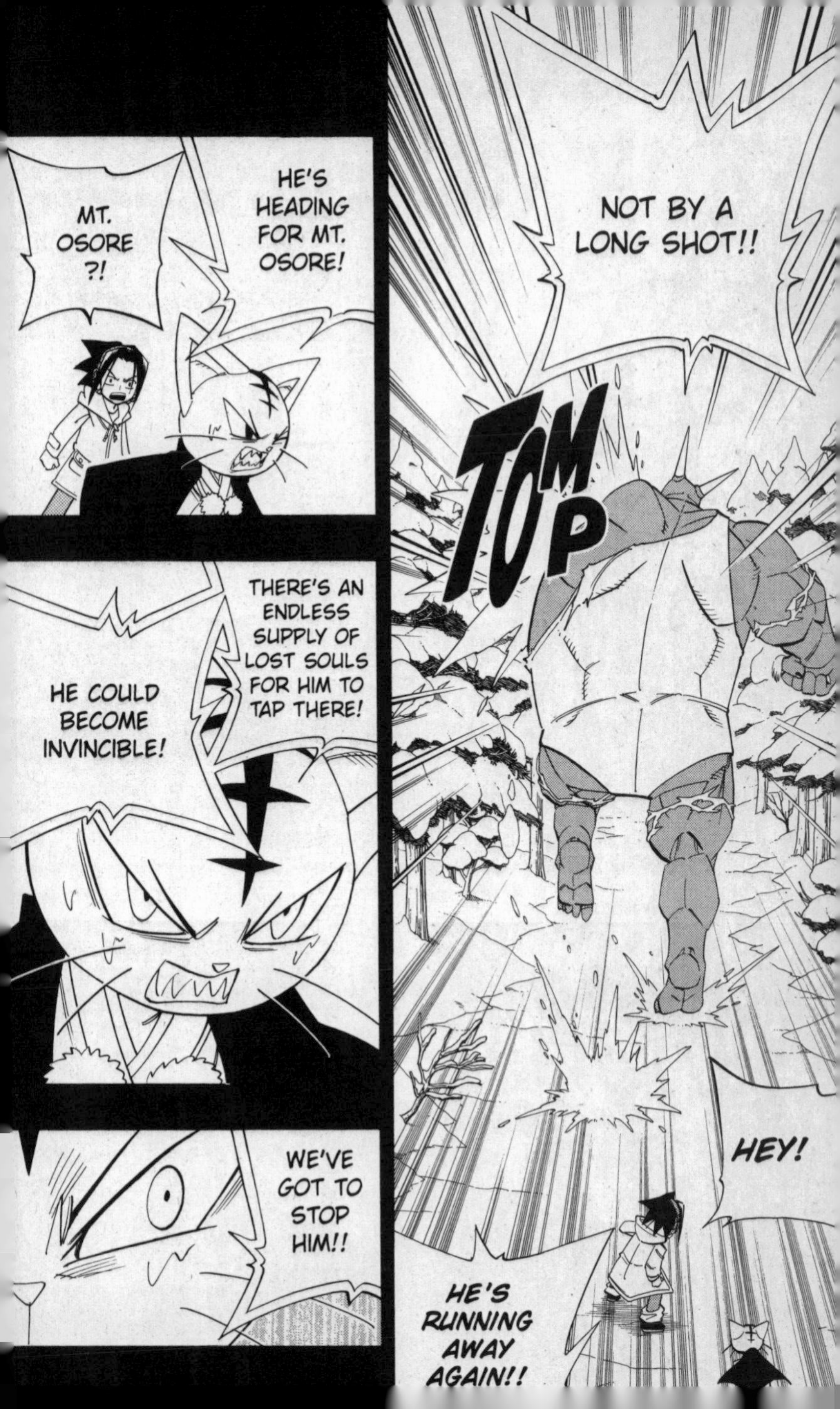
NOT BY A LONG SHOT!!
TOMP
HEY!
HE'S RUNNING AWAY AGAIN!!
HE'S HEADING FOR MT. OSORE!
MT. OSORE ?!
THERE'S AN ENDLESS SUPPLY OF LOST SOULS FOR HIM TO TAP THERE!
HE COULD BECOME INVINCIBLE!
WE'VE GOT TO STOP HIM!!

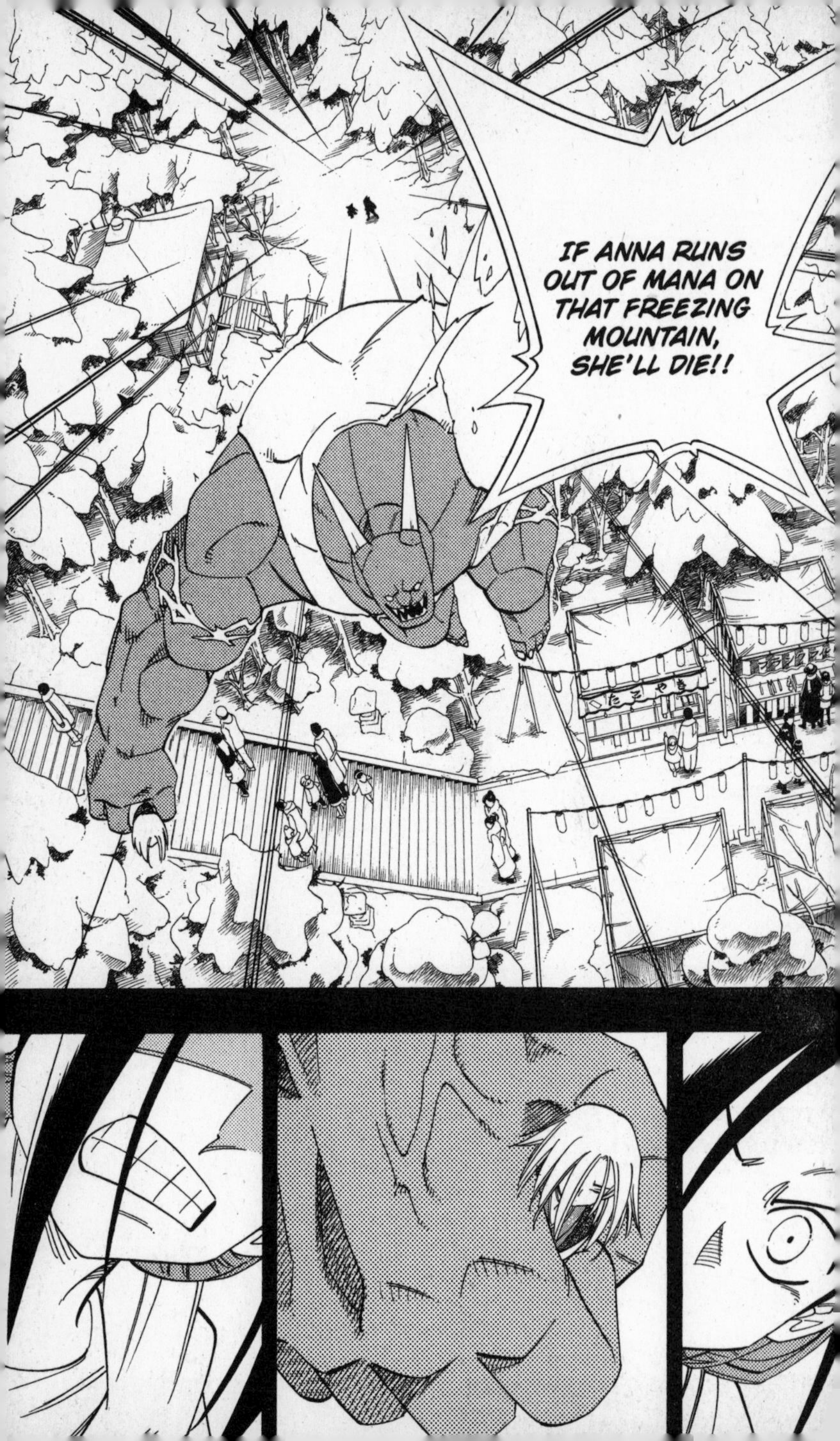
IF ANNA RUNS OUT OF MANA ON THAT FREEZING MOUNTAIN, SHE'LL DIE!!

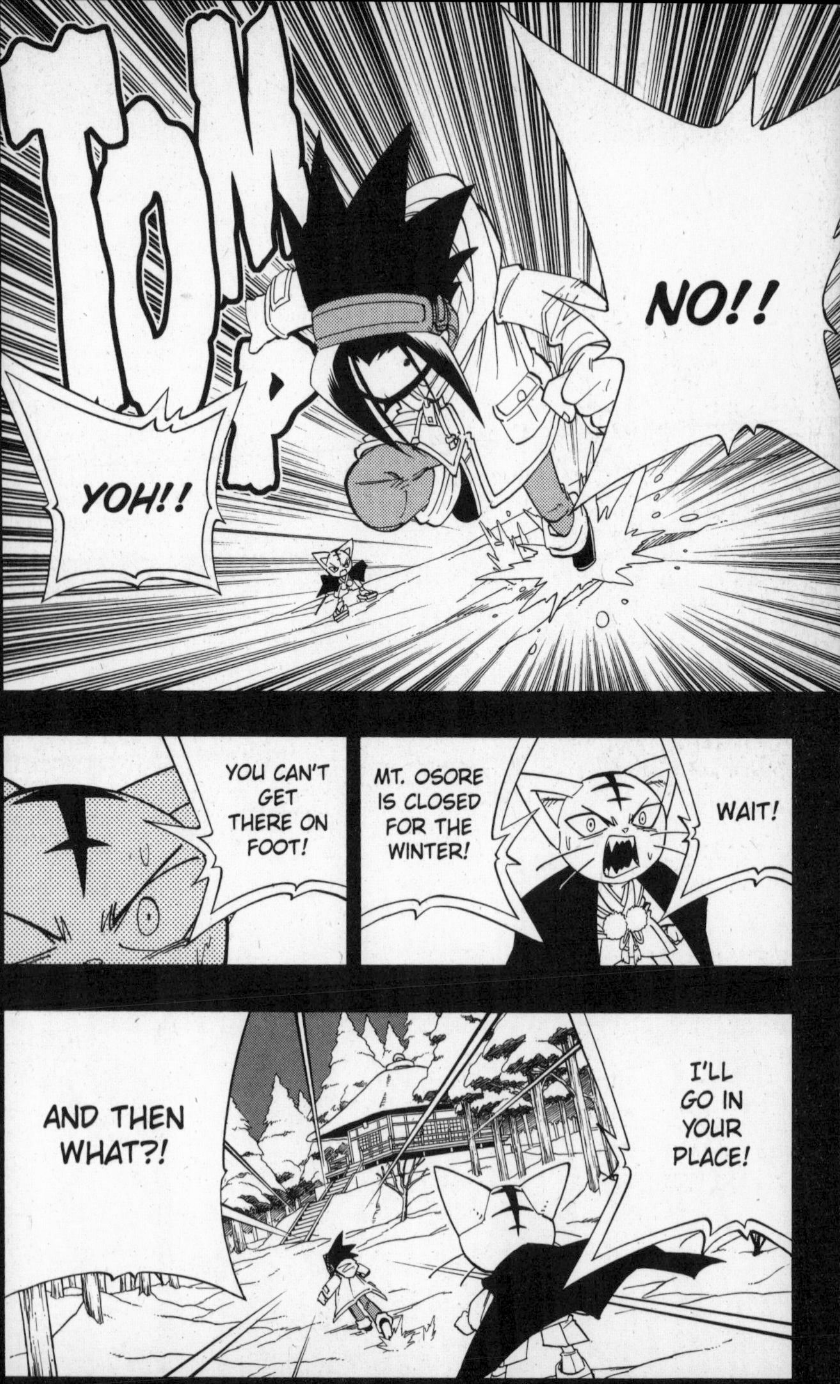
NO!!
TOMP
YOH!!
WAIT!
MT. OSORE IS CLOSED FOR THE WINTER!
YOU CAN'T GET THERE ON FOOT!
I'LL GO IN YOUR PLACE!
AND THEN WHAT?!

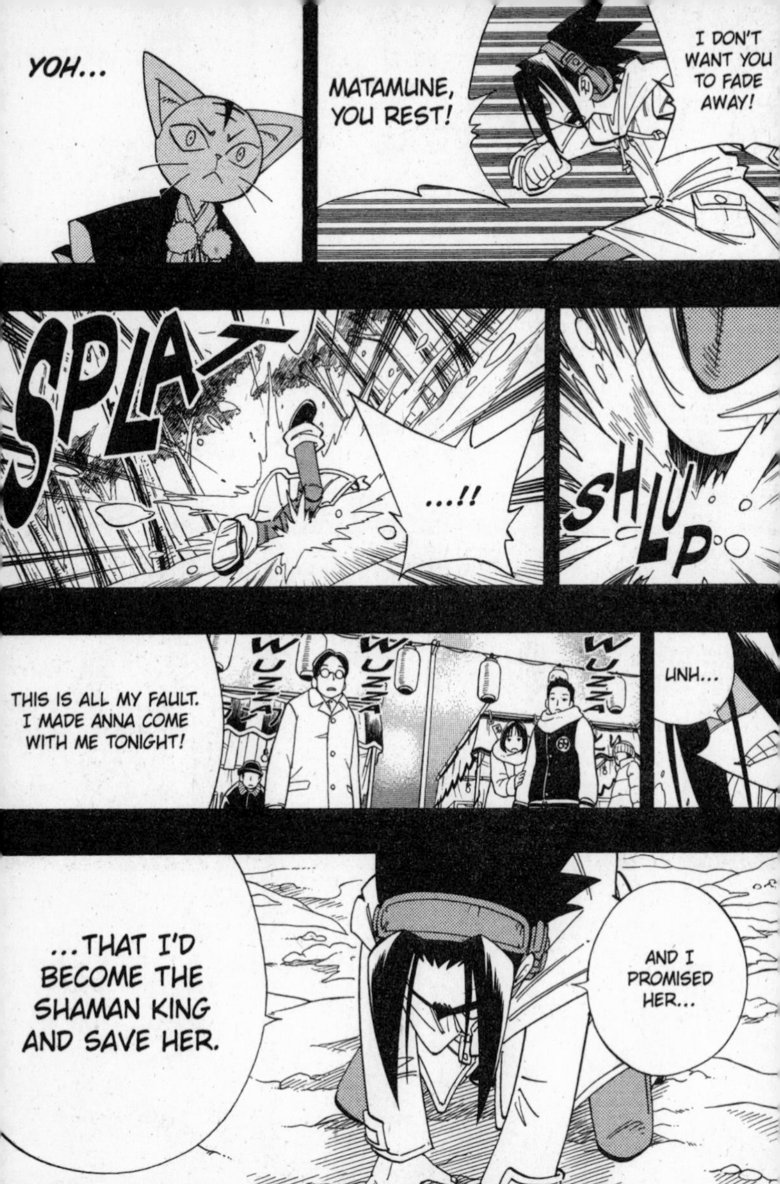
I DON'T WANT YOU TO FADE AWAY!
MATAMUNE, YOU REST!
YOH...
SHLULP
SPLAT
...!!
UNH...
WUNNA
WUNNA
WUNNA
THIS IS ALL MY FAULT. I MADE ANNA COME WITH ME TONIGHT!
AND I PROMISED HER...
...THAT I'D BECOME THE SHAMAN KING AND SAVE HER.

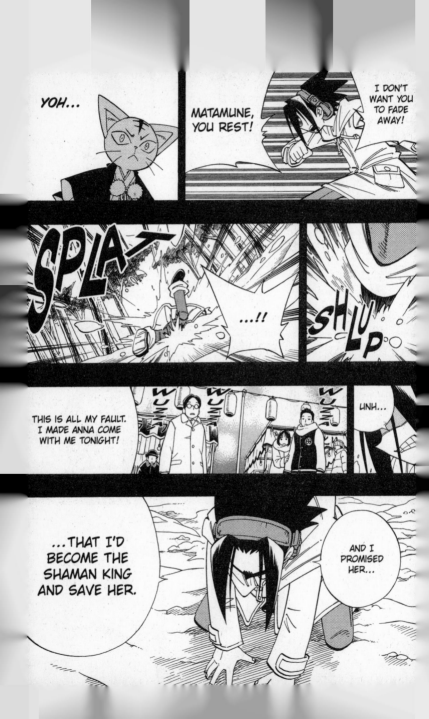

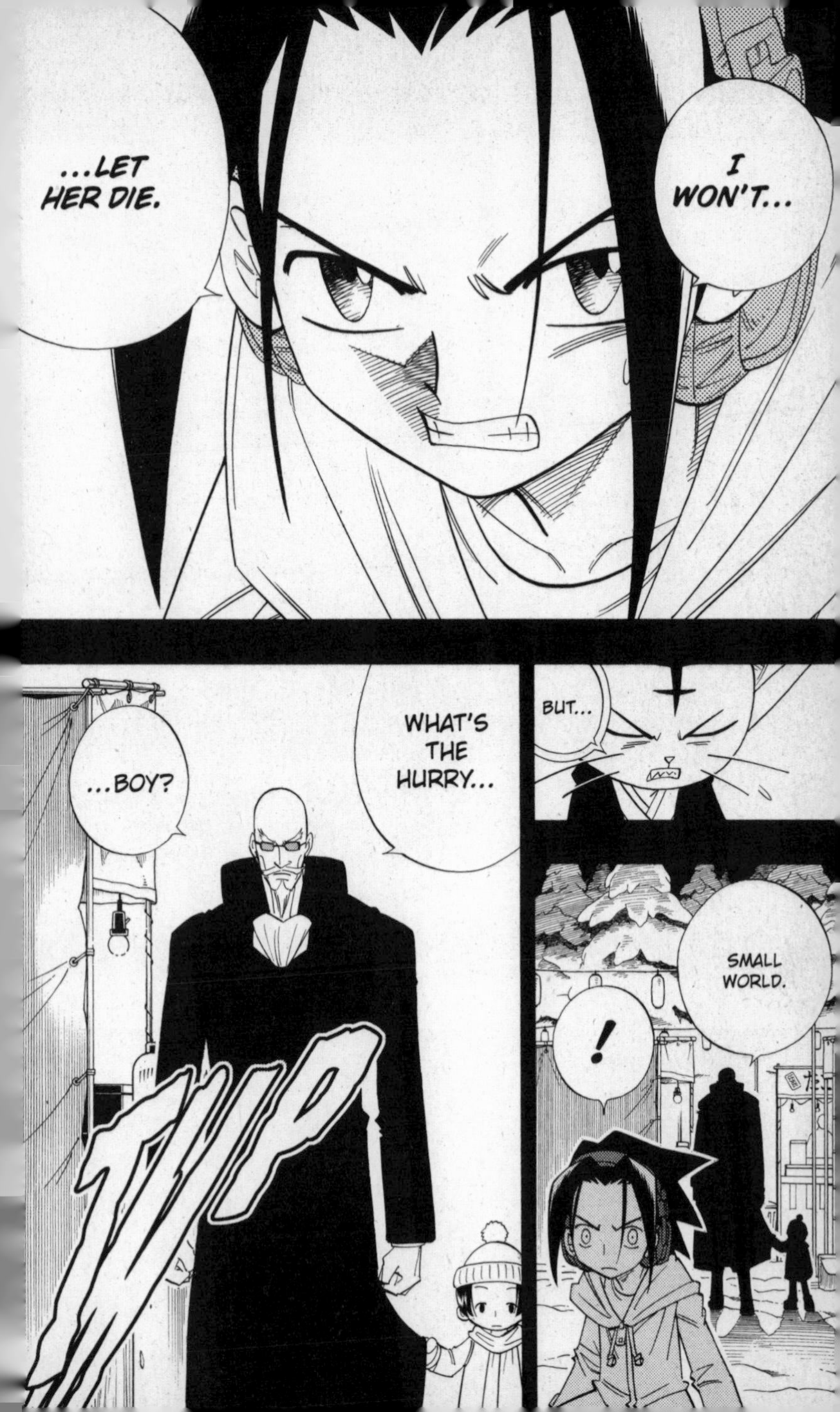
I WON'T...
...LET HER DIE.
BUT...
SMALL WORLD.
!
WHAT'S THE HURRY...
...BOY?

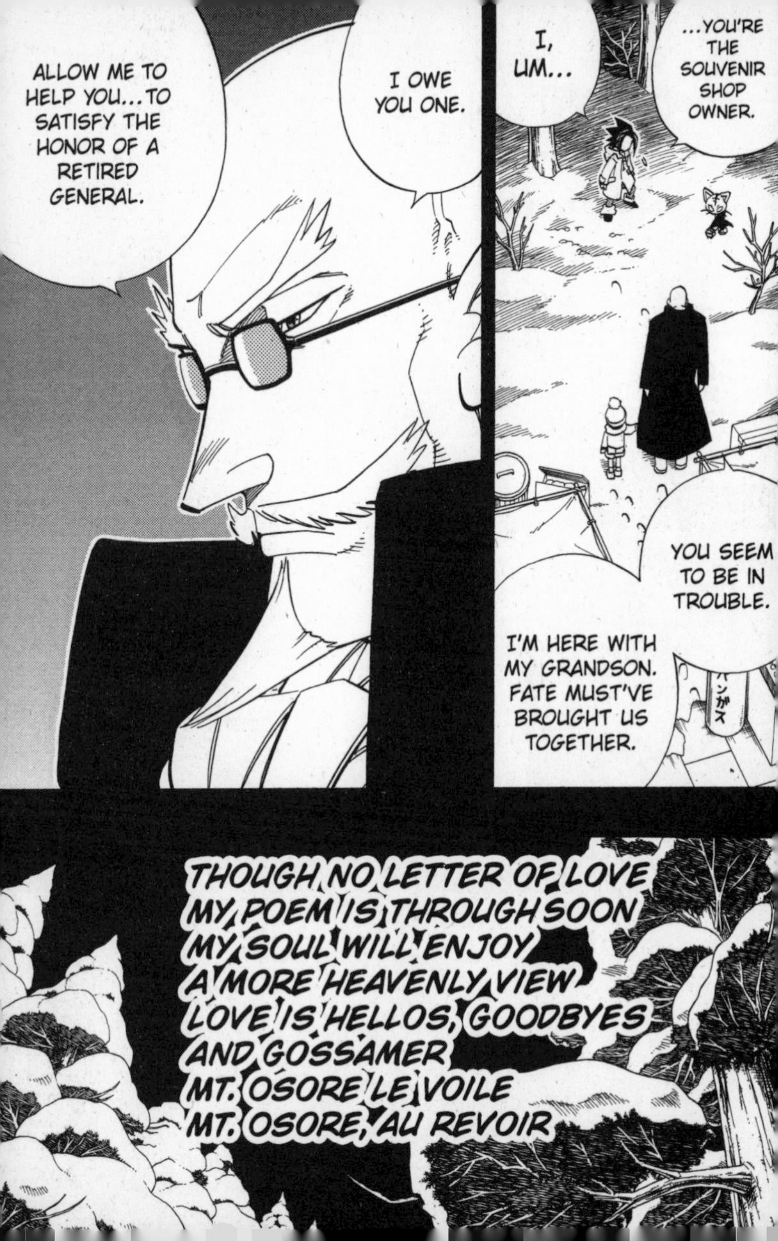
...YOU'RE THE SOUVENIR SHOP OWNER.
I, UM...
YOU SEEM TO BE IN TROUBLE.
I'M HERE WITH MY GRANDSON. FATE MUST'VE BROUGHT US TOGETHER.
I OWE YOU ONE.
ALLOW ME TO HELP YOU...TO SATISFY THE HONOR OF A RETIRED GENERAL.
THOUGH NO LETTER OF LOVE
MY POEM IS THROUGH SOON
MY SOUL WILL ENJOY
A MORE HEAVENLY VIEW
LOVE IS HELLOS, GOODBYES
AND GOSSAMER
MT. OSORE LE VOILE
MT. OSORE, AU REVOIR

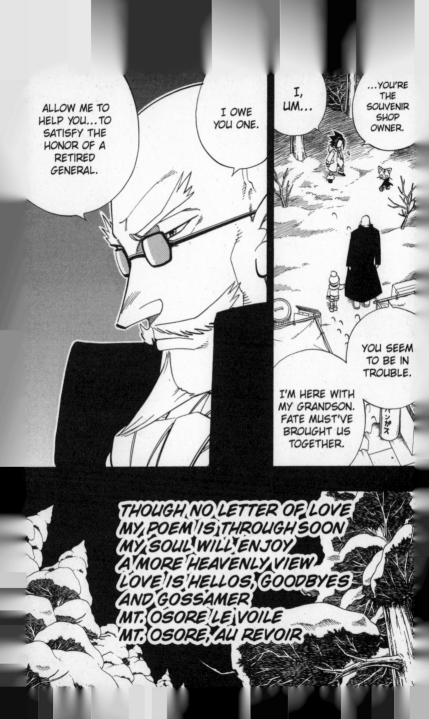

SHAMAN KING CHARACTER FILE No.106

大鬼

GIANT DEMON

1995
(DEC)

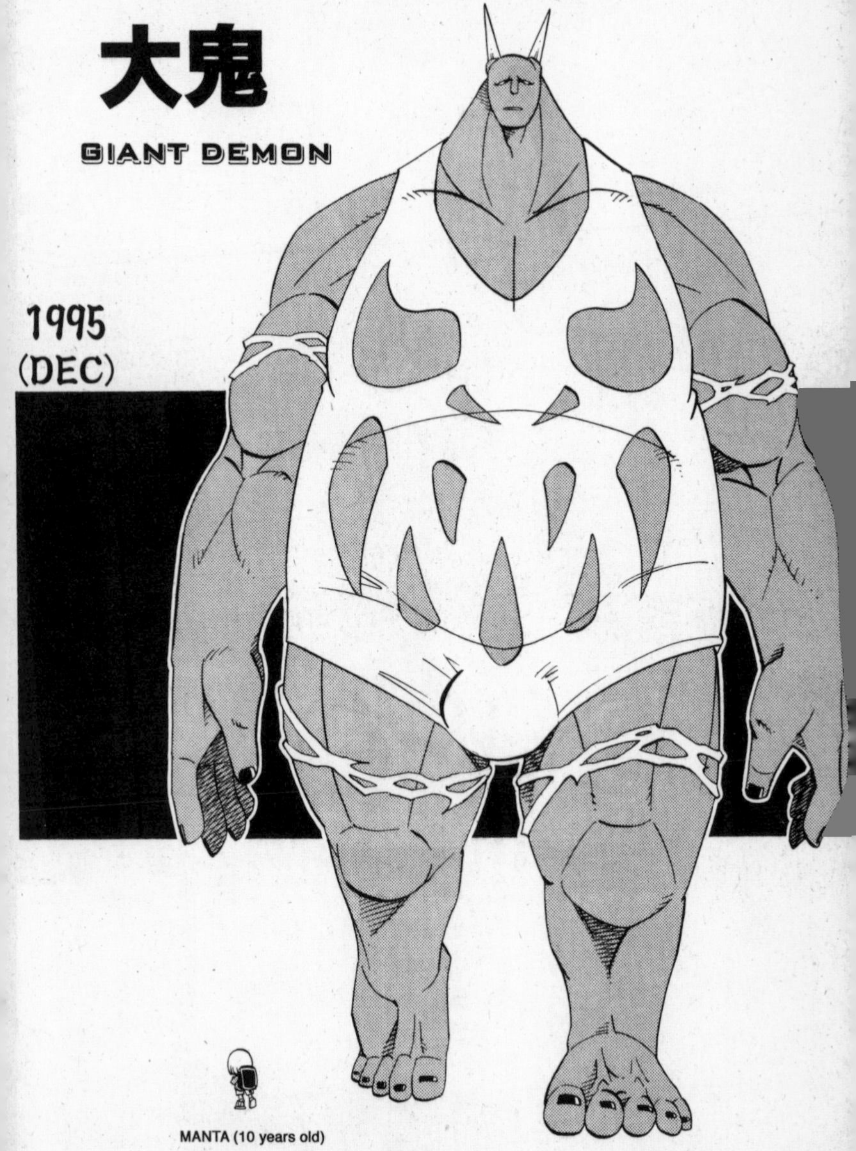

MANTA (10 years old)

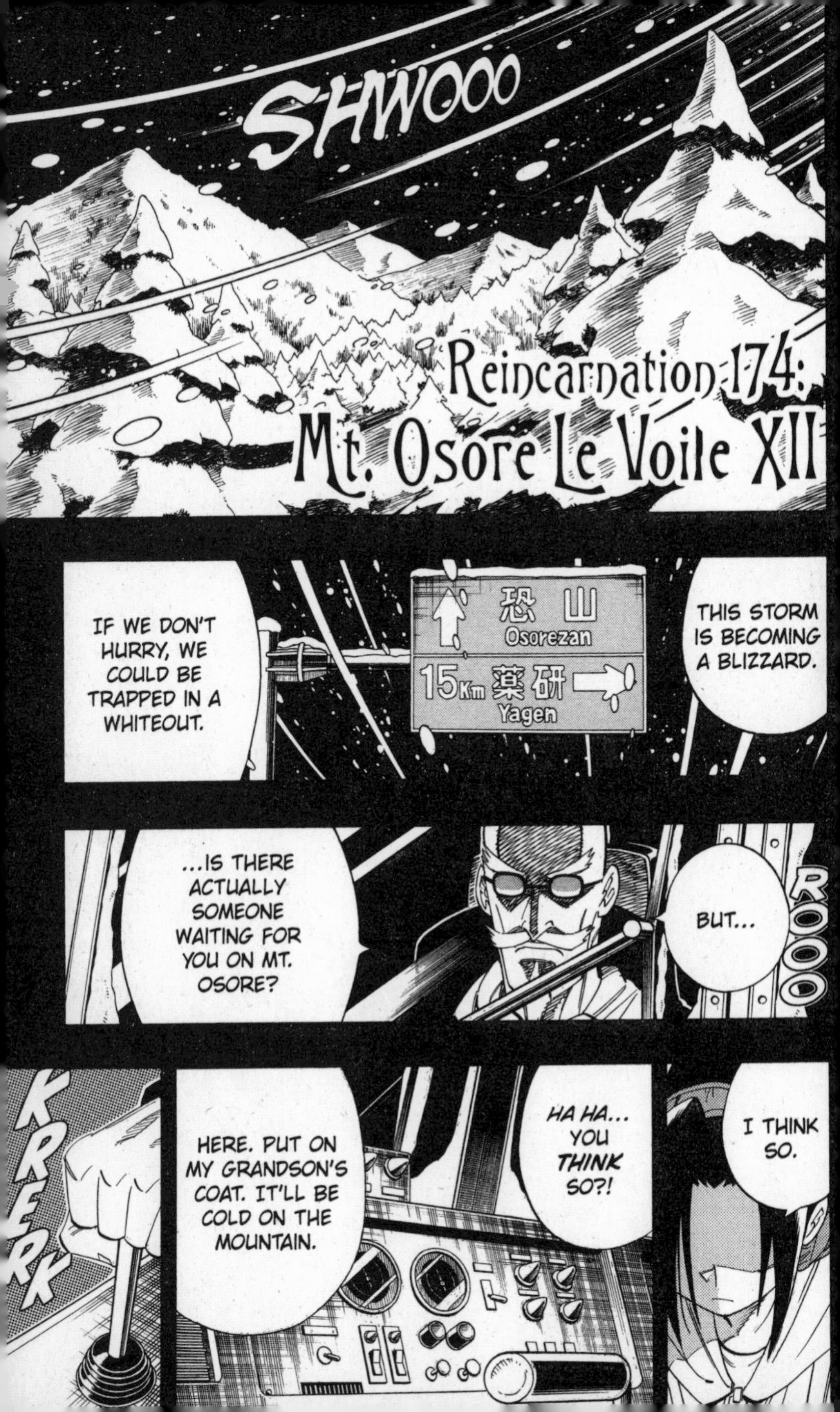
SHWOOO
Reincarnation 174: Mt. Osore Le Voile XII
THIS STORM IS BECOMING A BLIZZARD.
恐山
Osorezan
15Km 薬研
Yagen
IF WE DON'T HURRY, WE COULD BE TRAPPED IN A WHITEOUT.
ROOOO
BUT...
...IS THERE ACTUALLY SOMEONE WAITING FOR YOU ON MT. OSORE?
I THINK SO.
HA HA... YOU *THINK* SO?!
HERE. PUT ON MY GRANDSON'S COAT. IT'LL BE COLD ON THE MOUNTAIN.
KRERK

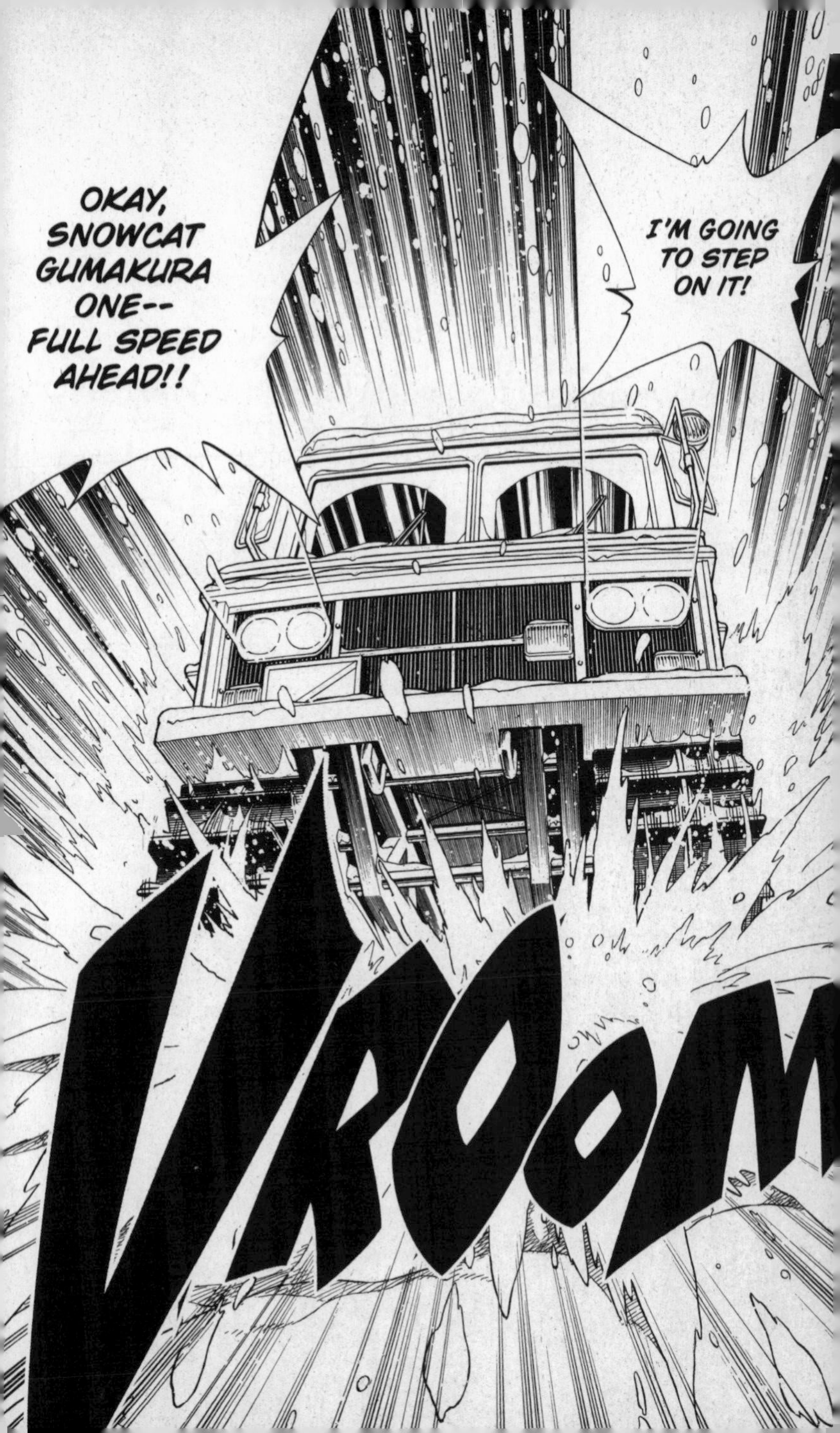
I'M GOING TO STEP ON IT!
OKAY, SNOWCAT GUMAKURA ONE-- FULL SPEED AHEAD!!
VROOM

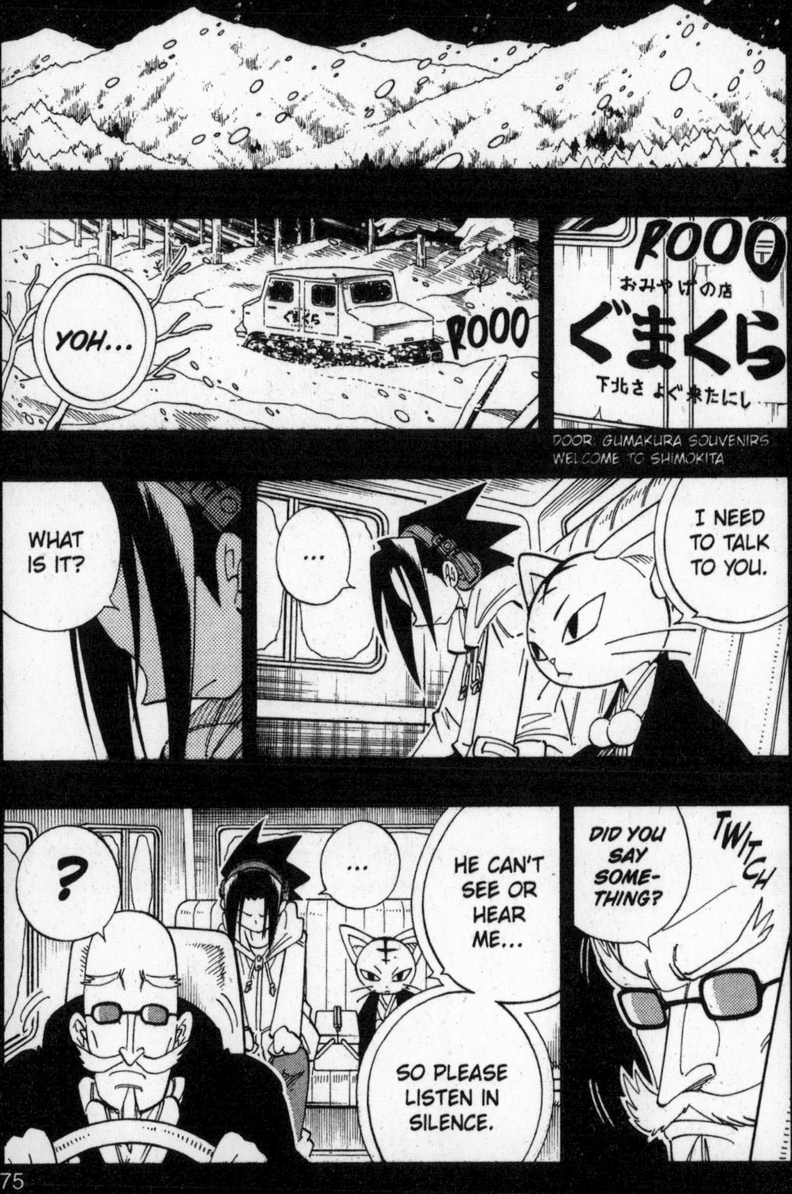
ROOO
おみやげの店
ぐまくら
下北さ よぐ 来たにし
DOOR: GUMAKURA SOUVENIRS
WELCOME TO SHIMOKITA
ROOO
YOH...
I NEED TO TALK TO YOU.
...
WHAT IS IT?
TWITCH
DID YOU SAY SOME-THING?
HE CAN'T SEE OR HEAR ME...
SO PLEASE LISTEN IN SILENCE.
...
?

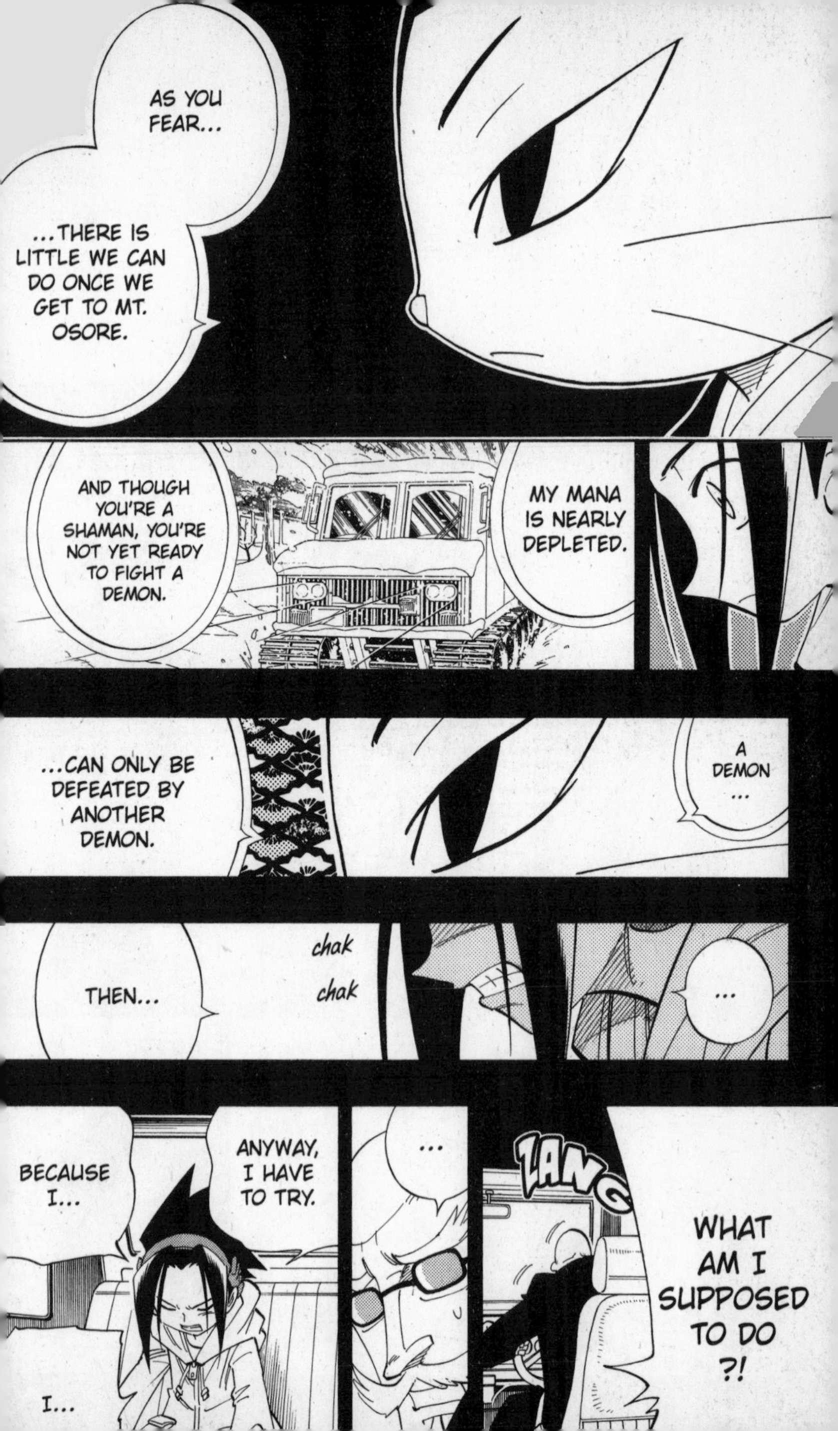
AS YOU FEAR...
...THERE IS LITTLE WE CAN DO ONCE WE GET TO MT. OSORE.
MY MANA IS NEARLY DEPLETED.
AND THOUGH YOU'RE A SHAMAN, YOU'RE NOT YET READY TO FIGHT A DEMON.
A DEMON ...
...CAN ONLY BE DEFEATED BY ANOTHER DEMON.
...
chak
chak
THEN...
ZANG
WHAT AM I SUPPOSED TO DO ?!
...
ANYWAY, I HAVE TO TRY.
BECAUSE I...
I...

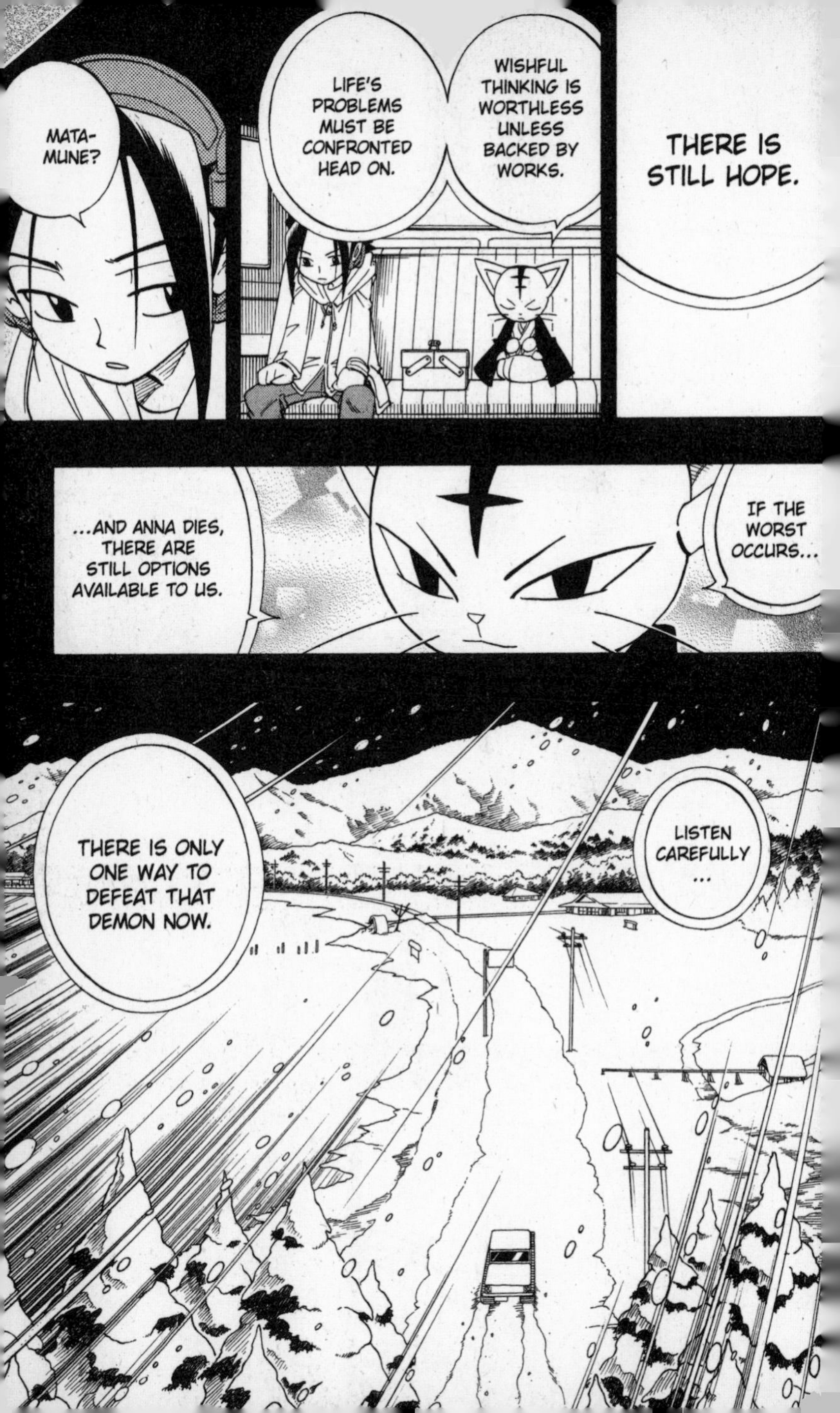
THERE IS STILL HOPE.
WISHFUL THINKING IS WORTHLESS UNLESS BACKED BY WORKS.
LIFE'S PROBLEMS MUST BE CONFRONTED HEAD ON.
MATA-MUNE?
IF THE WORST OCCURS...
...AND ANNA DIES, THERE ARE STILL OPTIONS AVAILABLE TO US.
LISTEN CAREFULLY ...
THERE IS ONLY ONE WAY TO DEFEAT THAT DEMON NOW.

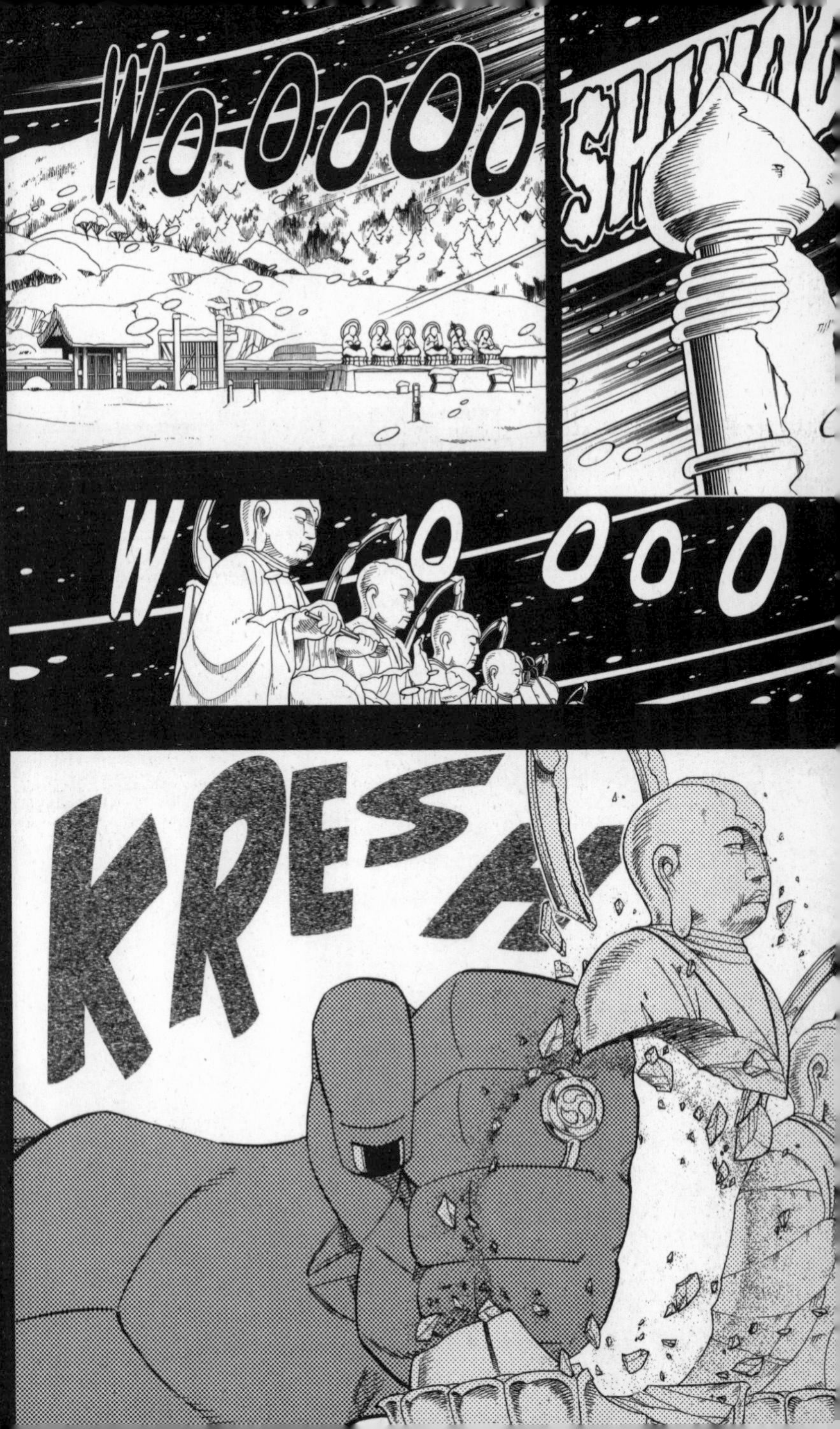
WO-OOOO
WOOOO
KRES

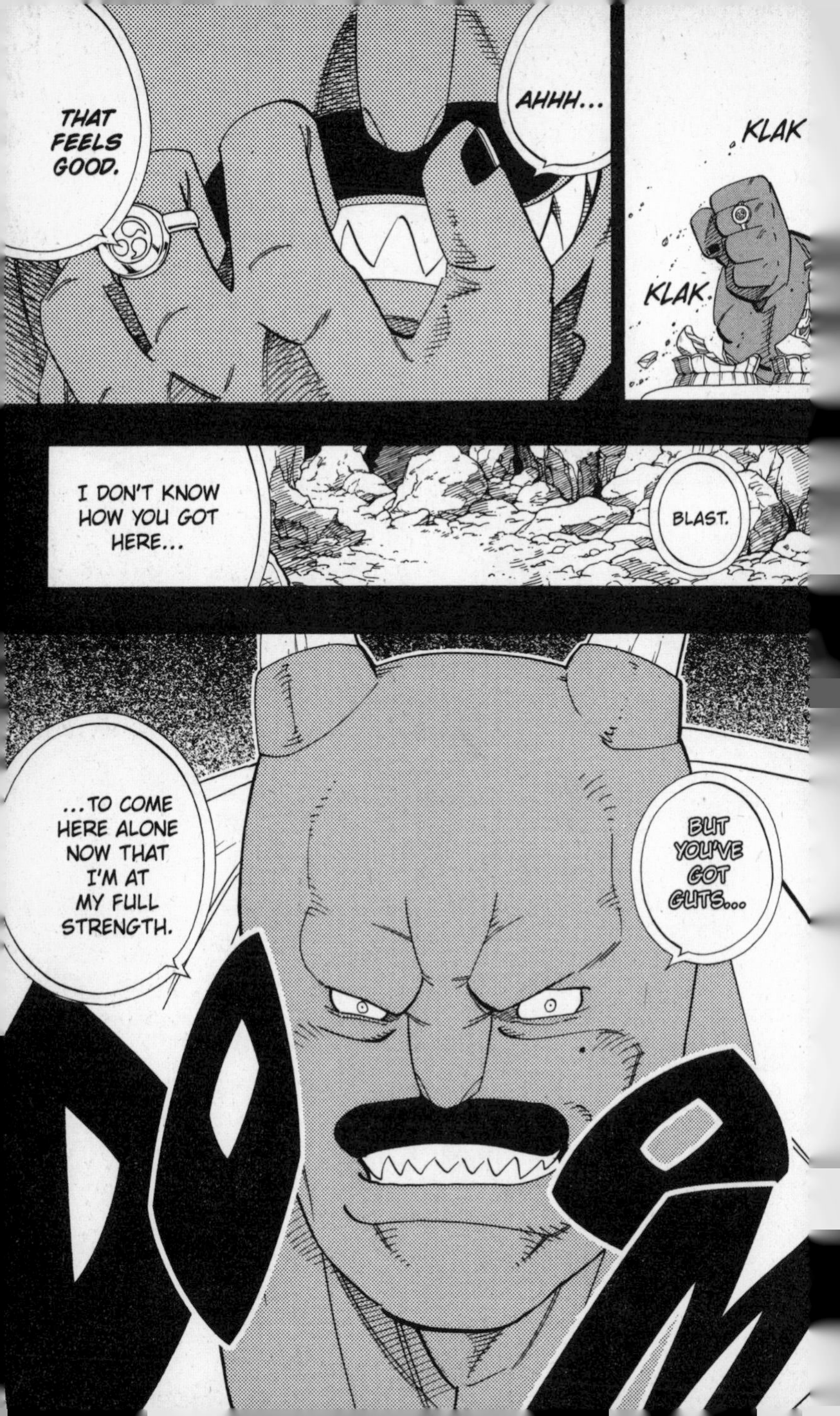
KLAK
KLAK.
AHHH...
THAT FEELS GOOD.
BLAST.
I DON'T KNOW HOW YOU GOT HERE...
BUT YOU'VE GOT GUTS...
...TO COME HERE ALONE NOW THAT I'M AT MY FULL STRENGTH.
DOOM

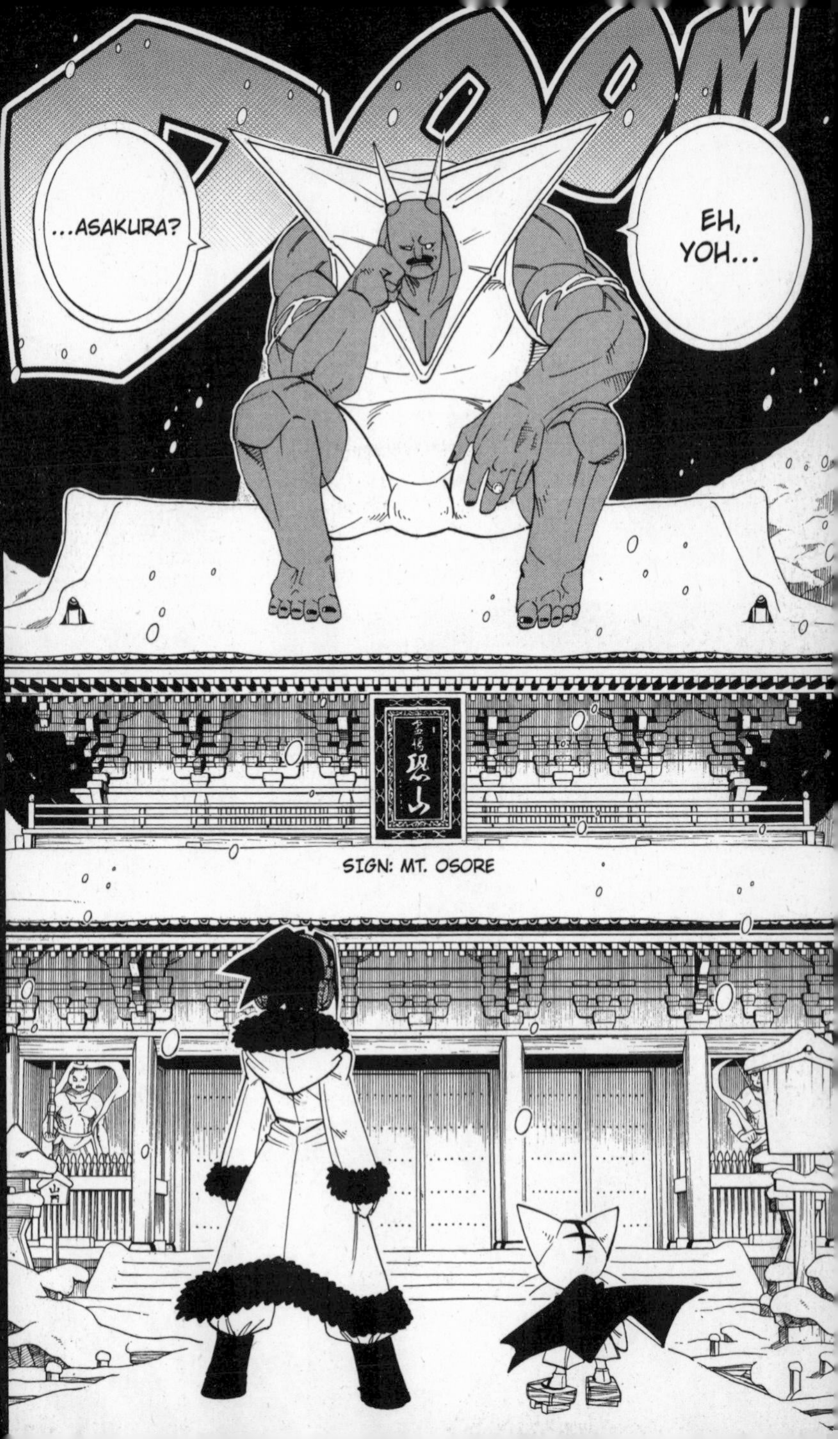
DOOM
EH, YOH...
...ASAKURA?
霊場 恐山
SIGN: MT. OSORE

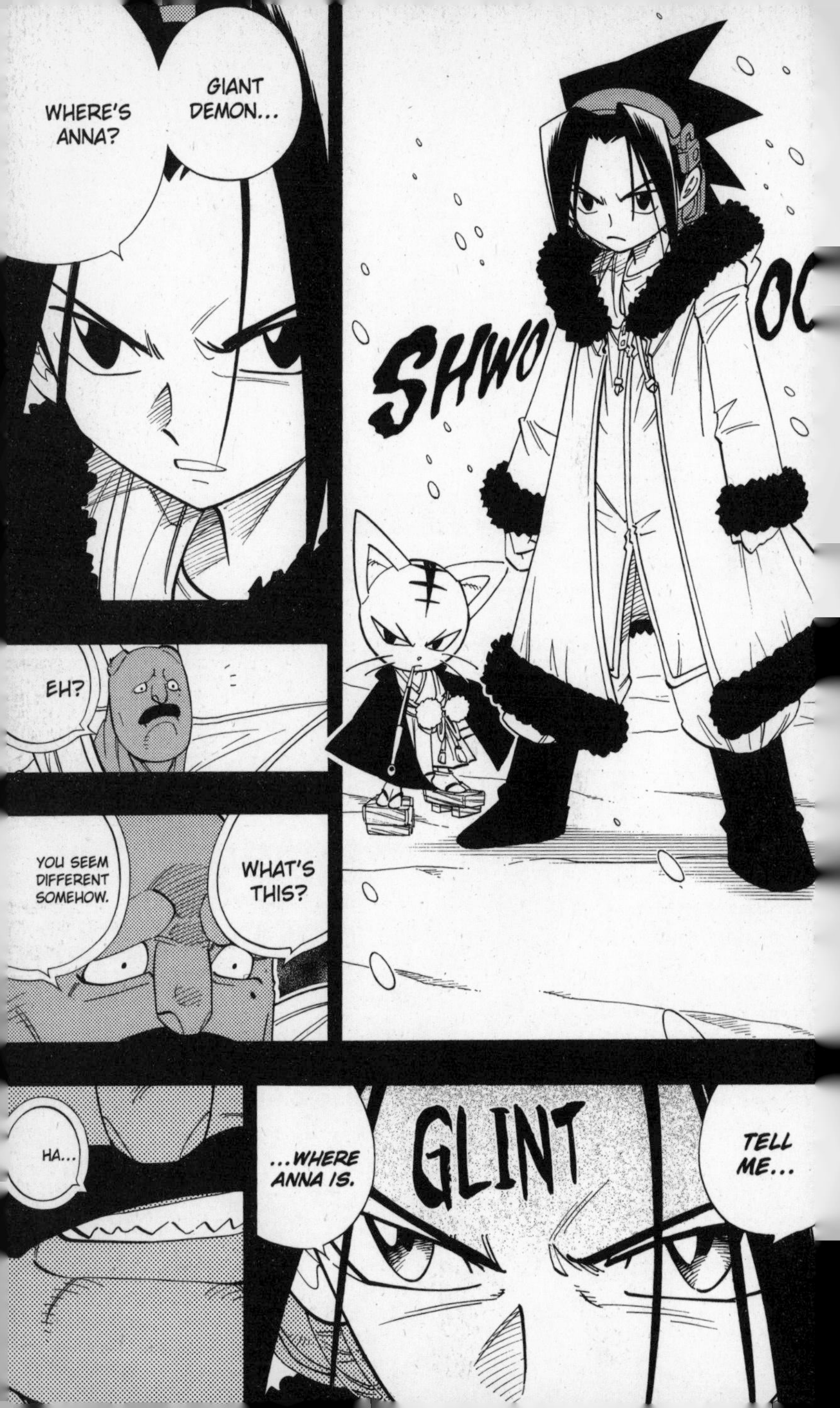

SHWOOO
GIANT DEMON...
WHERE'S ANNA?
EH?
WHAT'S THIS?
YOU SEEM DIFFERENT SOMEHOW.
TELL ME...
GLINT
...WHERE ANNA IS.
HA...

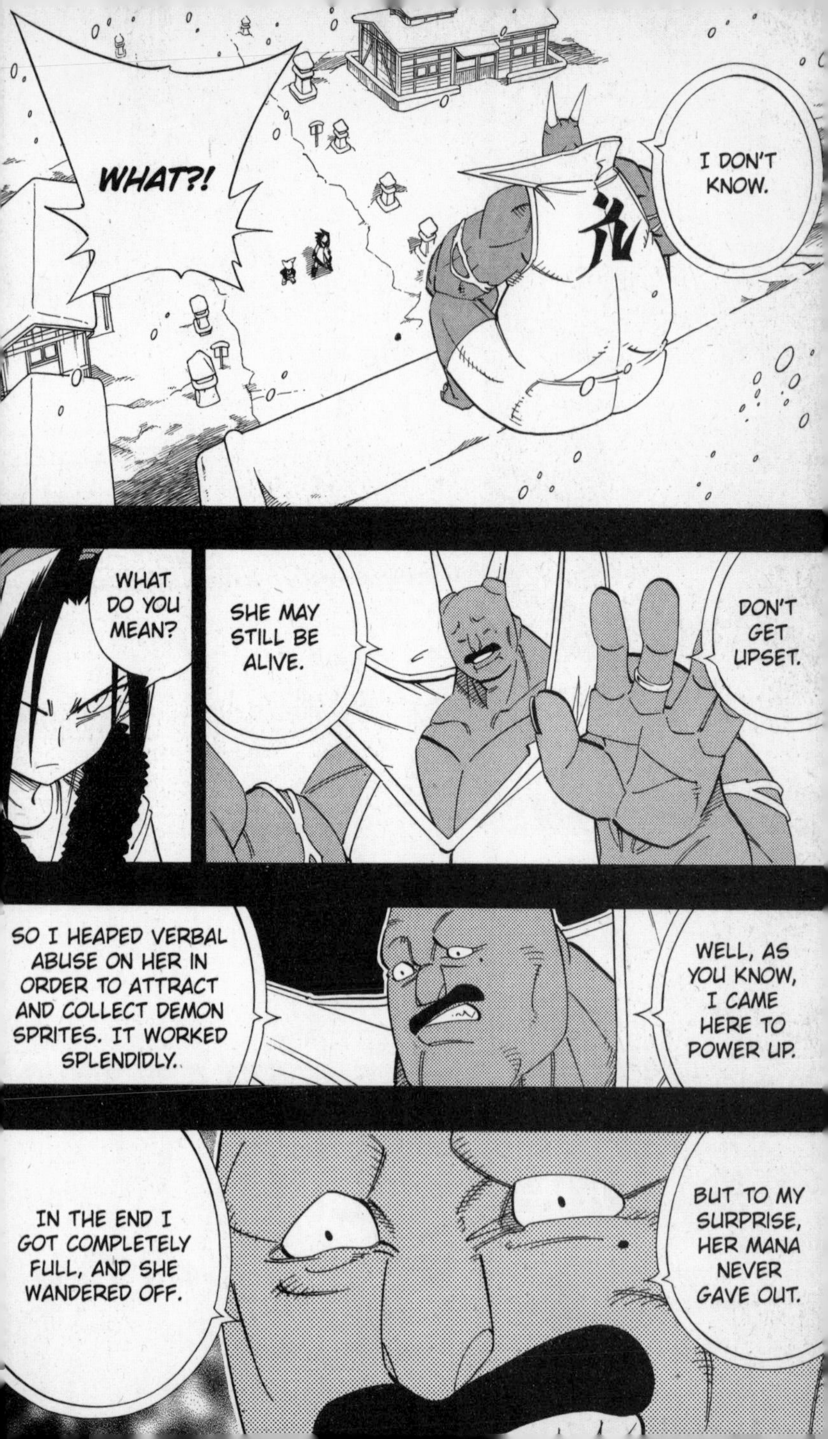
I DON'T KNOW.
WHAT?!
DON'T GET UPSET.
SHE MAY STILL BE ALIVE.
WHAT DO YOU MEAN?
WELL, AS YOU KNOW, I CAME HERE TO POWER UP.
SO I HEAPED VERBAL ABUSE ON HER IN ORDER TO ATTRACT AND COLLECT DEMON SPRITES. IT WORKED SPLENDIDLY.
BUT TO MY SURPRISE, HER MANA NEVER GAVE OUT.
IN THE END I GOT COMPLETELY FULL, AND SHE WANDERED OFF.

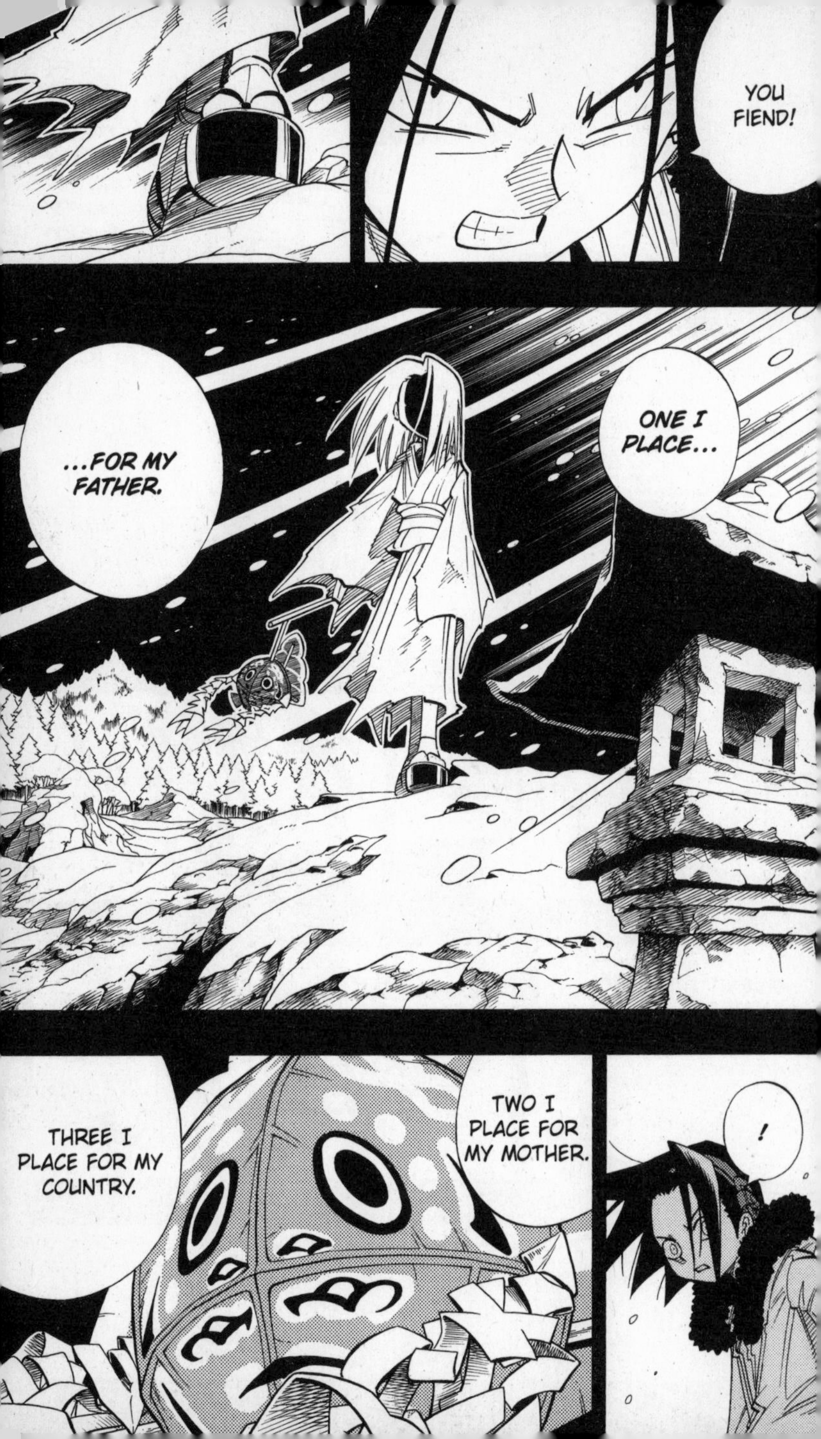
YOU FIEND!
ONE I PLACE...
...FOR MY FATHER.
!
TWO I PLACE FOR MY MOTHER.
THREE I PLACE FOR MY COUNTRY.

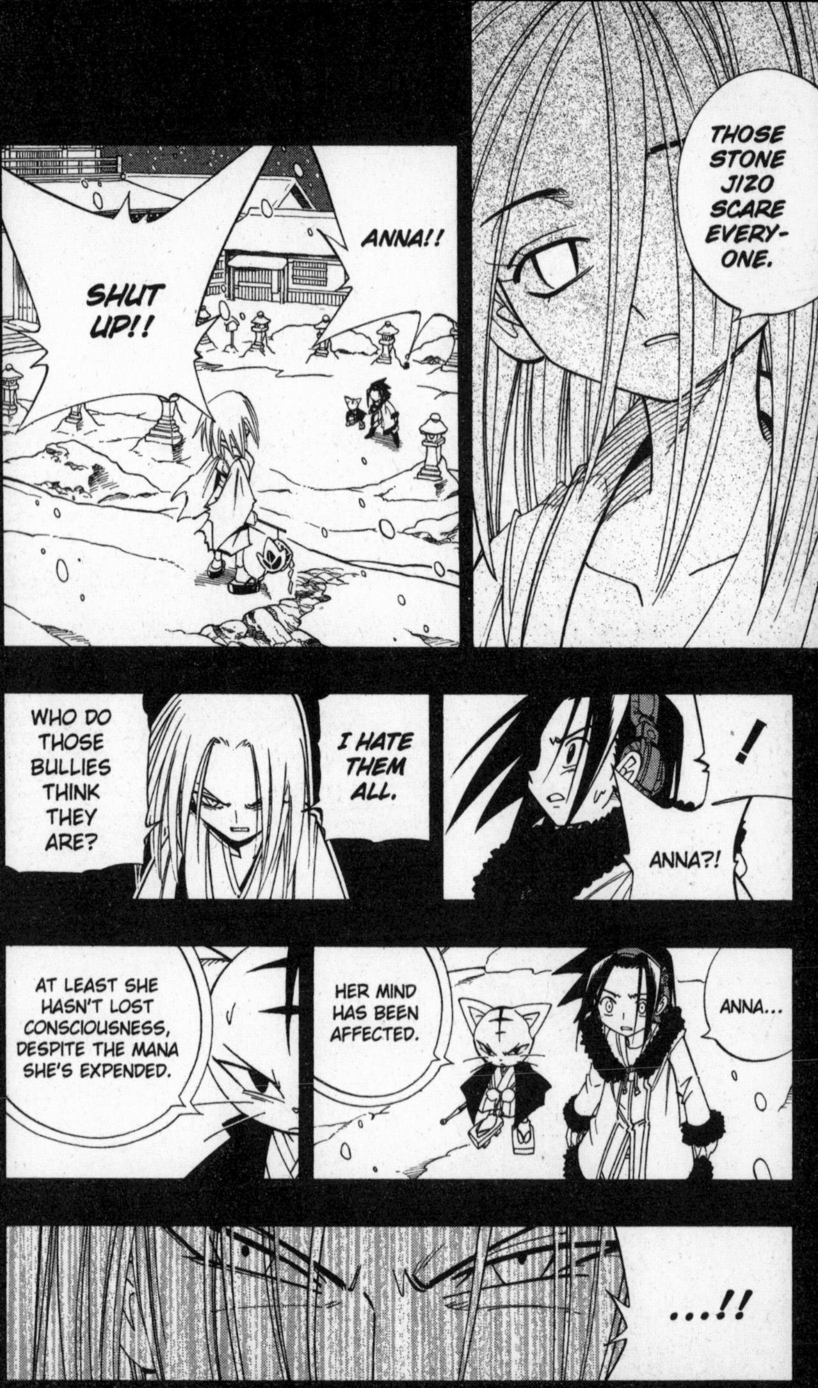

THOSE STONE JIZO SCARE EVERY-ONE.
ANNA!!
SHUT UP!!
!
ANNA?!
I HATE THEM ALL.
WHO DO THOSE BULLIES THINK THEY ARE?
ANNA...
HER MIND HAS BEEN AFFECTED.
AT LEAST SHE HASN'T LOST CONSCIOUSNESS, DESPITE THE MANA SHE'S EXPENDED.
...!!

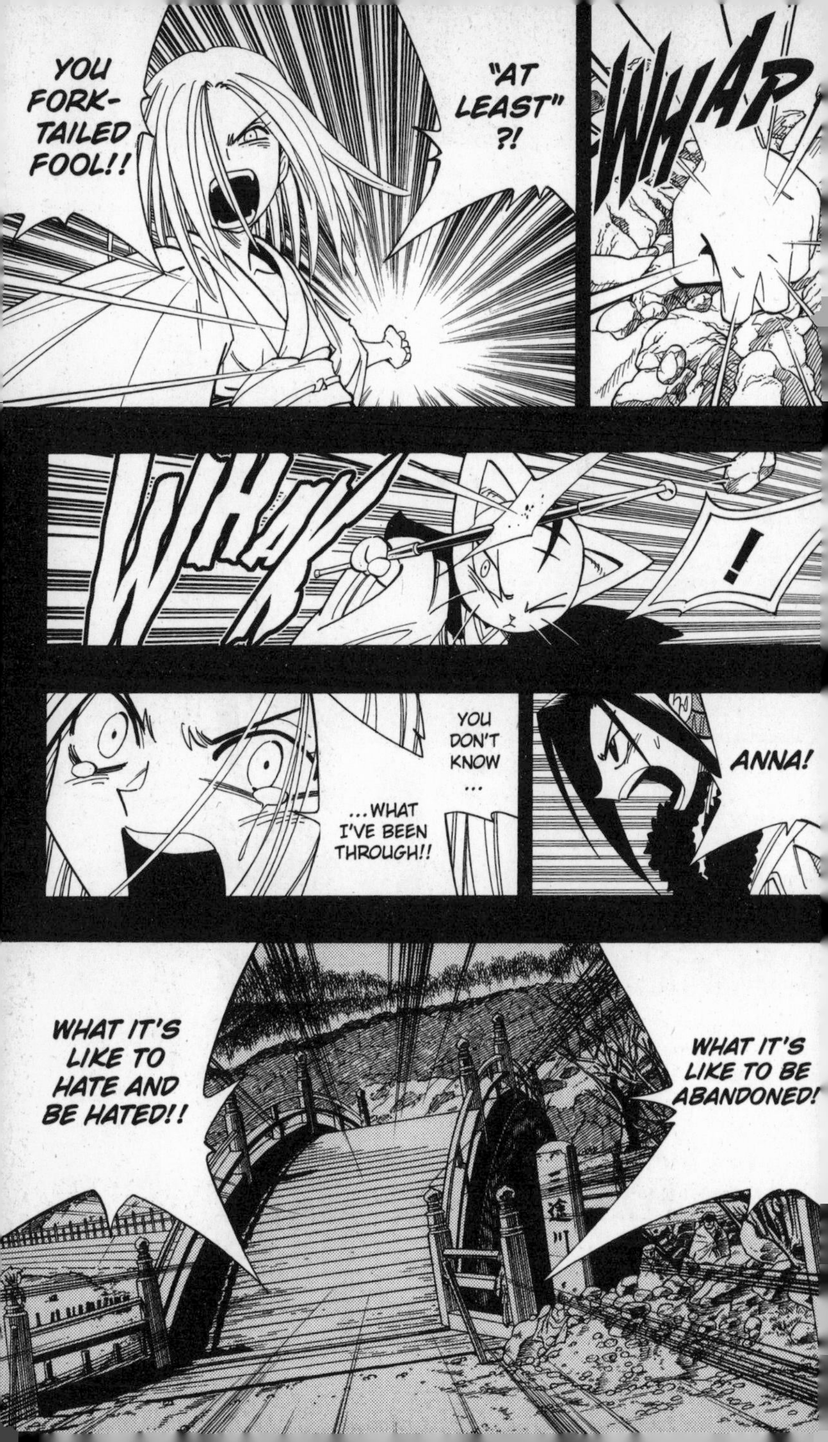
WHAP
"AT LEAST" ?!
YOU FORK-TAILED FOOL!!
!
WHAK
ANNA!
YOU DON'T KNOW ...
...WHAT I'VE BEEN THROUGH!!
WHAT IT'S LIKE TO BE ABANDONED!
WHAT IT'S LIKE TO HATE AND BE HATED!!

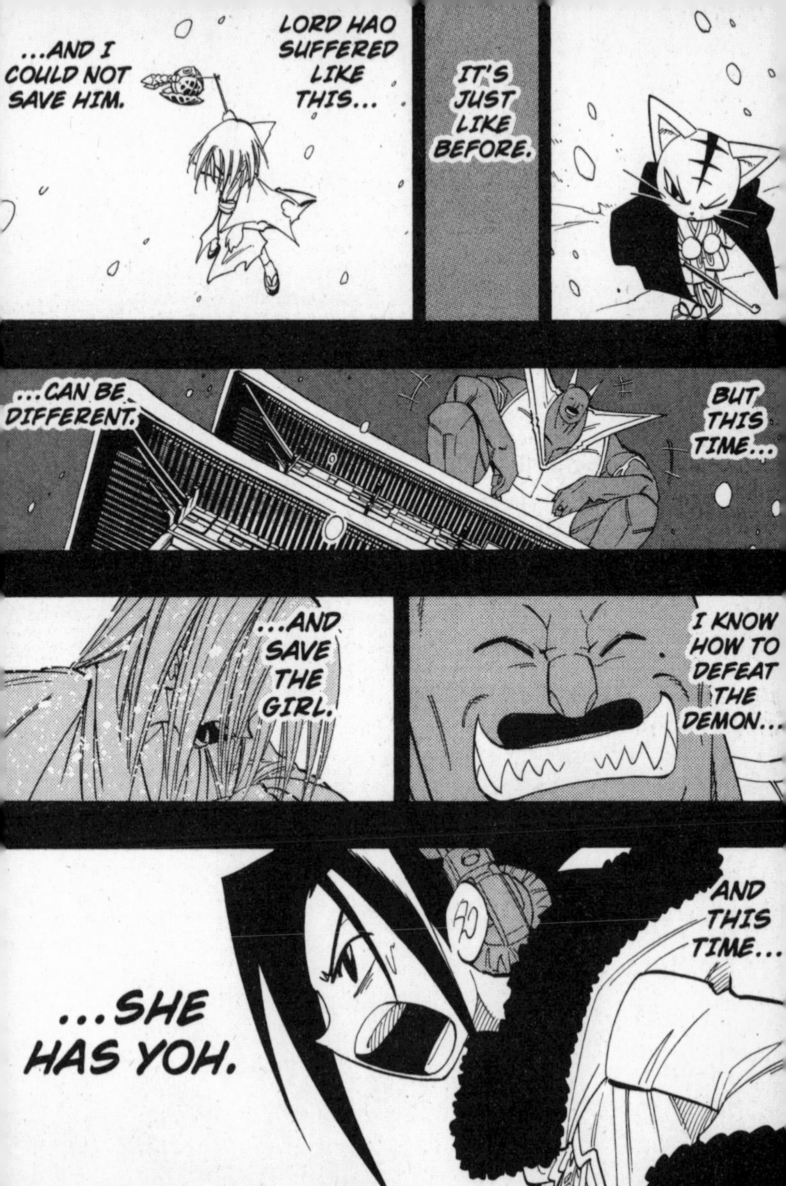
IT'S JUST LIKE BEFORE.
LORD HAO SUFFERED LIKE THIS...
...AND I COULD NOT SAVE HIM.
BUT THIS TIME...
...CAN BE DIFFERENT.
I KNOW HOW TO DEFEAT THE DEMON...
...AND SAVE THE GIRL.
AND THIS TIME...
...SHE HAS YOH.

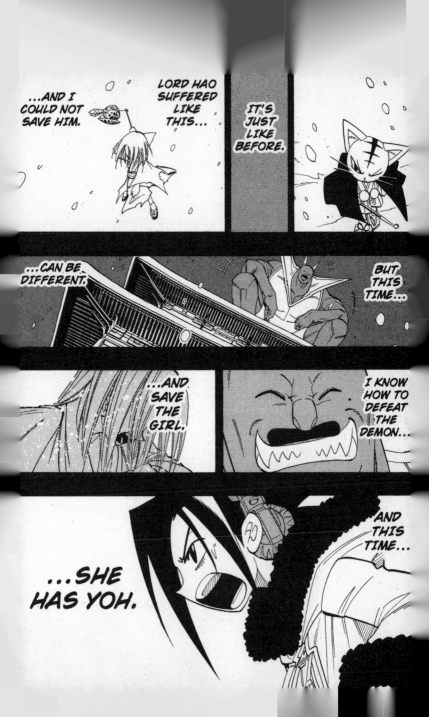

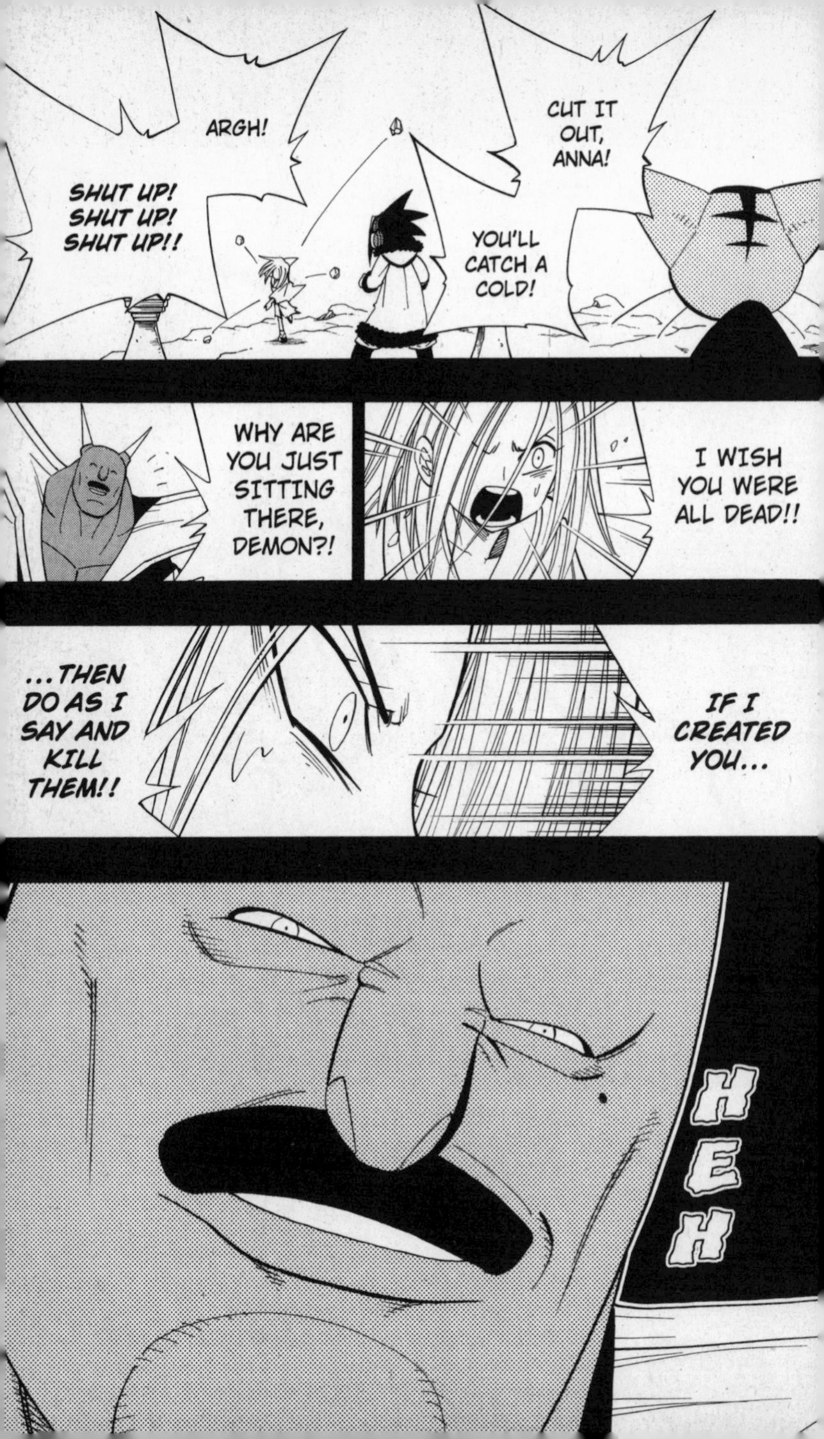
CUT IT OUT, ANNA!
YOU'LL CATCH A COLD!
ARGH!
SHUT UP! SHUT UP! SHUT UP!!
I WISH YOU WERE ALL DEAD!!
WHY ARE YOU JUST SITTING THERE, DEMON?!
IF I CREATED YOU...
...THEN DO AS I SAY AND KILL THEM!!
HEH

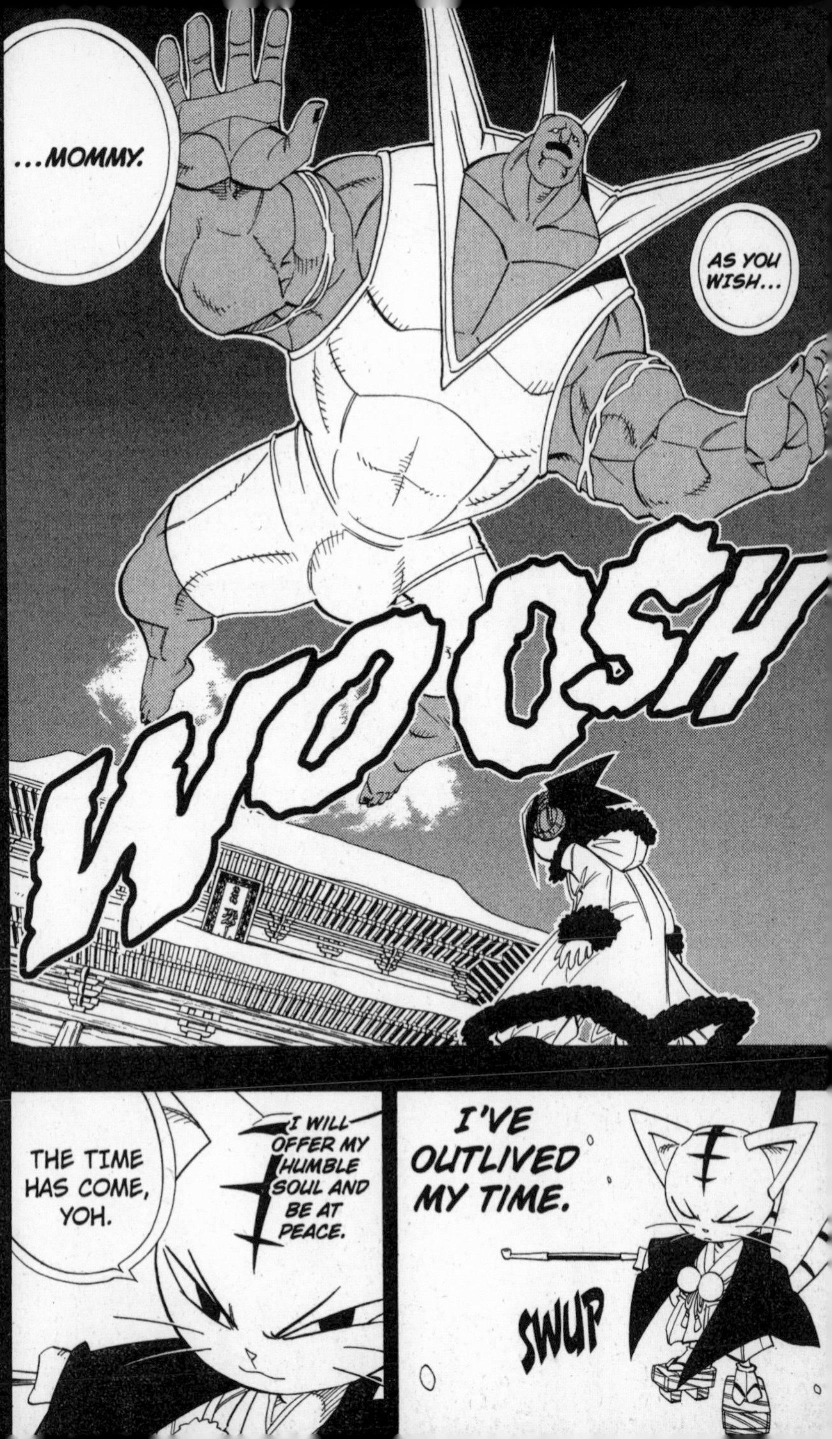
...MOMMY.
AS YOU WISH...
WOOSH
I'VE OUTLIVED MY TIME.
SWUP
I WILL OFFER MY HUMBLE SOUL AND BE AT PEACE.
THE TIME HAS COME, YOH.

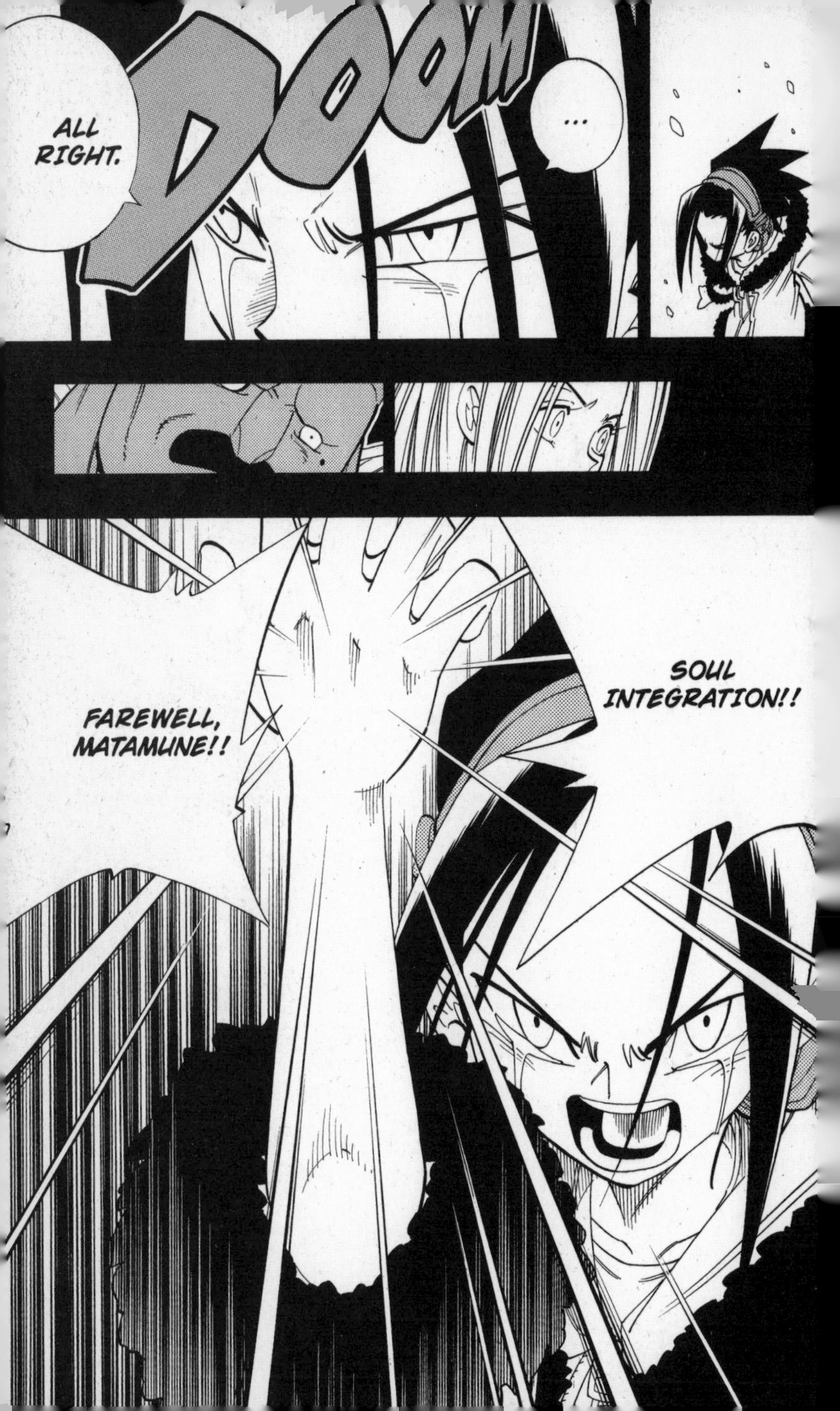
...
DOOM
ALL RIGHT.
SOUL INTEGRATION!!
FAREWELL, MATAMUNE!!

SHAMAN KING CHARACTER FILE No.107

ぐまくらいさお

ISAO GUMAKURA

1995
(DIC)

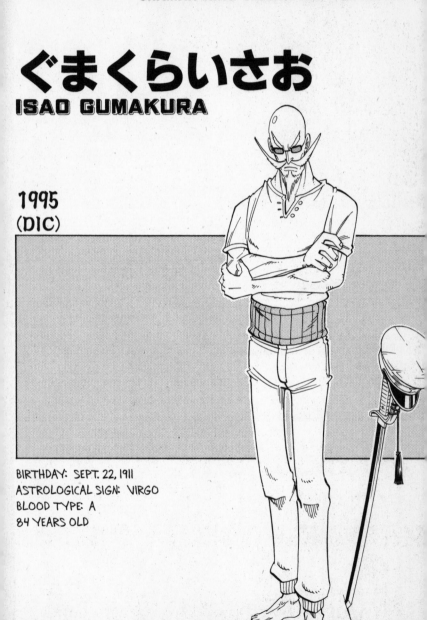

BIRTHDAY: SEPT. 22, 1911
ASTROLOGICAL SIGN: VIRGO
BLOOD TYPE: A
84 YEARS OLD

Reincarnation 175: Mt. Osore Le Voile XIII

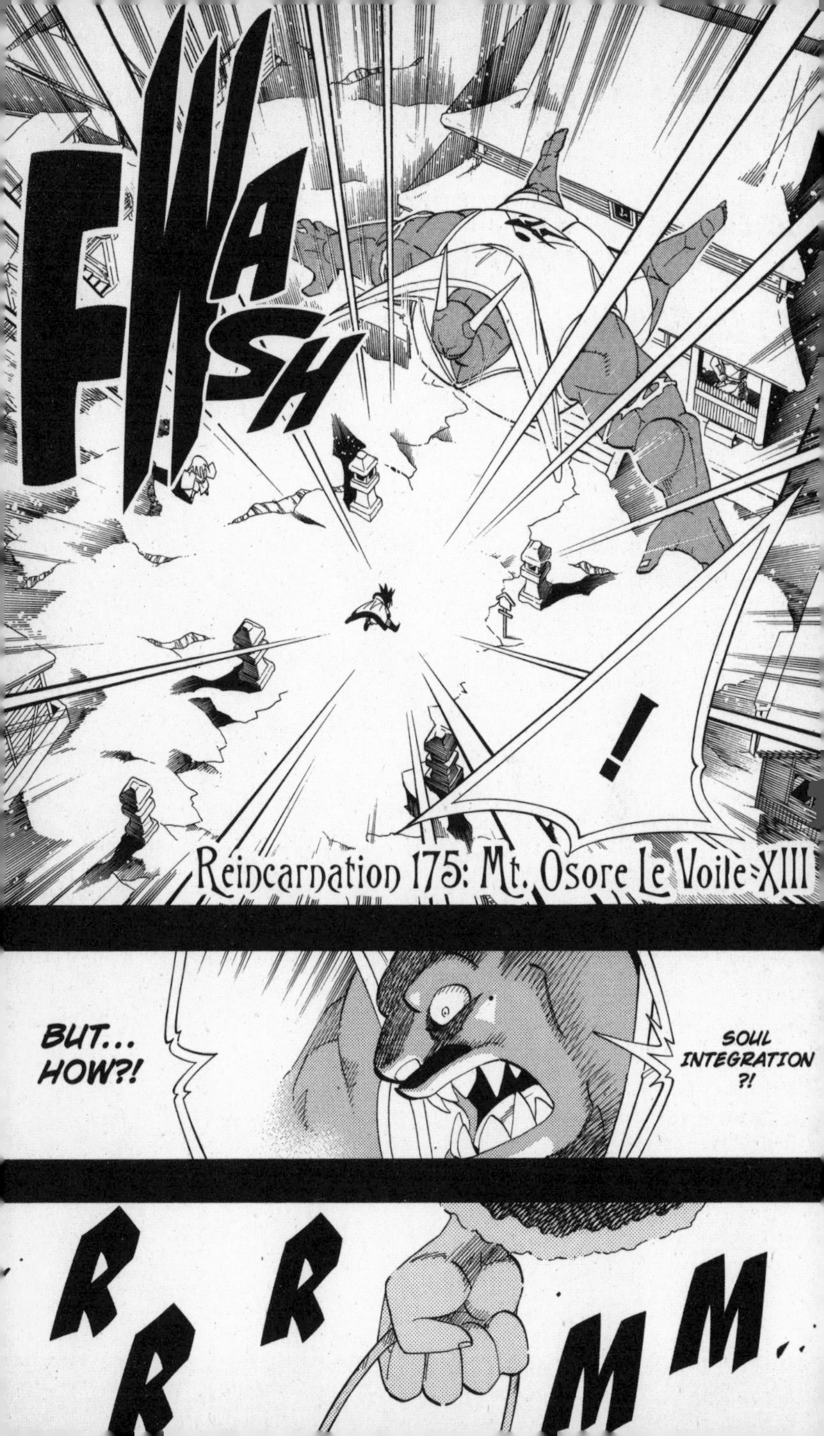
FWASH
!
SOUL INTEGRATION ?!
BUT... HOW?!
RRRRMM..

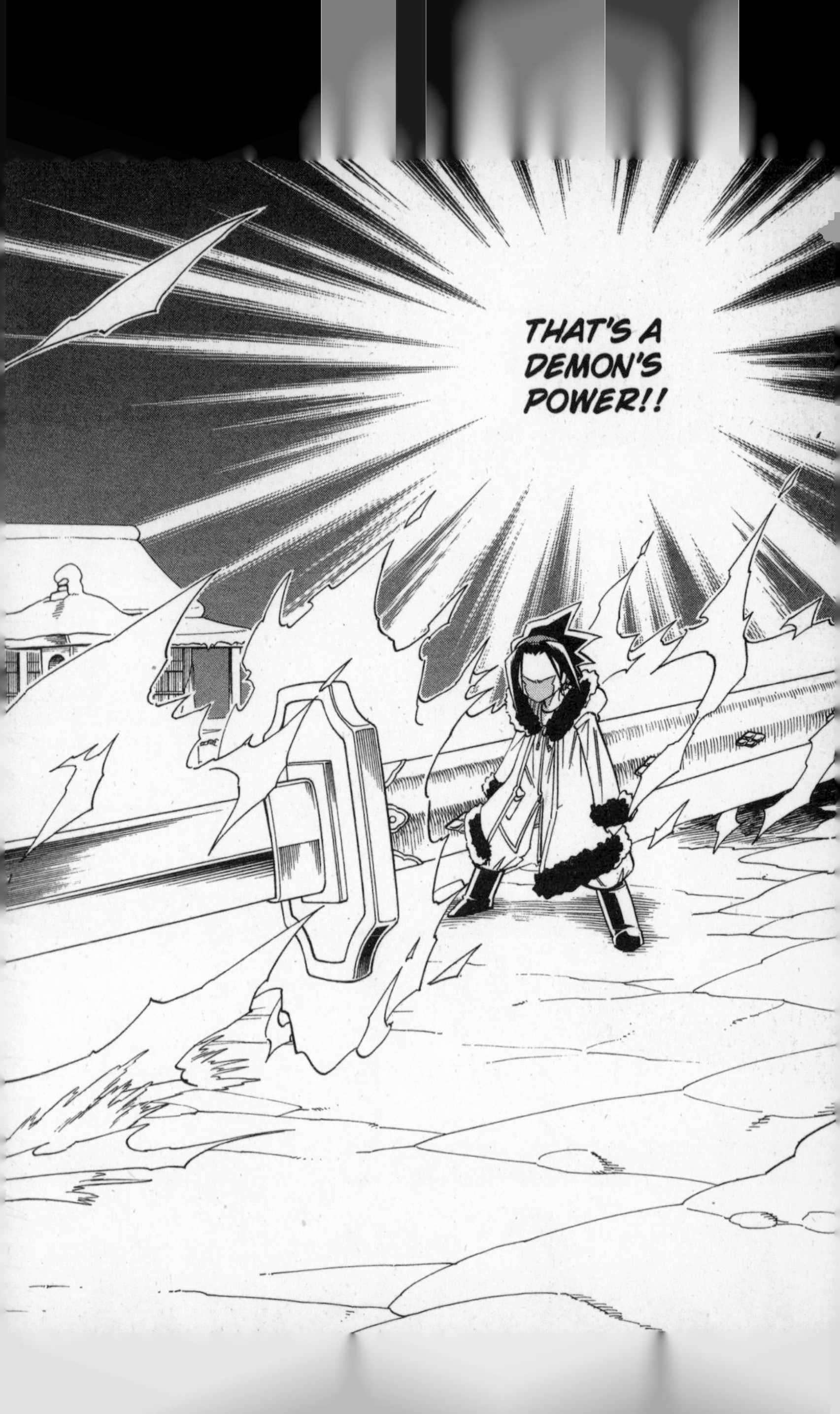
THAT'S A DEMON'S POWER!!

Reincarnation 175: Mt. Osore Le Voile XIII

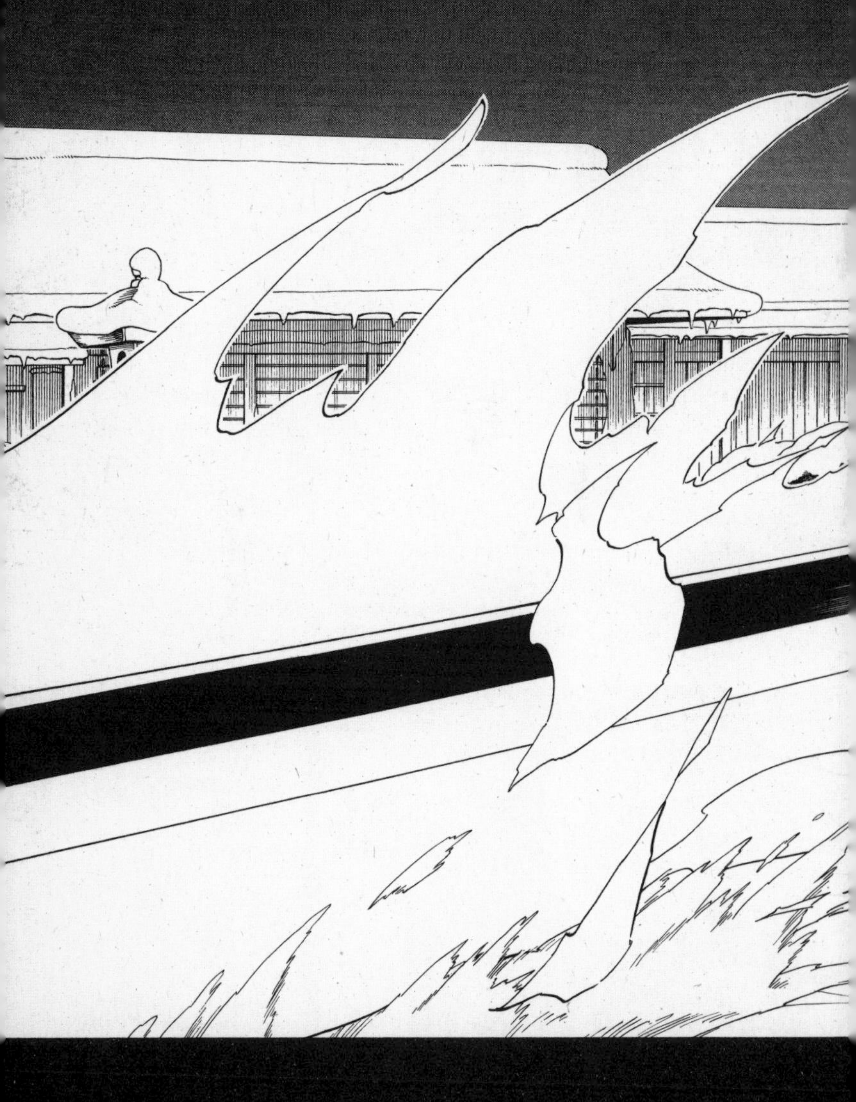

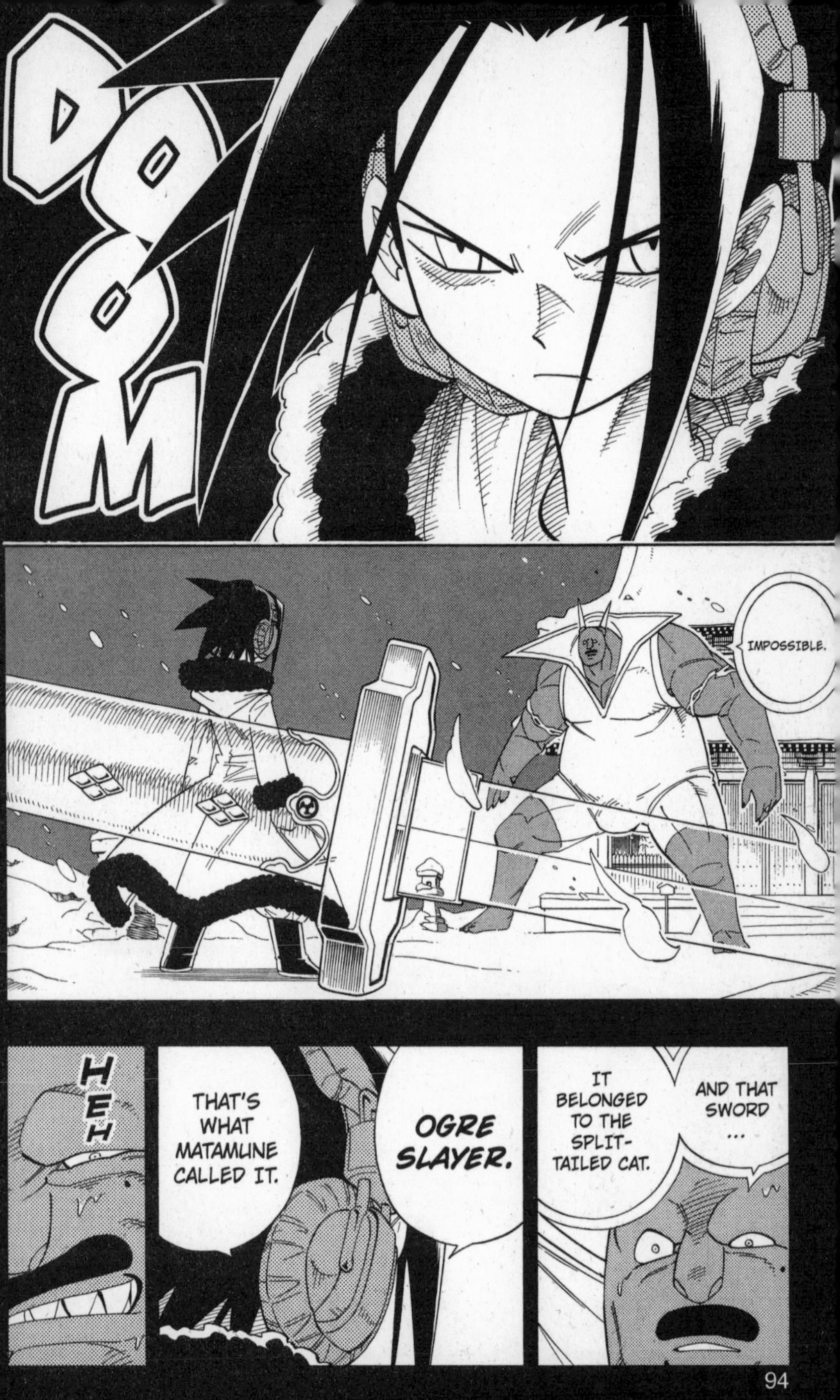
DOOOM
IMPOSSIBLE.
AND THAT SWORD ...
IT BELONGED TO THE SPLIT-TAILED CAT.
OGRE SLAYER.
THAT'S WHAT MATAMUNE CALLED IT.
HEH

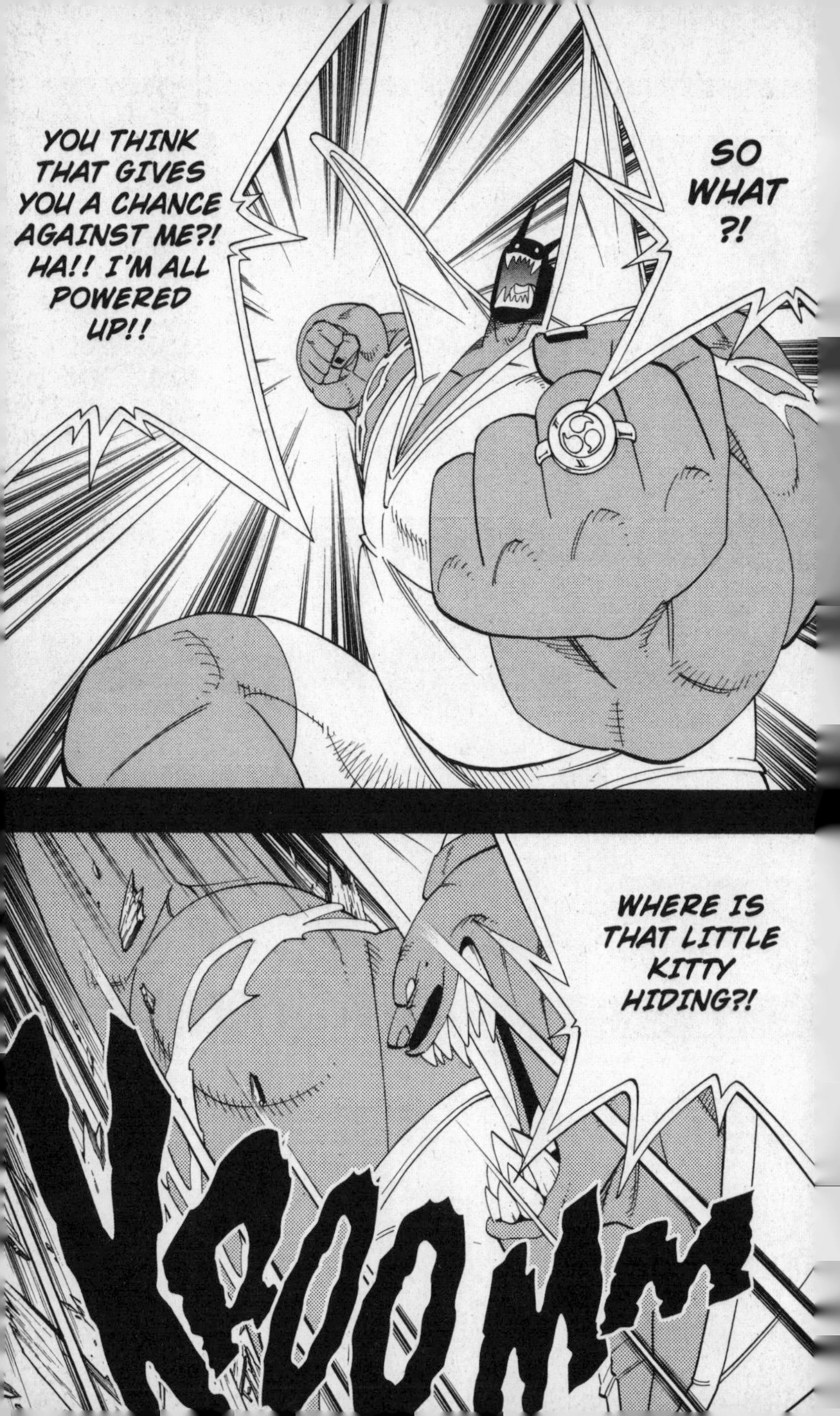
SO WHAT?!
YOU THINK THAT GIVES YOU A CHANCE AGAINST ME?! HA!! I'M ALL POWERED UP!!
WHERE IS THAT LITTLE KITTY HIDING?!
KROOM

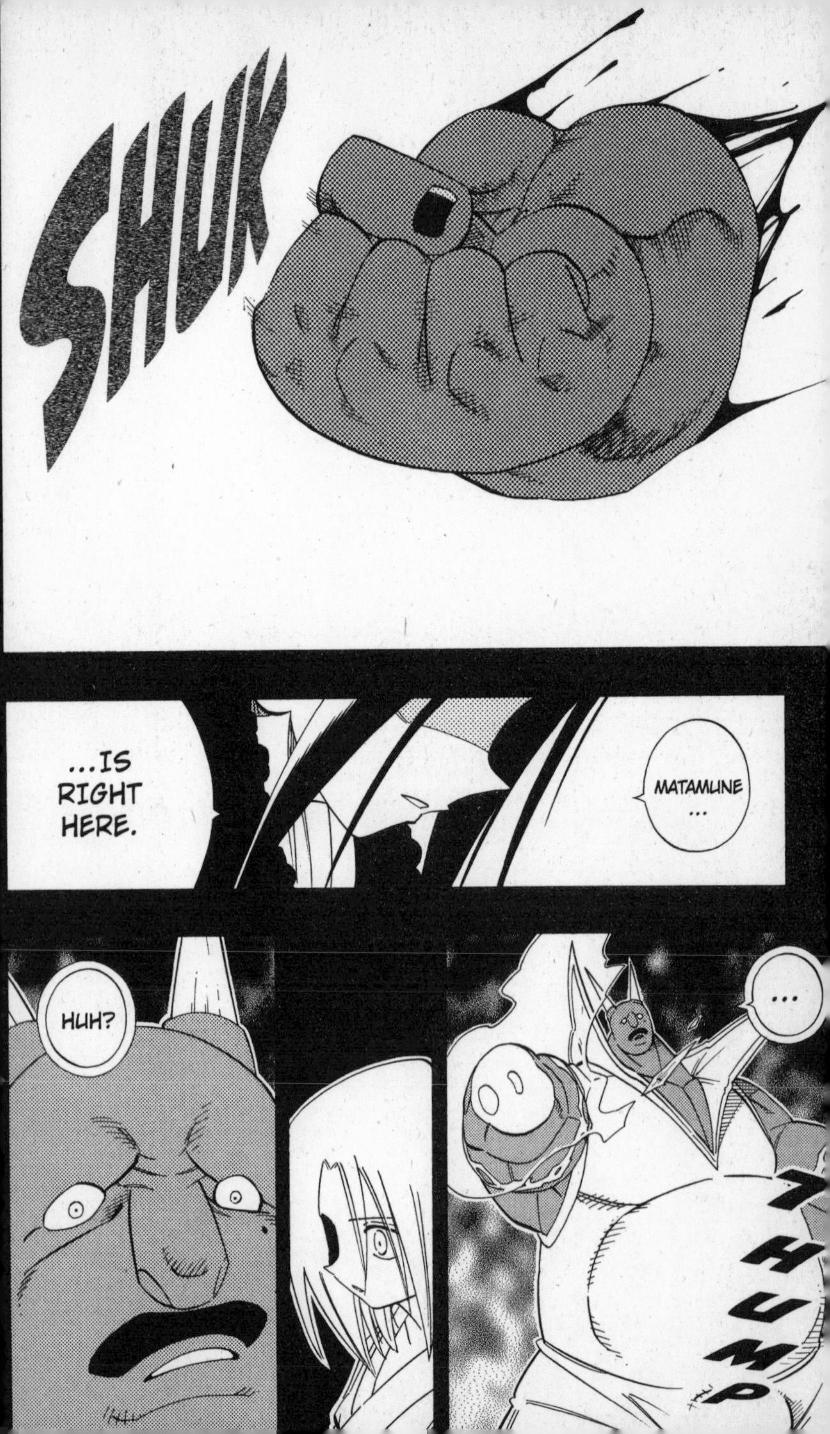
SHUK
MATAMUNE ...
...IS RIGHT HERE.
...
THUMP
HUH?

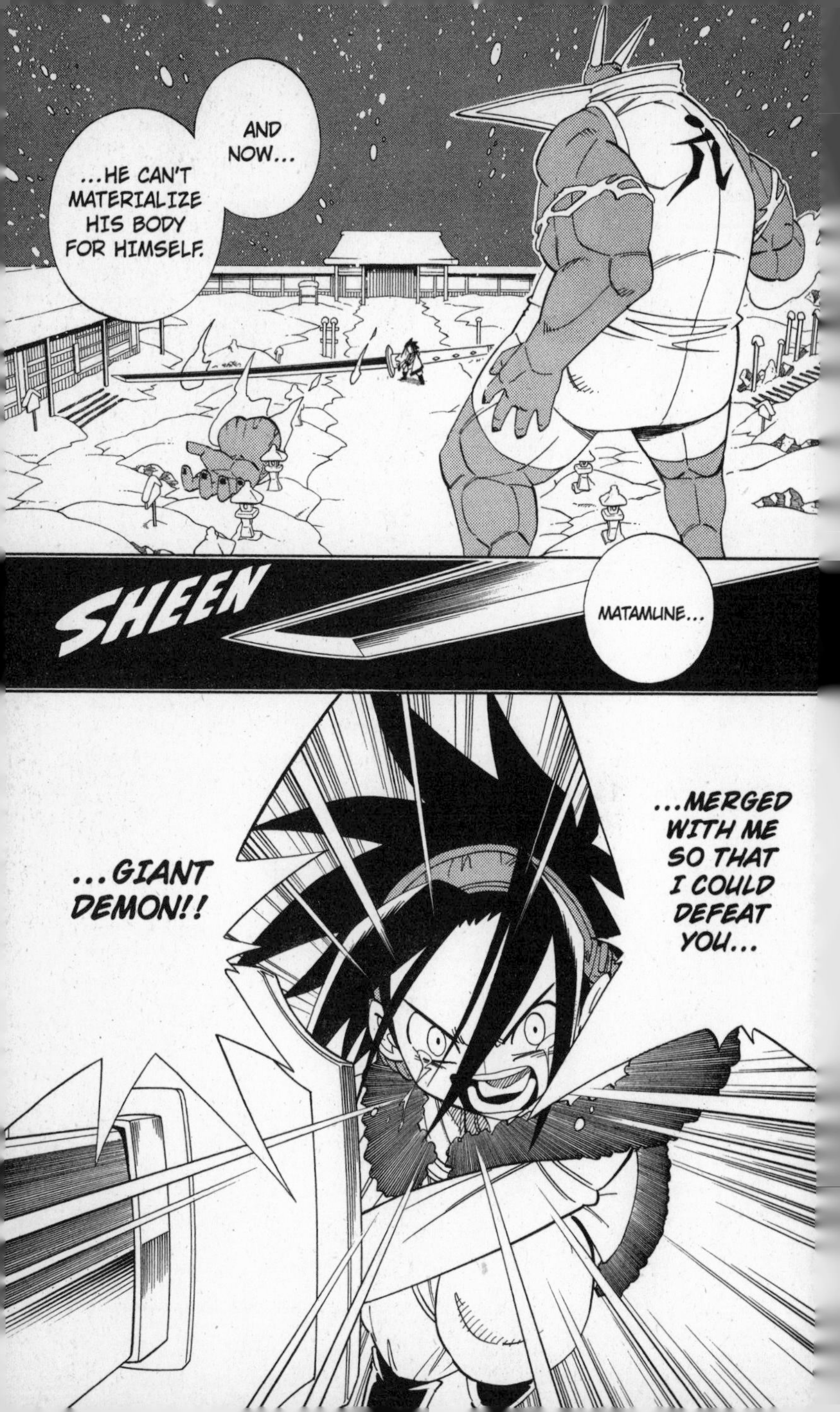
AND NOW...
...HE CAN'T MATERIALIZE HIS BODY FOR HIMSELF.
MATAMUNE...
SHEEN
...MERGED WITH ME SO THAT I COULD DEFEAT YOU...
...GIANT DEMON!!

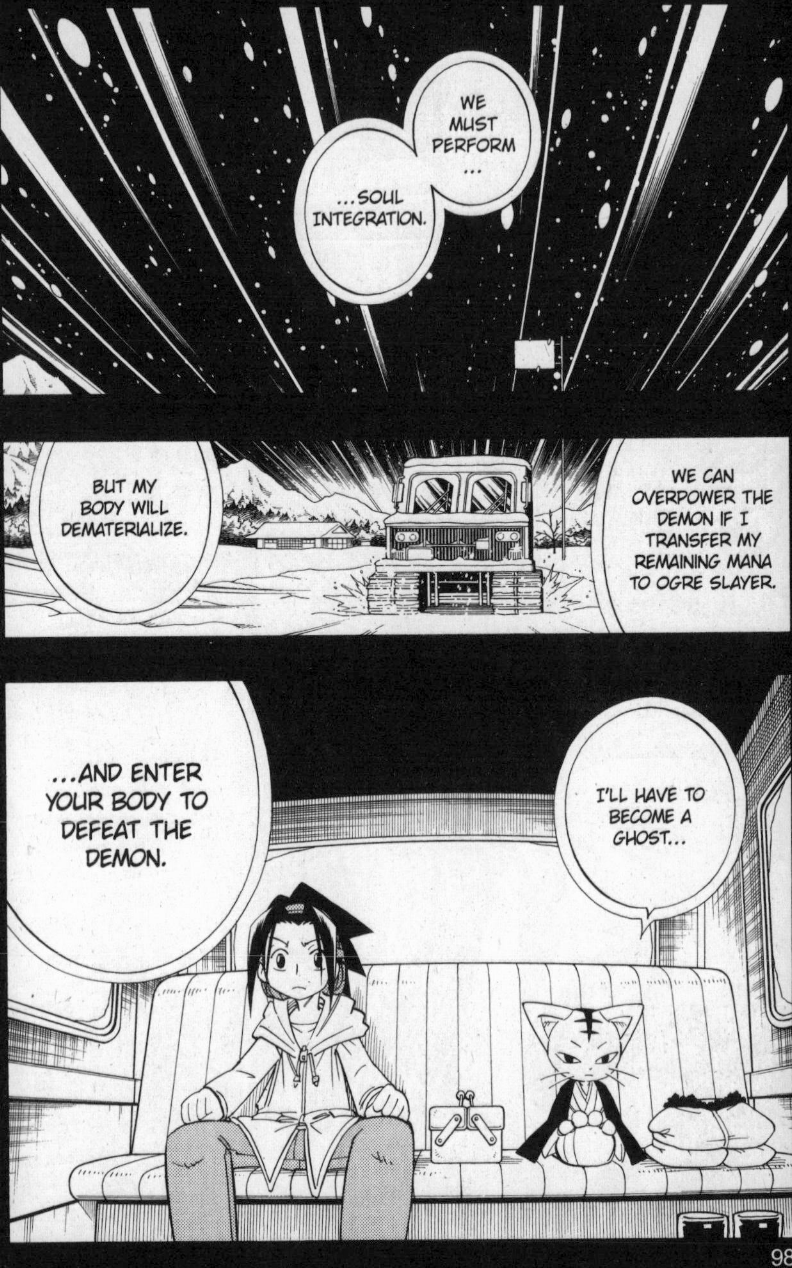
WE MUST PERFORM ...
...SOUL INTEGRATION.
WE CAN OVERPOWER THE DEMON IF I TRANSFER MY REMAINING MANA TO OGRE SLAYER.
BUT MY BODY WILL DEMATERIALIZE.
I'LL HAVE TO BECOME A GHOST...
...AND ENTER YOUR BODY TO DEFEAT THE DEMON.

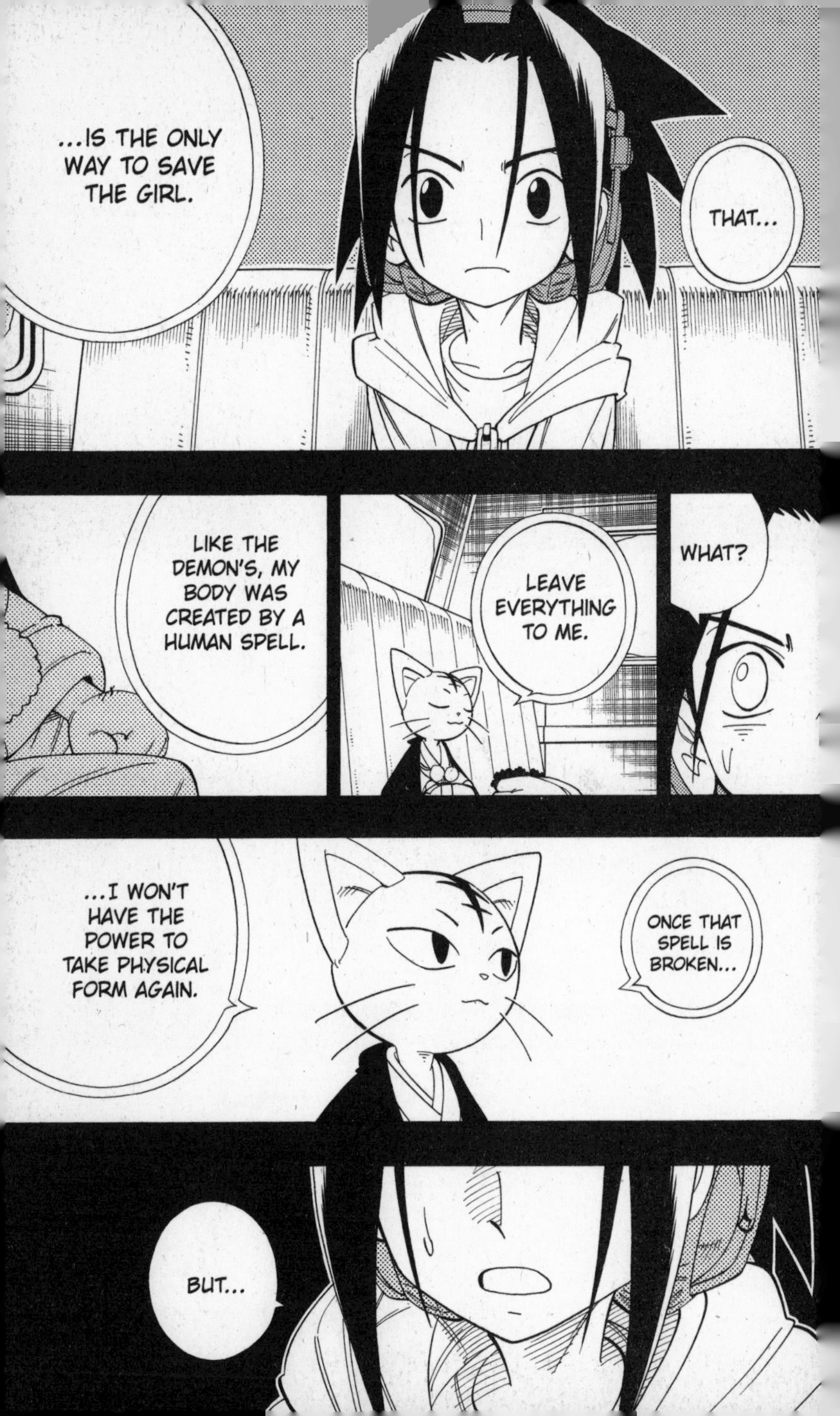
THAT...
...IS THE ONLY WAY TO SAVE THE GIRL.
WHAT?
LEAVE EVERYTHING TO ME.
LIKE THE DEMON'S, MY BODY WAS CREATED BY A HUMAN SPELL.
ONCE THAT SPELL IS BROKEN...
...I WON'T HAVE THE POWER TO TAKE PHYSICAL FORM AGAIN.
BUT...

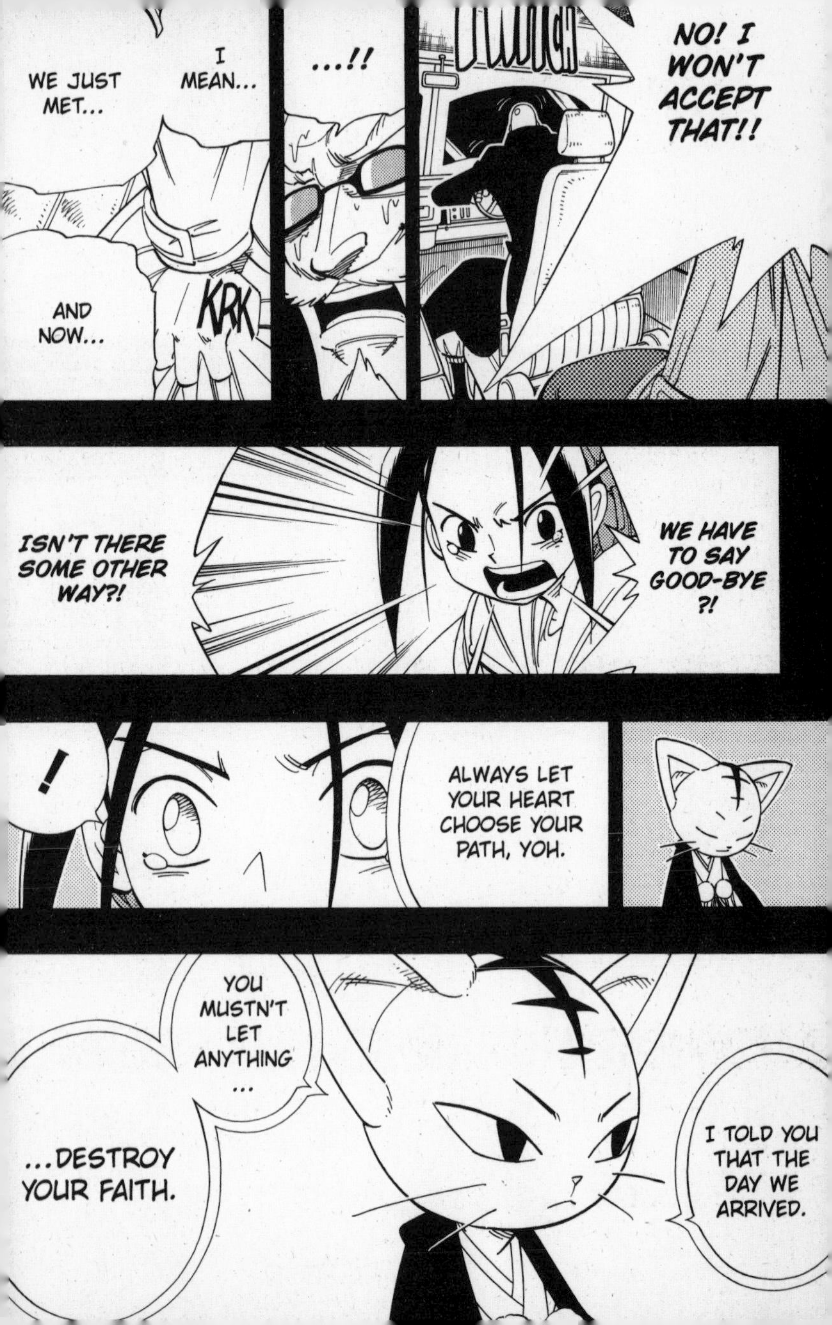
NO! I WON'T ACCEPT THAT!!
...!!
I MEAN...
WE JUST MET...
KRK
AND NOW...
WE HAVE TO SAY GOOD-BYE ?!
ISN'T THERE SOME OTHER WAY?!
ALWAYS LET YOUR HEART CHOOSE YOUR PATH, YOH.
!
I TOLD YOU THAT THE DAY WE ARRIVED.
YOU MUSTN'T LET ANYTHING ...
...DESTROY YOUR FAITH.

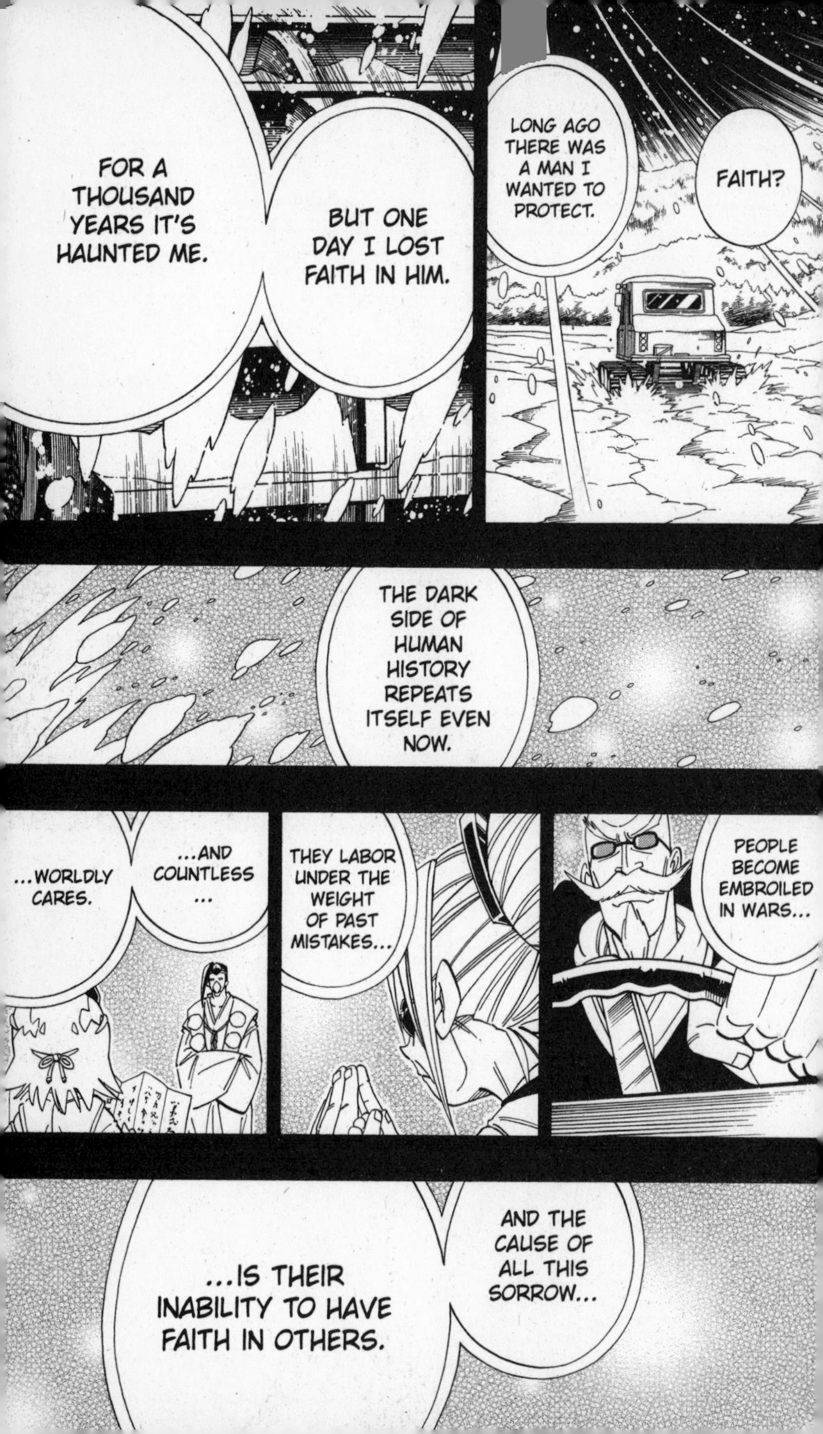
FAITH?
LONG AGO THERE WAS A MAN I WANTED TO PROTECT.
BUT ONE DAY I LOST FAITH IN HIM.
FOR A THOUSAND YEARS IT'S HAUNTED ME.
THE DARK SIDE OF HUMAN HISTORY REPEATS ITSELF EVEN NOW.
PEOPLE BECOME EMBROILED IN WARS...
THEY LABOR UNDER THE WEIGHT OF PAST MISTAKES...
...AND COUNTLESS ...
...WORLDLY CARES.
AND THE CAUSE OF ALL THIS SORROW...
...IS THEIR INABILITY TO HAVE FAITH IN OTHERS.

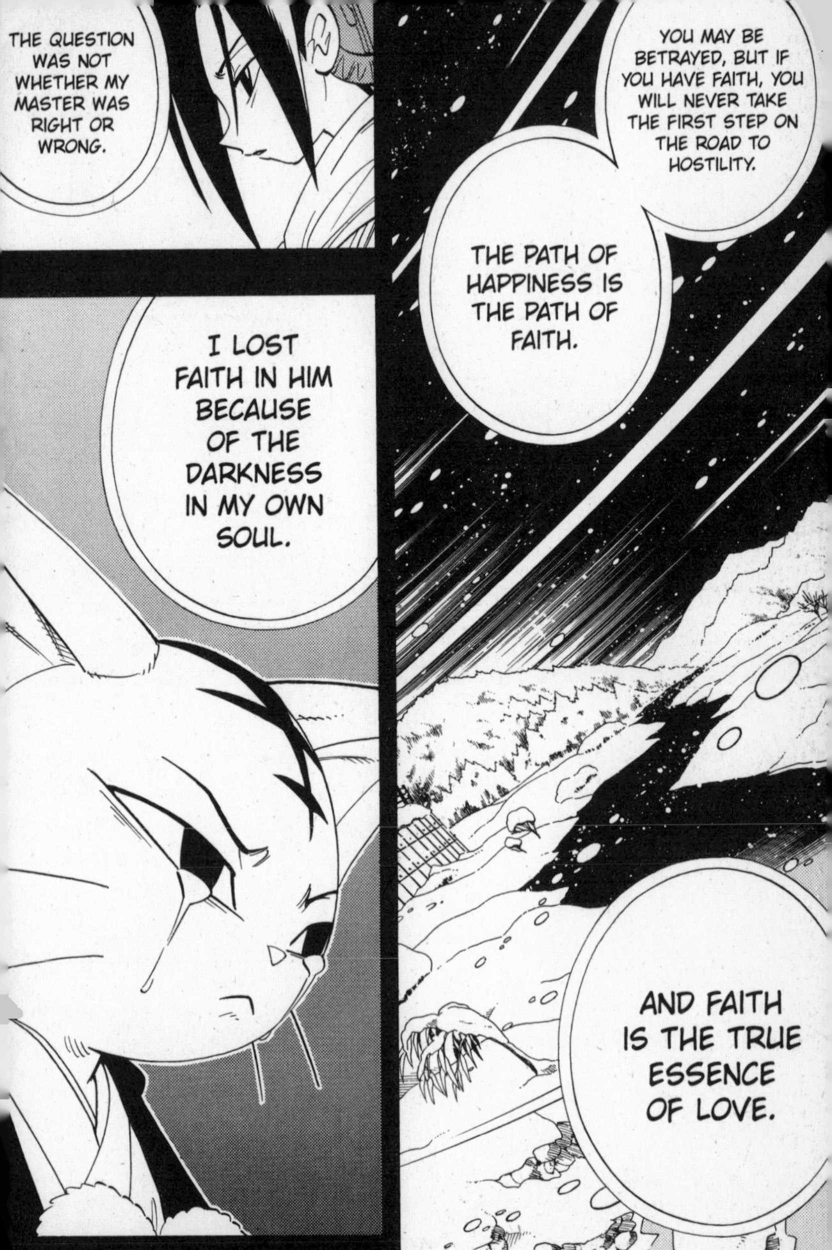
YOU MAY BE BETRAYED, BUT IF YOU HAVE FAITH, YOU WILL NEVER TAKE THE FIRST STEP ON THE ROAD TO HOSTILITY.
THE PATH OF HAPPINESS IS THE PATH OF FAITH.
AND FAITH IS THE TRUE ESSENCE OF LOVE.
THE QUESTION WAS NOT WHETHER MY MASTER WAS RIGHT OR WRONG.
I LOST FAITH IN HIM BECAUSE OF THE DARKNESS IN MY OWN SOUL.

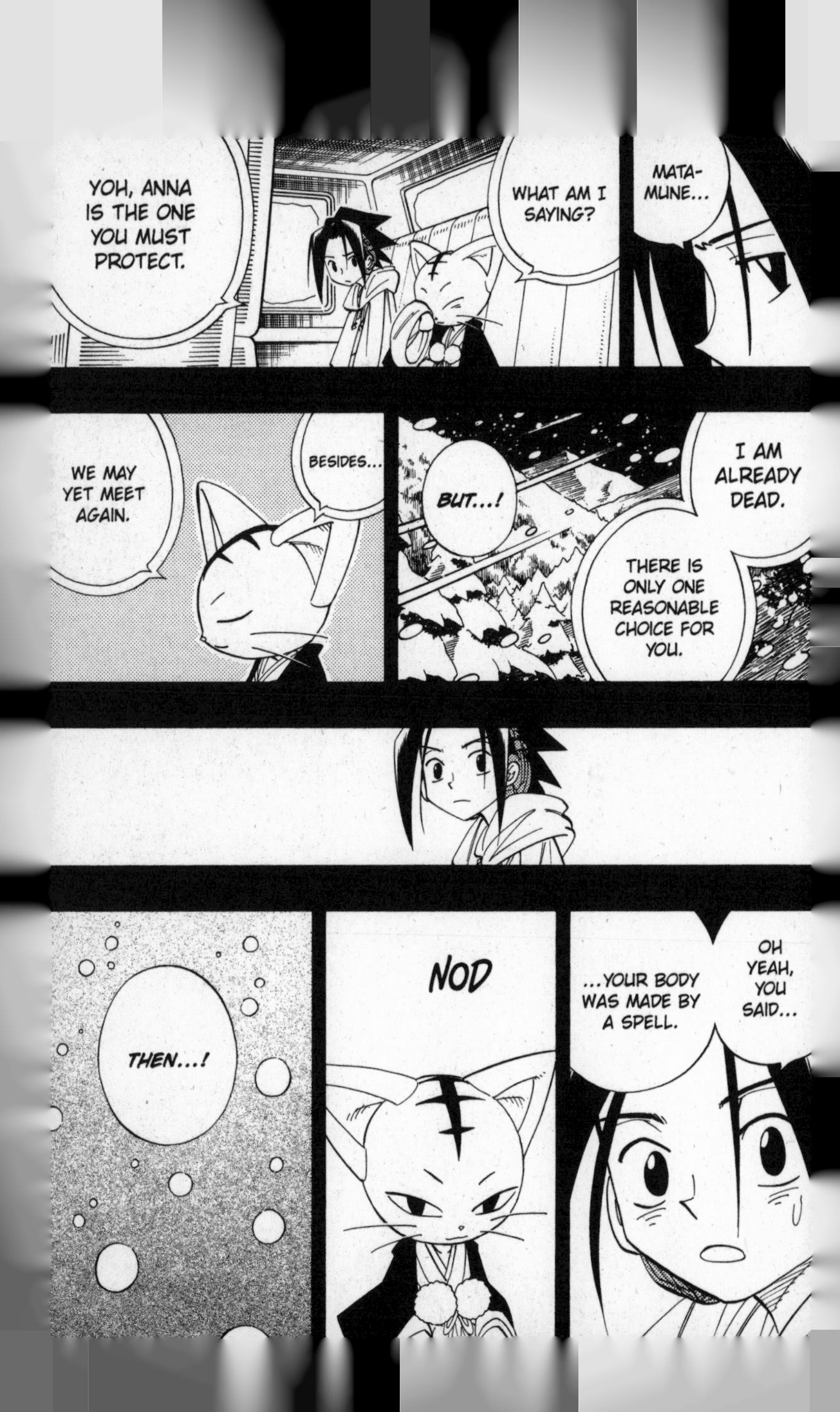
MATA-MUNE...
WHAT AM I SAYING?
YOH, ANNA IS THE ONE YOU MUST PROTECT.
I AM ALREADY DEAD.
THERE IS ONLY ONE REASONABLE CHOICE FOR YOU.
BUT...!
BESIDES...
WE MAY YET MEET AGAIN.
OH YEAH, YOU SAID...
...YOUR BODY WAS MADE BY A SPELL.
NOD
THEN...!

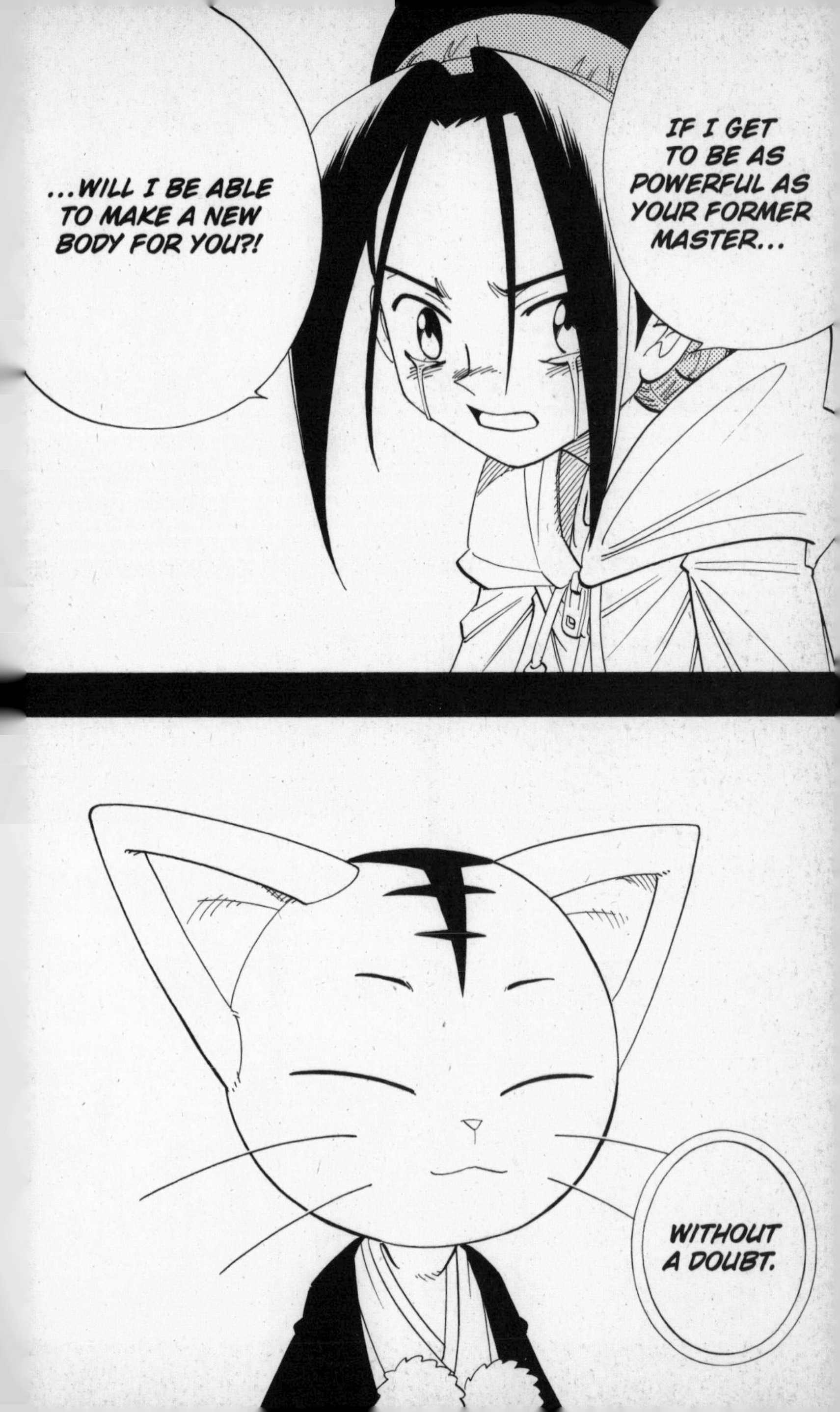
IF I GET TO BE AS POWERFUL AS YOUR FORMER MASTER...
...WILL I BE ABLE TO MAKE A NEW BODY FOR YOU?!
WITHOUT A DOUBT.

READ THIS WAY

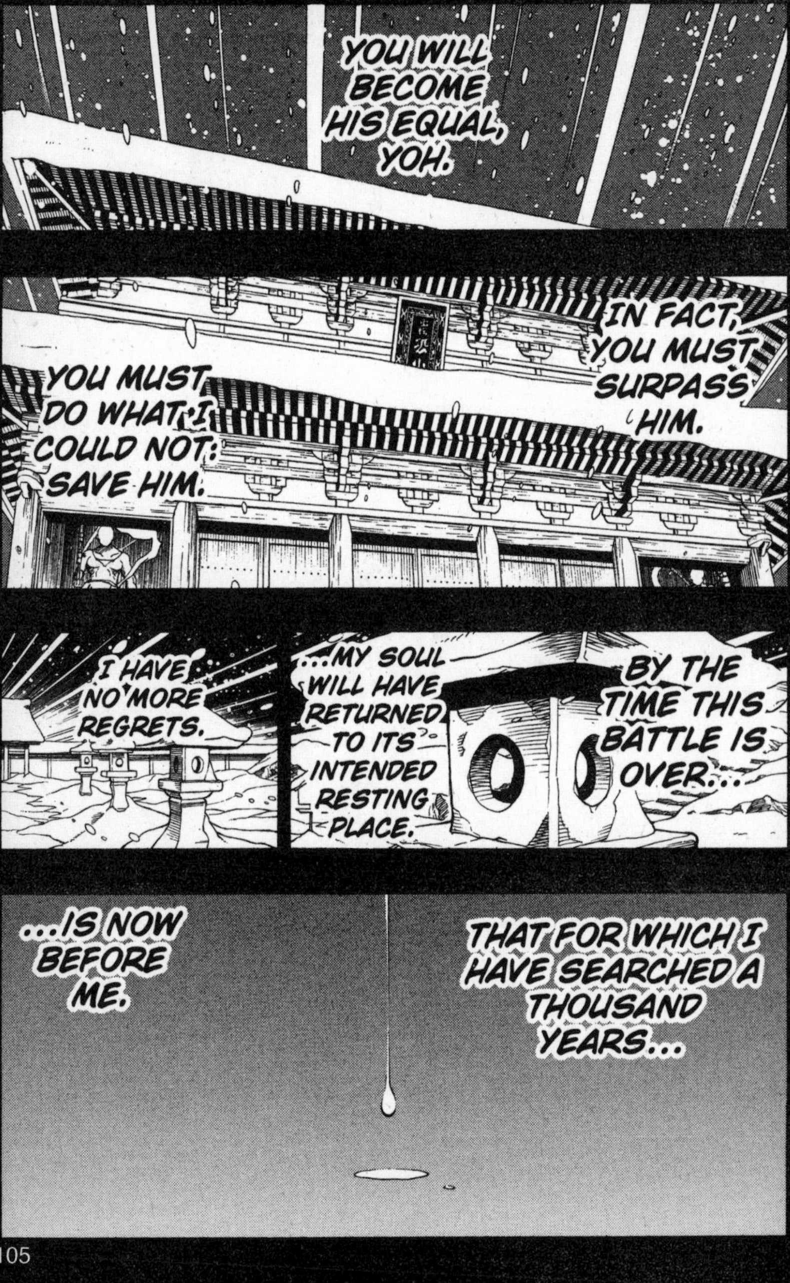
YOU WILL BECOME HIS EQUAL, YOH.
IN FACT, YOU MUST SURPASS HIM.
YOU MUST DO WHAT I COULD NOT: SAVE HIM.
BY THE TIME THIS BATTLE IS OVER...
...MY SOUL WILL HAVE RETURNED TO ITS INTENDED RESTING PLACE.
I HAVE NO MORE REGRETS.
THAT FOR WHICH I HAVE SEARCHED A THOUSAND YEARS...
...IS NOW BEFORE ME.

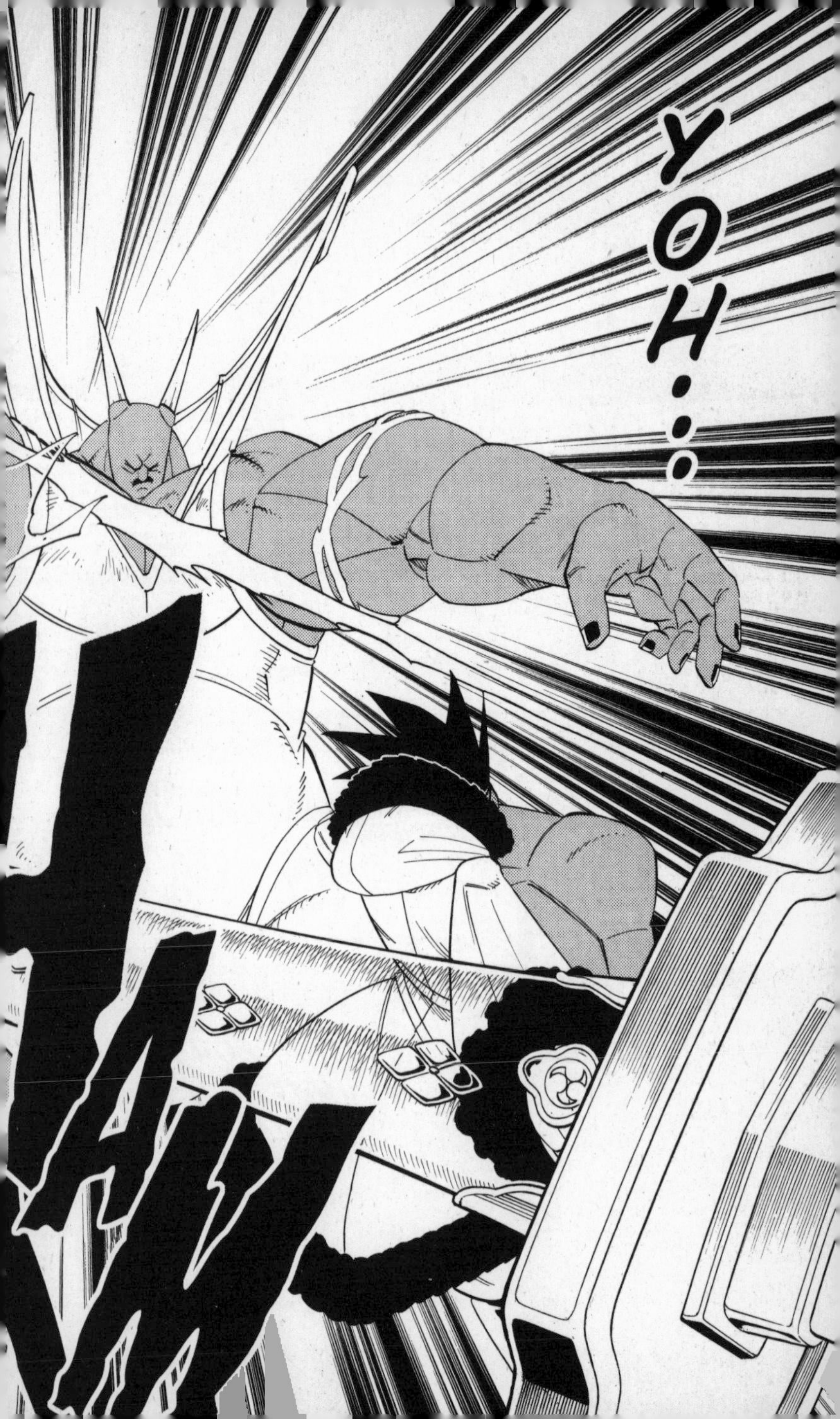
YOH...

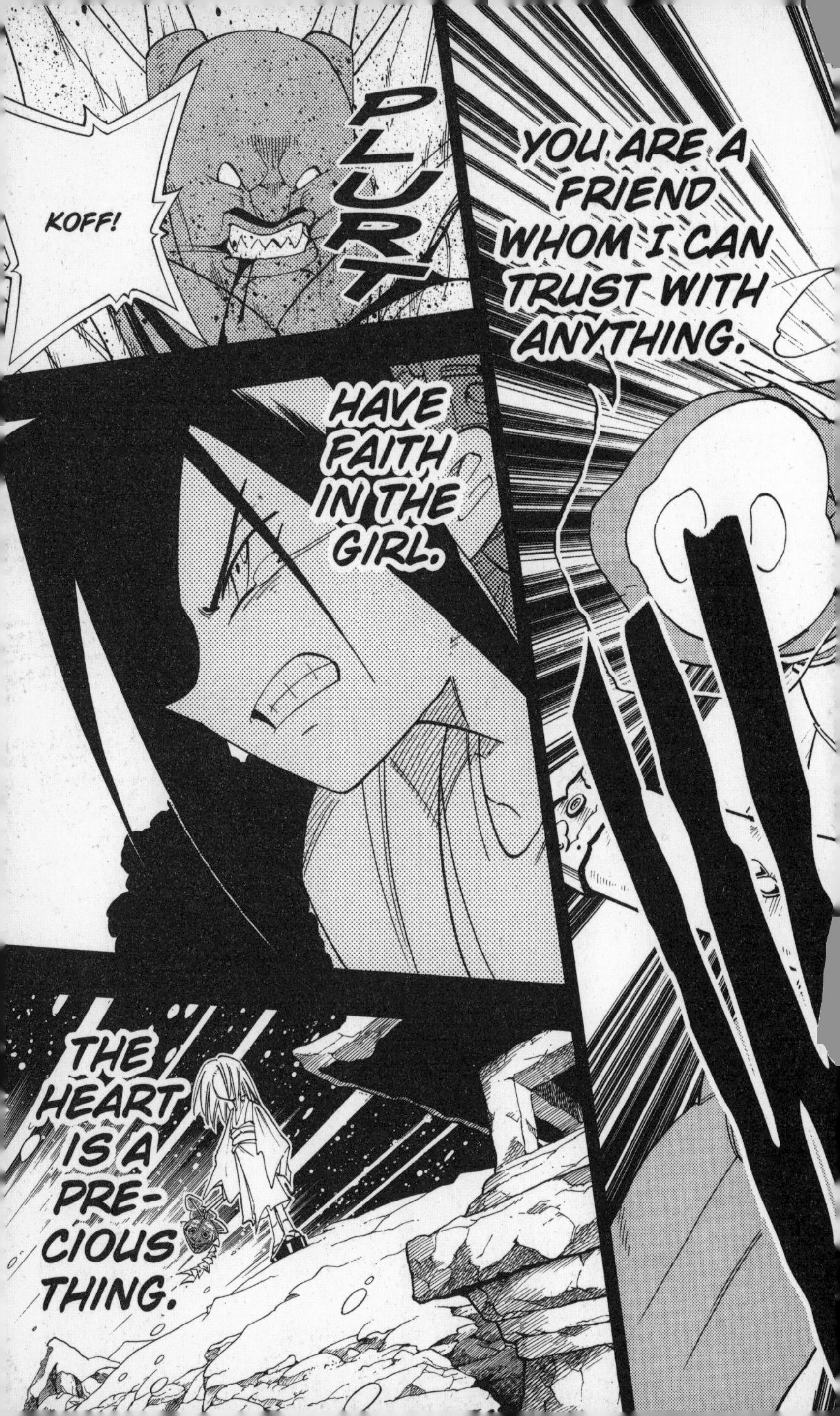
YOU ARE A FRIEND WHOM I CAN TRUST WITH ANYTHING.
PLURT
KOFF!
HAVE FAITH IN THE GIRL.
THE HEART IS A PRE-CIOUS THING.

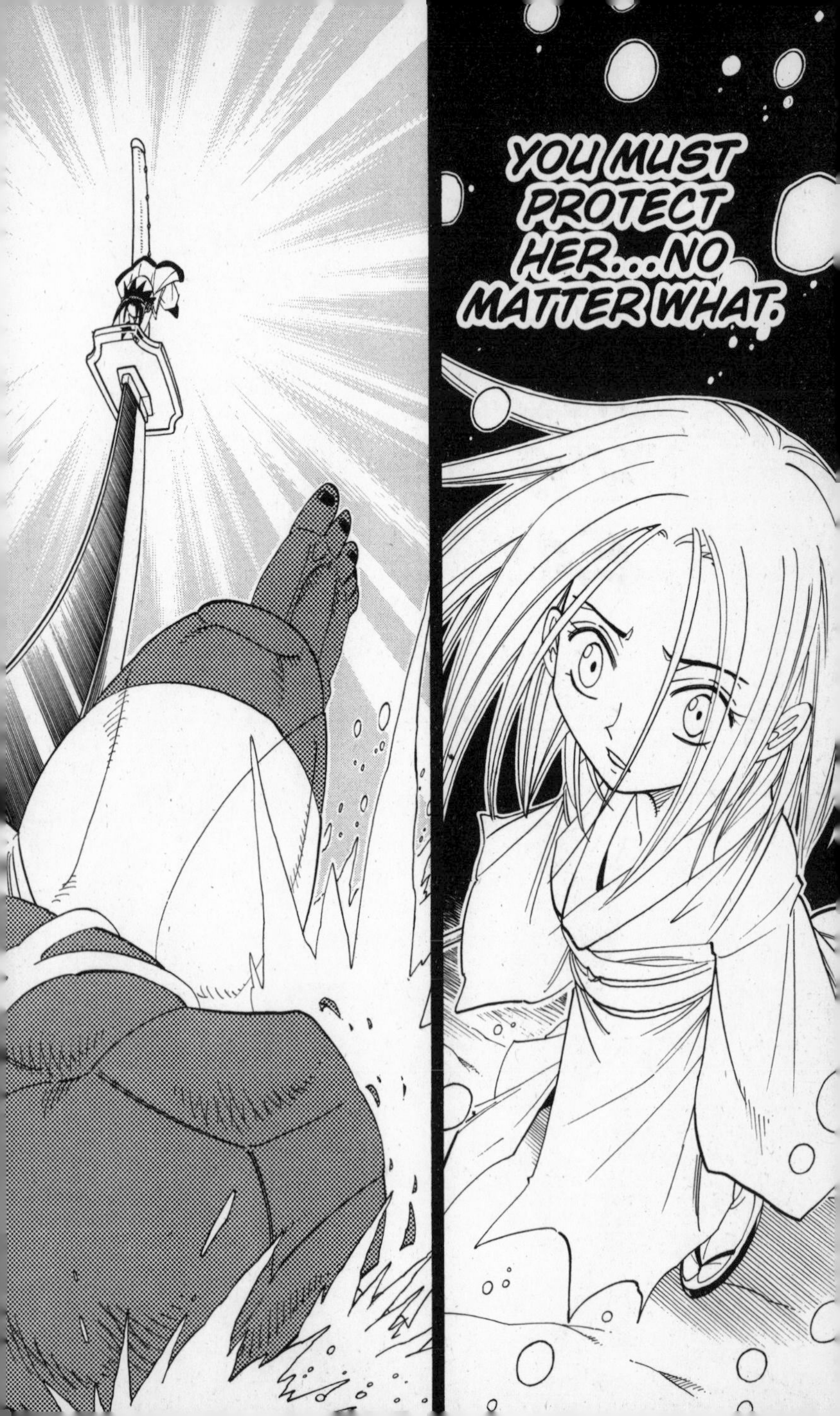
YOU MUST PROTECT HER...NO MATTER WHAT.

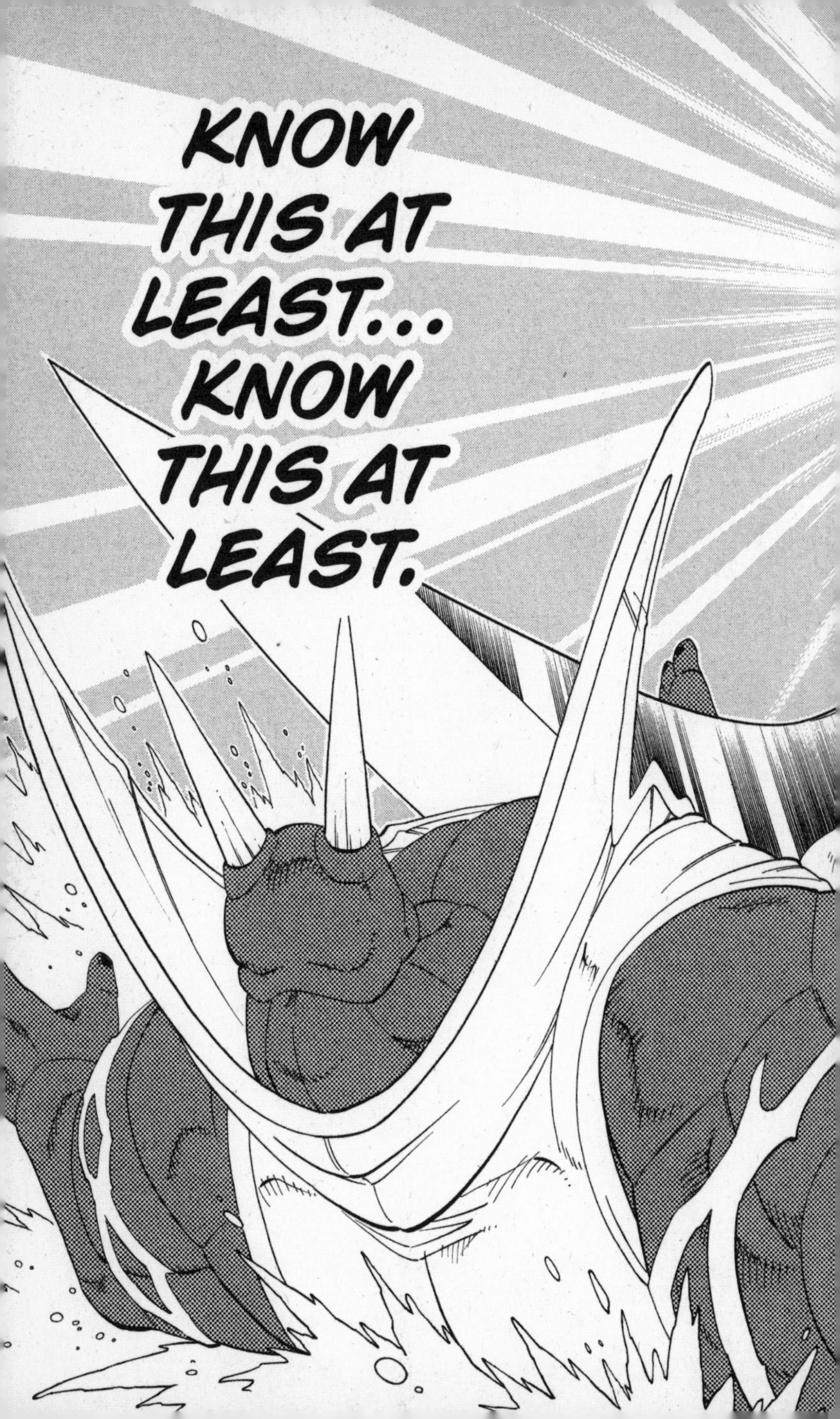
KNOW THIS AT LEAST... KNOW THIS AT LEAST.

SHAMAN KING CHARACTER FILE No.108

1995
(DEC)

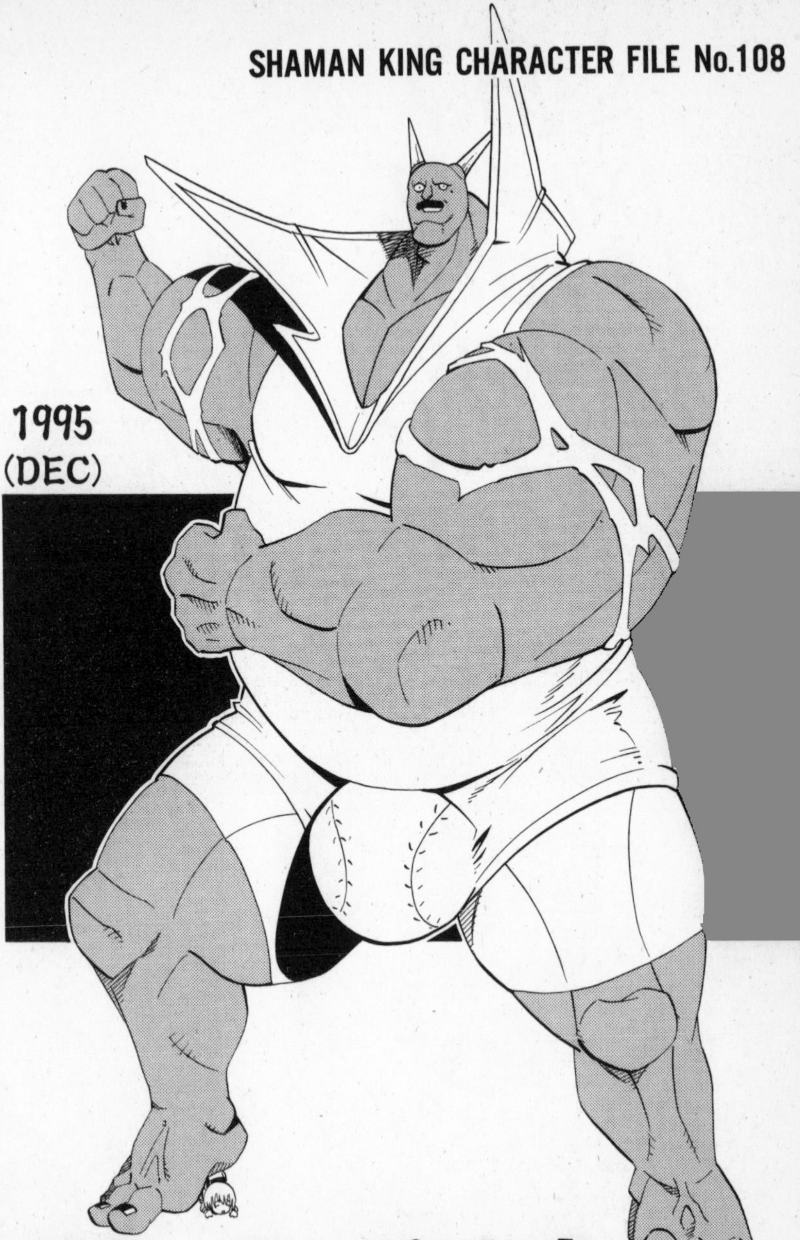

パワーアップ!大鬼

POWERED-UP GIANT DEMON

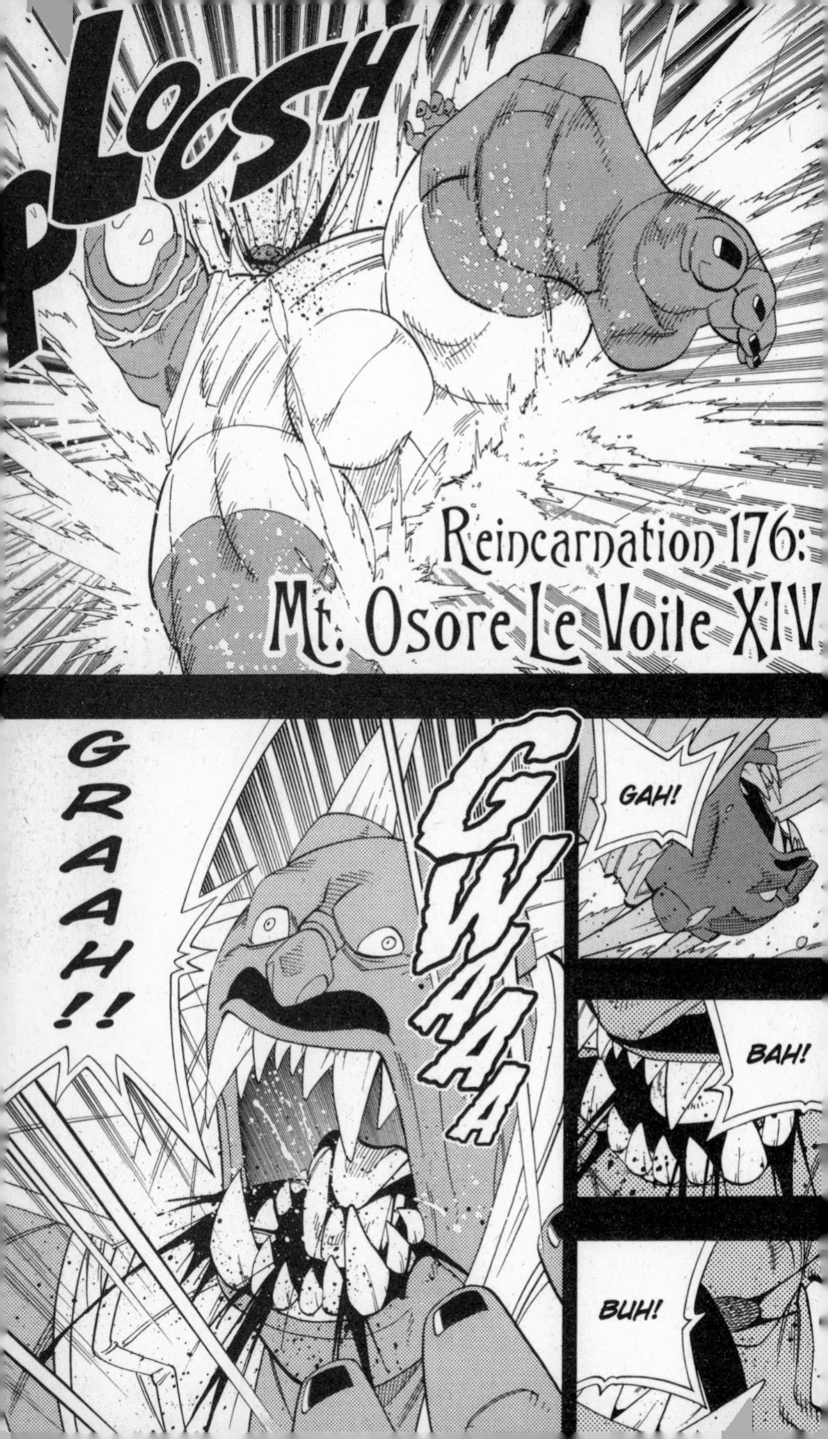
PLOOSH
Reincarnation 176:
Mt. Osore Le Voile XIV
GAH!
BAH!
BUH!
GWAAA
GRAAH!!

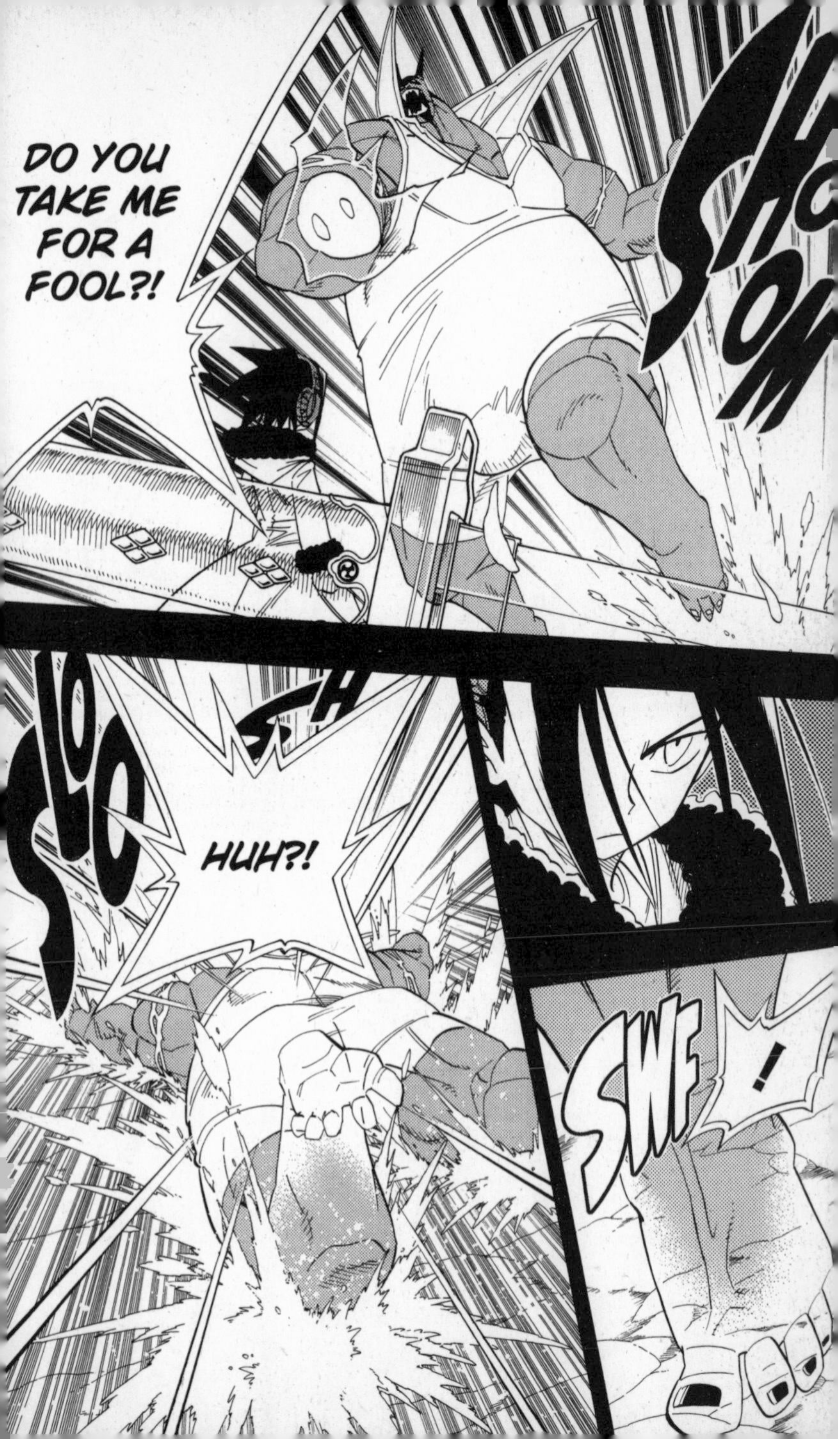
DO YOU TAKE ME FOR A FOOL?!
SWF
!
HUH?!

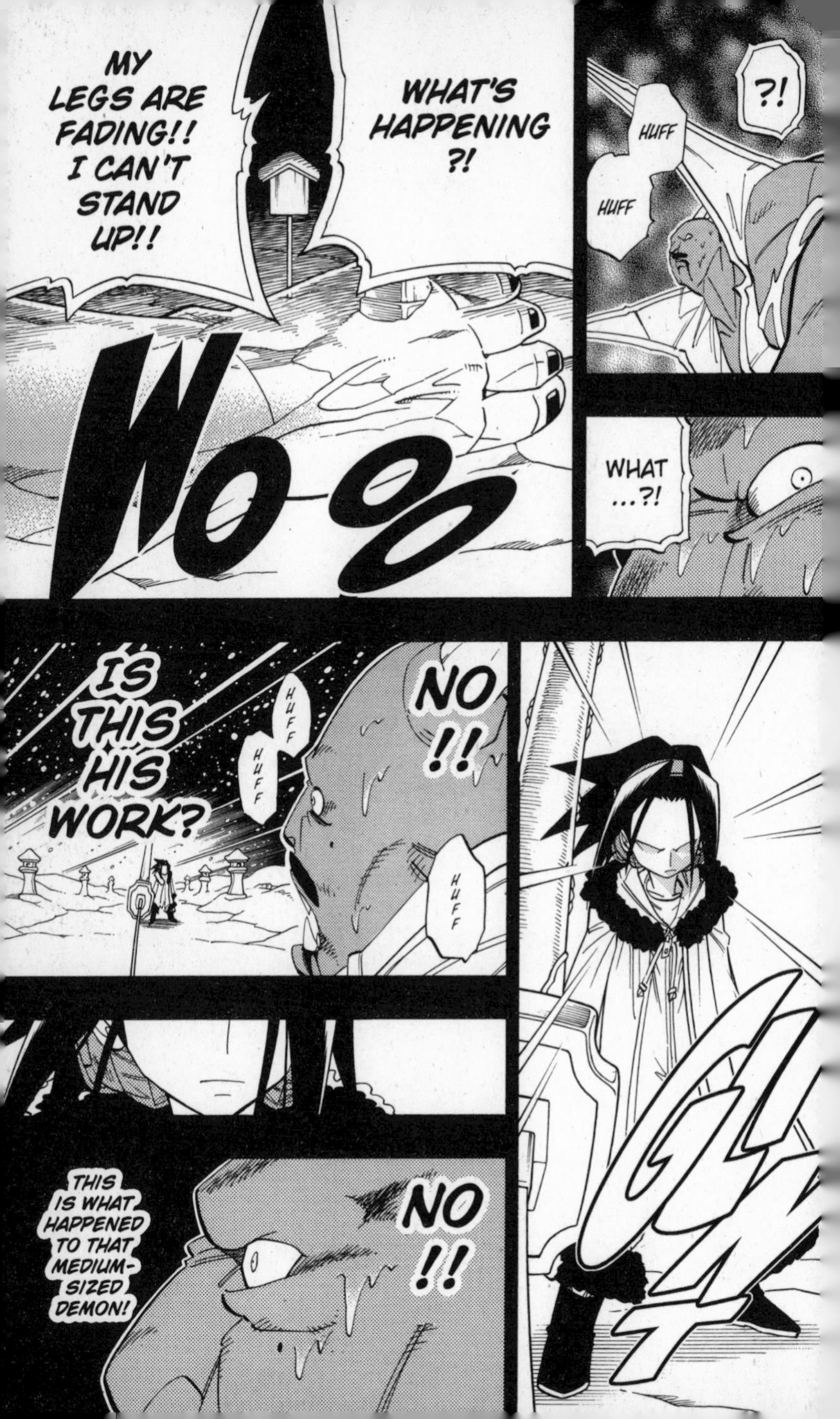
?!
HUFF
HUFF
WHAT ...?!
WHAT'S HAPPENING ?!
MY LEGS ARE FADING!! I CAN'T STAND UP!!
WOOO
NO !!
HUFF
HUFF
HUFF
IS THIS HIS WORK?
NO !!
THIS IS WHAT HAPPENED TO THAT MEDIUM-SIZED DEMON!

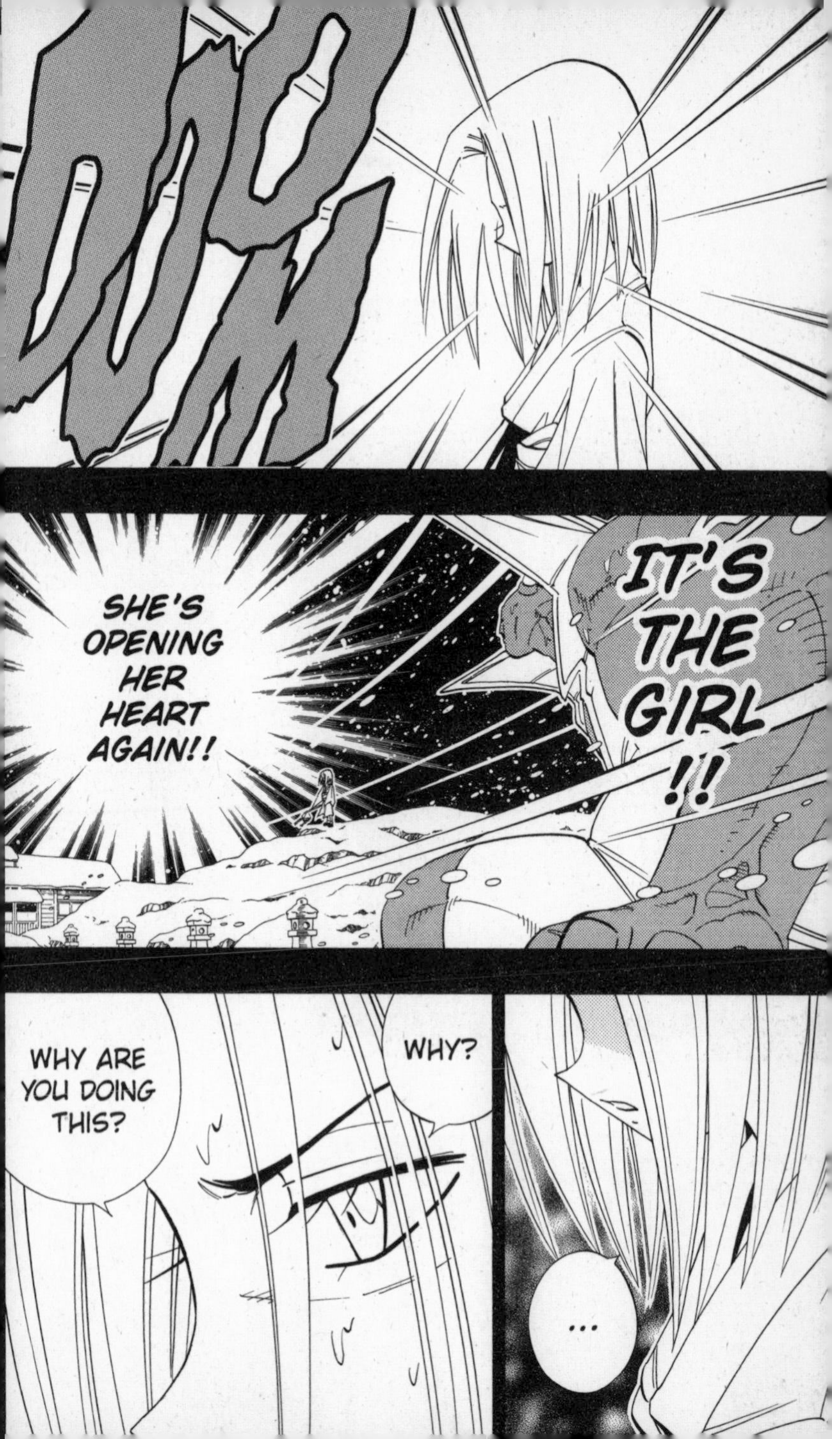
IT'S THE GIRL!!
SHE'S OPENING HER HEART AGAIN!!
...
WHY?
WHY ARE YOU DOING THIS?

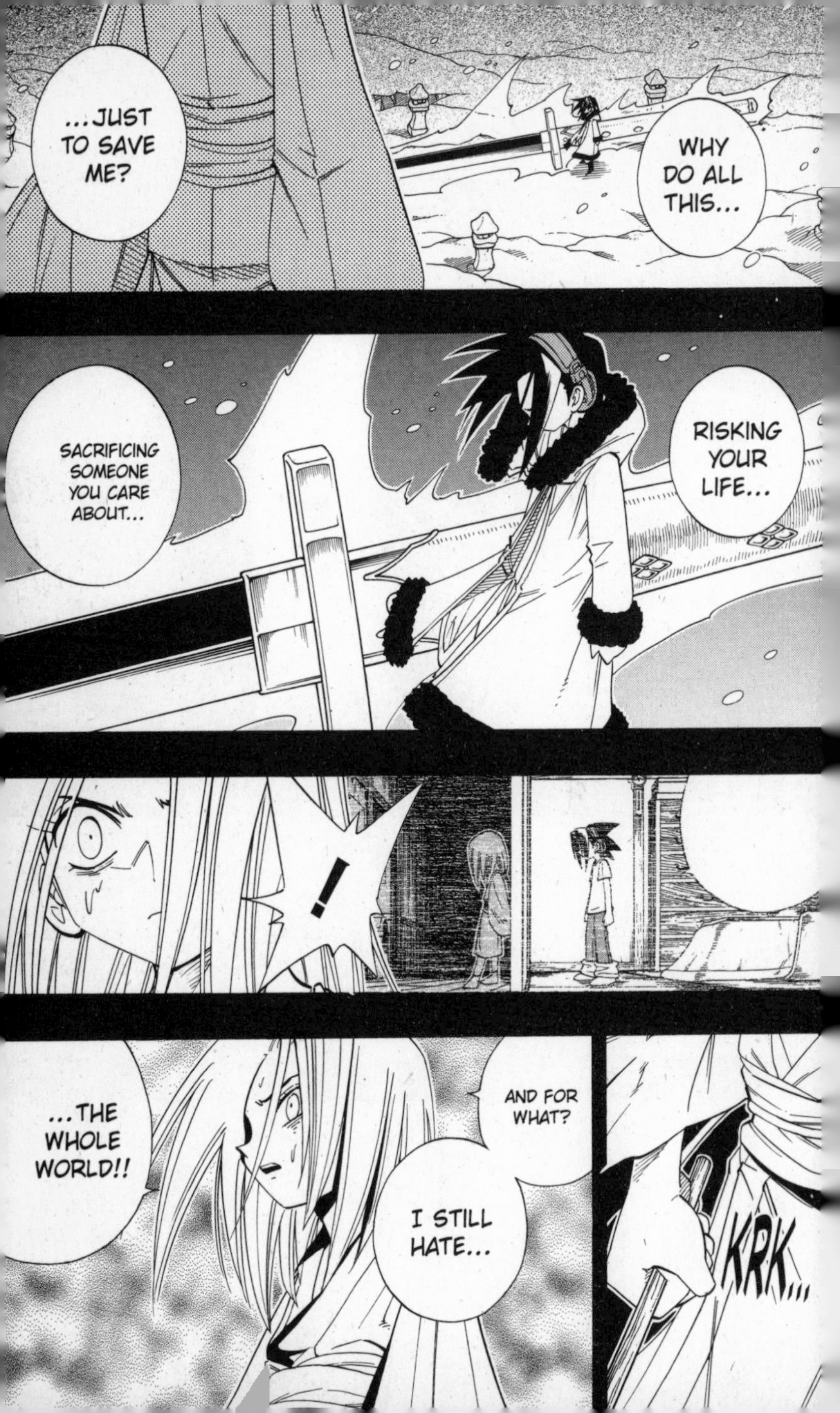
WHY DO ALL THIS...
...JUST TO SAVE ME?
RISKING YOUR LIFE...
SACRIFICING SOMEONE YOU CARE ABOUT...
!
KRK...
AND FOR WHAT?
I STILL HATE...
...THE WHOLE WORLD!!

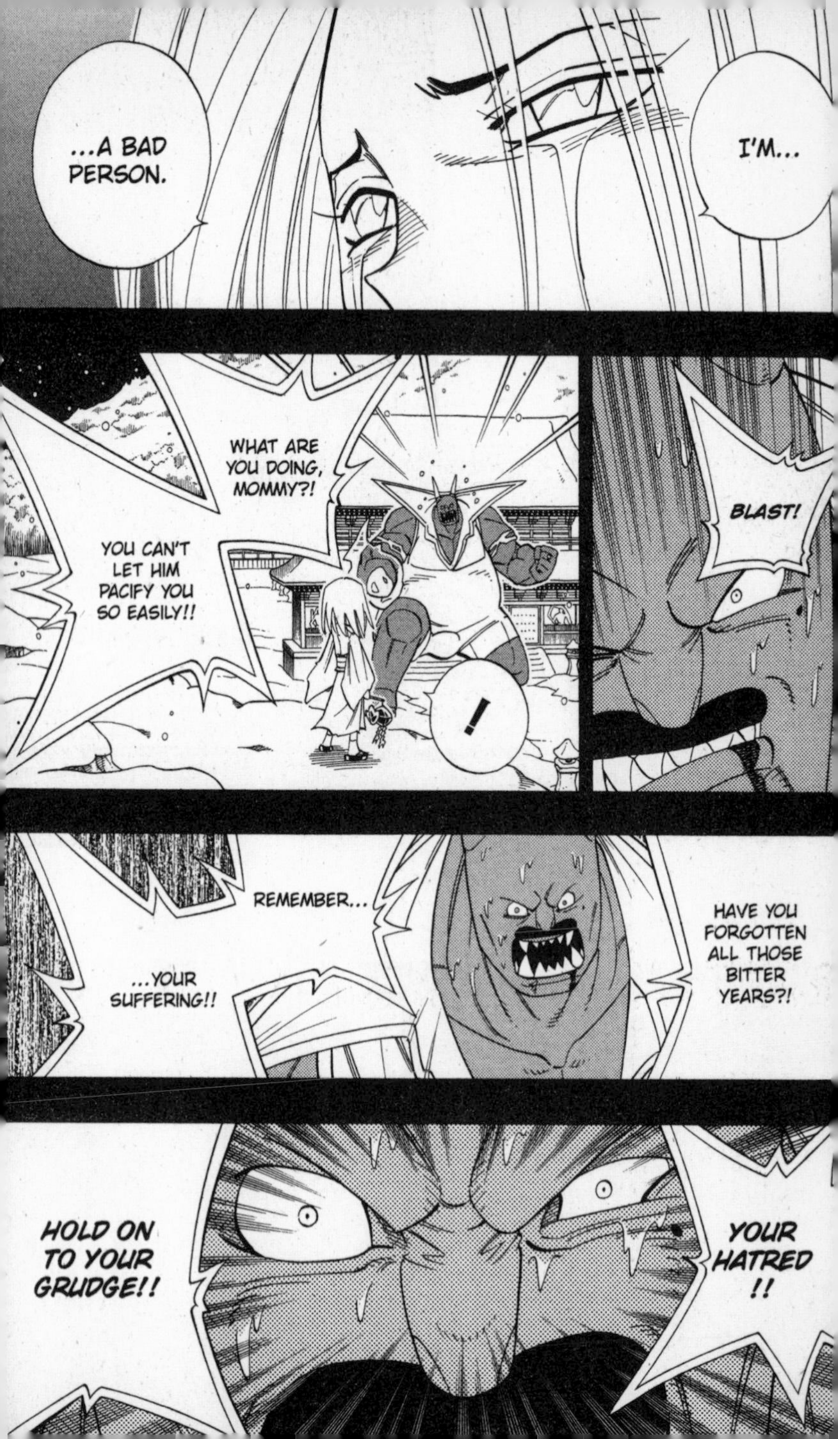
I'M...
...A BAD PERSON.
BLAST!
WHAT ARE YOU DOING, MOMMY?!
YOU CAN'T LET HIM PACIFY YOU SO EASILY!!
!
HAVE YOU FORGOTTEN ALL THOSE BITTER YEARS?!
REMEMBER...
...YOUR SUFFERING!!
YOUR HATRED !!
HOLD ON TO YOUR GRUDGE!!

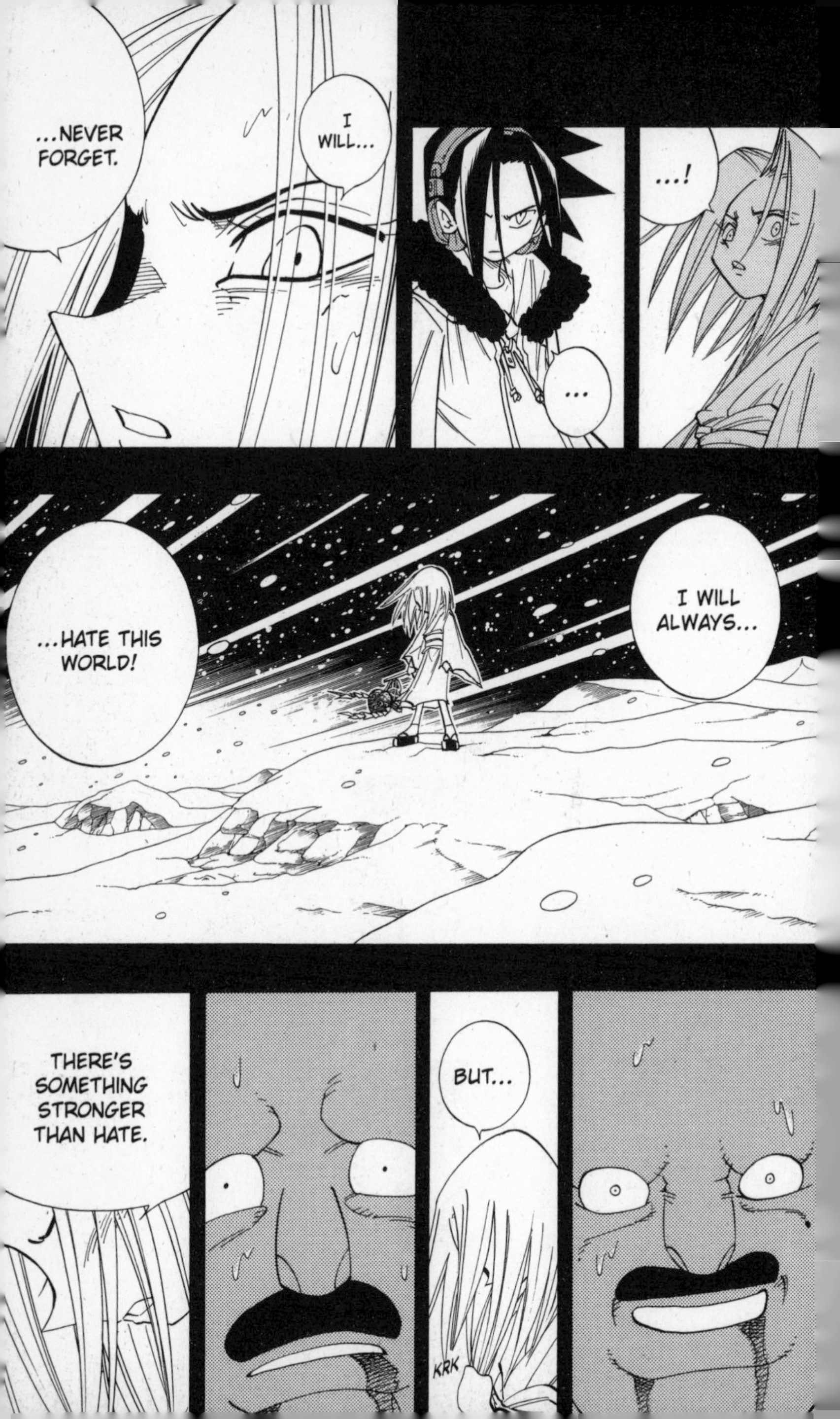
...!
...
I WILL...
...NEVER FORGET.
I WILL ALWAYS...
...HATE THIS WORLD!
BUT...
KRK
THERE'S SOMETHING STRONGER THAN HATE.

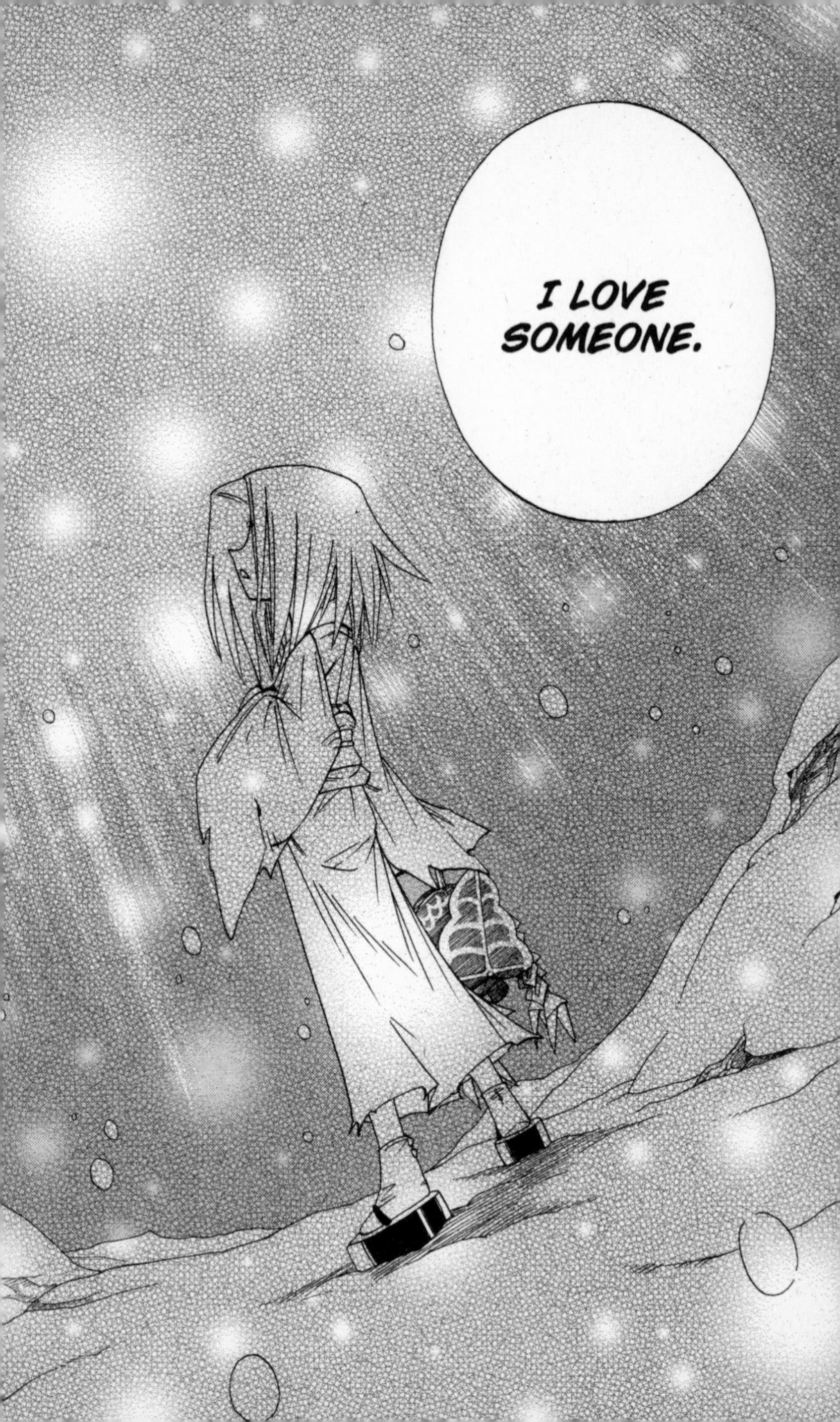
I LOVE SOMEONE.

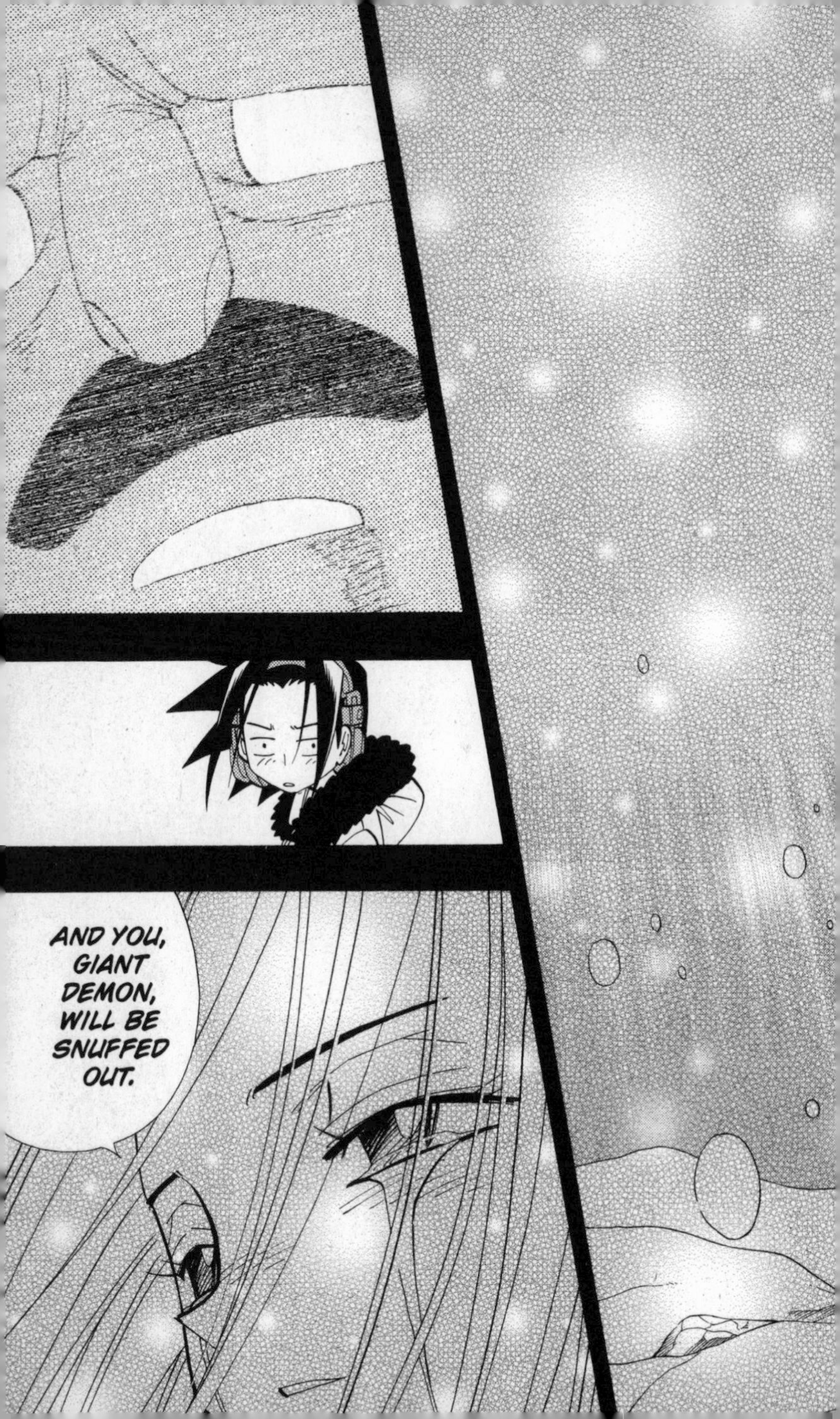
AND YOU, GIANT DEMON, WILL BE SNUFFED OUT.

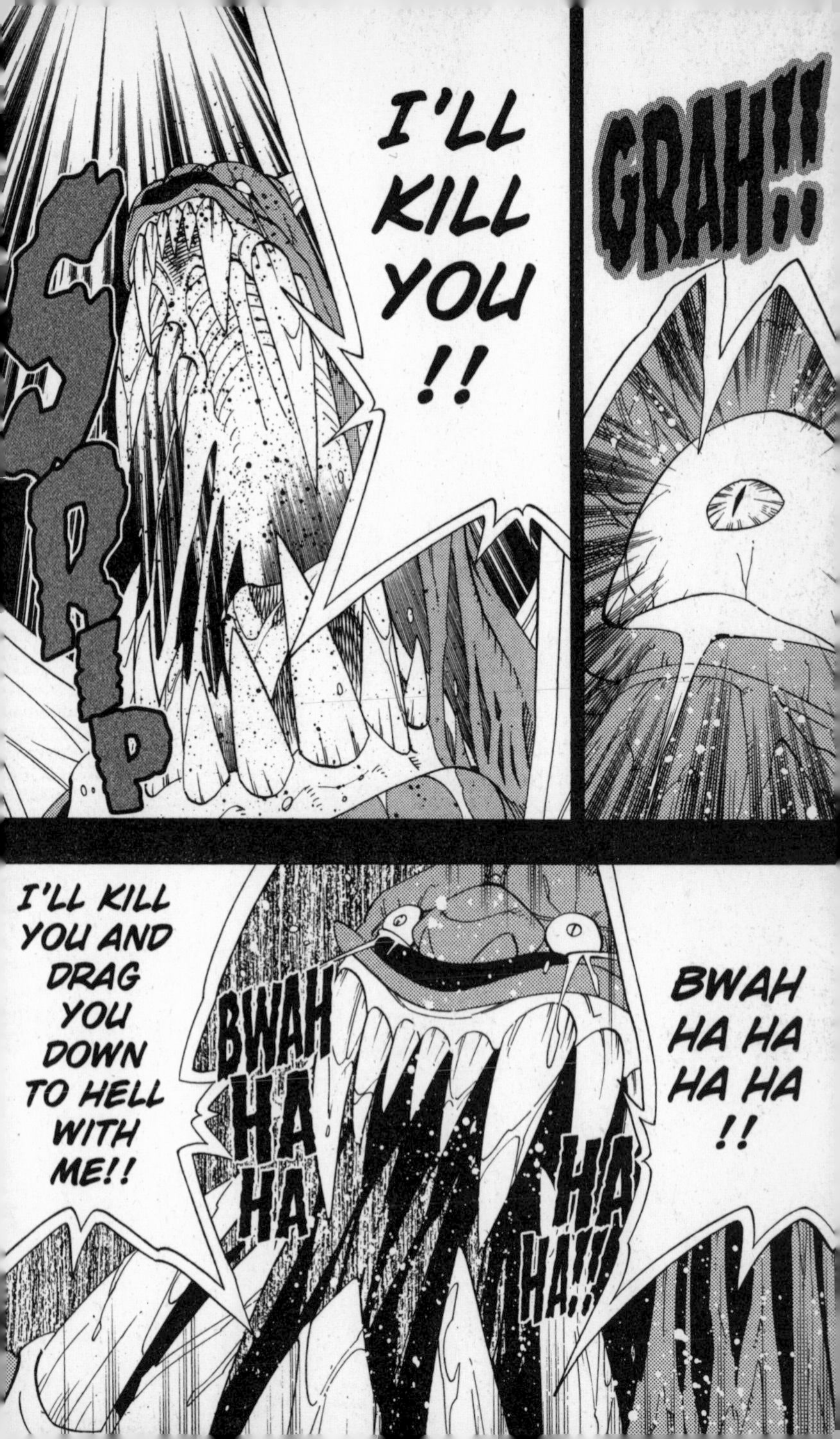
GRAH!!
I'LL KILL YOU!!
SRIP
BWAH HA HA HA HA!!
BWAH HA HA HA HA!!
I'LL KILL YOU AND DRAG YOU DOWN TO HELL WITH ME!!

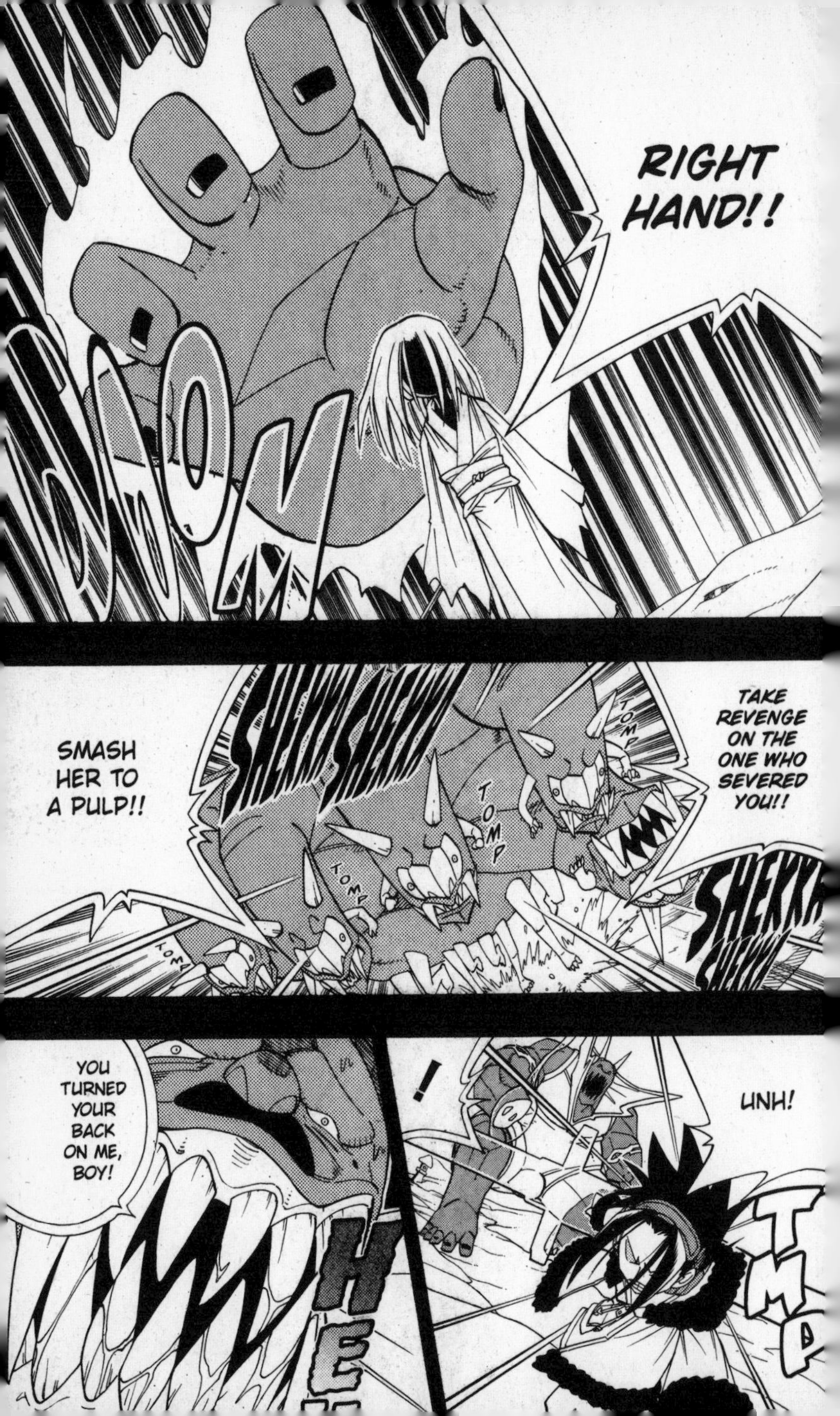
RIGHT HAND!!
TAKE REVENGE ON THE ONE WHO SEVERED YOU!!
TOMP
TOMP
SMASH HER TO A PULP!!
TOMP
TOMP
!
UNH!
TOMP
YOU TURNED YOUR BACK ON ME, BOY!

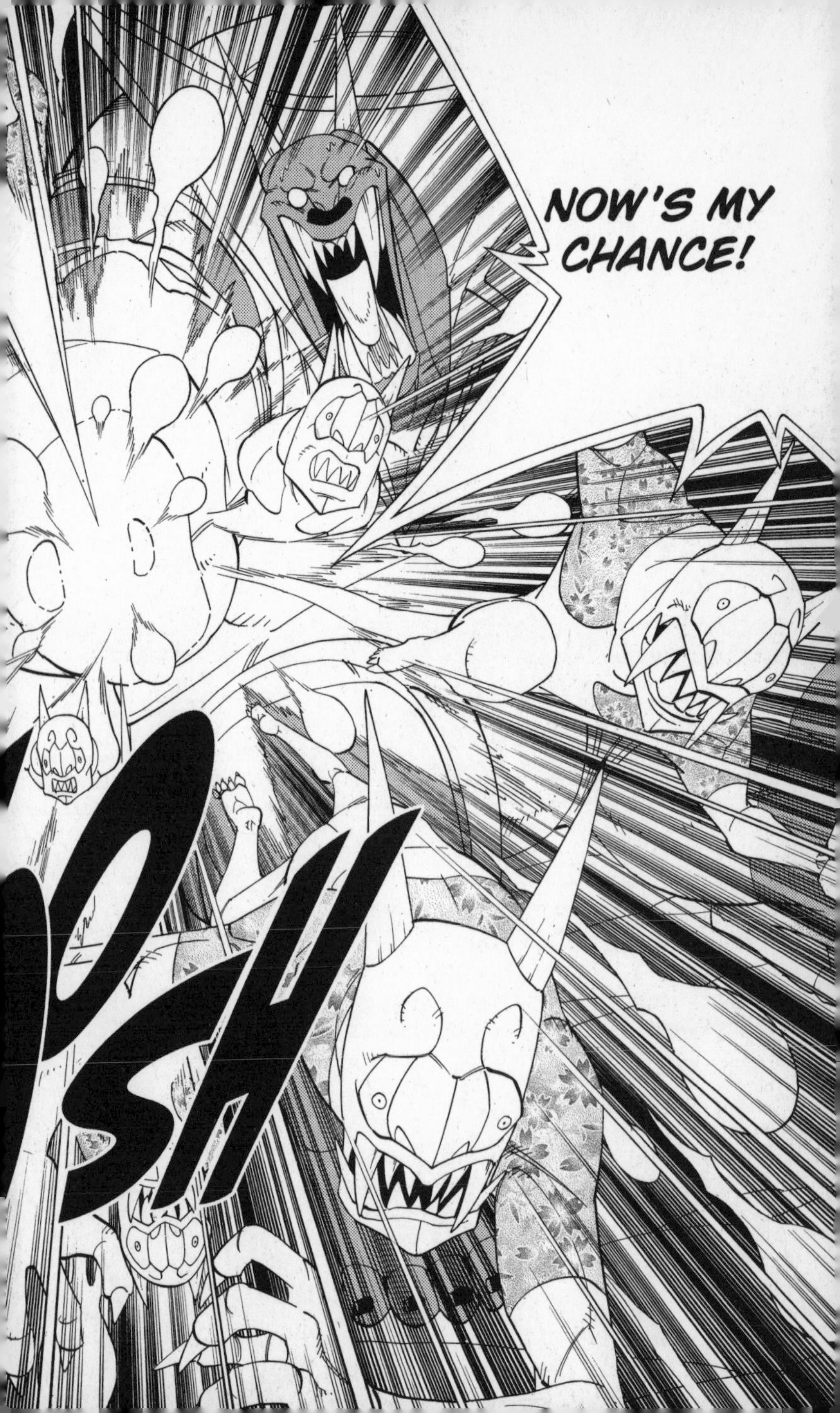
NOW'S MY CHANCE!

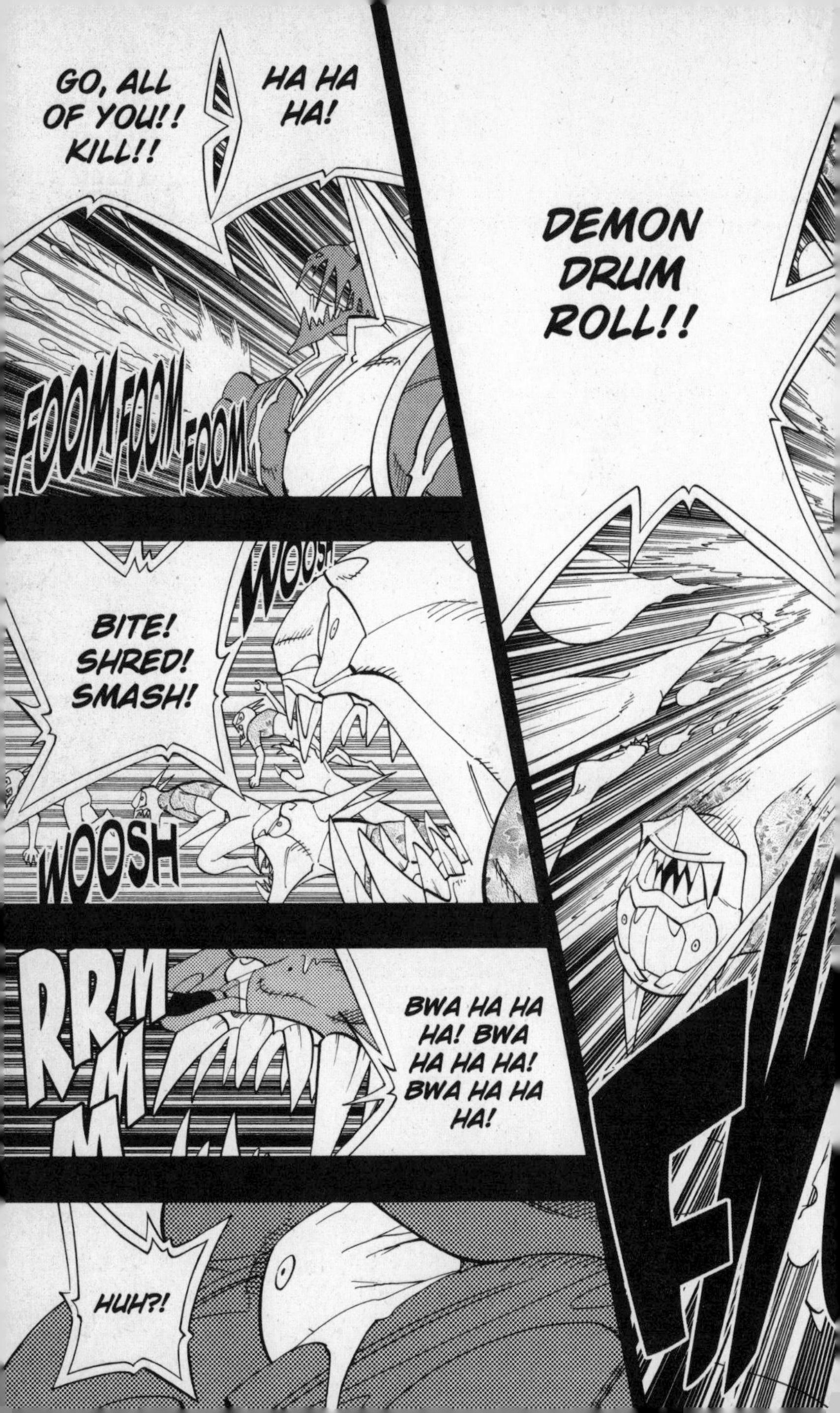
DEMON DRUM ROLL!!
HA HA HA!
GO, ALL OF YOU!! KILL!!
FOOM FOOM FOOM
WOOSH
BITE! SHRED! SMASH!
WOOSH
BWA HA HA HA! BWA HA HA HA! BWA HA HA HA!
RRMMM
HUH?!

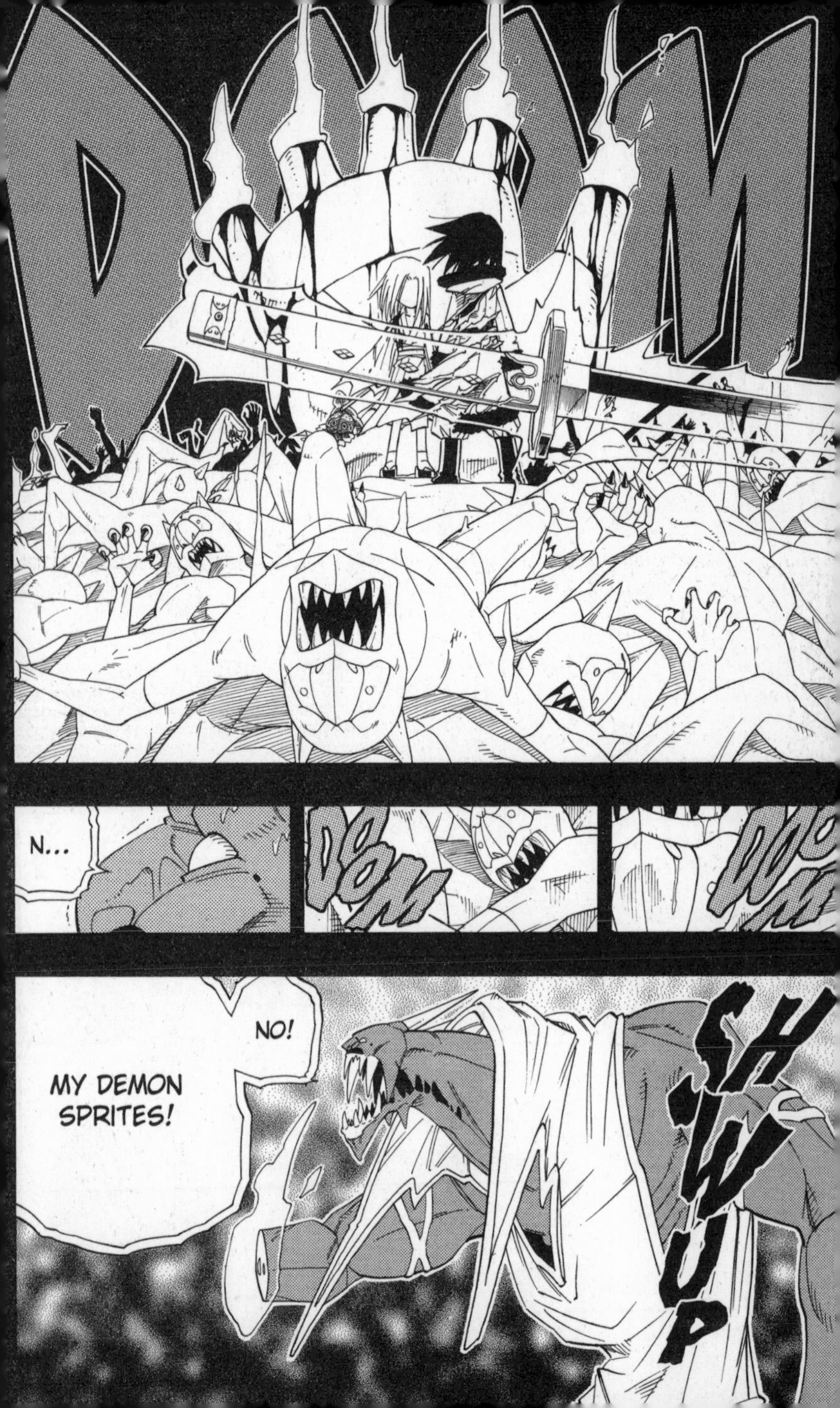
DOOM
DOOM
N...
NO!
MY DEMON SPRITES!
SHWUP

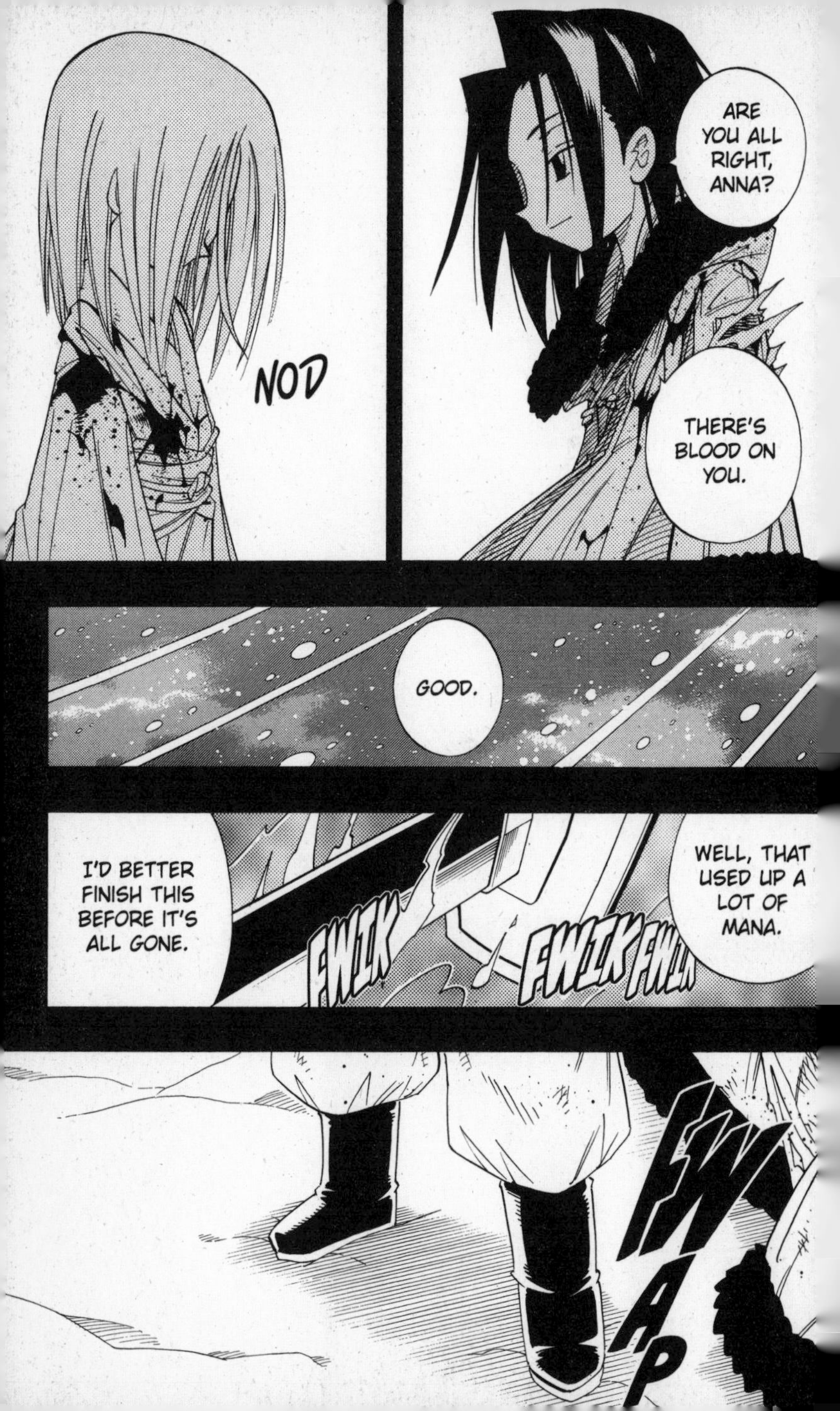
ARE YOU ALL RIGHT, ANNA?
THERE'S BLOOD ON YOU.
NOD
GOOD.
WELL, THAT USED UP A LOT OF MANA.
FWIK FWIK
FWIK
I'D BETTER FINISH THIS BEFORE IT'S ALL GONE.
FWAP

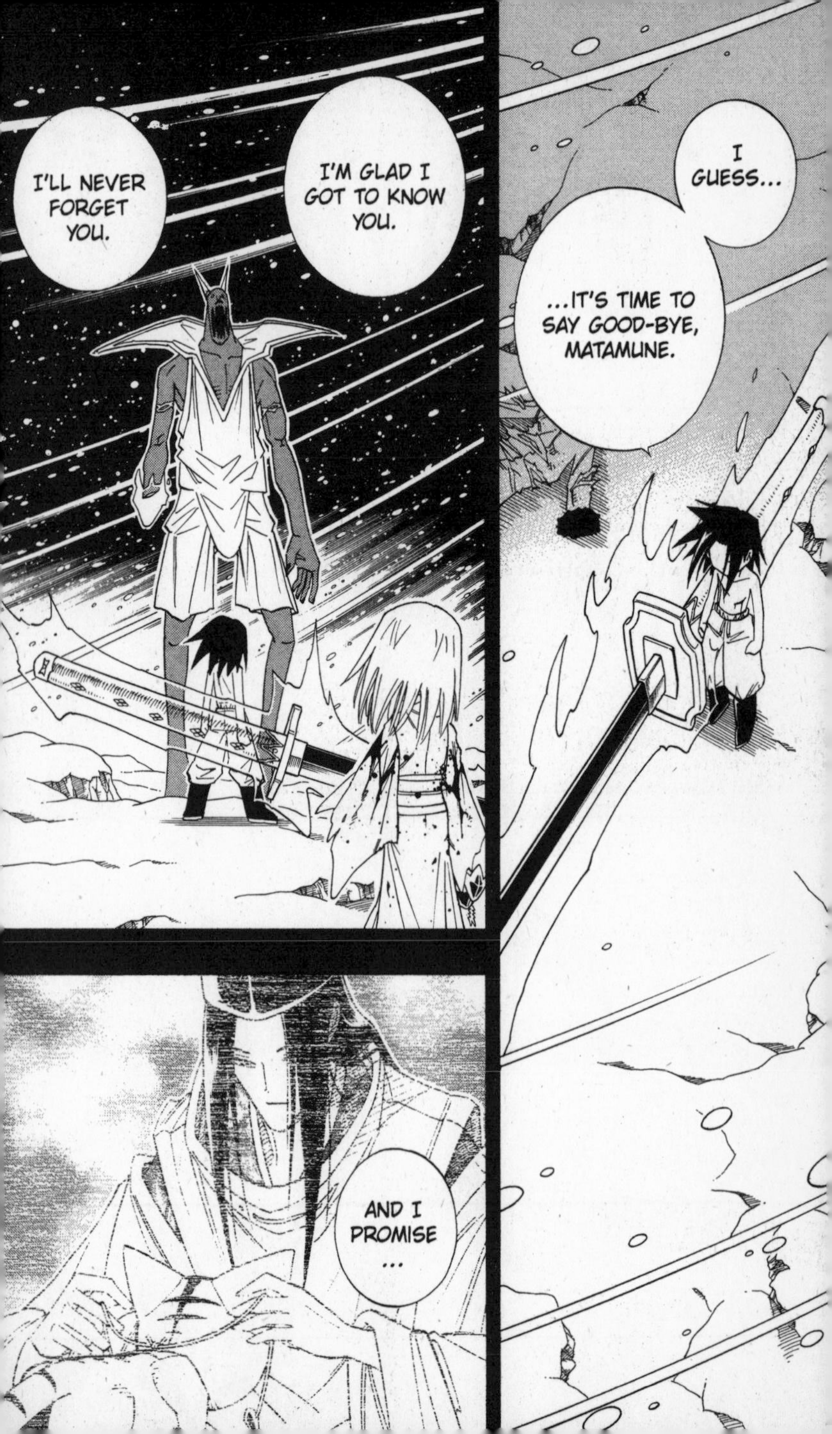
I GUESS...
...IT'S TIME TO SAY GOOD-BYE, MATAMUNE.
I'M GLAD I GOT TO KNOW YOU.
I'LL NEVER FORGET YOU.
AND I PROMISE ...

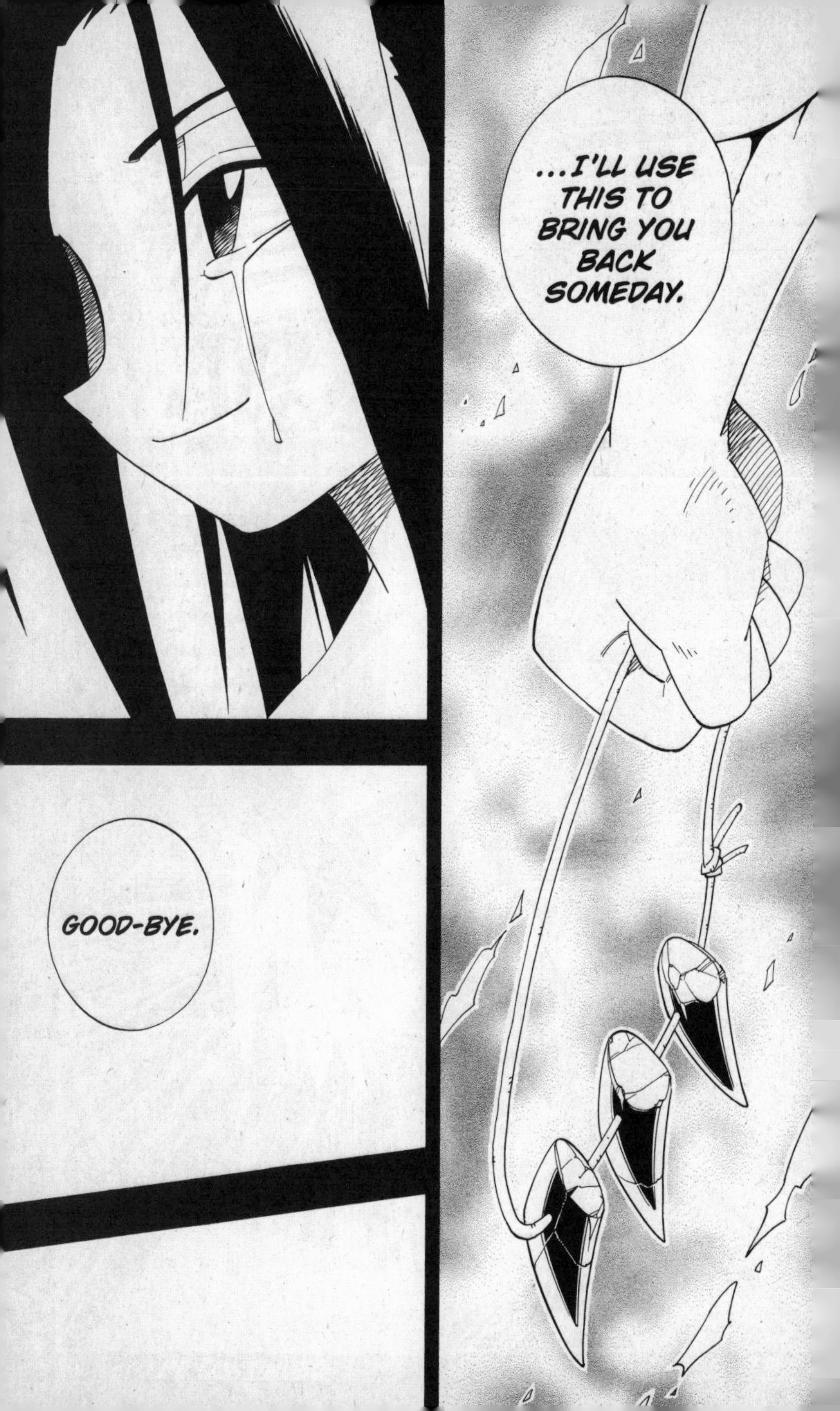
...I'LL USE THIS TO BRING YOU BACK SOMEDAY.
GOOD-BYE.

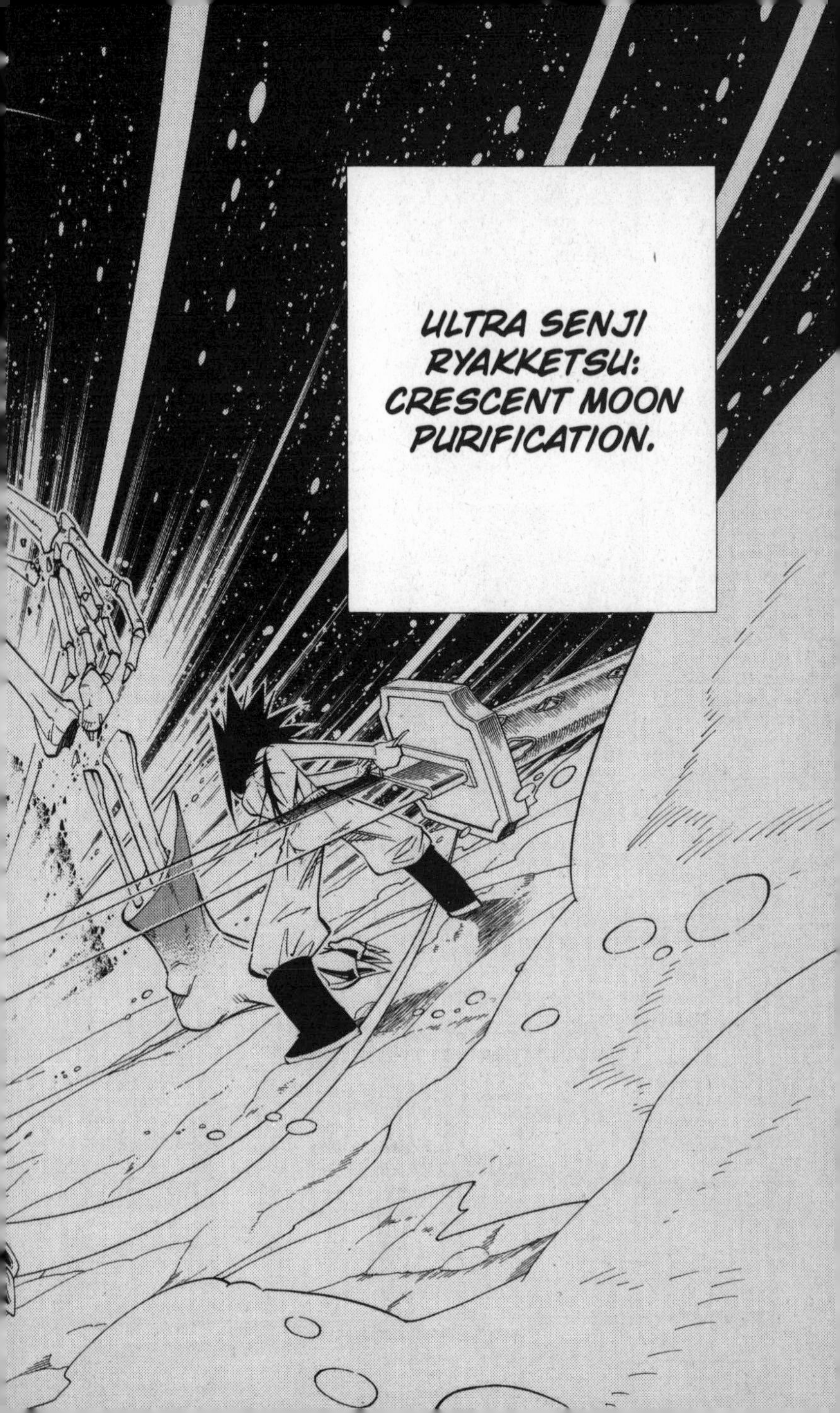
ULTRA SENJI RYAKKETSU: CRESCENT MOON PURIFICATION.

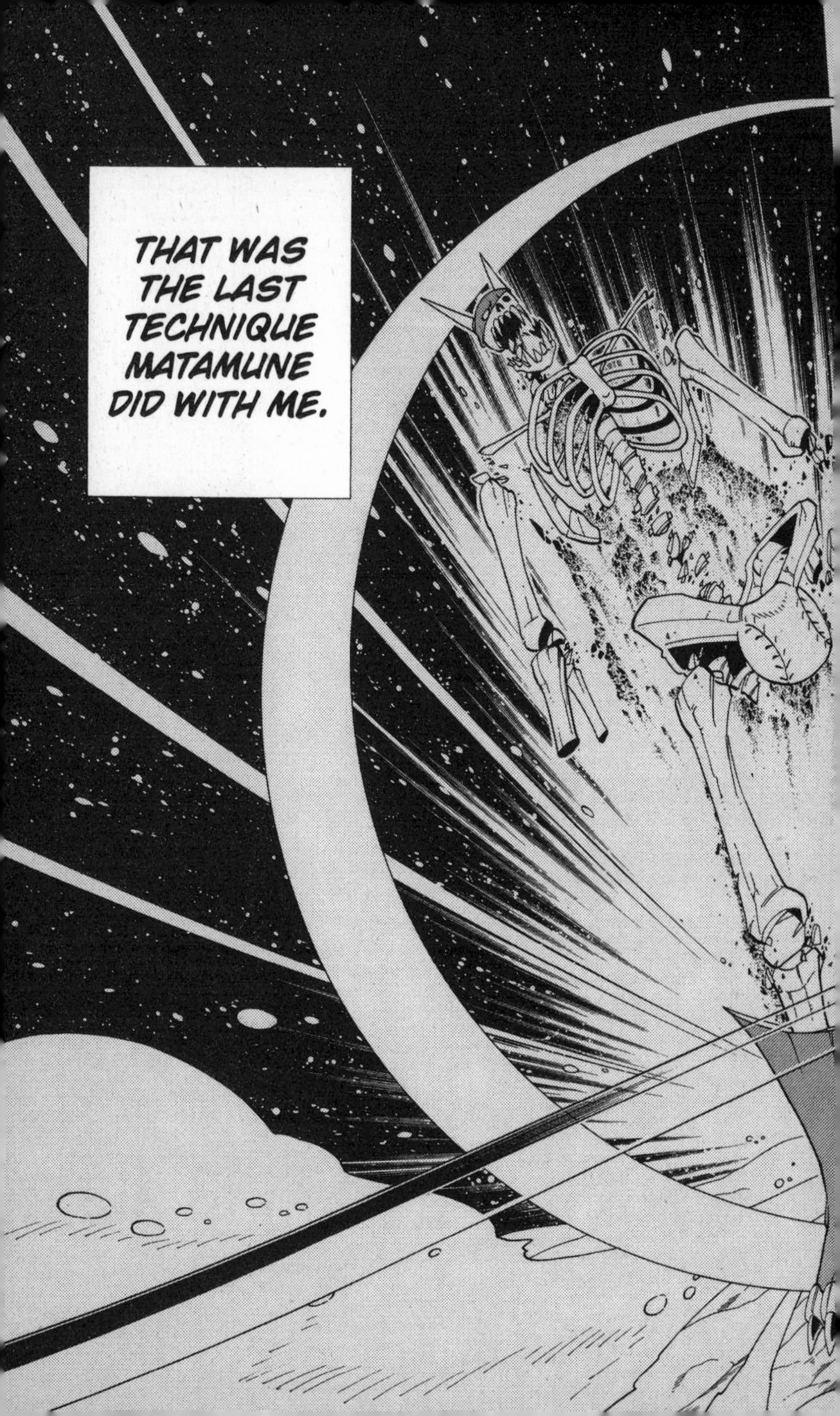
THAT WAS THE LAST TECHNIQUE MATAMUNE DID WITH ME.

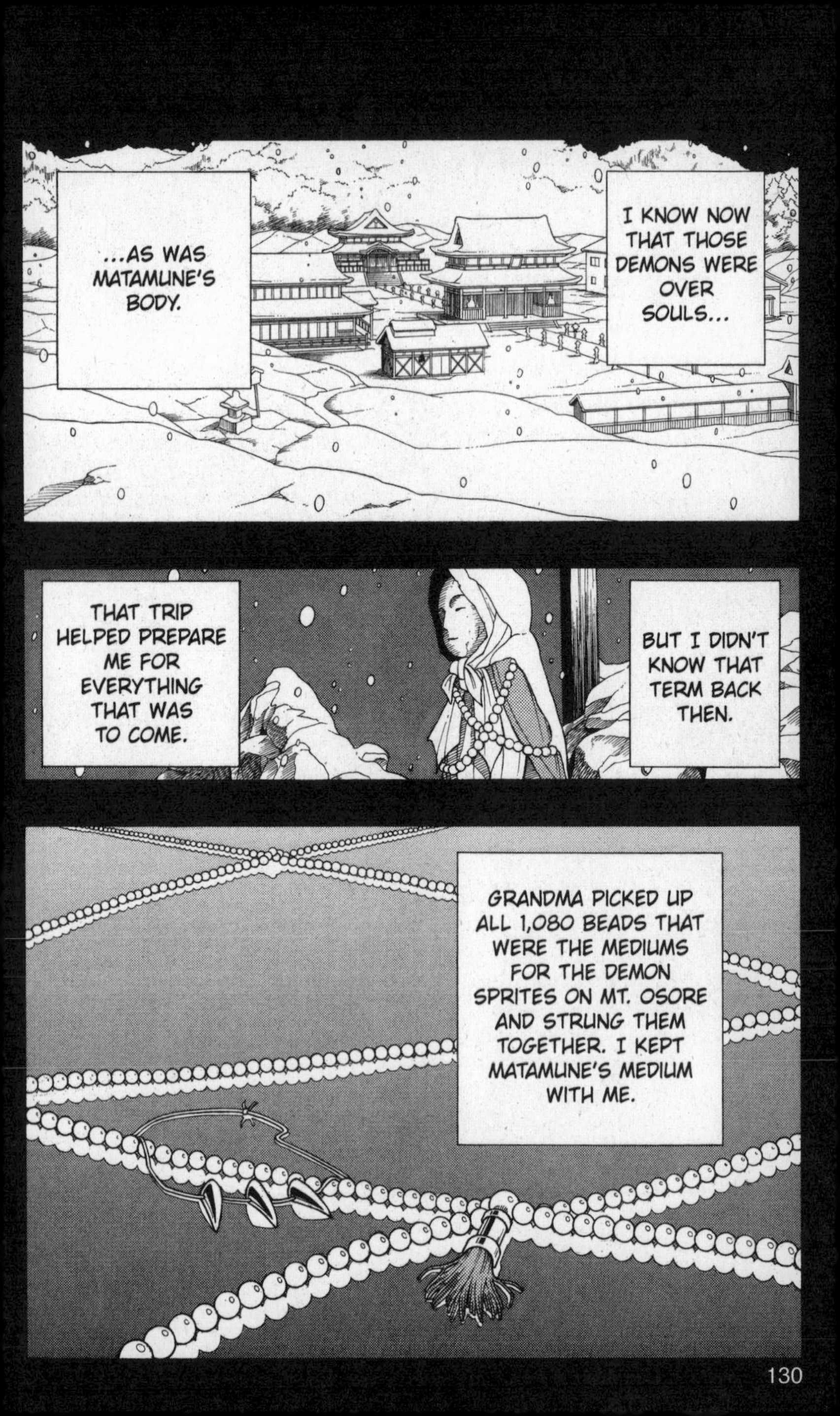
I KNOW NOW THAT THOSE DEMONS WERE OVER SOULS...
...AS WAS MATAMUNE'S BODY.
BUT I DIDN'T KNOW THAT TERM BACK THEN.
THAT TRIP HELPED PREPARE ME FOR EVERYTHING THAT WAS TO COME.
GRANDMA PICKED UP ALL 1,080 BEADS THAT WERE THE MEDIUMS FOR THE DEMON SPRITES ON MT. OSORE AND STRUNG THEM TOGETHER. I KEPT MATAMUNE'S MEDIUM WITH ME.

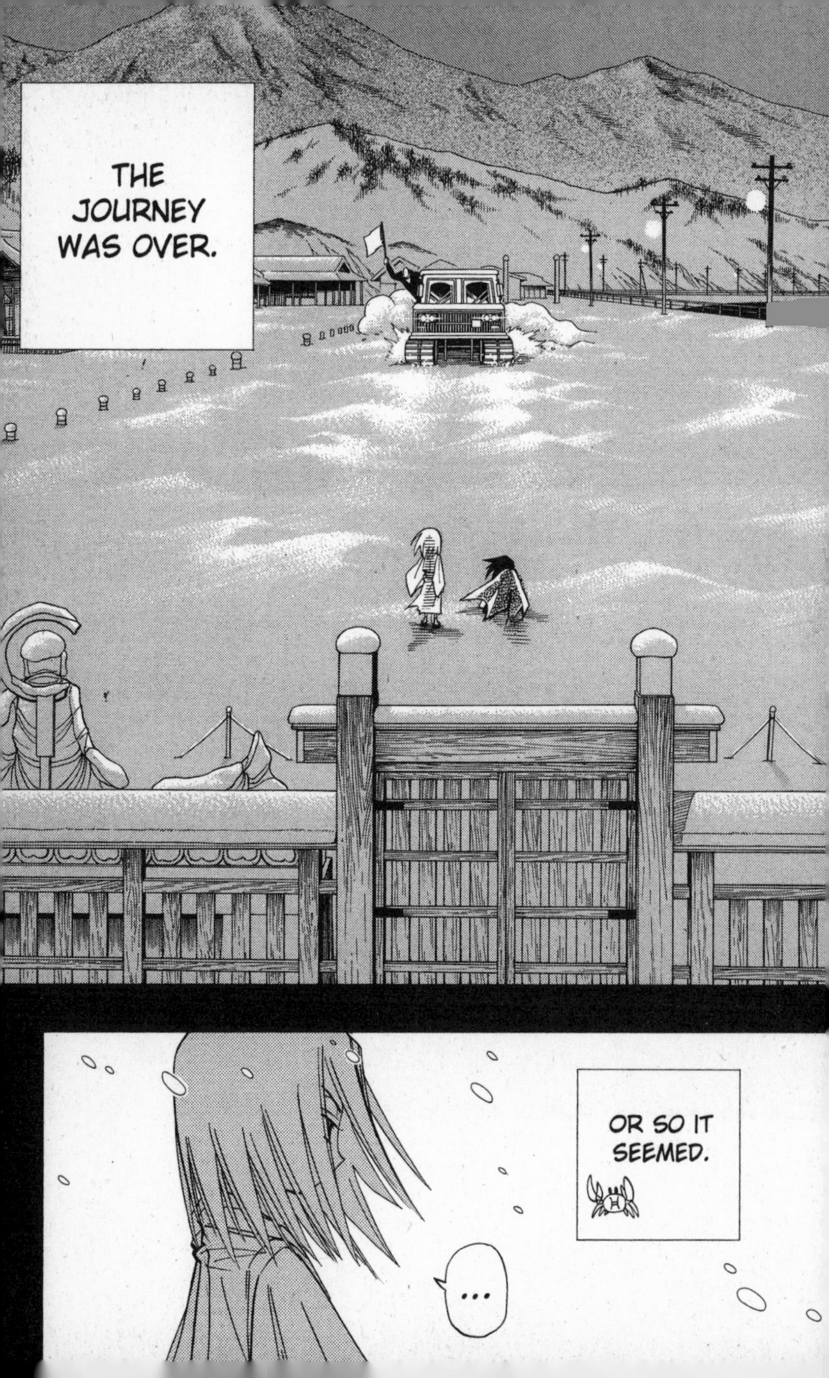
THE JOURNEY WAS OVER.
OR SO IT SEEMED.
...

SHAMAN KING CHARACTER FILE No.109

ノラマタムネ

STRAY MATAMUNE

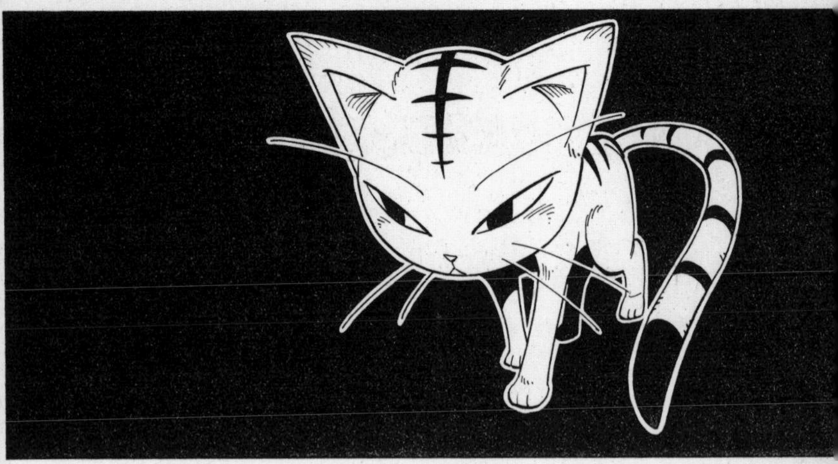

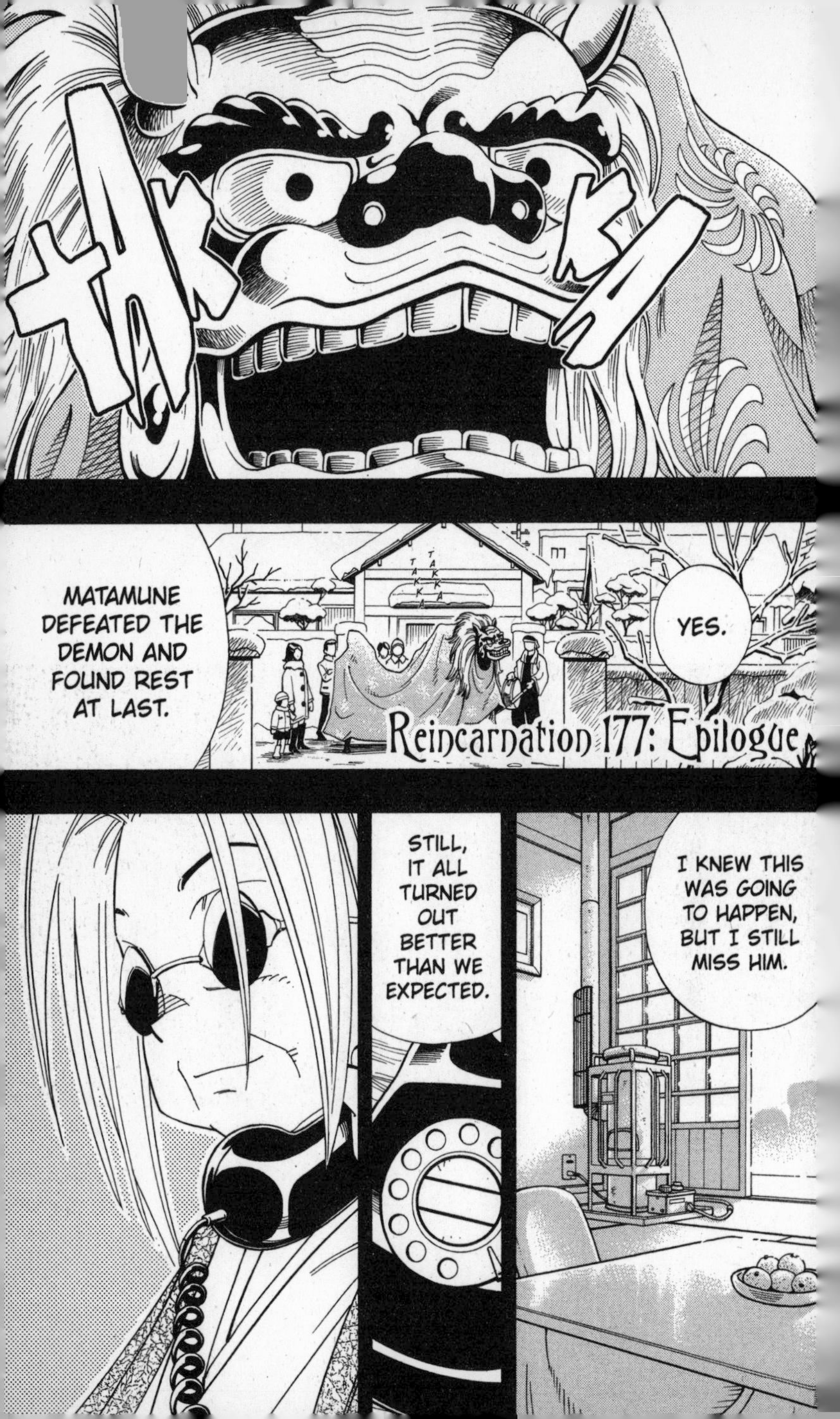

TAKKA
TAKKA
MATAMUNE DEFEATED THE DEMON AND FOUND REST AT LAST.
YES.
Reincarnation 177: Epilogue
I KNEW THIS WAS GOING TO HAPPEN, BUT I STILL MISS HIM.
STILL, IT ALL TURNED OUT BETTER THAN WE EXPECTED.

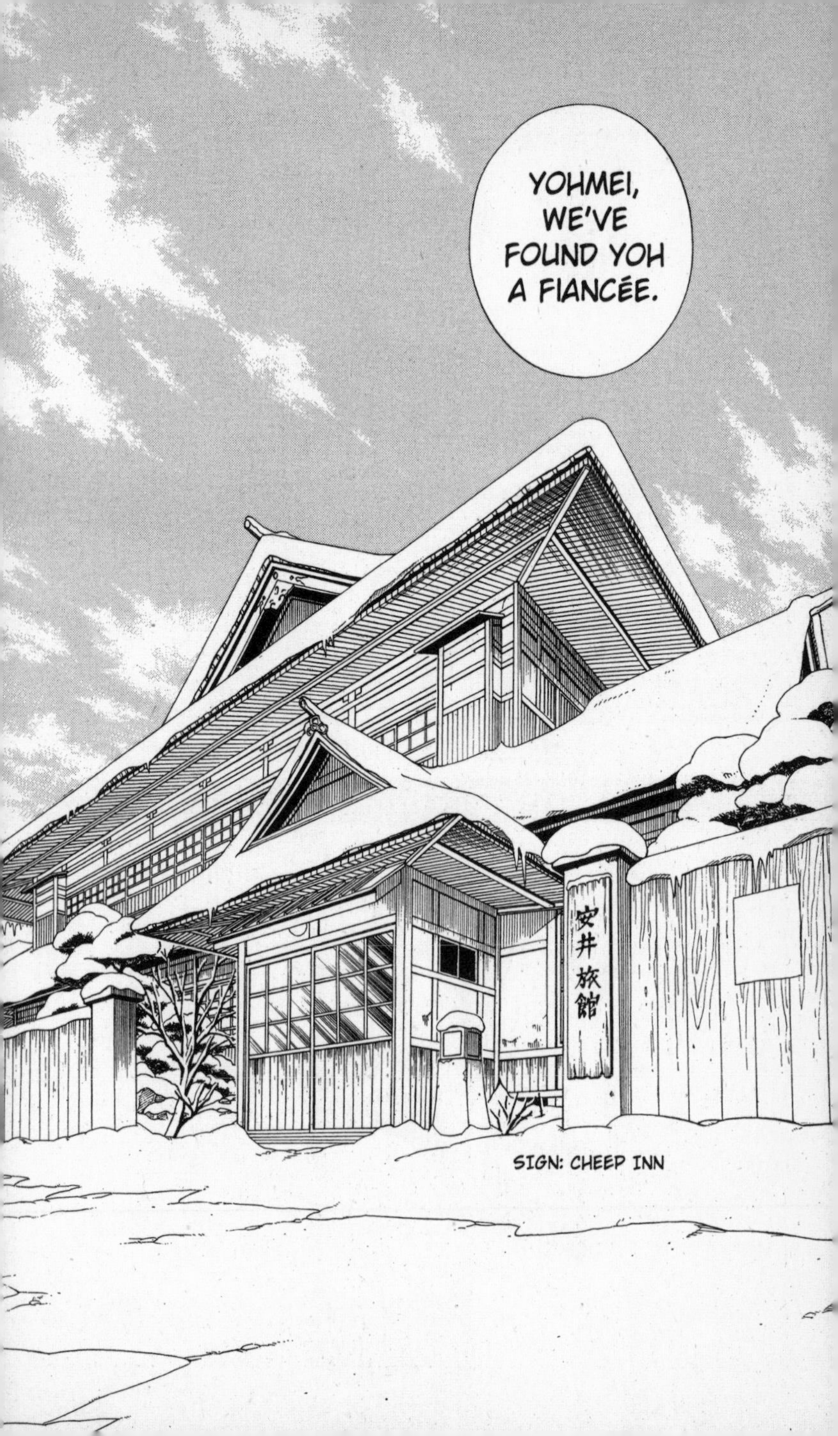
YOHMEI, WE'VE FOUND YOH A FIANCÉE.
安井旅館
SIGN: CHEEP INN

Reincarnation 177: Epilogue

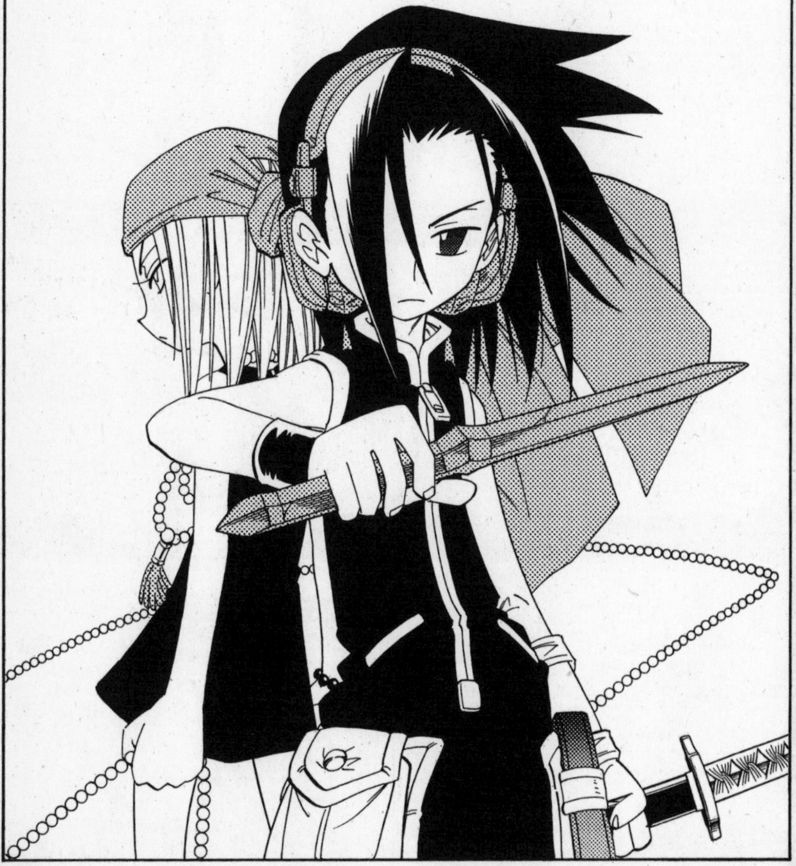

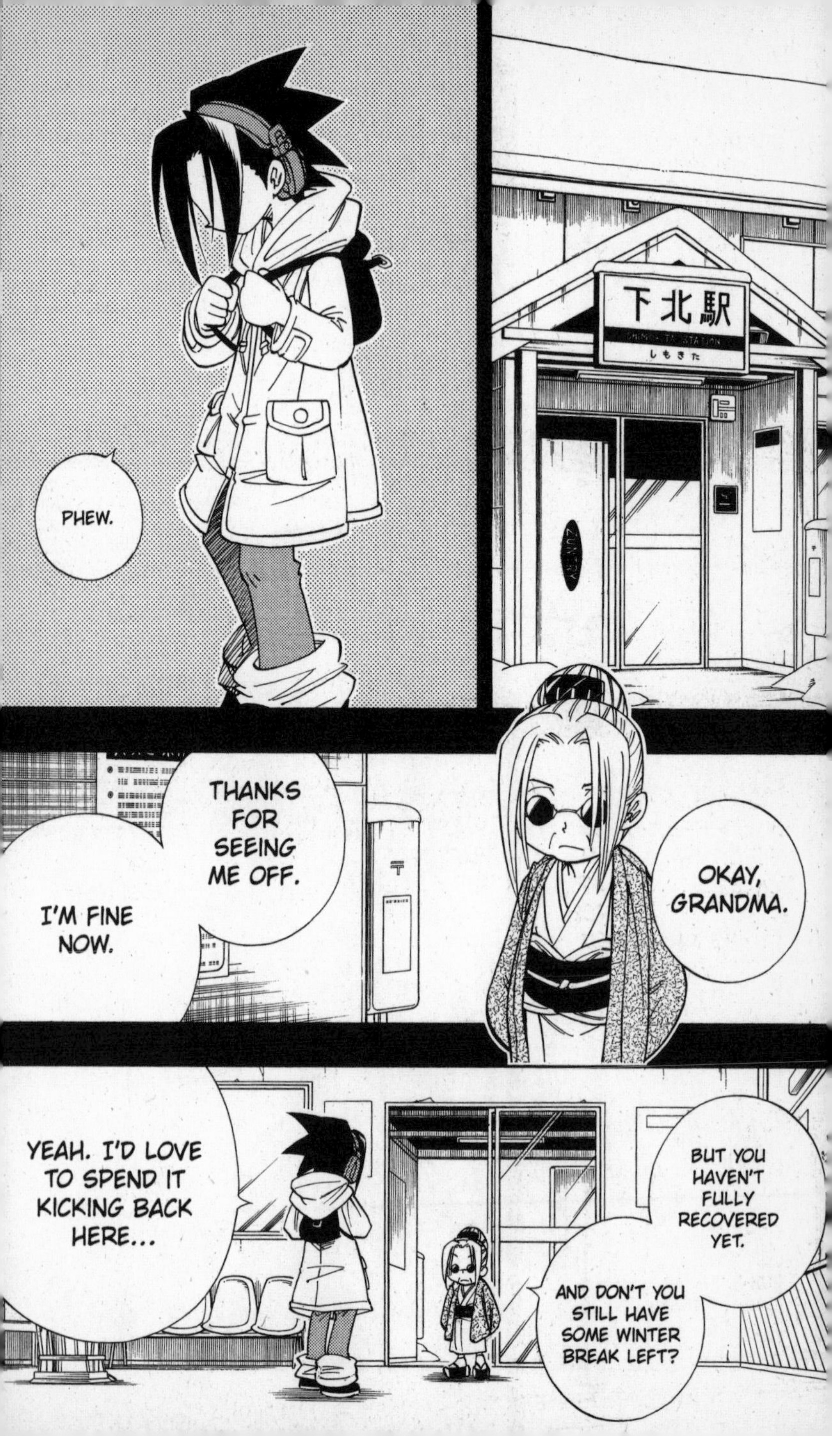
下北駅
しもきた
PHEW.
OKAY, GRANDMA.
THANKS FOR SEEING ME OFF.
I'M FINE NOW.
BUT YOU HAVEN'T FULLY RECOVERED YET.
AND DON'T YOU STILL HAVE SOME WINTER BREAK LEFT?
YEAH. I'D LOVE TO SPEND IT KICKING BACK HERE...

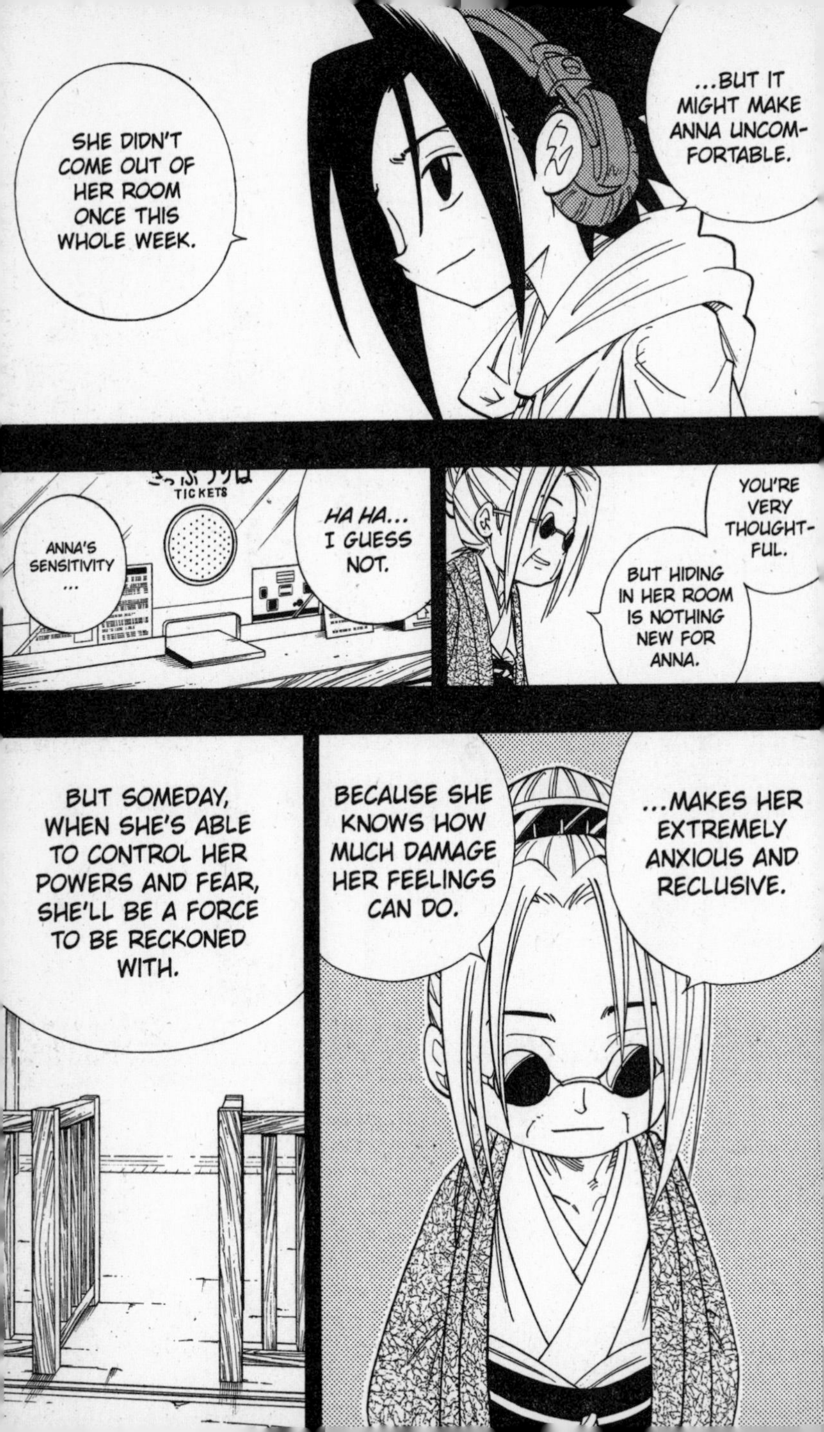
...BUT IT MIGHT MAKE ANNA UNCOM-FORTABLE.
SHE DIDN'T COME OUT OF HER ROOM ONCE THIS WHOLE WEEK.
YOU'RE VERY THOUGHT-FUL.
BUT HIDING IN HER ROOM IS NOTHING NEW FOR ANNA.
HA HA... I GUESS NOT.
TICKETS
ANNA'S SENSITIVITY ...
...MAKES HER EXTREMELY ANXIOUS AND RECLUSIVE.
BECAUSE SHE KNOWS HOW MUCH DAMAGE HER FEELINGS CAN DO.
BUT SOMEDAY, WHEN SHE'S ABLE TO CONTROL HER POWERS AND FEAR, SHE'LL BE A FORCE TO BE RECKONED WITH.

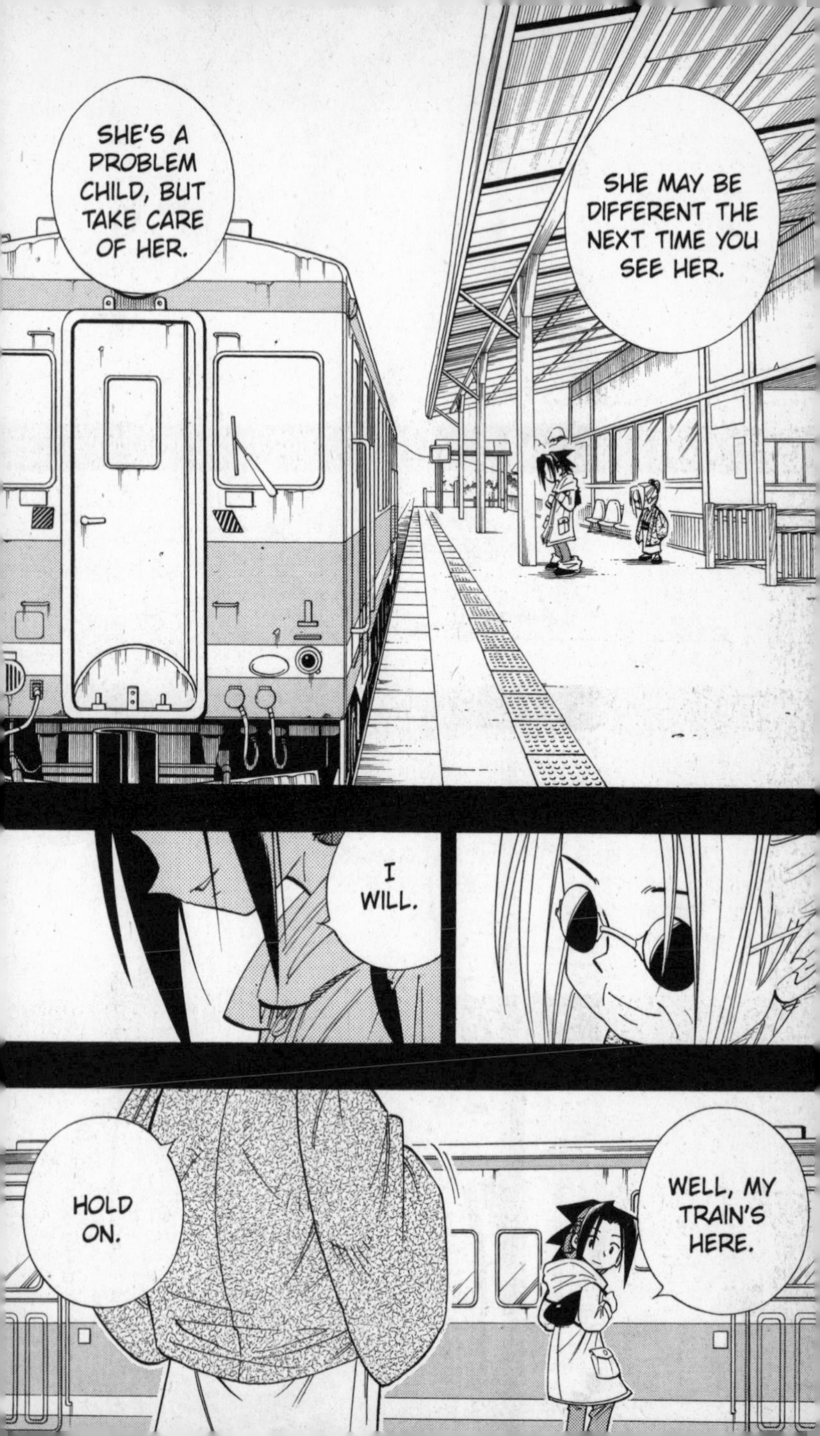
SHE MAY BE DIFFERENT THE NEXT TIME YOU SEE HER.
SHE'S A PROBLEM CHILD, BUT TAKE CARE OF HER.
I WILL.
WELL, MY TRAIN'S HERE.
HOLD ON.

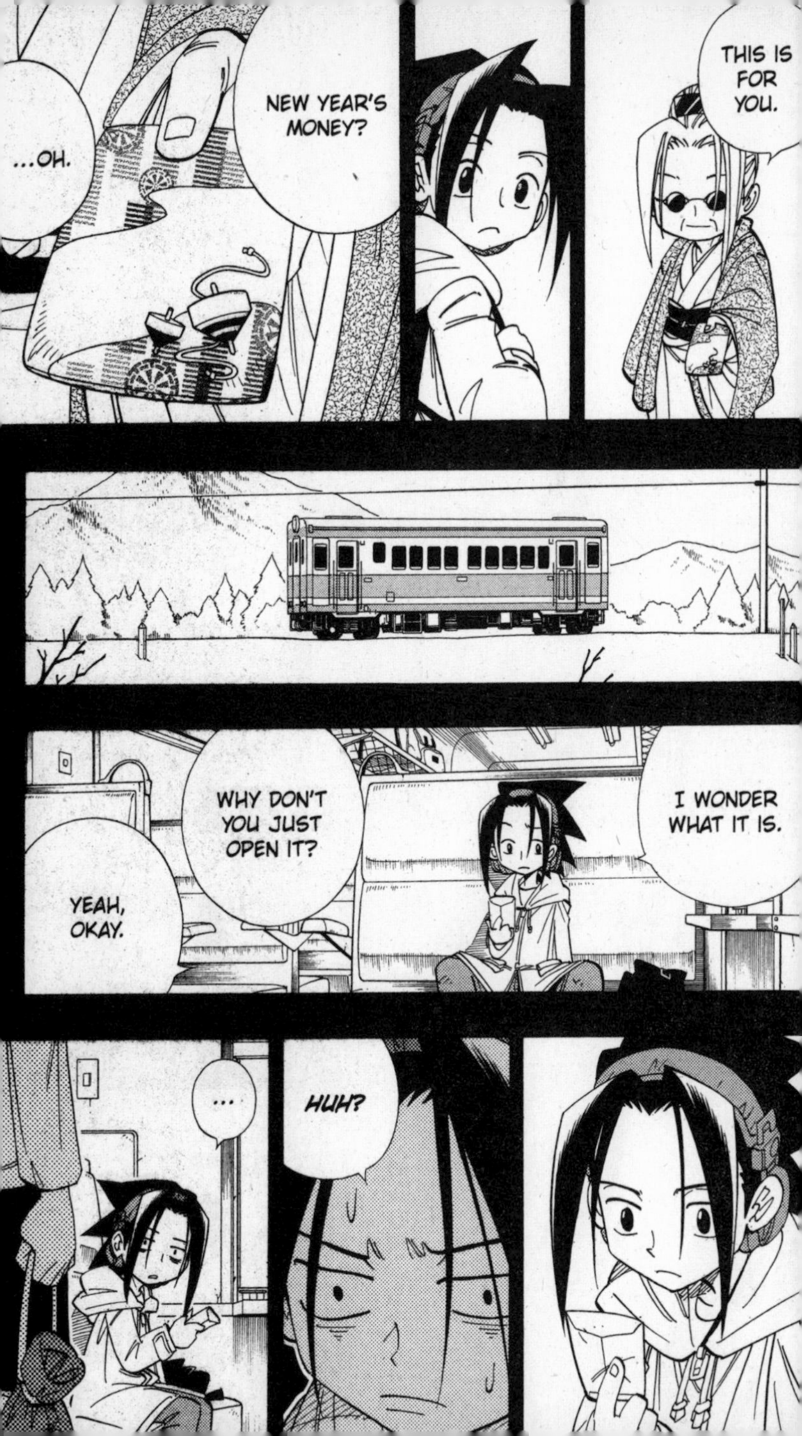
THIS IS FOR YOU.
NEW YEAR'S MONEY?
...OH.
I WONDER WHAT IT IS.
WHY DON'T YOU JUST OPEN IT?
YEAH, OKAY.
HUH?
...

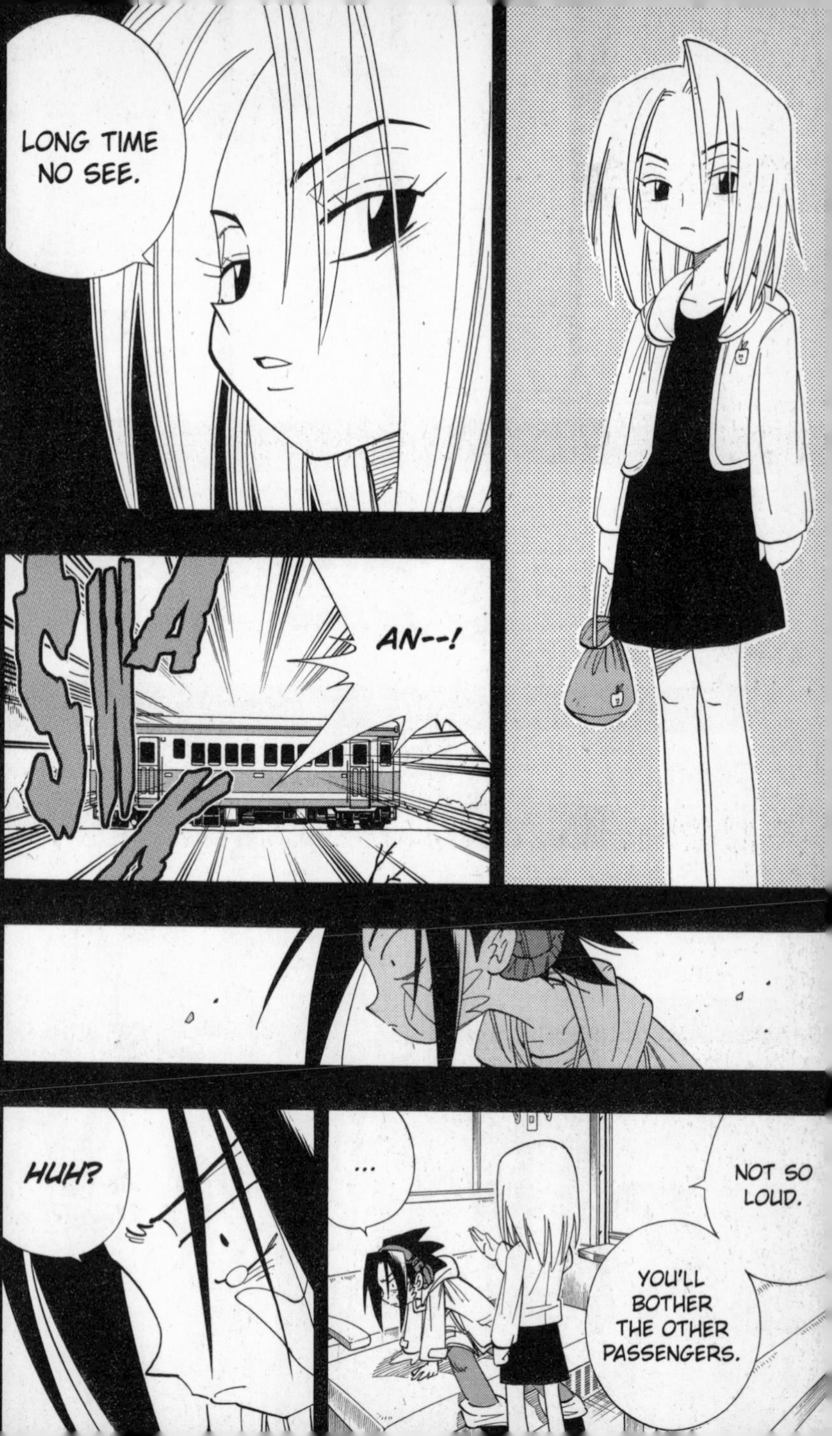
LONG TIME NO SEE.
AN--!
NOT SO LOUD.
...
YOU'LL BOTHER THE OTHER PASSENGERS.
HUH?

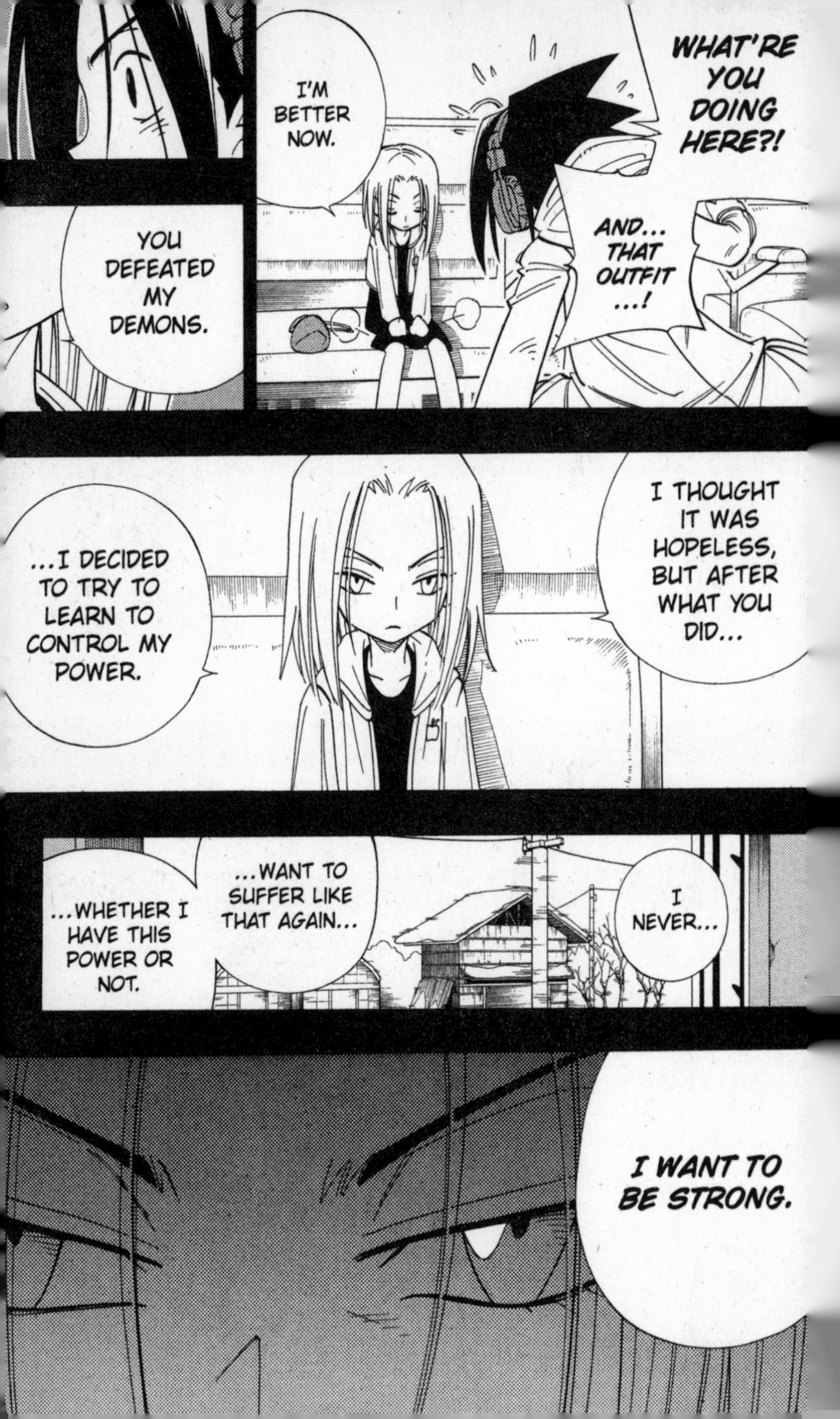
WHAT'RE YOU DOING HERE?!
AND... THAT OUTFIT ...!
I'M BETTER NOW.
YOU DEFEATED MY DEMONS.
I THOUGHT IT WAS HOPELESS, BUT AFTER WHAT YOU DID...
...I DECIDED TO TRY TO LEARN TO CONTROL MY POWER.
I NEVER...
...WANT TO SUFFER LIKE THAT AGAIN...
...WHETHER I HAVE THIS POWER OR NOT.
I WANT TO BE STRONG.

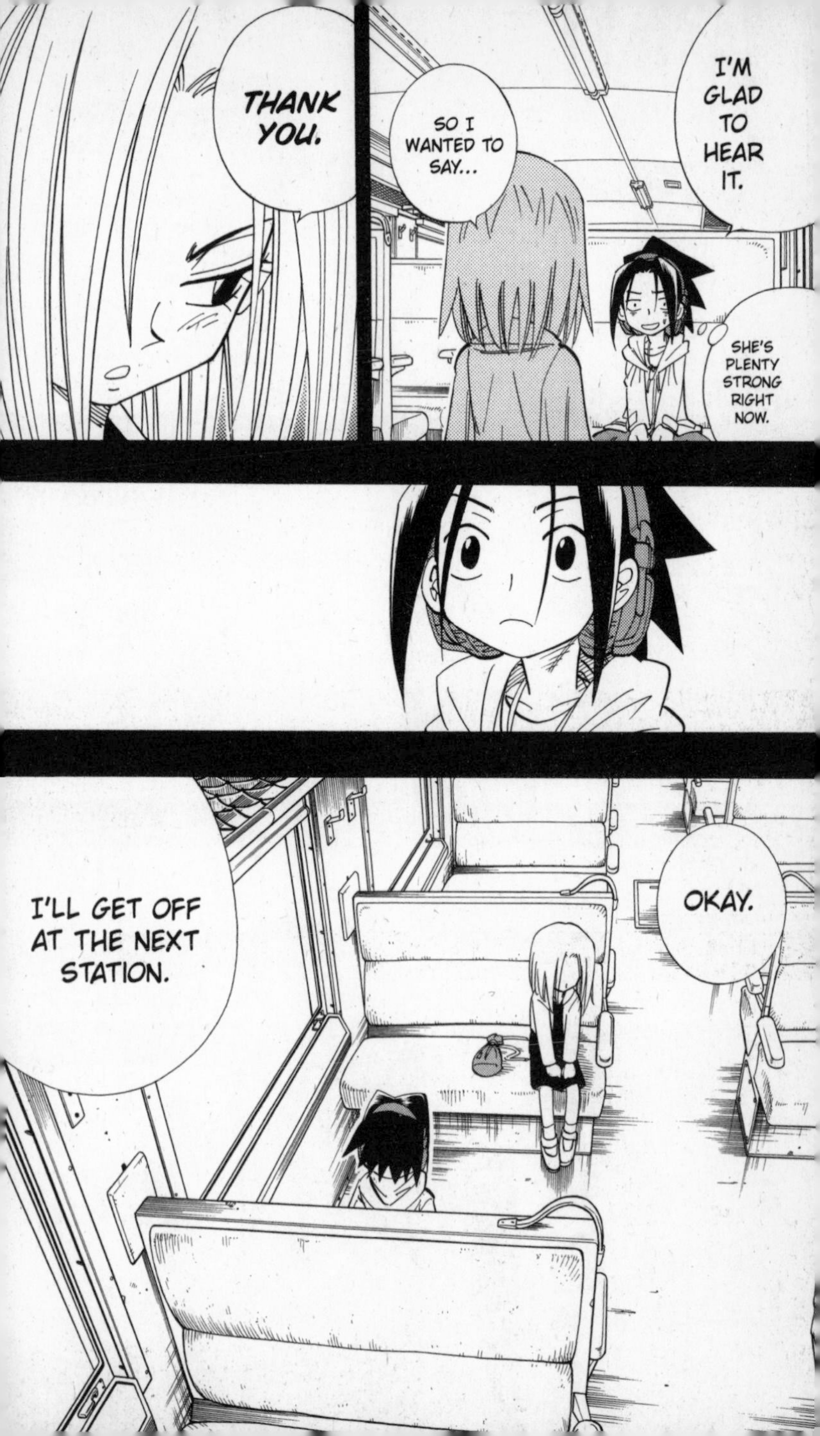
I'M GLAD TO HEAR IT.
SO I WANTED TO SAY...
SHE'S PLENTY STRONG RIGHT NOW.
THANK YOU.
OKAY.
I'LL GET OFF AT THE NEXT STATION.

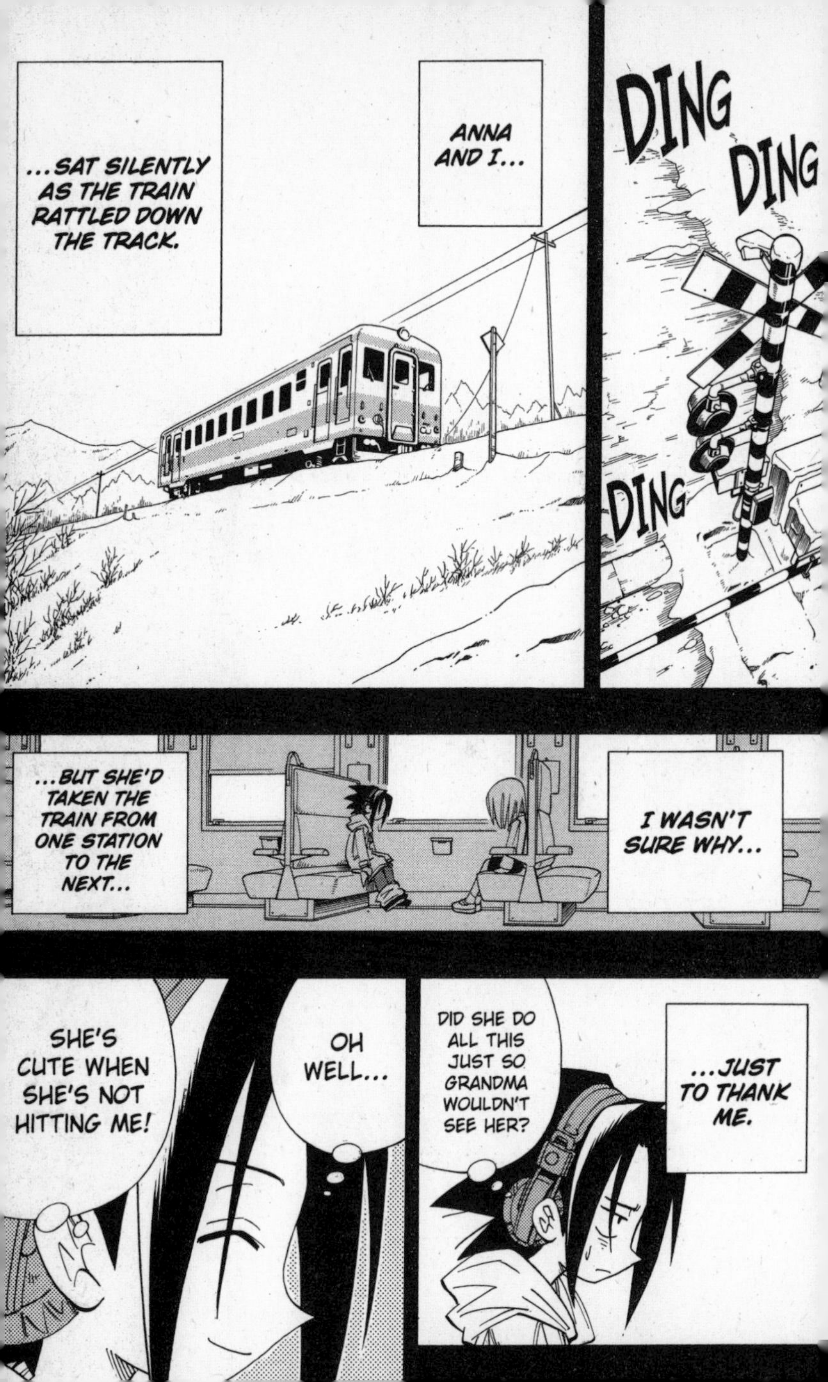
DING
DING
DING
ANNA AND I...
...SAT SILENTLY AS THE TRAIN RATTLED DOWN THE TRACK.
I WASN'T SURE WHY...
...BUT SHE'D TAKEN THE TRAIN FROM ONE STATION TO THE NEXT...
...JUST TO THANK ME.
DID SHE DO ALL THIS JUST SO GRANDMA WOULDN'T SEE HER?
OH WELL...
SHE'S CUTE WHEN SHE'S NOT HITTING ME!

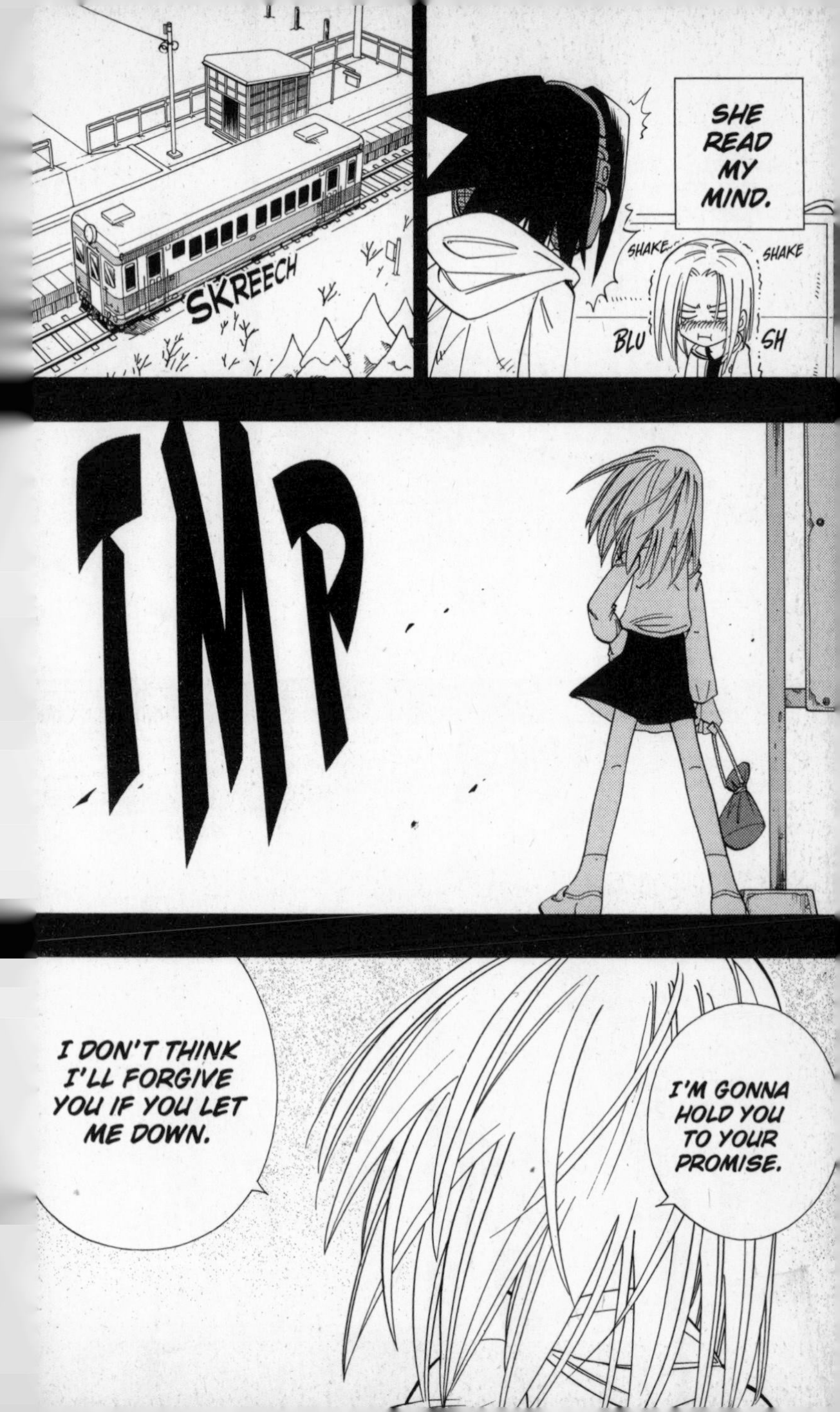
SHE READ MY MIND.
SHAKE SHAKE
BLU SH
SKREECH
TMP
I'M GONNA HOLD YOU TO YOUR PROMISE.
I DON'T THINK I'LL FORGIVE YOU IF YOU LET ME DOWN.

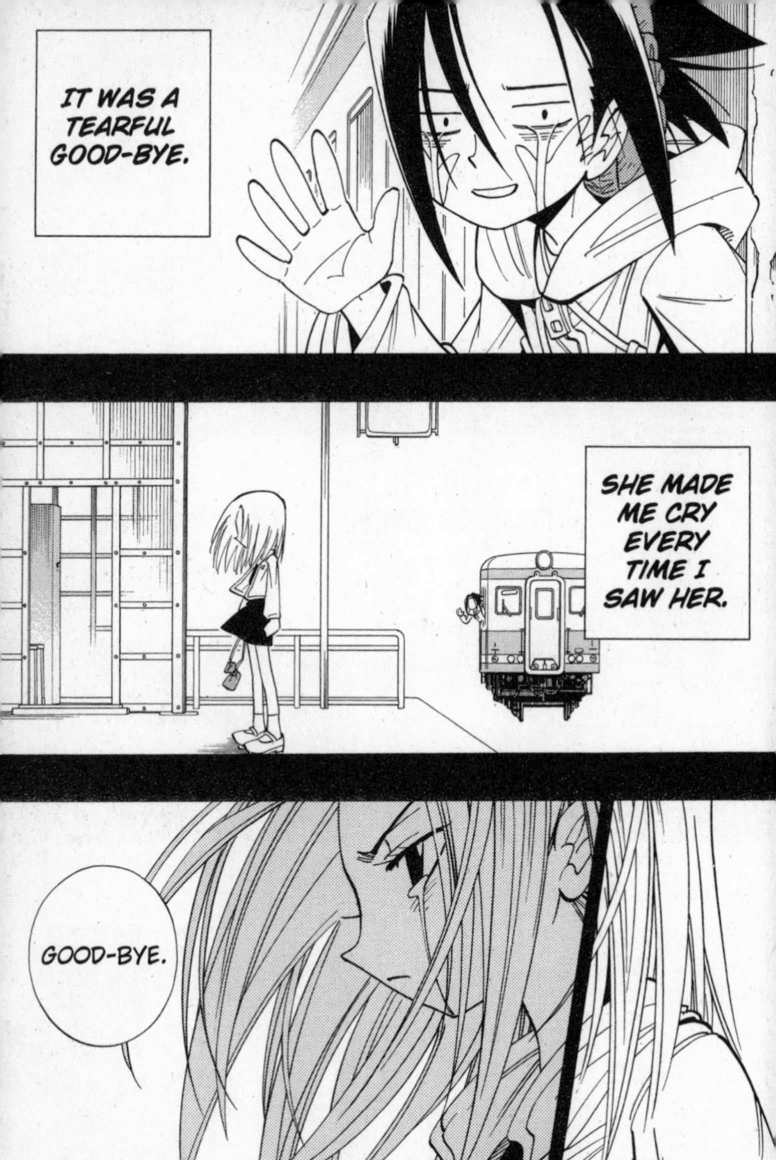
IT WAS A TEARFUL GOOD-BYE.
SHE MADE ME CRY EVERY TIME I SAW HER.
GOOD-BYE.

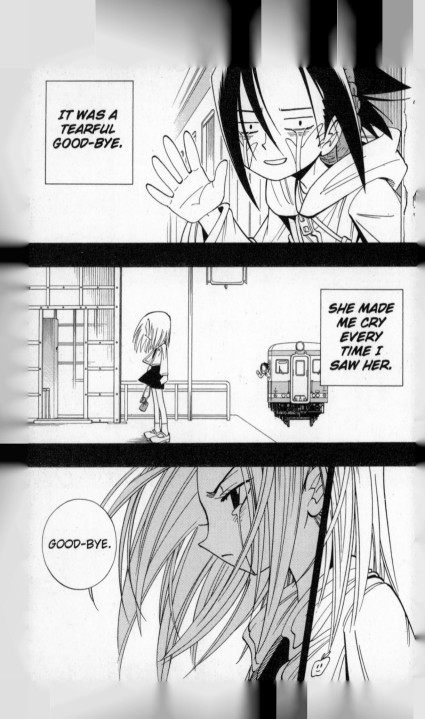

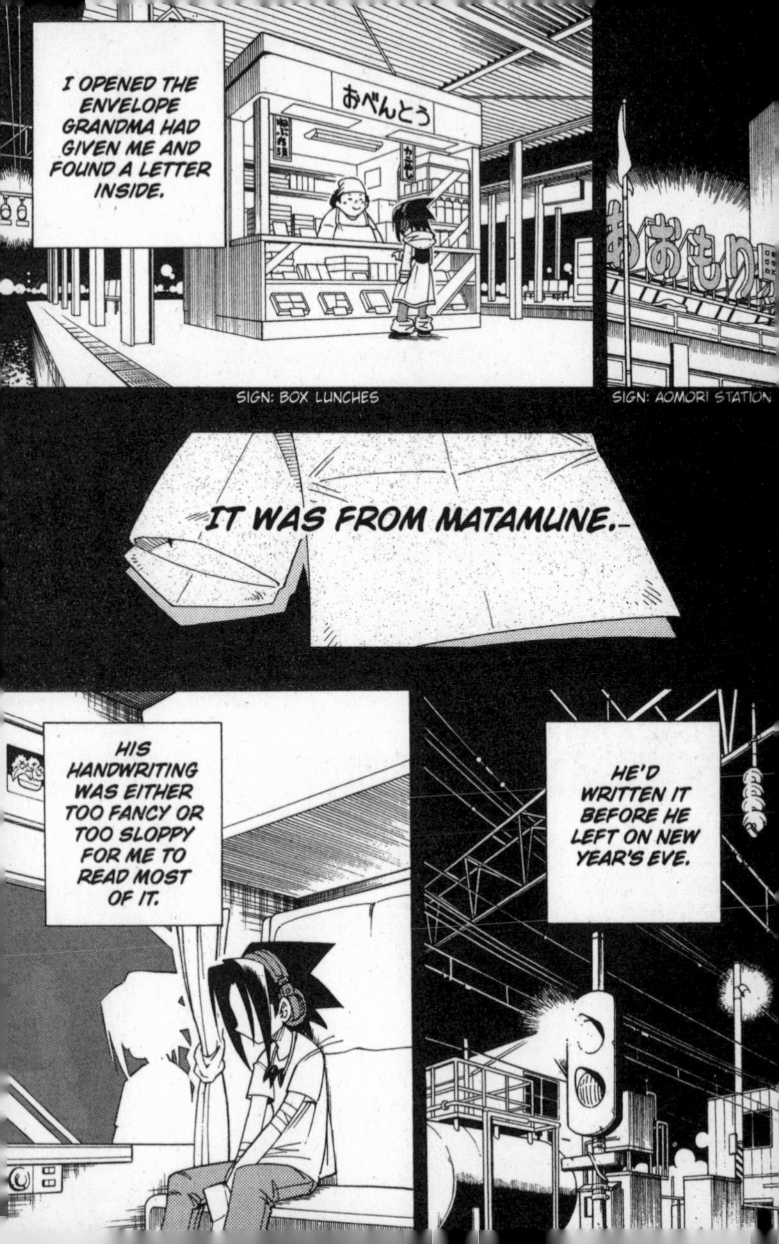

SIGN: AOMORI STATION
I OPENED THE ENVELOPE GRANDMA HAD GIVEN ME AND FOUND A LETTER INSIDE.
おべんとう
SIGN: BOX LUNCHES
IT WAS FROM MATAMUNE.
HE'D WRITTEN IT BEFORE HE LEFT ON NEW YEAR'S EVE.
HIS HANDWRITING WAS EITHER TOO FANCY OR TOO SLOPPY FOR ME TO READ MOST OF IT.

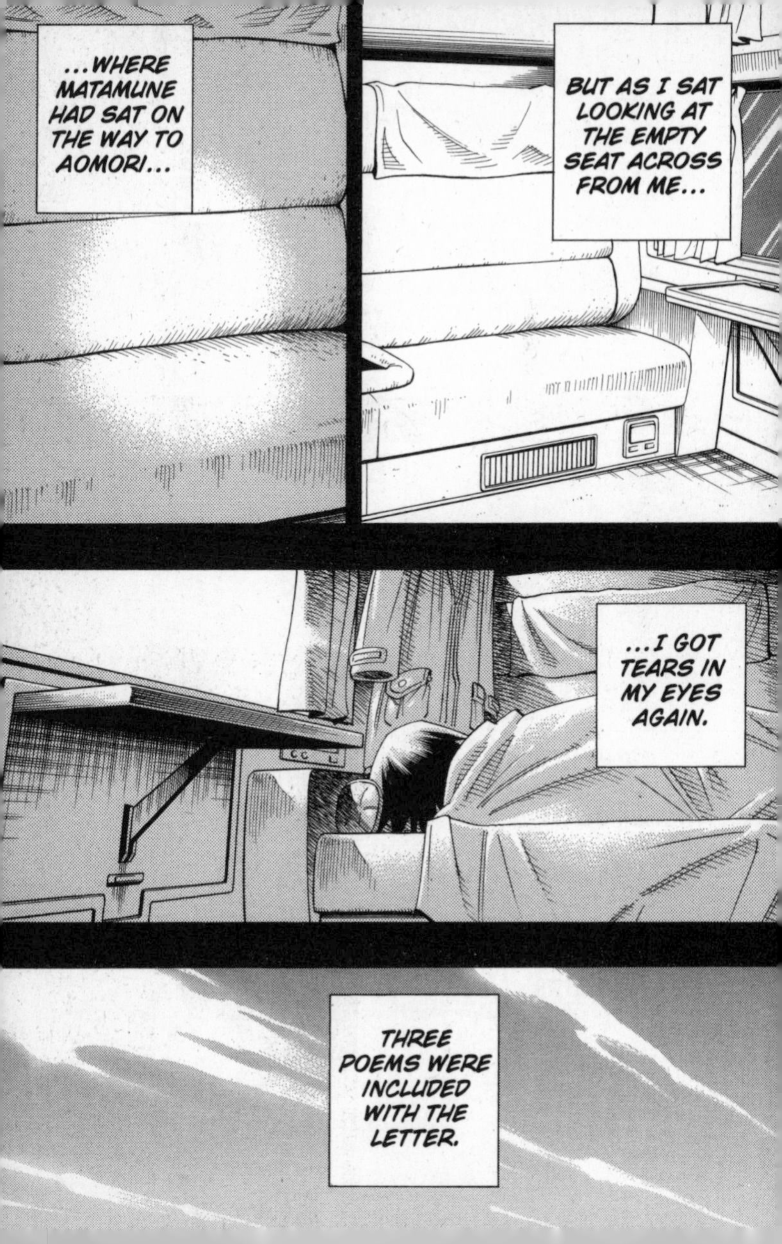
BUT AS I SAT LOOKING AT THE EMPTY SEAT ACROSS FROM ME...
...WHERE MATAMUNE HAD SAT ON THE WAY TO AOMORI...
...I GOT TEARS IN MY EYES AGAIN.
THREE POEMS WERE INCLUDED WITH THE LETTER.

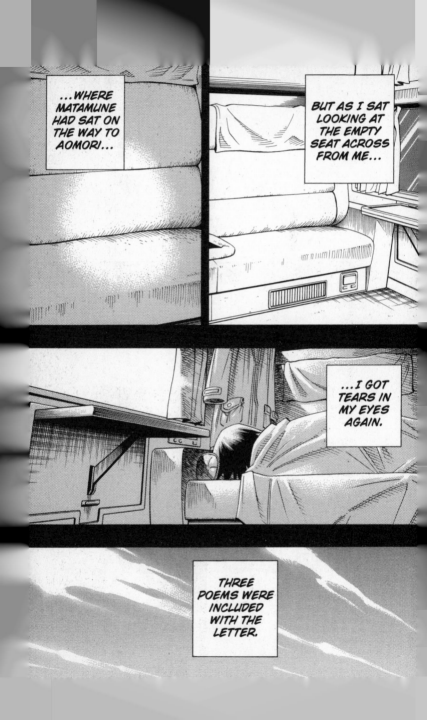

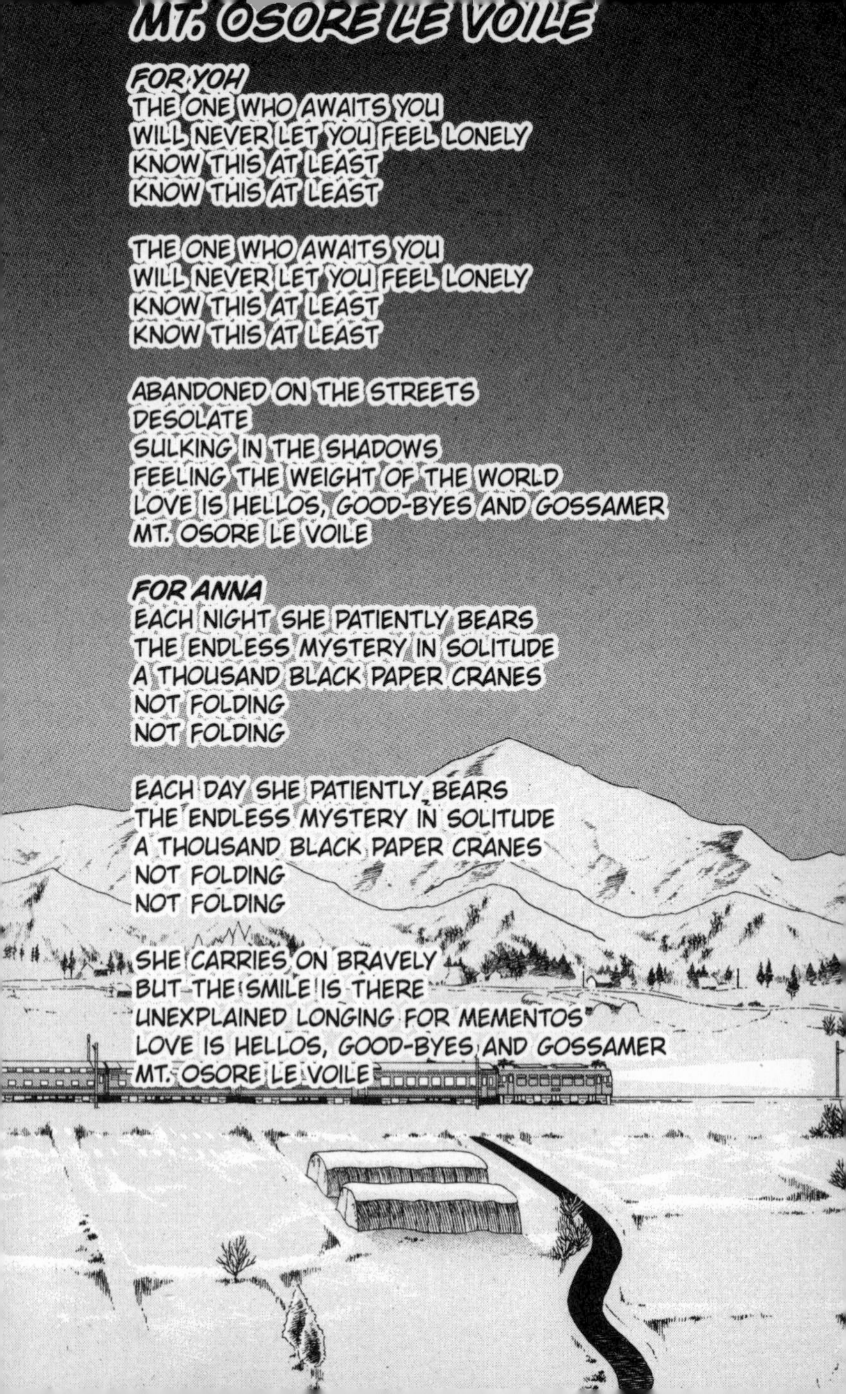
MT. OSORE LE VOILE
FOR YOH
THE ONE WHO AWAITS YOU
WILL NEVER LET YOU FEEL LONELY
KNOW THIS AT LEAST
KNOW THIS AT LEAST
THE ONE WHO AWAITS YOU
WILL NEVER LET YOU FEEL LONELY
KNOW THIS AT LEAST
KNOW THIS AT LEAST
ABANDONED ON THE STREETS
DESOLATE
SULKING IN THE SHADOWS
FEELING THE WEIGHT OF THE WORLD
LOVE IS HELLOS, GOOD-BYES AND GOSSAMER
MT. OSORE LE VOILE
FOR ANNA
EACH NIGHT SHE PATIENTLY BEARS
THE ENDLESS MYSTERY IN SOLITUDE
A THOUSAND BLACK PAPER CRANES
NOT FOLDING
NOT FOLDING
EACH DAY SHE PATIENTLY BEARS
THE ENDLESS MYSTERY IN SOLITUDE
A THOUSAND BLACK PAPER CRANES
NOT FOLDING
NOT FOLDING
SHE CARRIES ON BRAVELY
BUT THE SMILE IS THERE
UNEXPLAINED LONGING FOR MEMENTOS
LOVE IS HELLOS, GOOD-BYES AND GOSSAMER
MT. OSORE LE VOILE

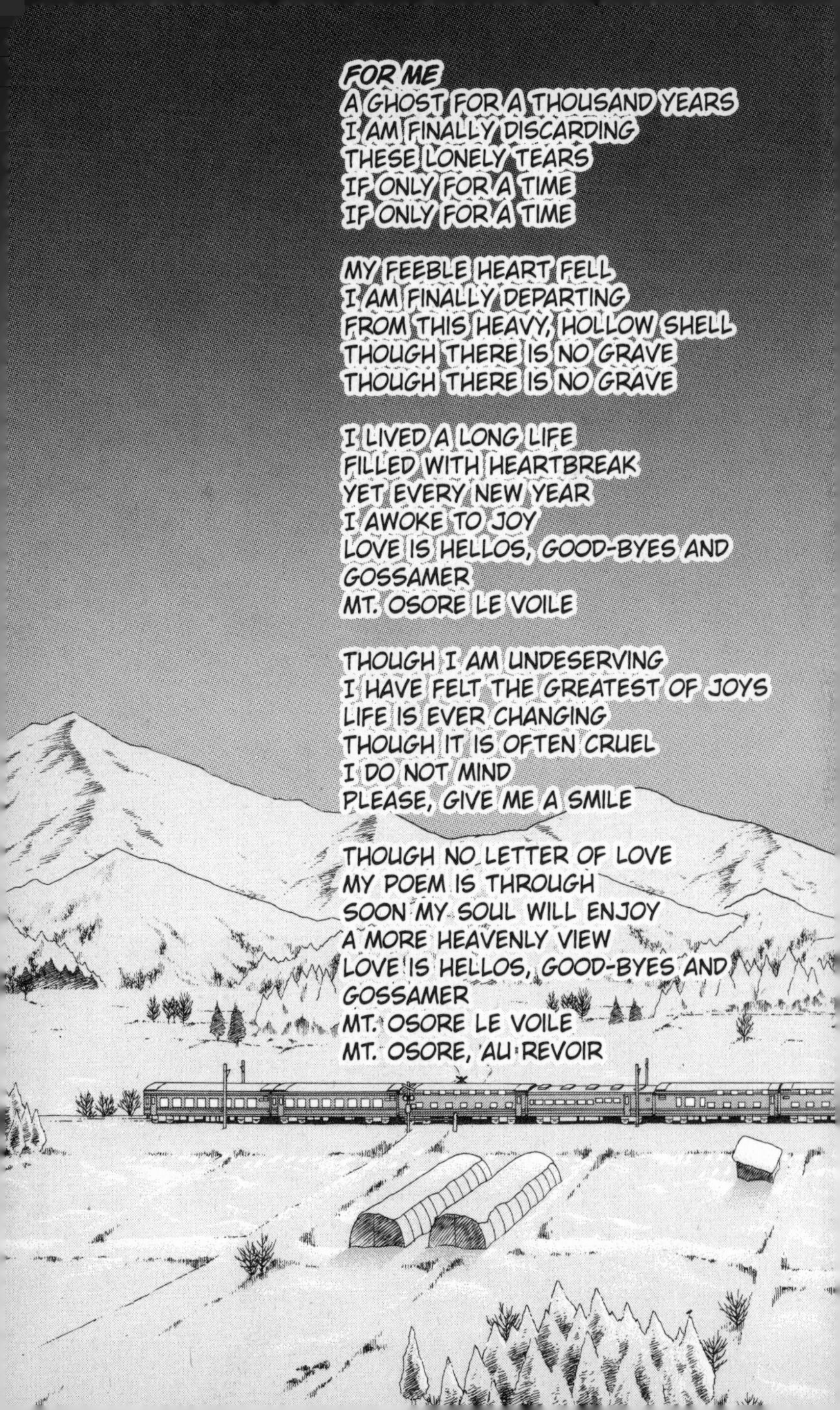
FOR ME
A GHOST FOR A THOUSAND YEARS
I AM FINALLY DISCARDING
THESE LONELY TEARS
IF ONLY FOR A TIME
IF ONLY FOR A TIME

MY FEEBLE HEART FELL
I AM FINALLY DEPARTING
FROM THIS HEAVY, HOLLOW SHELL
THOUGH THERE IS NO GRAVE
THOUGH THERE IS NO GRAVE

I LIVED A LONG LIFE
FILLED WITH HEARTBREAK
YET EVERY NEW YEAR
I AWOKE TO JOY
LOVE IS HELLOS, GOOD-BYES AND
GOSSAMER
MT. OSORE LE VOILE

THOUGH I AM UNDESERVING
I HAVE FELT THE GREATEST OF JOYS
LIFE IS EVER CHANGING
THOUGH IT IS OFTEN CRUEL
I DO NOT MIND
PLEASE, GIVE ME A SMILE

THOUGH NO LETTER OF LOVE
MY POEM IS THROUGH
SOON MY SOUL WILL ENJOY
A MORE HEAVENLY VIEW
LOVE IS HELLOS, GOOD-BYES AND
GOSSAMER
MT. OSORE LE VOILE
MT. OSORE, AU REVOIR

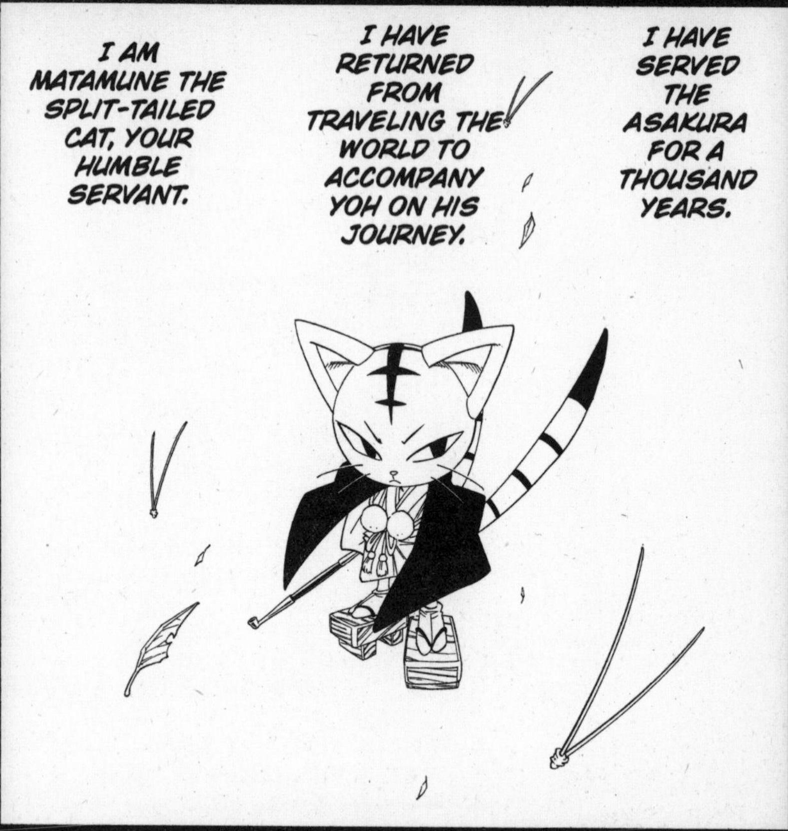
I HAVE SERVED THE ASAKURA FOR A THOUSAND YEARS.
I HAVE RETURNED FROM TRAVELING THE WORLD TO ACCOMPANY YOH ON HIS JOURNEY.
I AM MATAMUNE THE SPLIT-TAILED CAT, YOUR HUMBLE SERVANT.

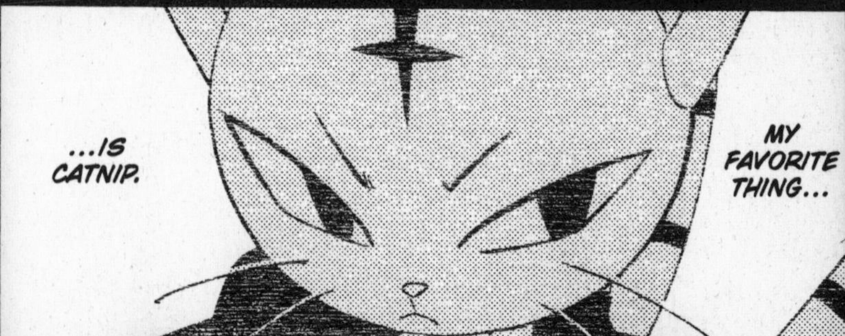
MY FAVORITE THING...
...IS CATNIP.

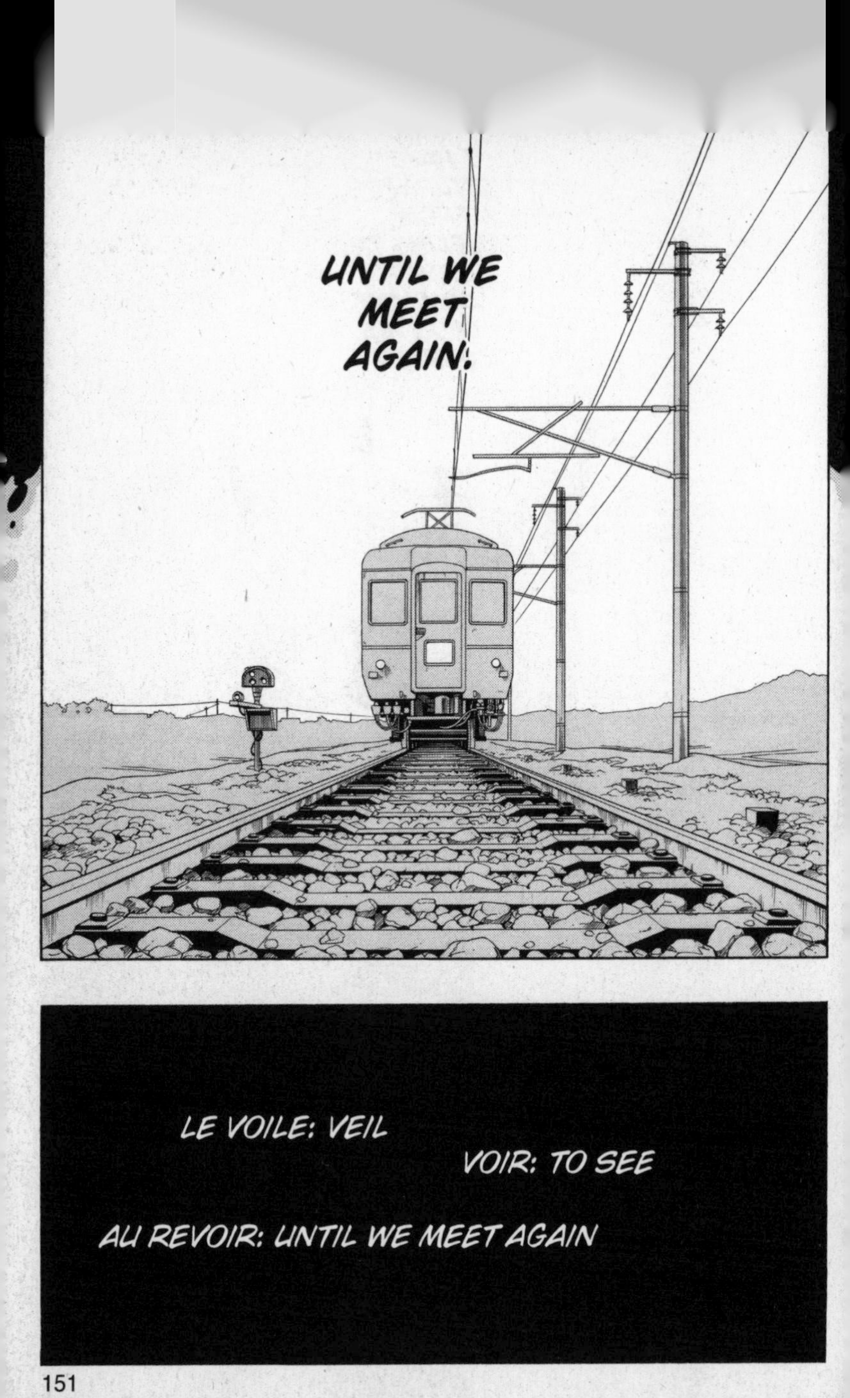
UNTIL WE MEET AGAIN.

LE VOILE: VEIL

VOIR: TO SEE

AU REVOIR: UNTIL WE MEET AGAIN

Mt. Osore Le Voile

Reincarnation 178: Epilogue II

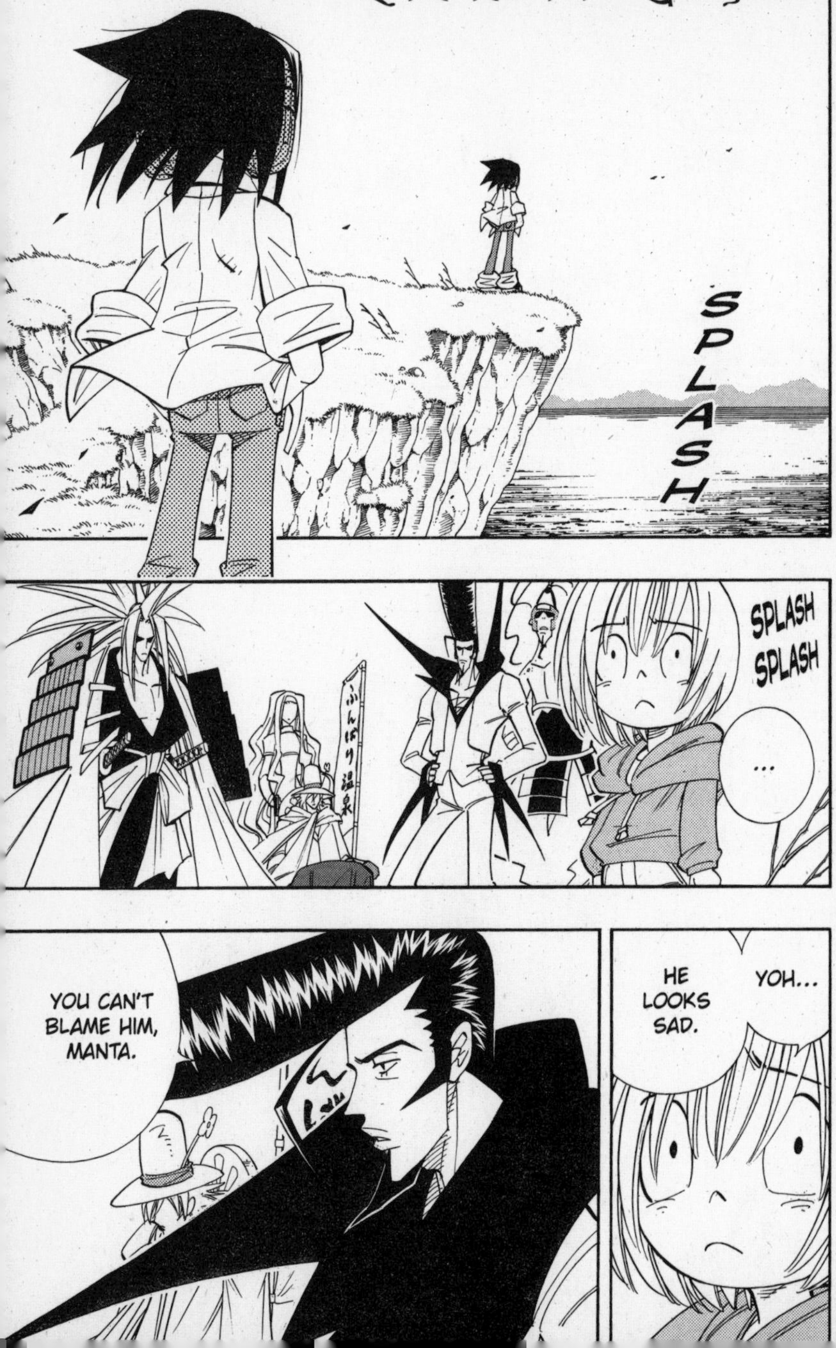
SPLASH
SPLASH
SPLASH
...
ふんばり温泉
YOH...
HE LOOKS SAD.
YOU CAN'T BLAME HIM, MANTA.

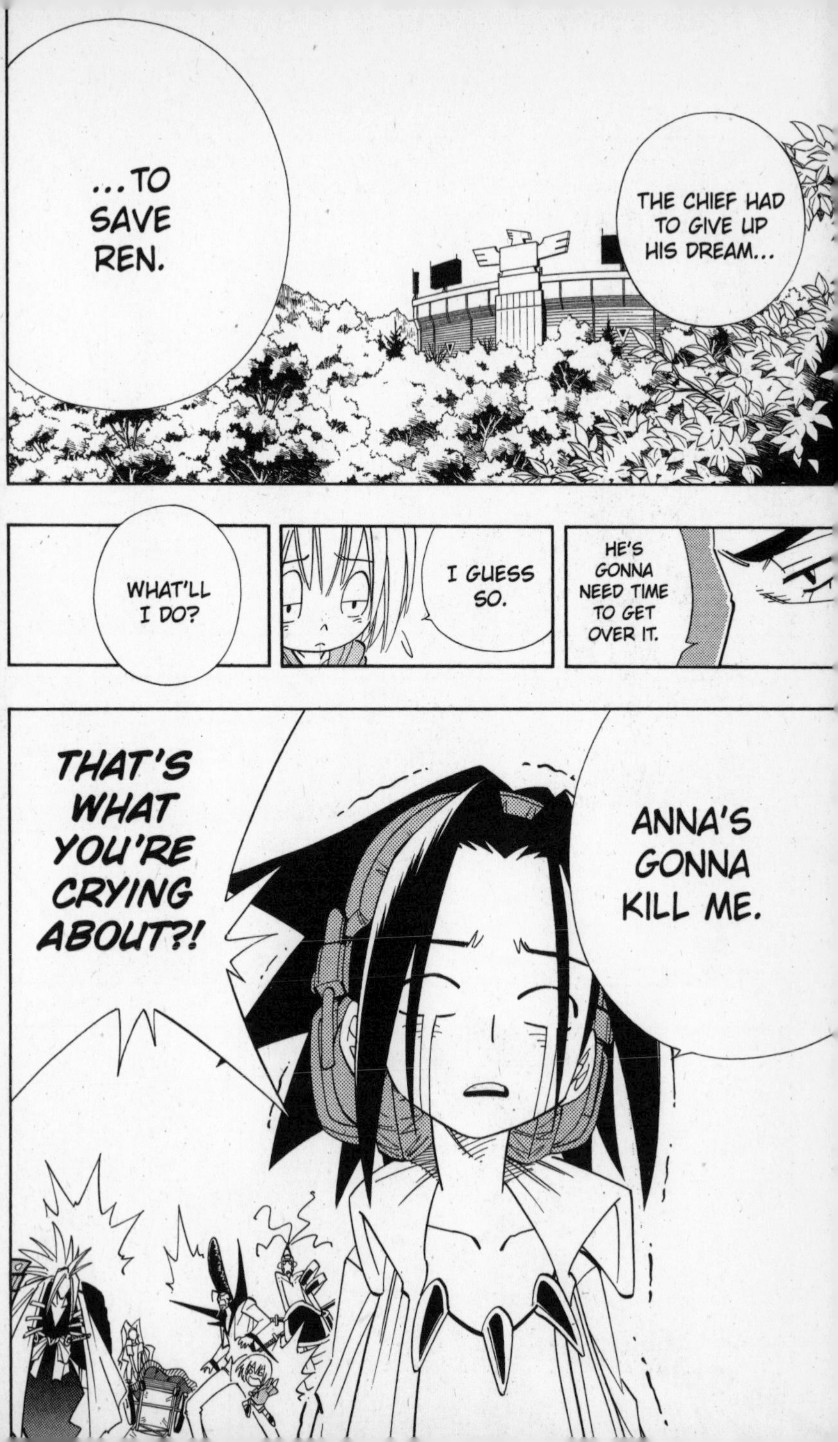
THE CHIEF HAD TO GIVE UP HIS DREAM...
...TO SAVE REN.
HE'S GONNA NEED TIME TO GET OVER IT.
I GUESS SO.
WHAT'LL I DO?
ANNA'S GONNA KILL ME.
THAT'S WHAT YOU'RE CRYING ABOUT?!

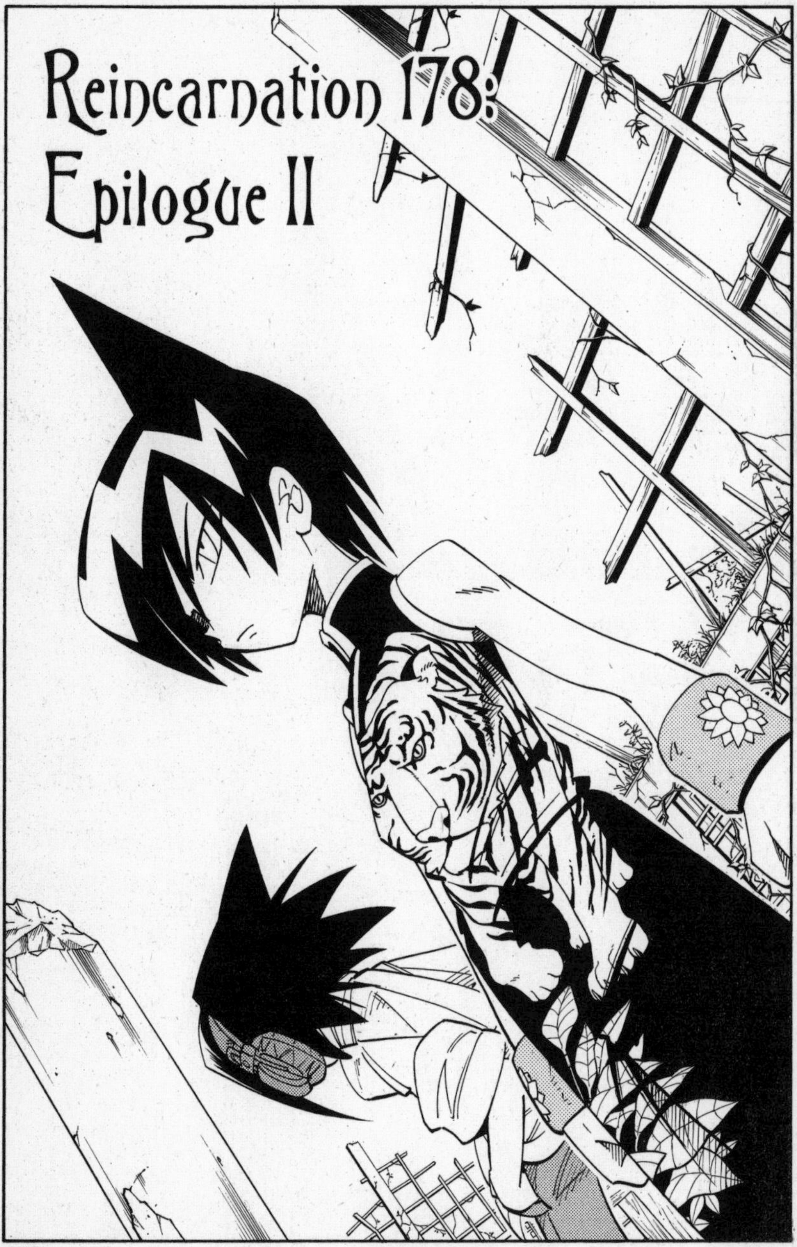
Reincarnation 178:
Epilogue II

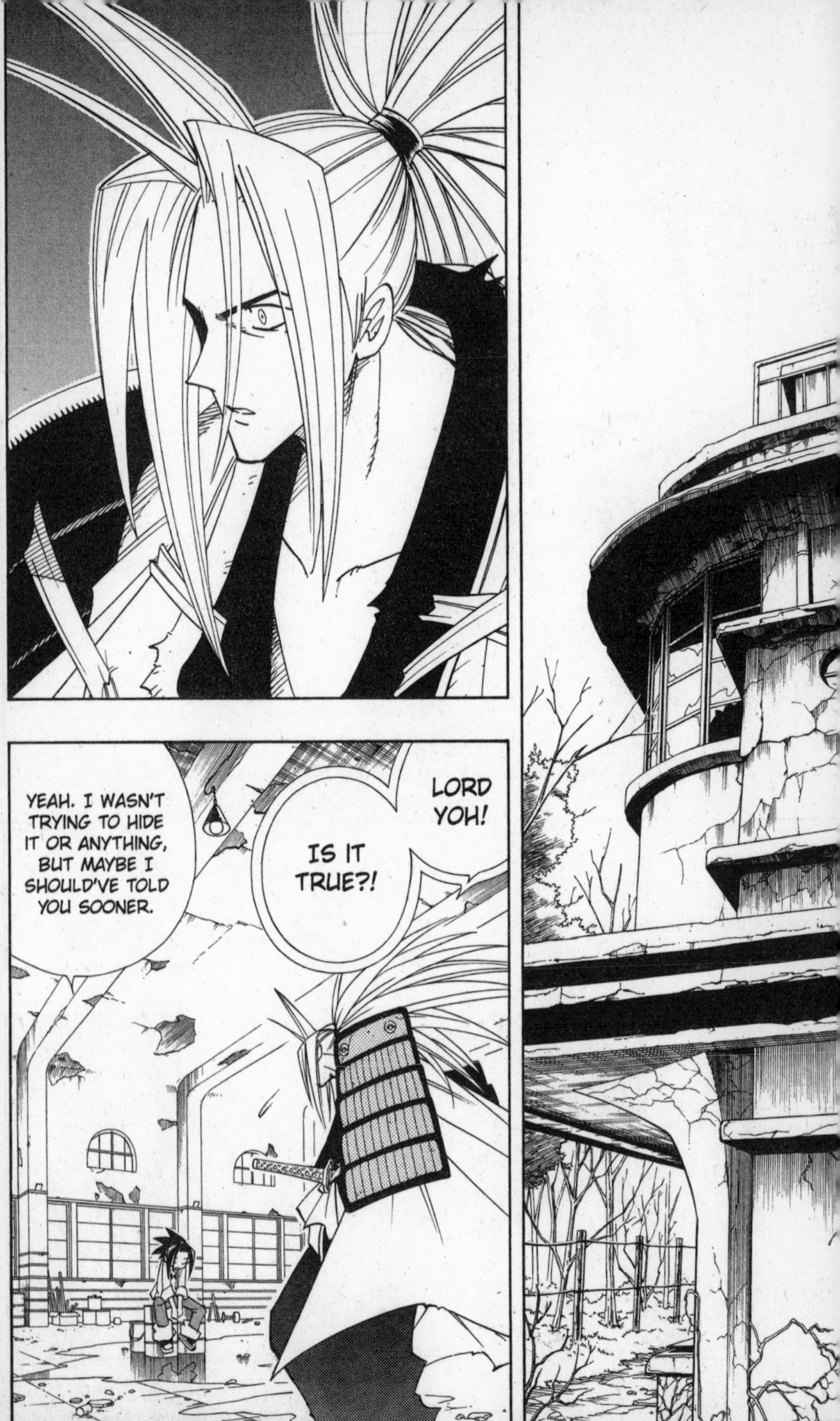
LORD YOH!
IS IT TRUE?!
YEAH. I WASN'T TRYING TO HIDE IT OR ANYTHING, BUT MAYBE I SHOULD'VE TOLD YOU SOONER.

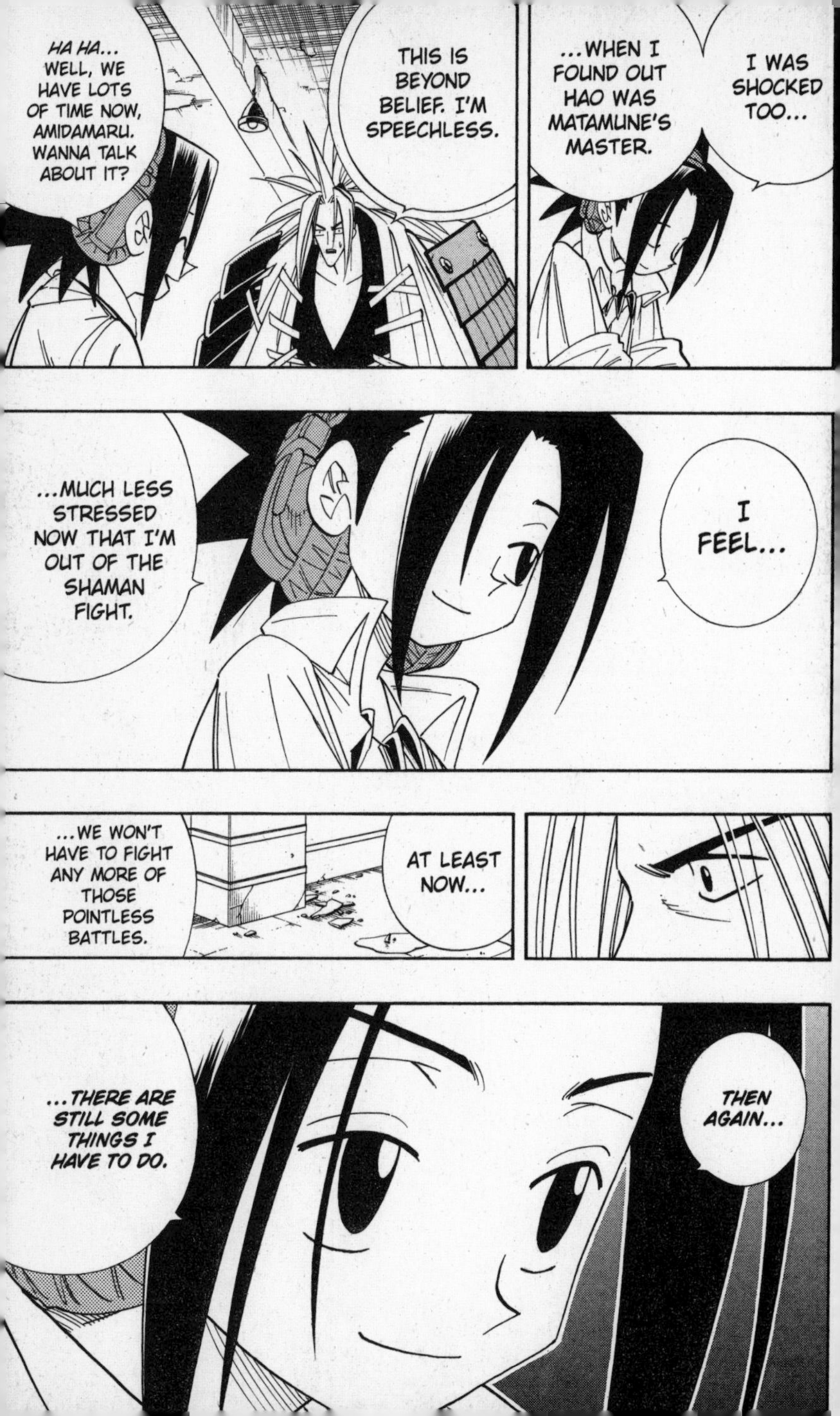
I WAS SHOCKED TOO...
...WHEN I FOUND OUT HAO WAS MATAMUNE'S MASTER.
THIS IS BEYOND BELIEF. I'M SPEECHLESS.
HA HA... WELL, WE HAVE LOTS OF TIME NOW, AMIDAMARU. WANNA TALK ABOUT IT?
I FEEL...
...MUCH LESS STRESSED NOW THAT I'M OUT OF THE SHAMAN FIGHT.
AT LEAST NOW...
...WE WON'T HAVE TO FIGHT ANY MORE OF THOSE POINTLESS BATTLES.
THEN AGAIN...
...THERE ARE STILL SOME THINGS I HAVE TO DO.

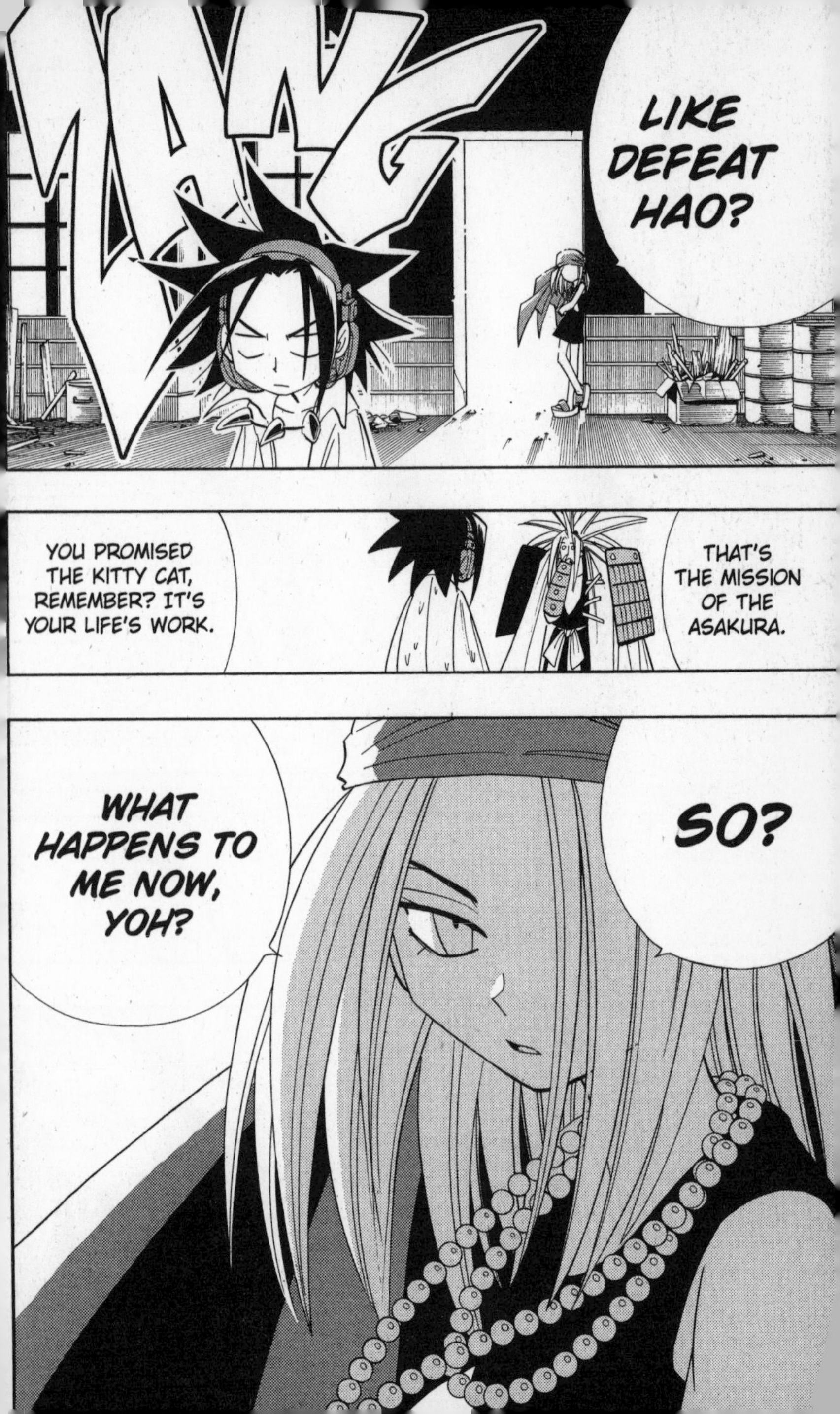
LIKE DEFEAT HAO?
THAT'S THE MISSION OF THE ASAKURA.
YOU PROMISED THE KITTY CAT, REMEMBER? IT'S YOUR LIFE'S WORK.
SO?
WHAT HAPPENS TO ME NOW, YOH?

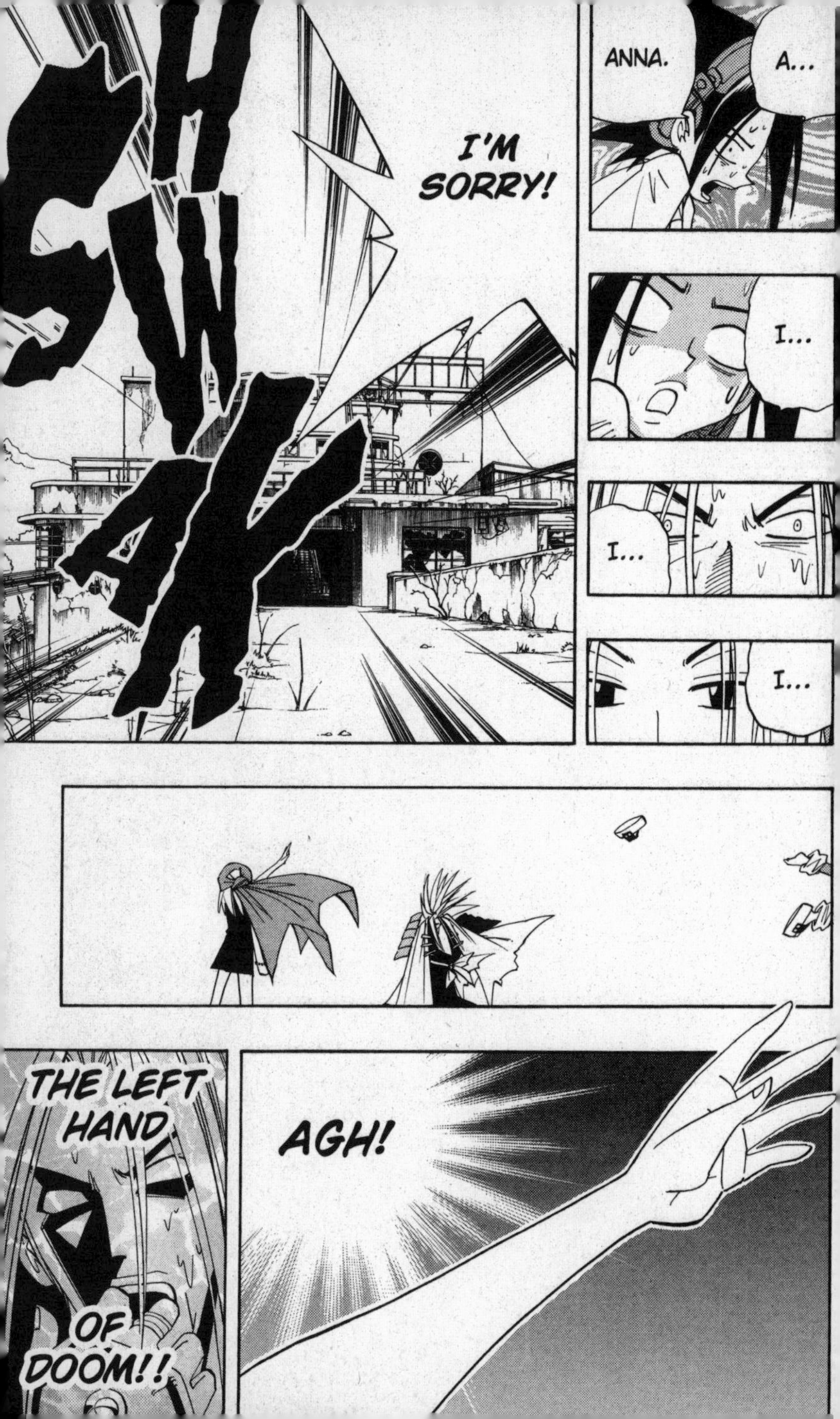
A...
ANNA.
I...
I...
I...
I'M SORRY!
AGH!
THE LEFT HAND
OF DOOM!!

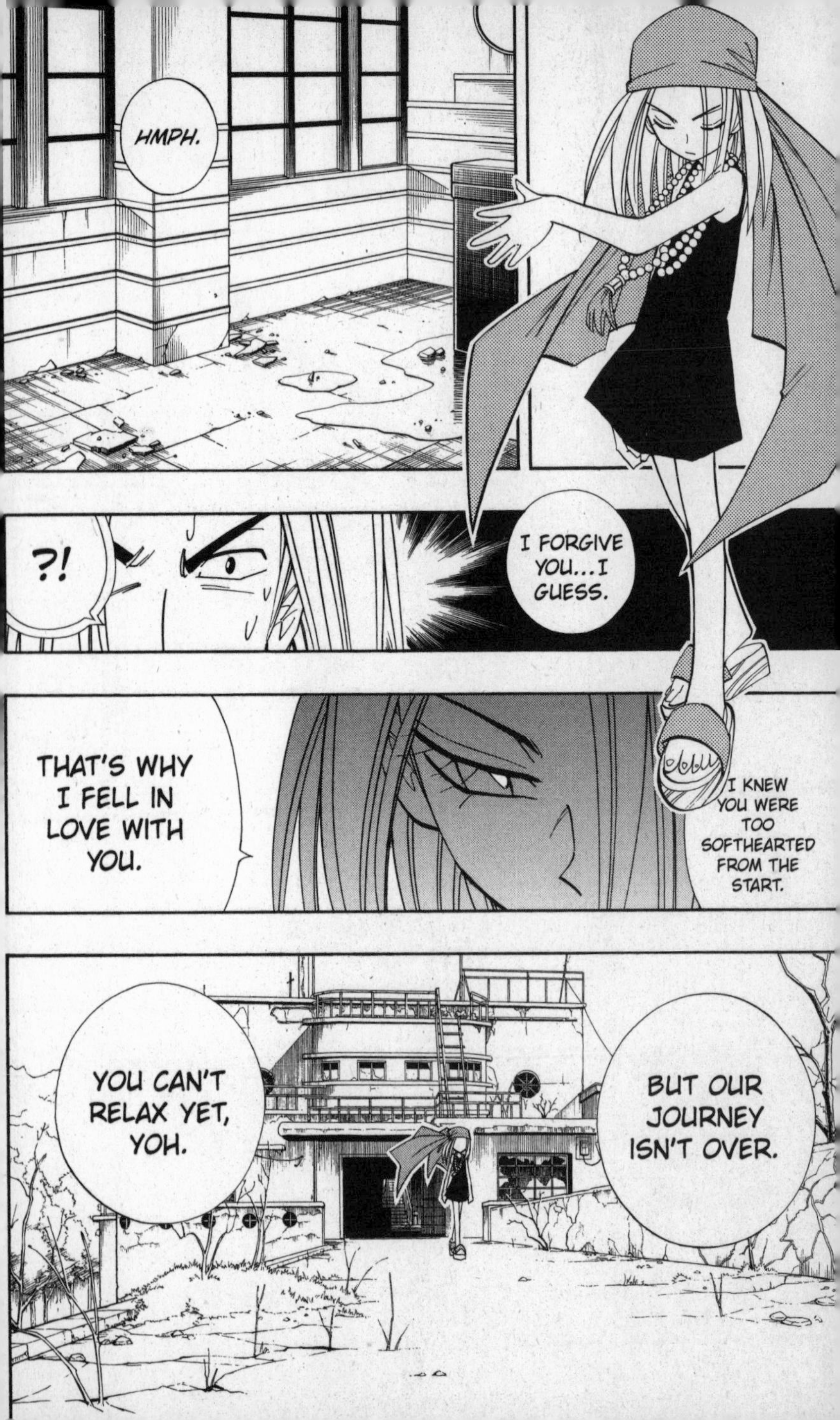
I FORGIVE YOU...I GUESS.
HMPH.
?!
I KNEW YOU WERE TOO SOFTHEARTED FROM THE START.
THAT'S WHY I FELL IN LOVE WITH YOU.
BUT OUR JOURNEY ISN'T OVER.
YOU CAN'T RELAX YET, YOH.

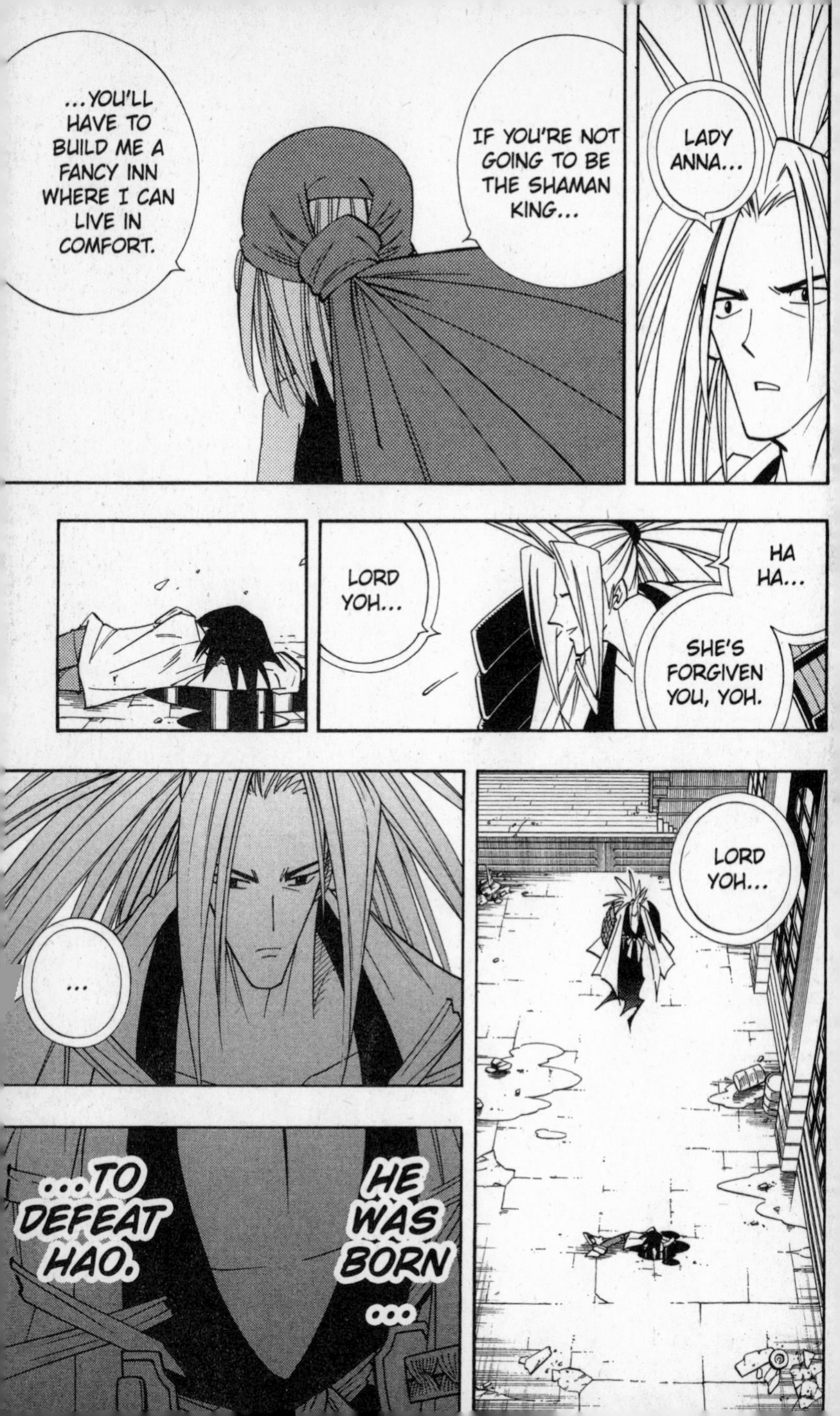
LADY ANNA...
IF YOU'RE NOT GOING TO BE THE SHAMAN KING...
...YOU'LL HAVE TO BUILD ME A FANCY INN WHERE I CAN LIVE IN COMFORT.
HA HA...
SHE'S FORGIVEN YOU, YOH.
LORD YOH...
LORD YOH...
...
HE WAS BORN...
...TO DEFEAT HAO.

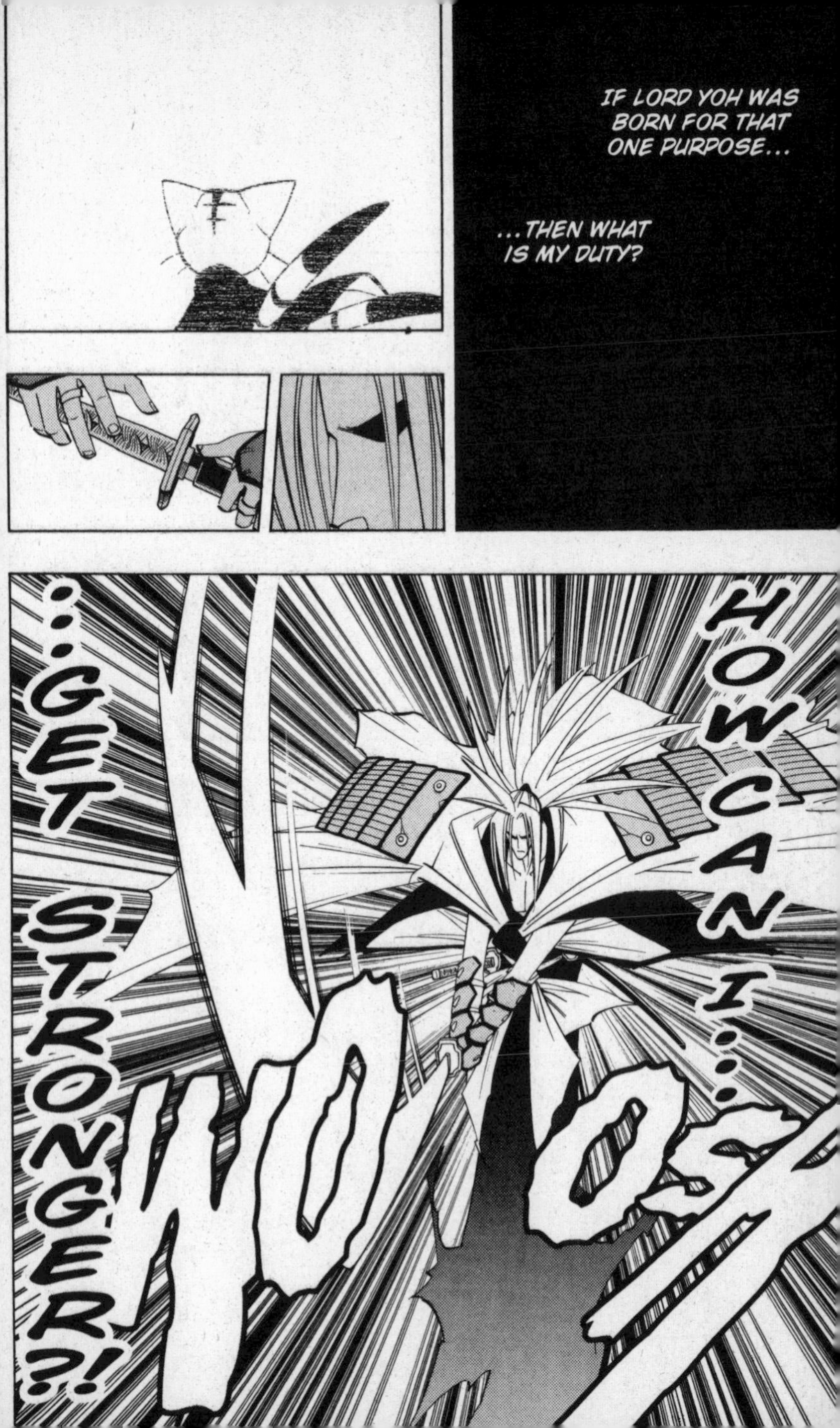
IF LORD YOH WAS BORN FOR THAT ONE PURPOSE...
...THEN WHAT IS MY DUTY?
HOW CAN I...
...GET STRONGER?!

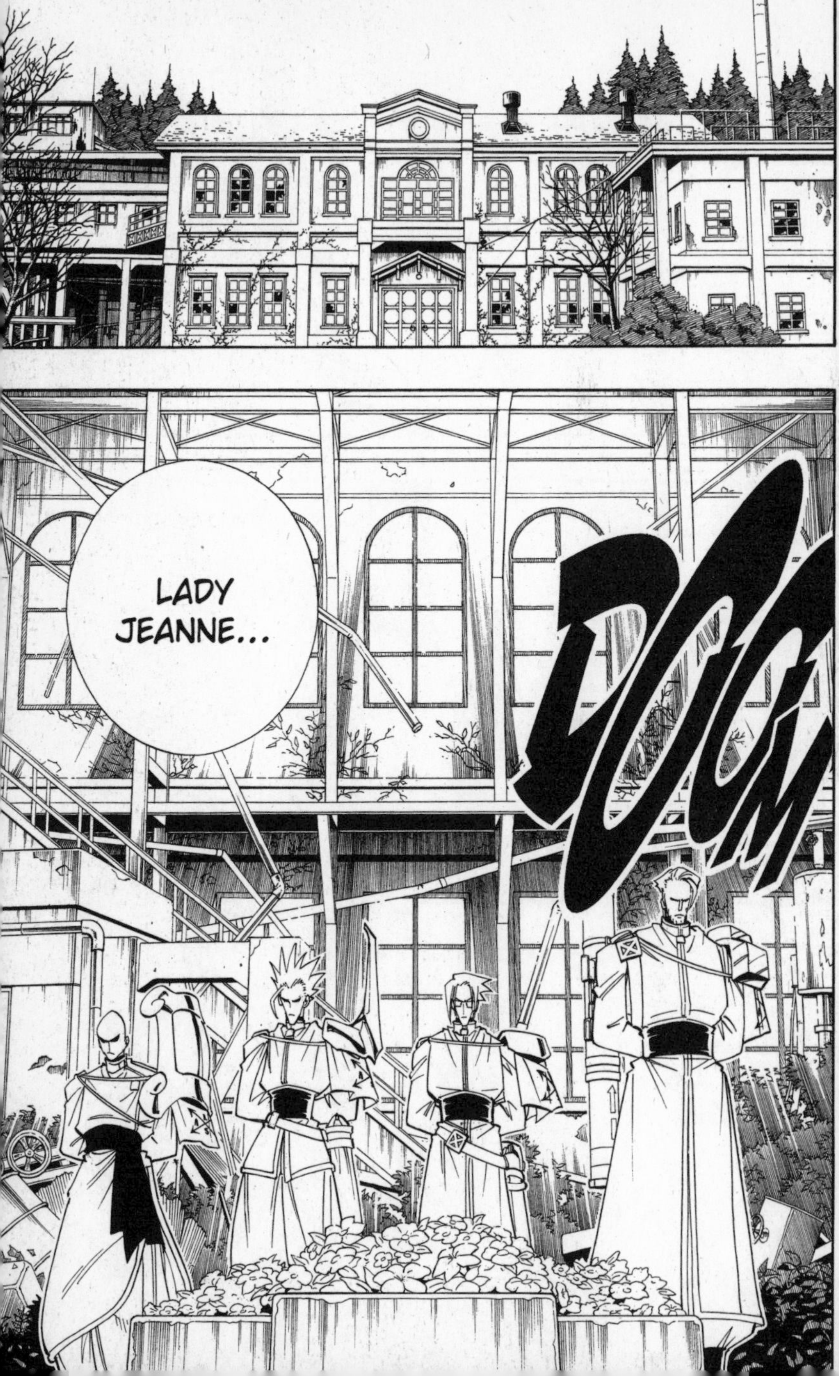

LADY JEANNE...
DOOM

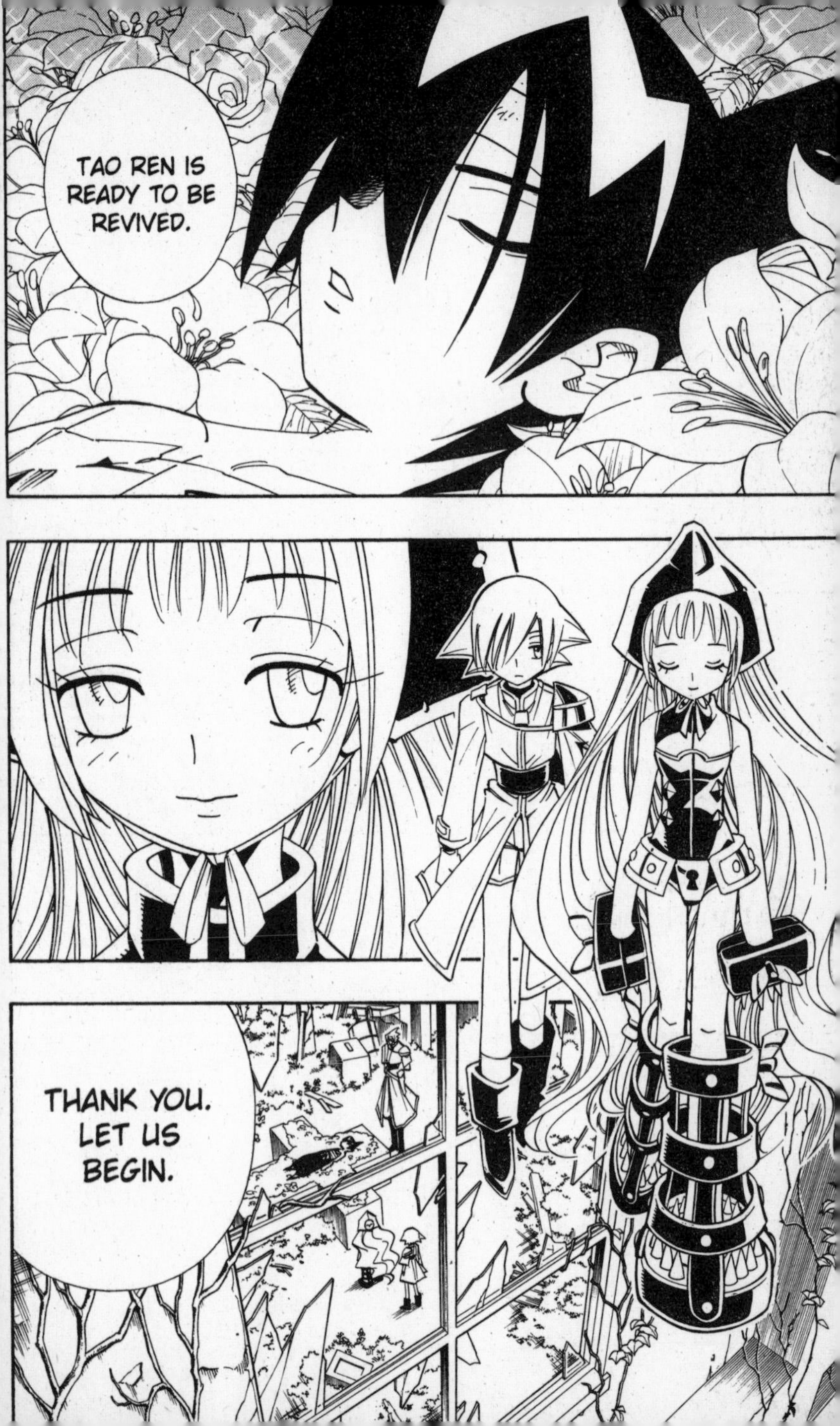
TAO REN IS READY TO BE REVIVED.
THANK YOU. LET US BEGIN.

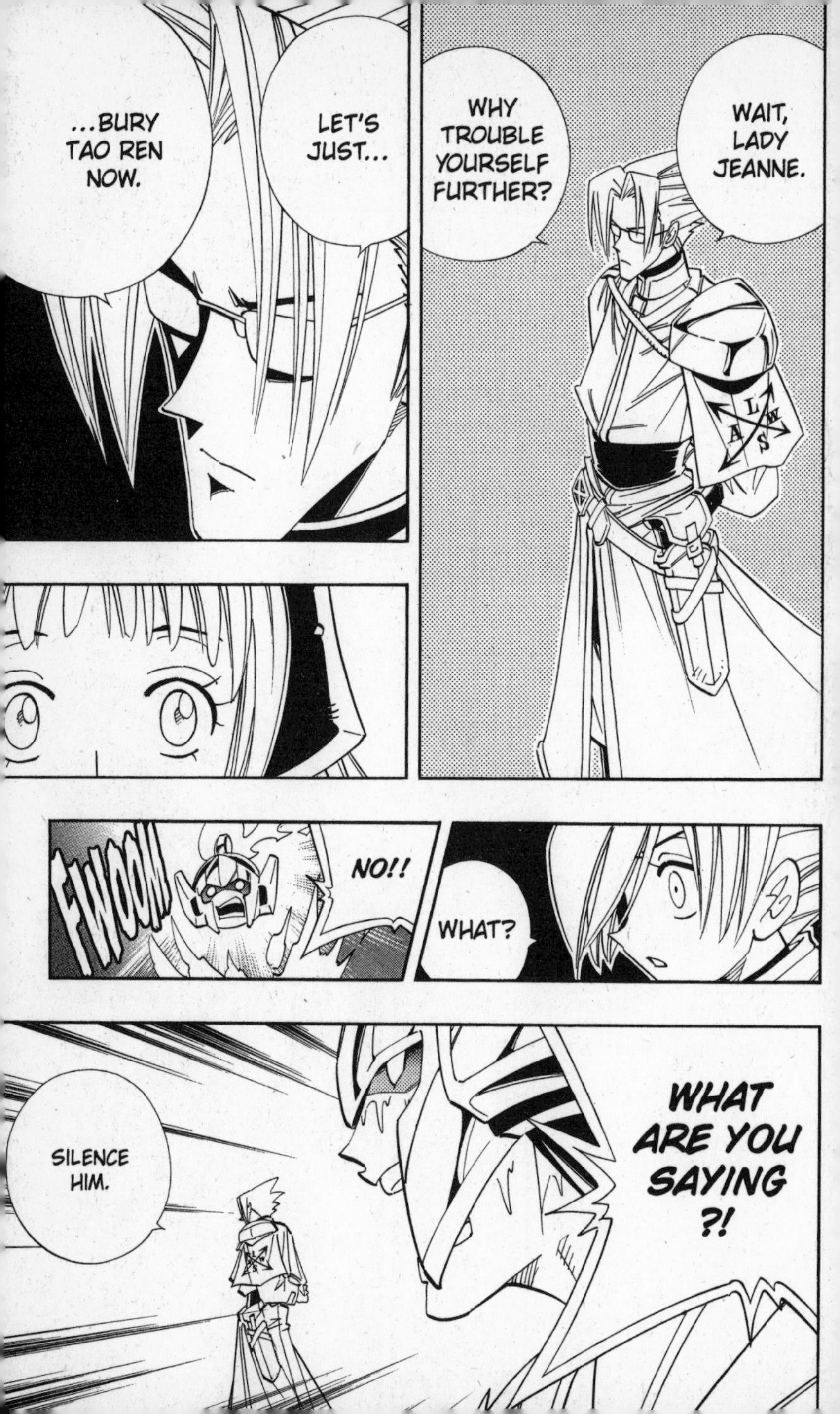
WAIT, LADY JEANNE.
WHY TROUBLE YOURSELF FURTHER?
LET'S JUST...
...BURY TAO REN NOW.
WHAT?
NO!!
FWOOM
WHAT ARE YOU SAYING ?!
SILENCE HIM.

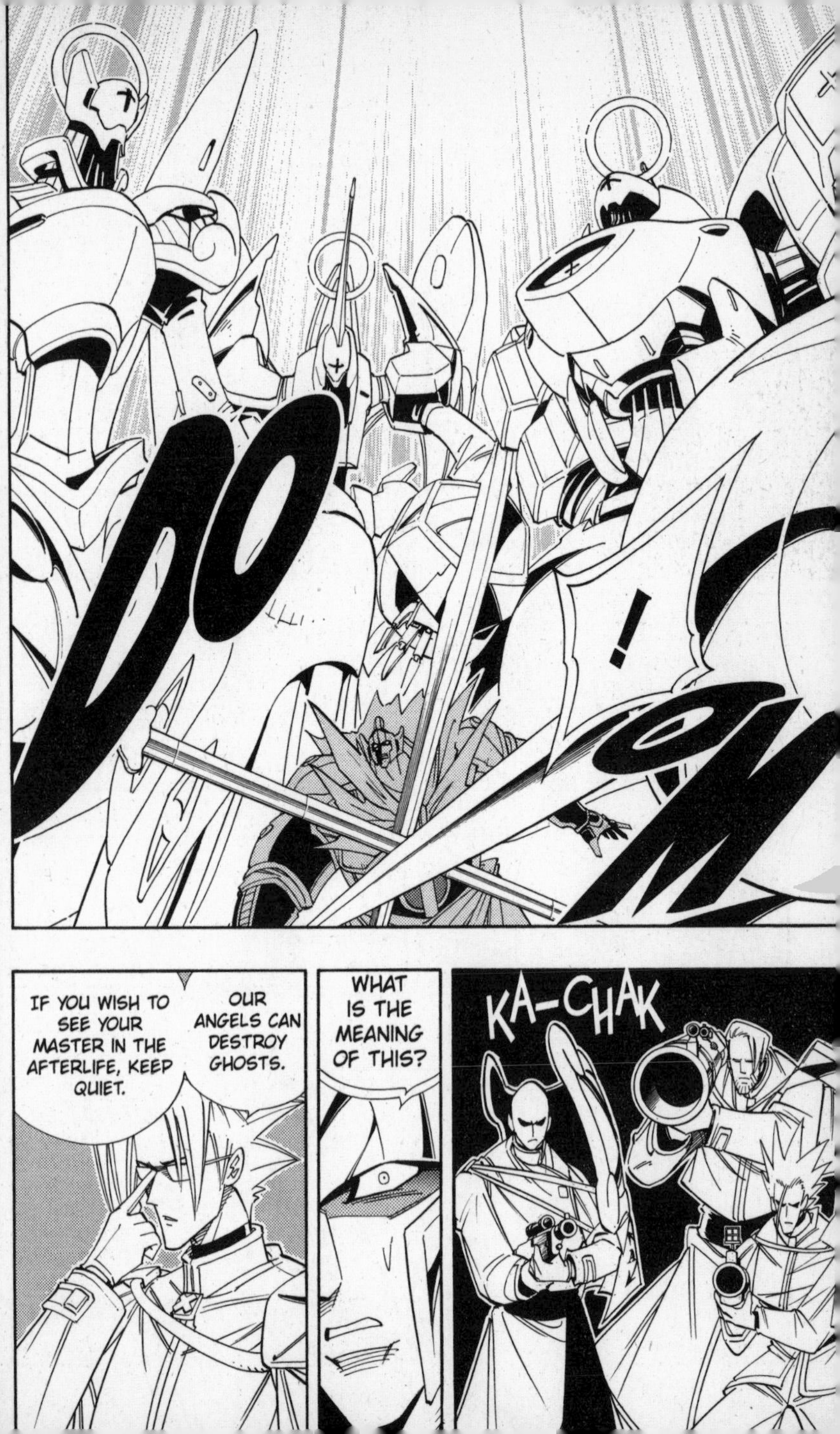
KA-CHAK
WHAT IS THE MEANING OF THIS?
OUR ANGELS CAN DESTROY GHOSTS.
IF YOU WISH TO SEE YOUR MASTER IN THE AFTERLIFE, KEEP QUIET.

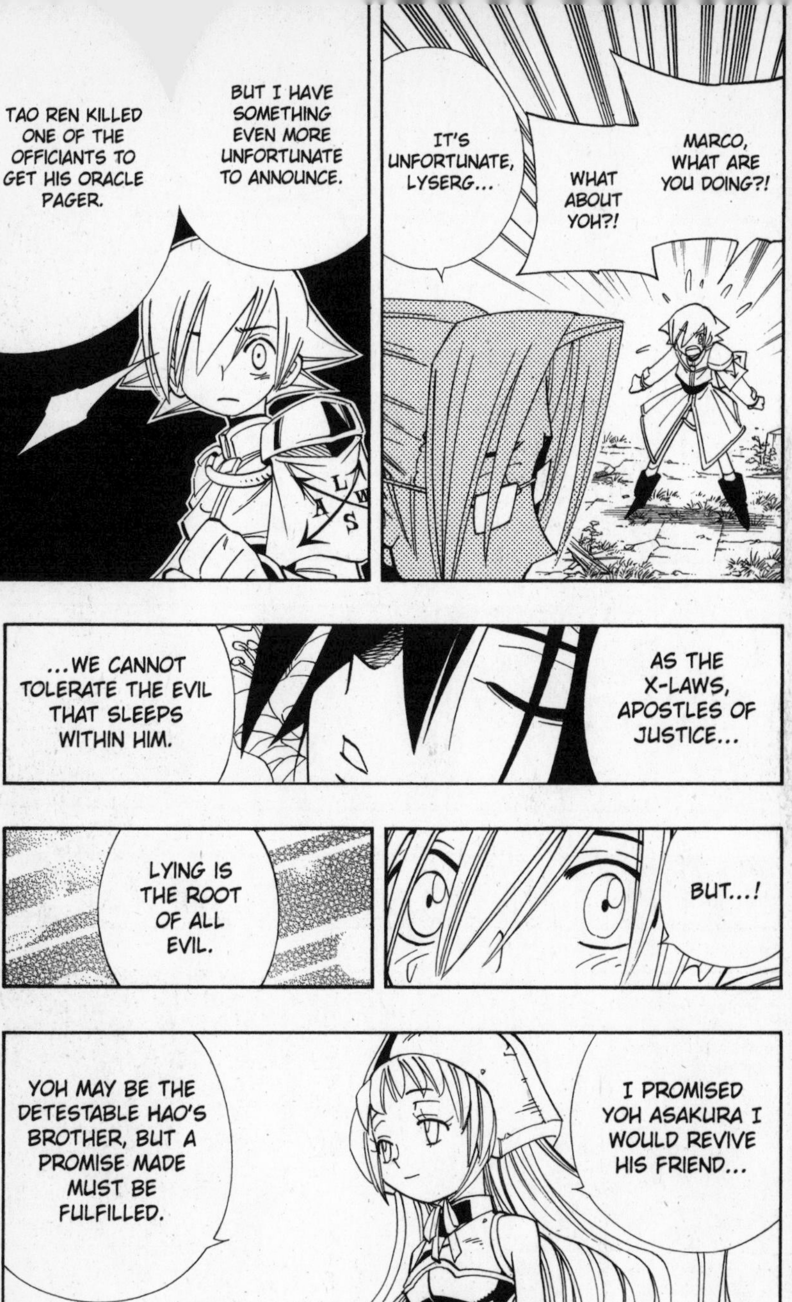
MARCO, WHAT ARE YOU DOING?!
WHAT ABOUT YOH?!
IT'S UNFORTUNATE, LYSERG...
BUT I HAVE SOMETHING EVEN MORE UNFORTUNATE TO ANNOUNCE.
TAO REN KILLED ONE OF THE OFFICIANTS TO GET HIS ORACLE PAGER.
AS THE X-LAWS, APOSTLES OF JUSTICE...
...WE CANNOT TOLERATE THE EVIL THAT SLEEPS WITHIN HIM.
BUT...!
LYING IS THE ROOT OF ALL EVIL.
I PROMISED YOH ASAKURA I WOULD REVIVE HIS FRIEND...
YOH MAY BE THE DETESTABLE HAO'S BROTHER, BUT A PROMISE MADE MUST BE FULFILLED.

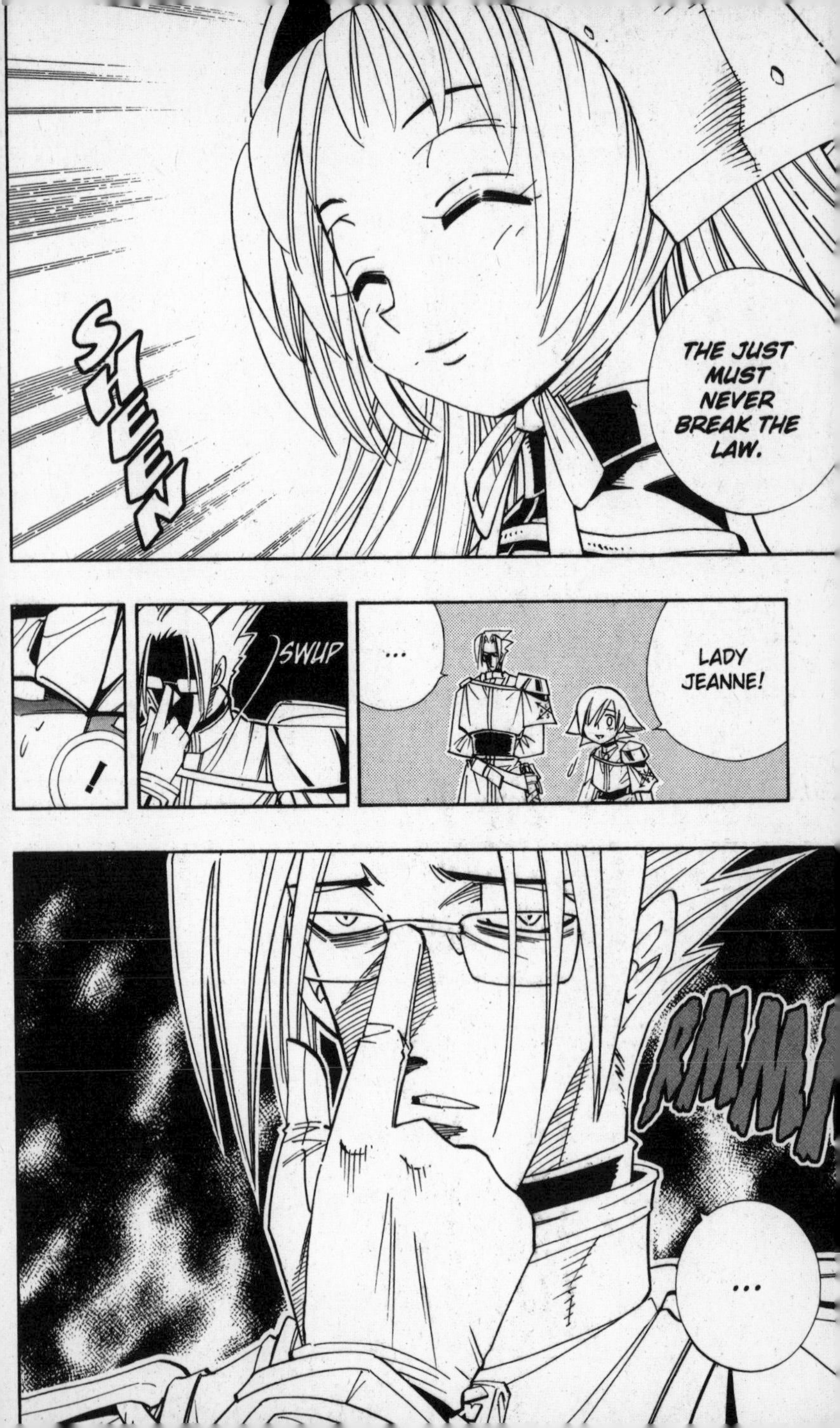
THE JUST MUST NEVER BREAK THE LAW.
SHEEN
LADY JEANNE!
...
SWUP
!
RMMM
...

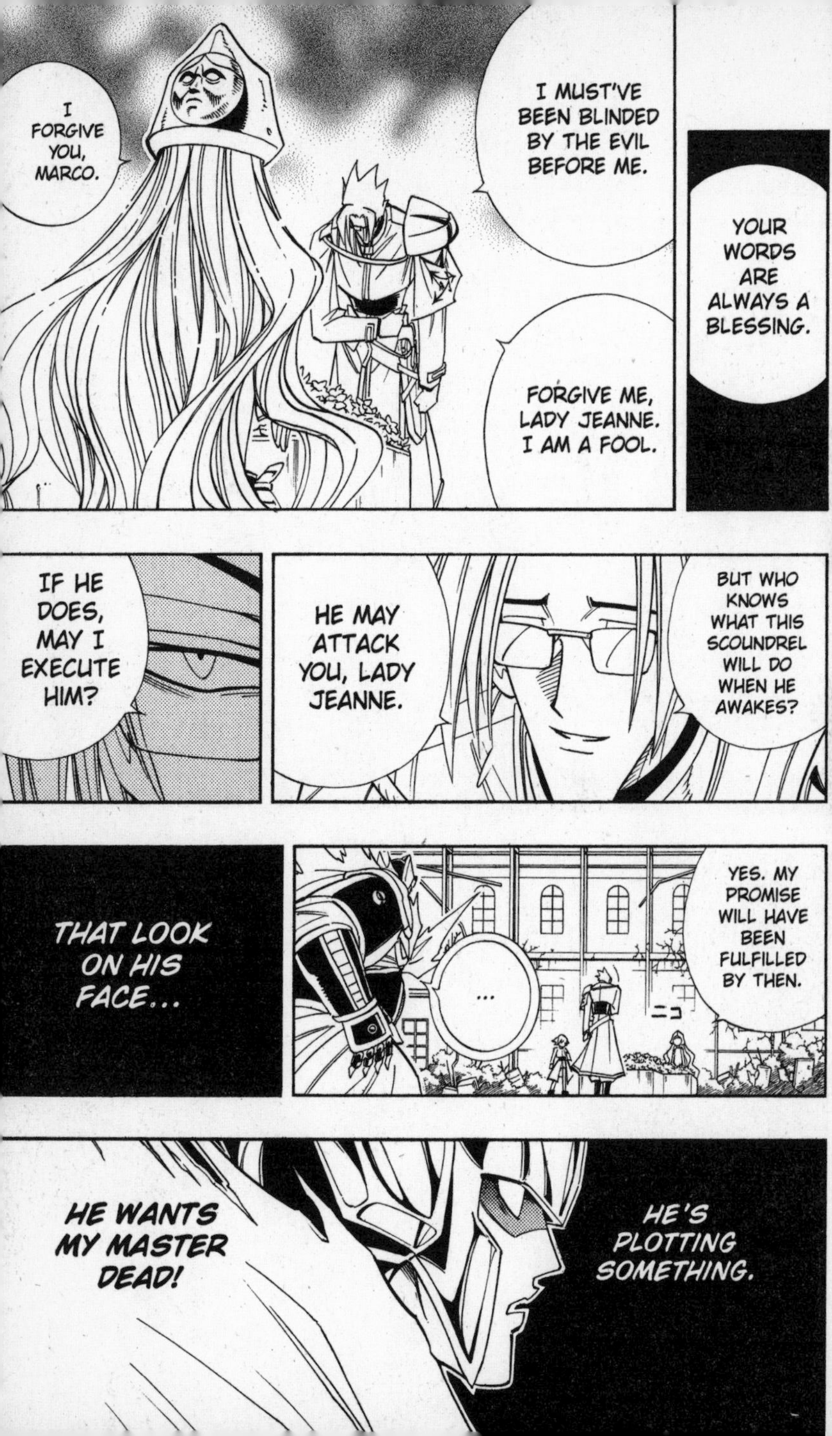
YOUR WORDS ARE ALWAYS A BLESSING.
I MUST'VE BEEN BLINDED BY THE EVIL BEFORE ME.
FORGIVE ME, LADY JEANNE. I AM A FOOL.
I FORGIVE YOU, MARCO.
BUT WHO KNOWS WHAT THIS SCOUNDREL WILL DO WHEN HE AWAKES?
HE MAY ATTACK YOU, LADY JEANNE.
IF HE DOES, MAY I EXECUTE HIM?
YES. MY PROMISE WILL HAVE BEEN FULFILLED BY THEN.
ニコ
...
THAT LOOK ON HIS FACE...
HE'S PLOTTING SOMETHING.
HE WANTS MY MASTER DEAD!

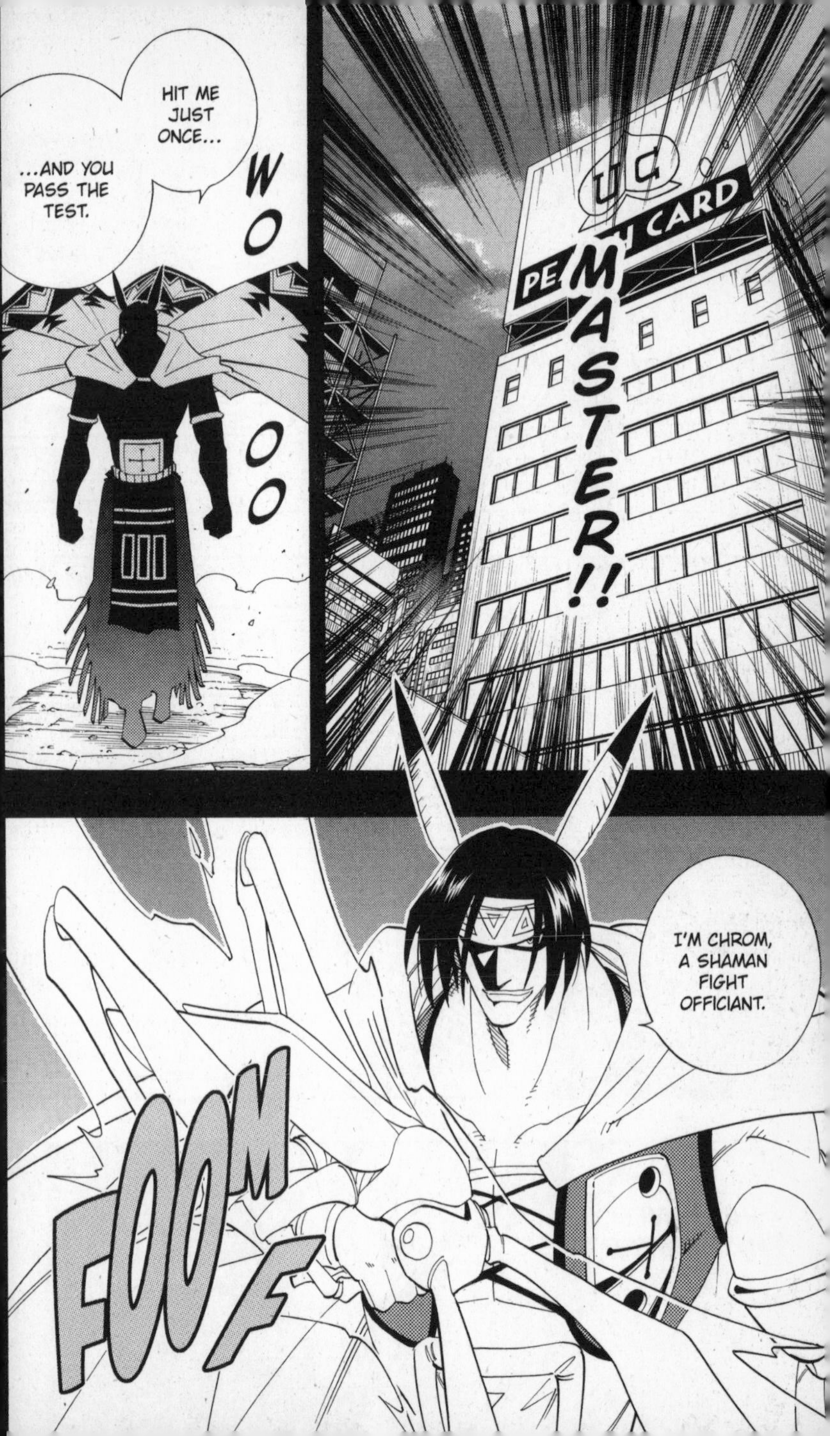
UG
CARD
MASTER!!
HIT ME JUST ONCE...
...AND YOU PASS THE TEST.
WOOO
I'M CHROM, A SHAMAN FIGHT OFFICIANT.
FOOMF

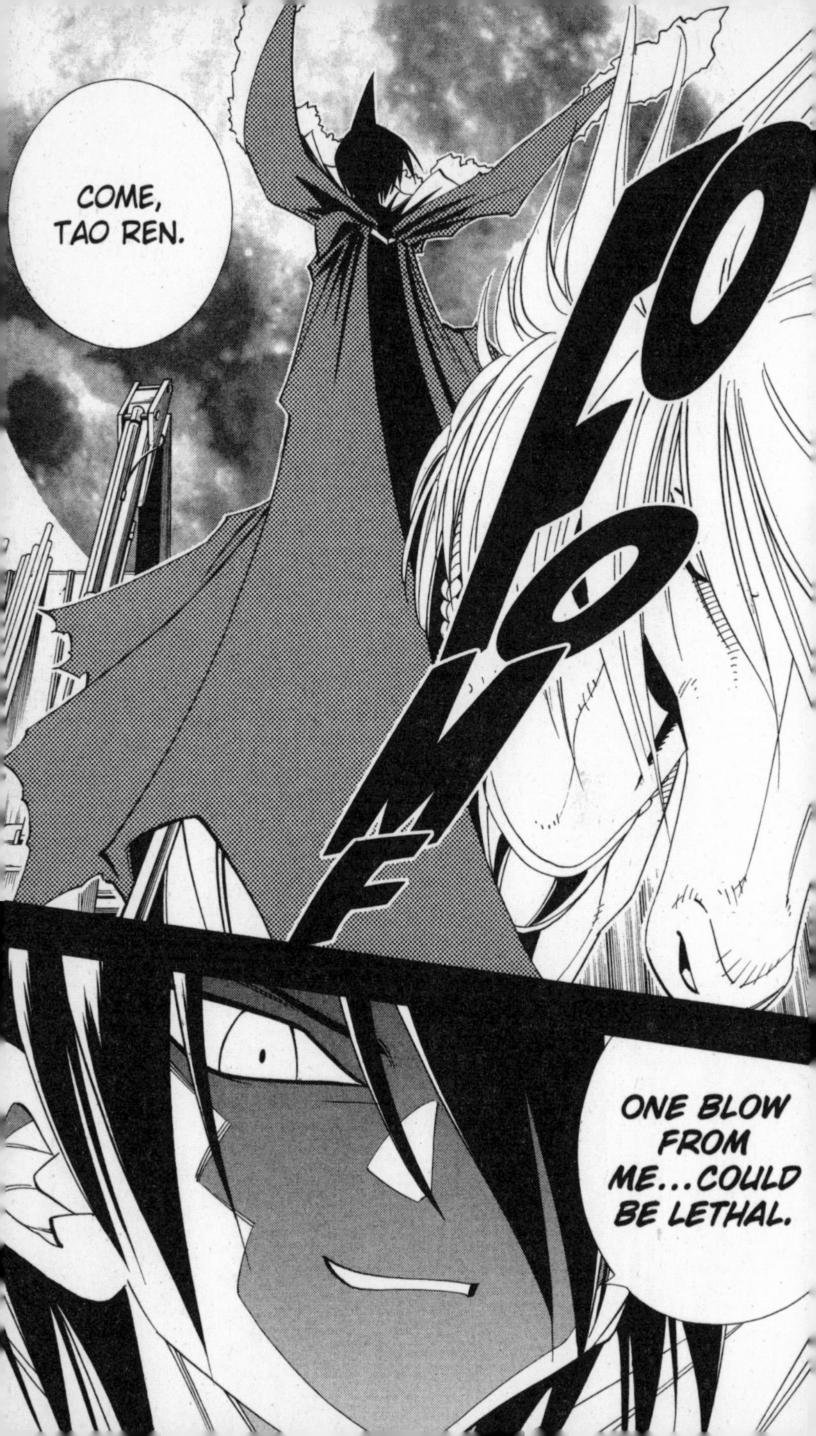
COME, TAO REN.
ONE BLOW FROM ME...COULD BE LETHAL.

SHAMAN KING ITEM FILE No.53

SWORD NO-001

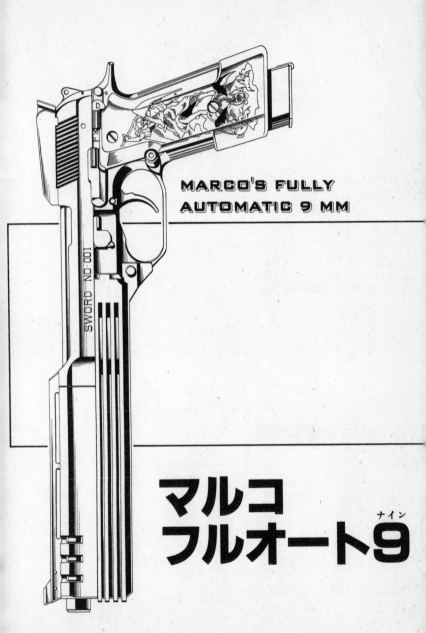

MARCO'S FULLY AUTOMATIC 9 MM

マルコ
フルオート9（ナイン）

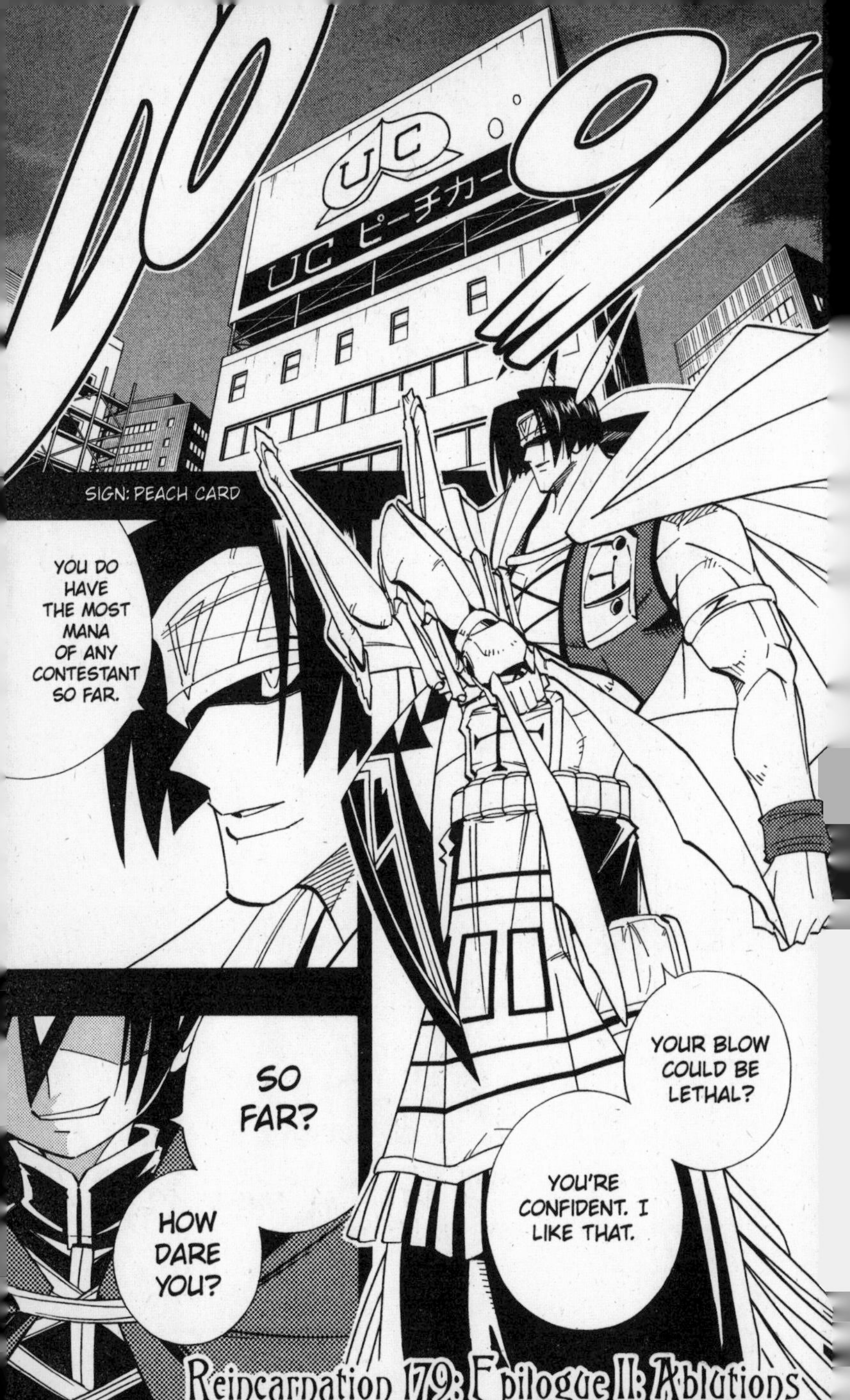
UC
UC ピーチカード
SIGN: PEACH CARD
YOU DO HAVE THE MOST MANA OF ANY CONTESTANT SO FAR.
SO FAR?
HOW DARE YOU?
YOUR BLOW COULD BE LETHAL?
YOU'RE CONFIDENT. I LIKE THAT.

Reincarnation 179: Epilogue II: Ablutions

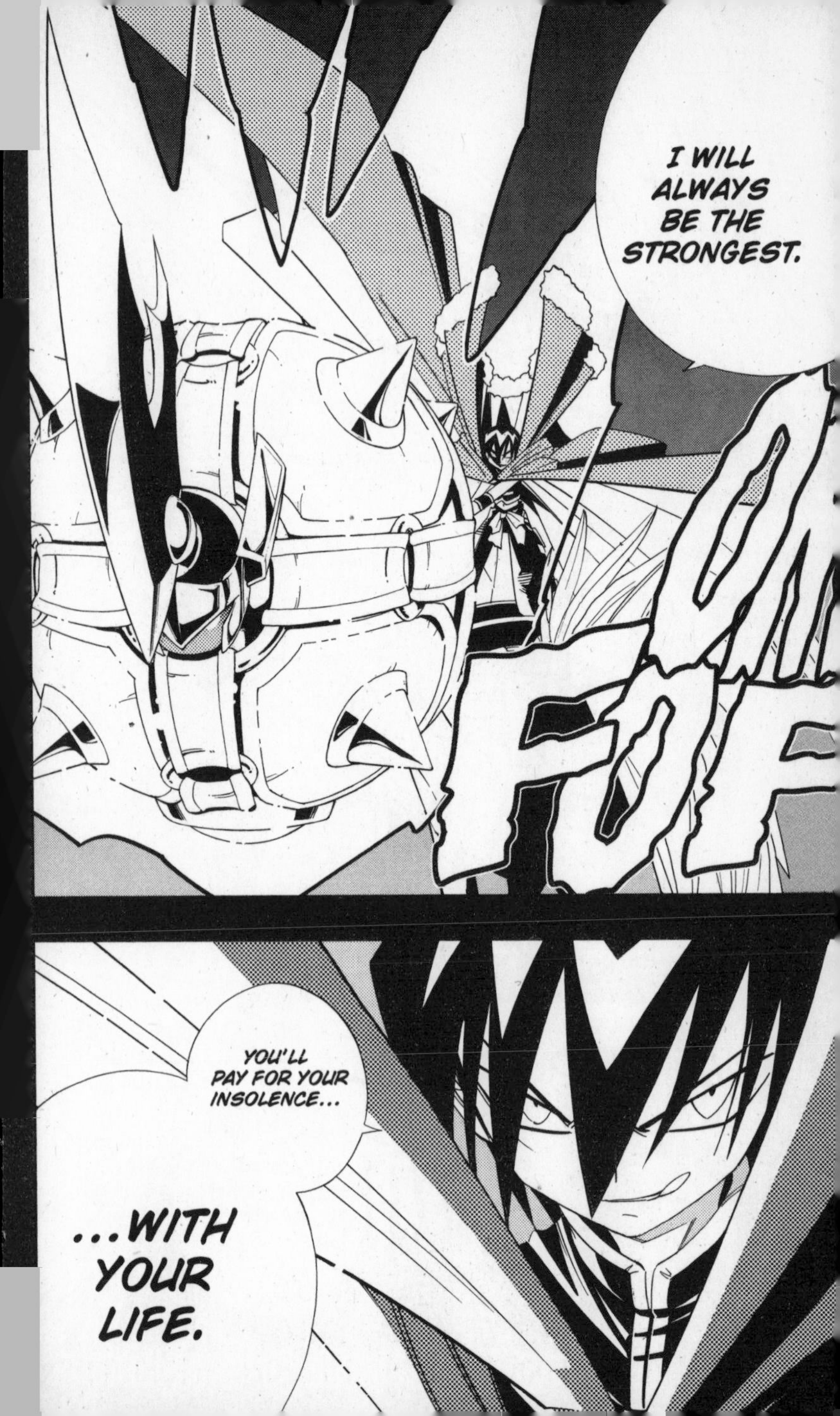
I WILL ALWAYS BE THE STRONGEST.
YOU'LL PAY FOR YOUR INSOLENCE...
...WITH YOUR LIFE.

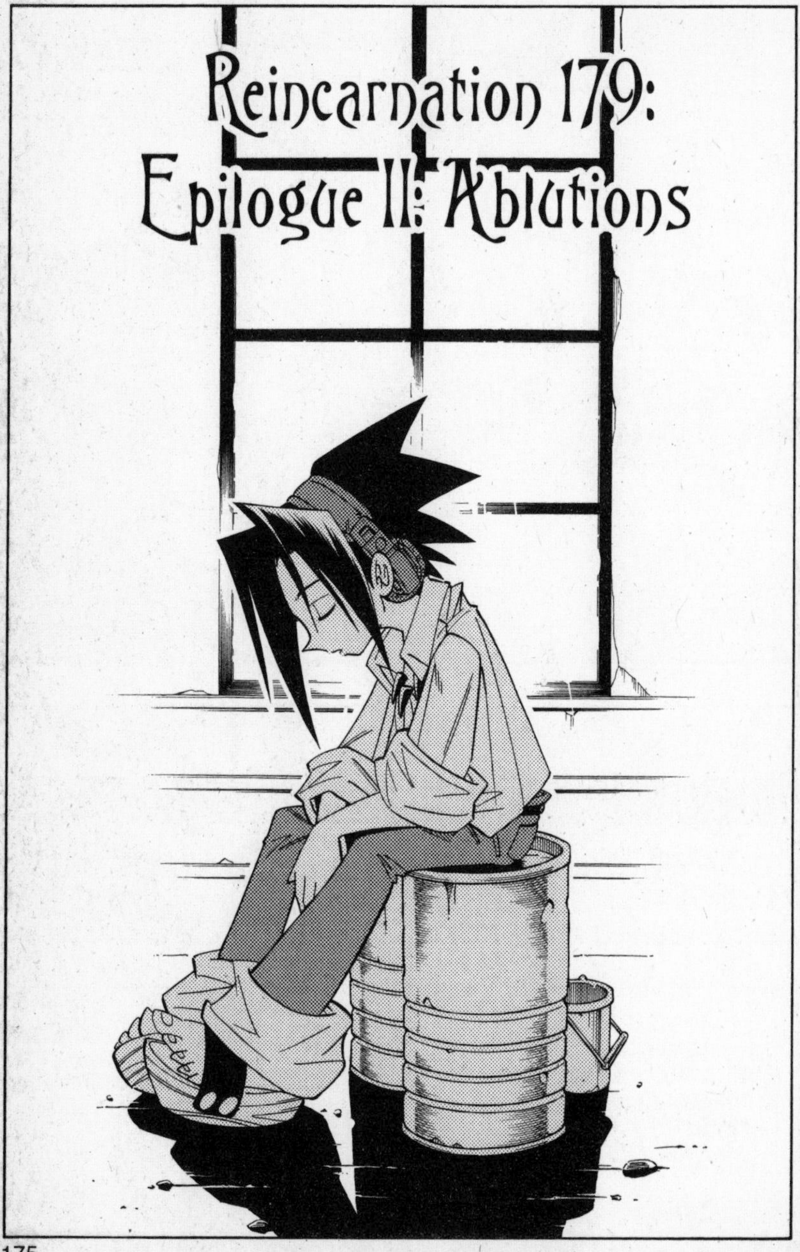
Reincarnation 179:
Epilogue II: Ablutions

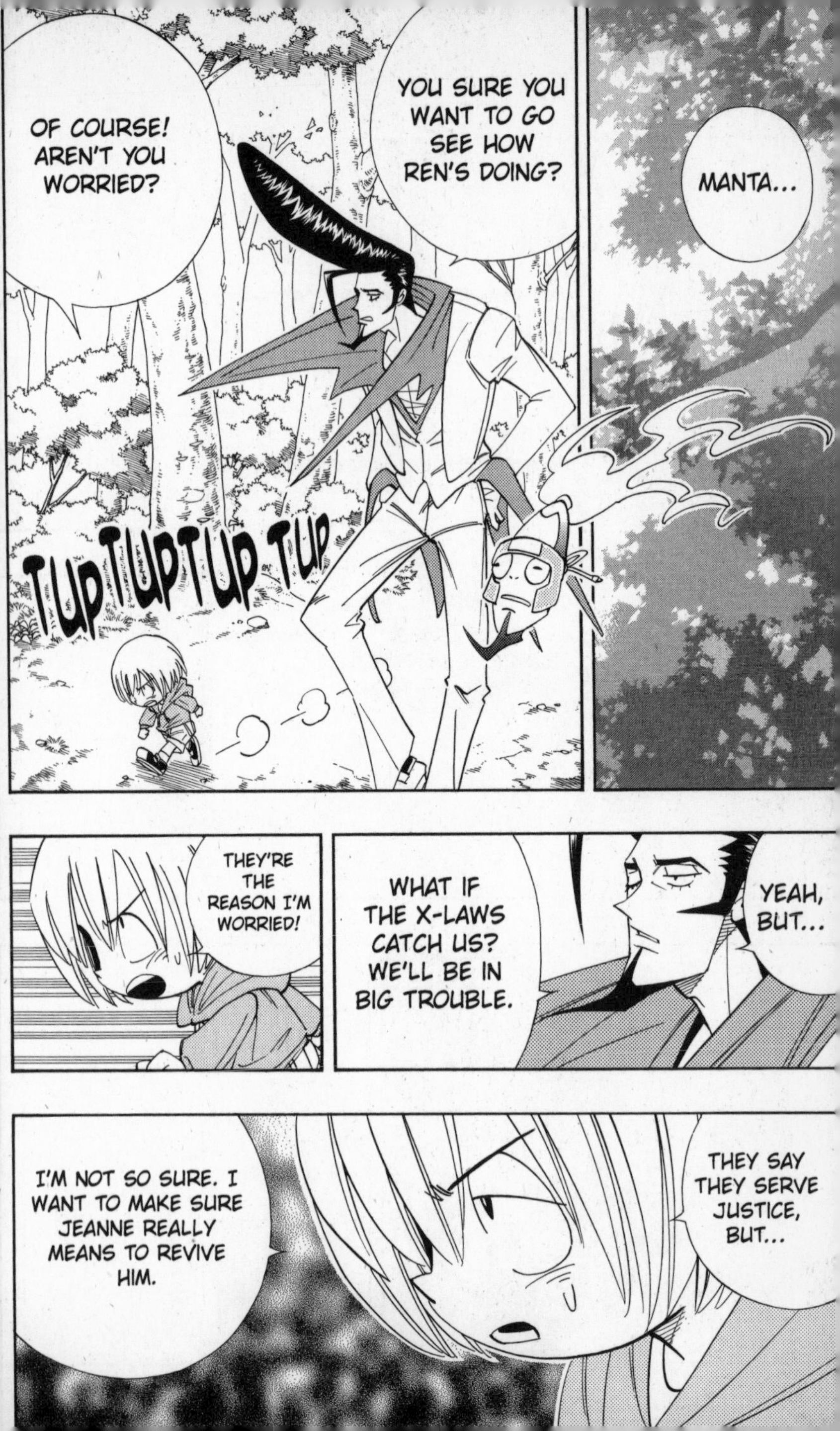
MANTA...
YOU SURE YOU WANT TO GO SEE HOW REN'S DOING?
OF COURSE! AREN'T YOU WORRIED?
TUP TUP TUP TUP
YEAH, BUT...
WHAT IF THE X-LAWS CATCH US? WE'LL BE IN BIG TROUBLE.
THEY'RE THE REASON I'M WORRIED!
THEY SAY THEY SERVE JUSTICE, BUT...
I'M NOT SO SURE. I WANT TO MAKE SURE JEANNE REALLY MEANS TO REVIVE HIM.

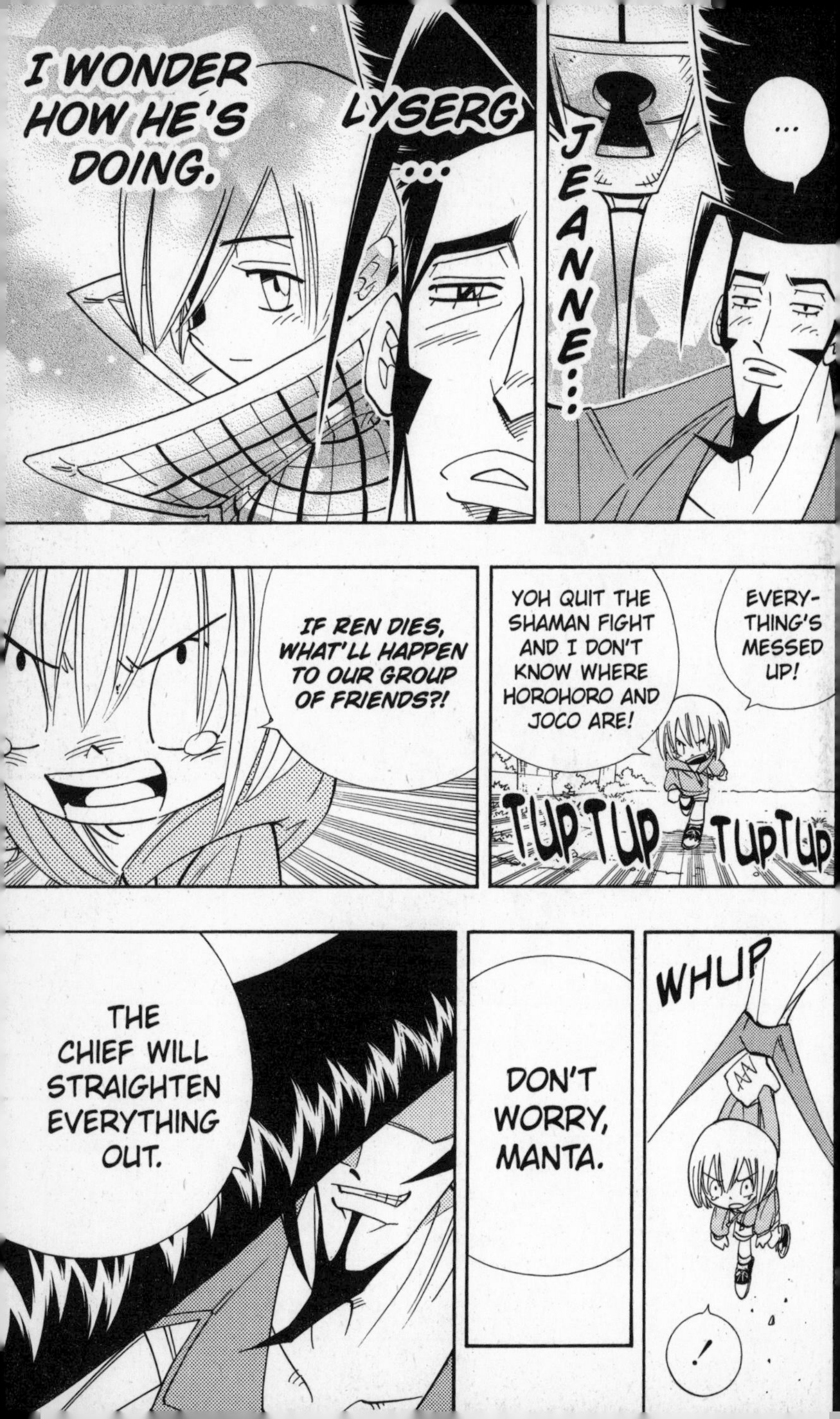
...
JEANNE...
LYSERG...
I WONDER HOW HE'S DOING.
EVERY-THING'S MESSED UP!
YOH QUIT THE SHAMAN FIGHT AND I DON'T KNOW WHERE HOROHORO AND JOCO ARE!
TUP TUP
TUP TUP
IF REN DIES, WHAT'LL HAPPEN TO OUR GROUP OF FRIENDS?!
WHUP
!
DON'T WORRY, MANTA.
THE CHIEF WILL STRAIGHTEN EVERYTHING OUT.

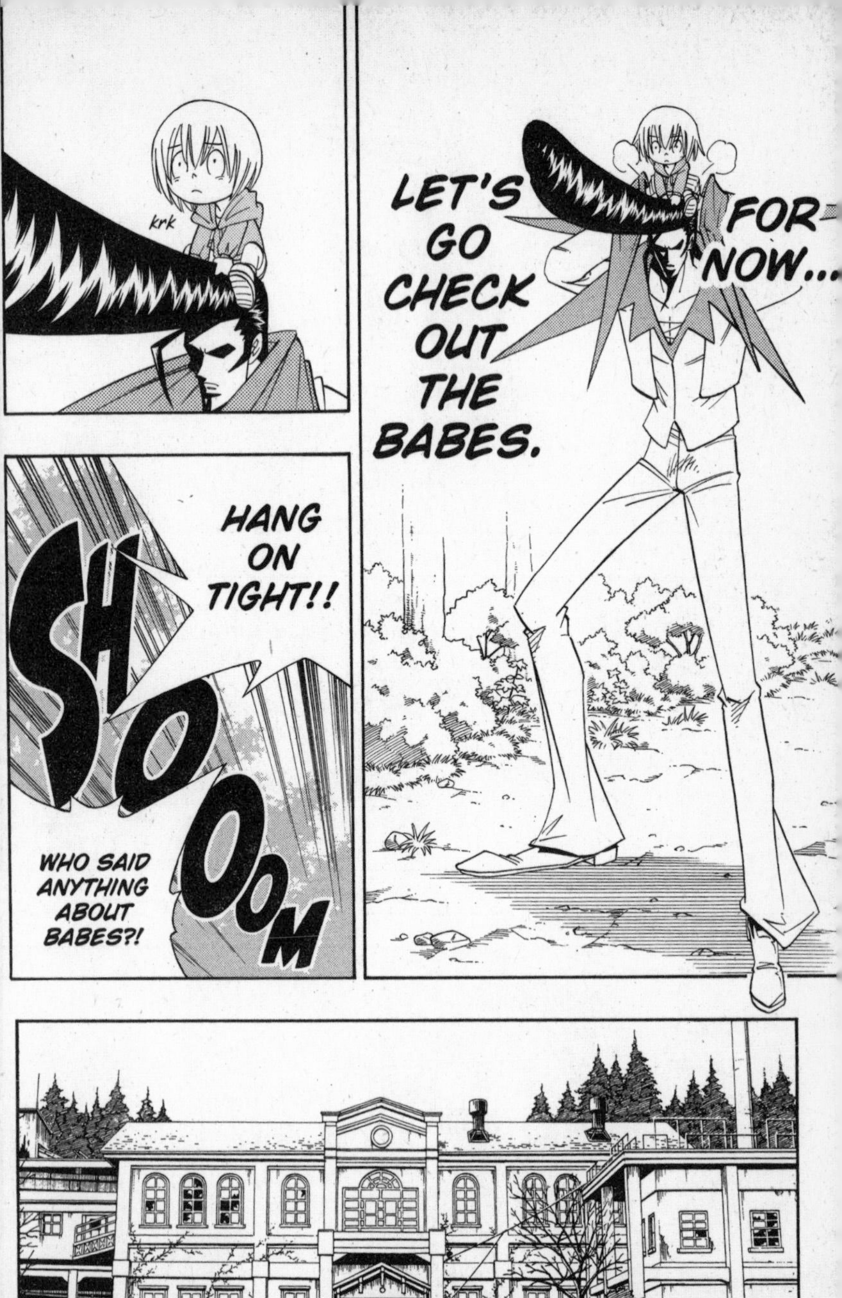
FOR NOW...
LET'S GO CHECK OUT THE BABES.
krk
HANG ON TIGHT!!
SHOOOOM
WHO SAID ANYTHING ABOUT BABES?!

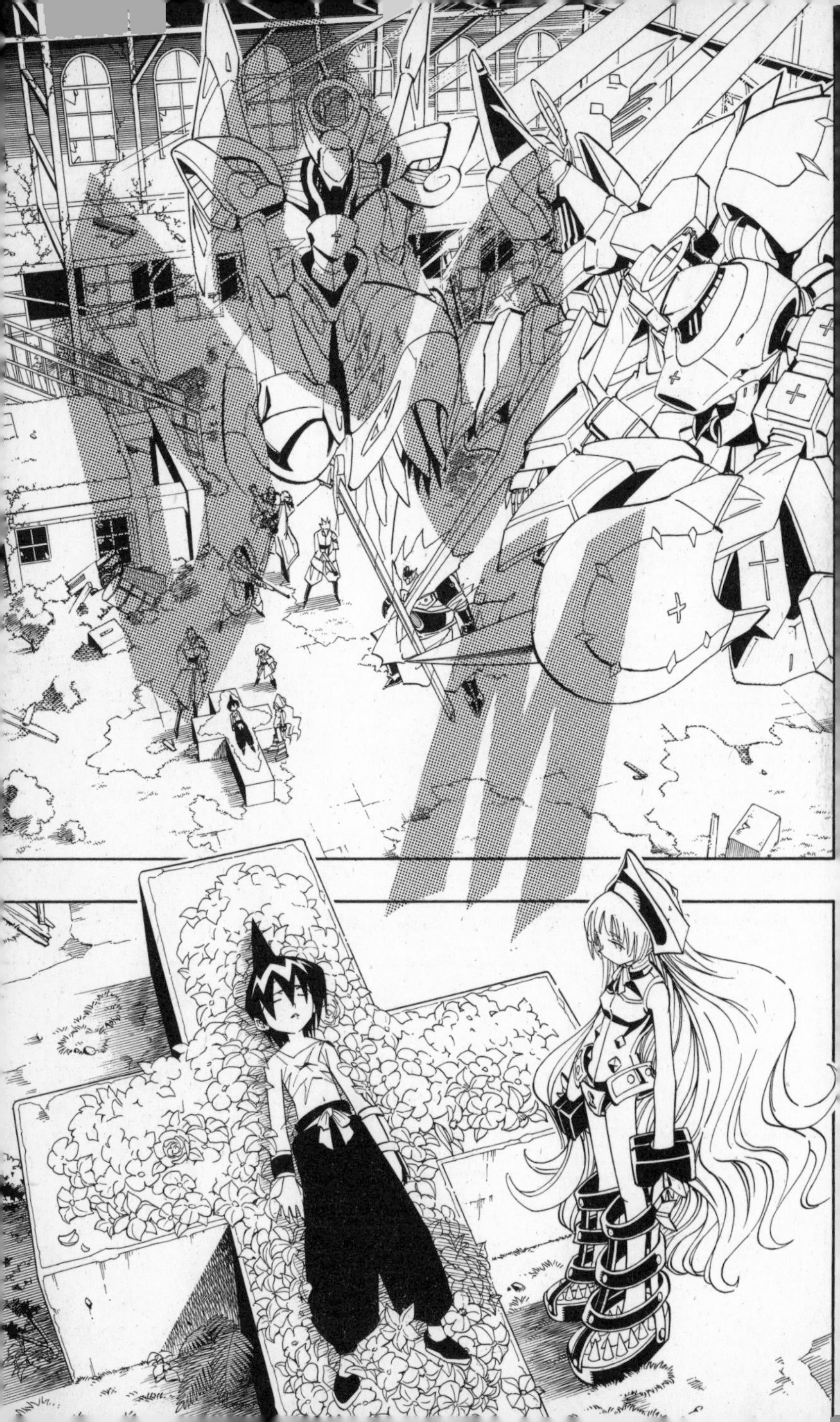

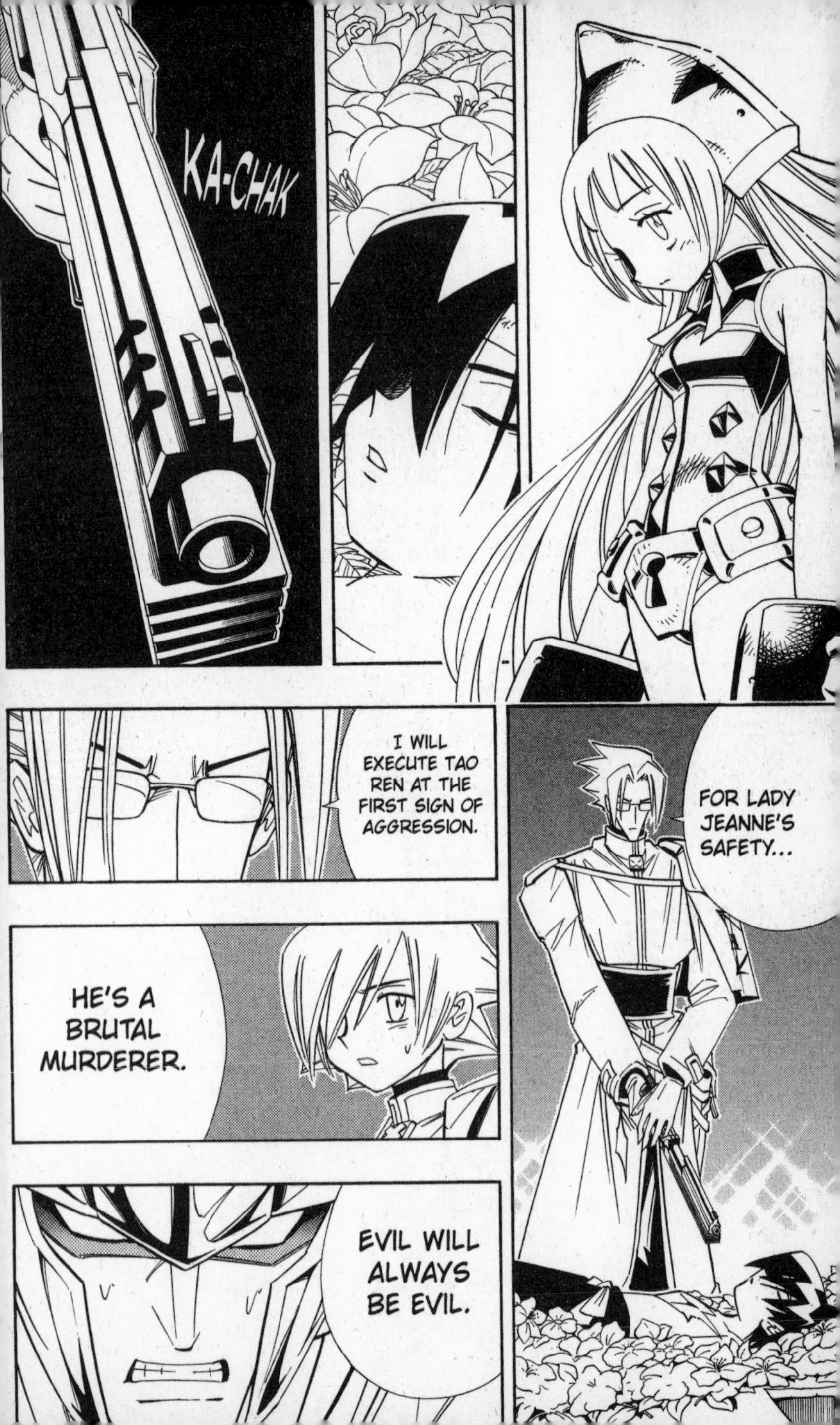
KA-CHAK
FOR LADY JEANNE'S SAFETY...
I WILL EXECUTE TAO REN AT THE FIRST SIGN OF AGGRESSION.
HE'S A BRUTAL MURDERER.
EVIL WILL ALWAYS BE EVIL.

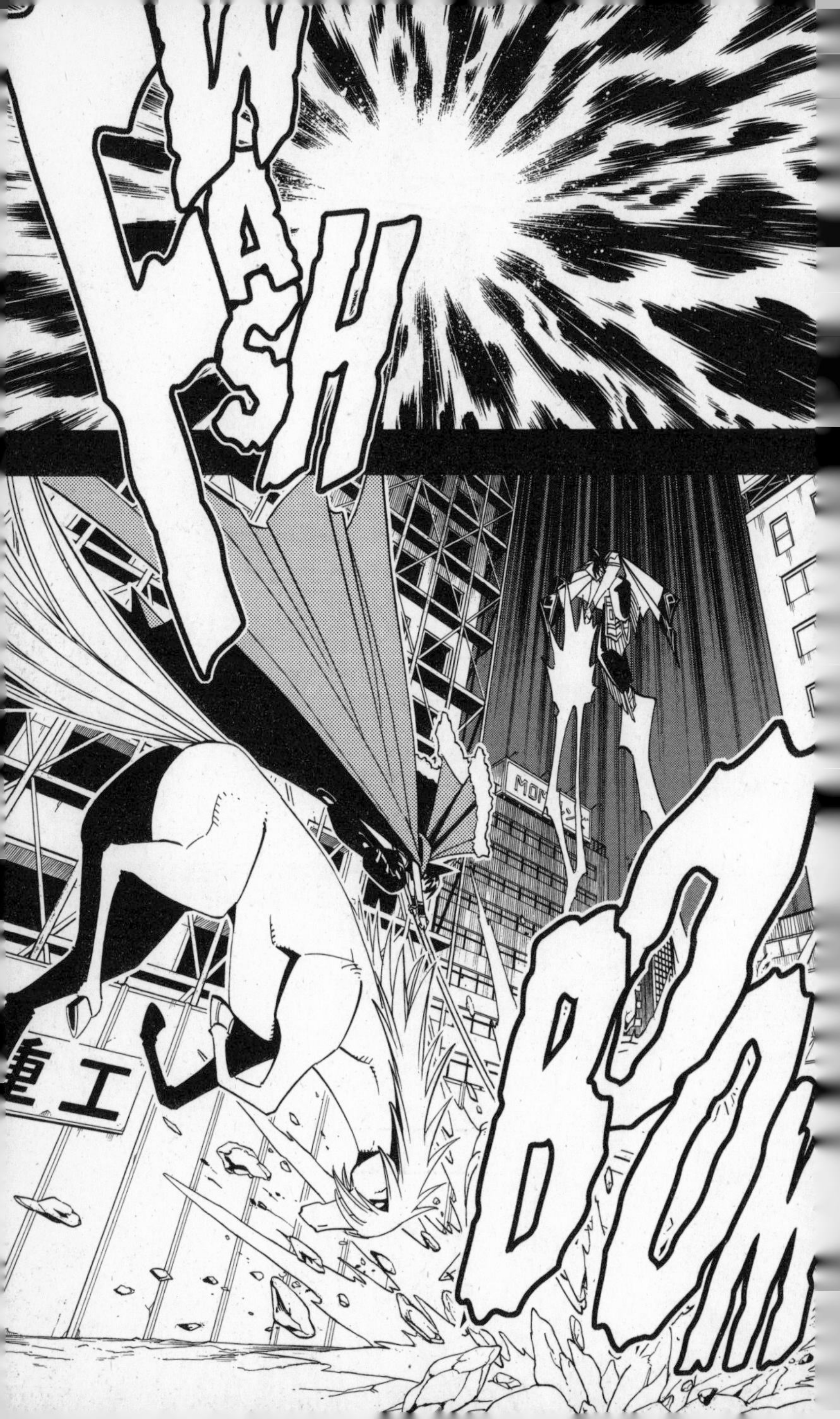

WASH
重工

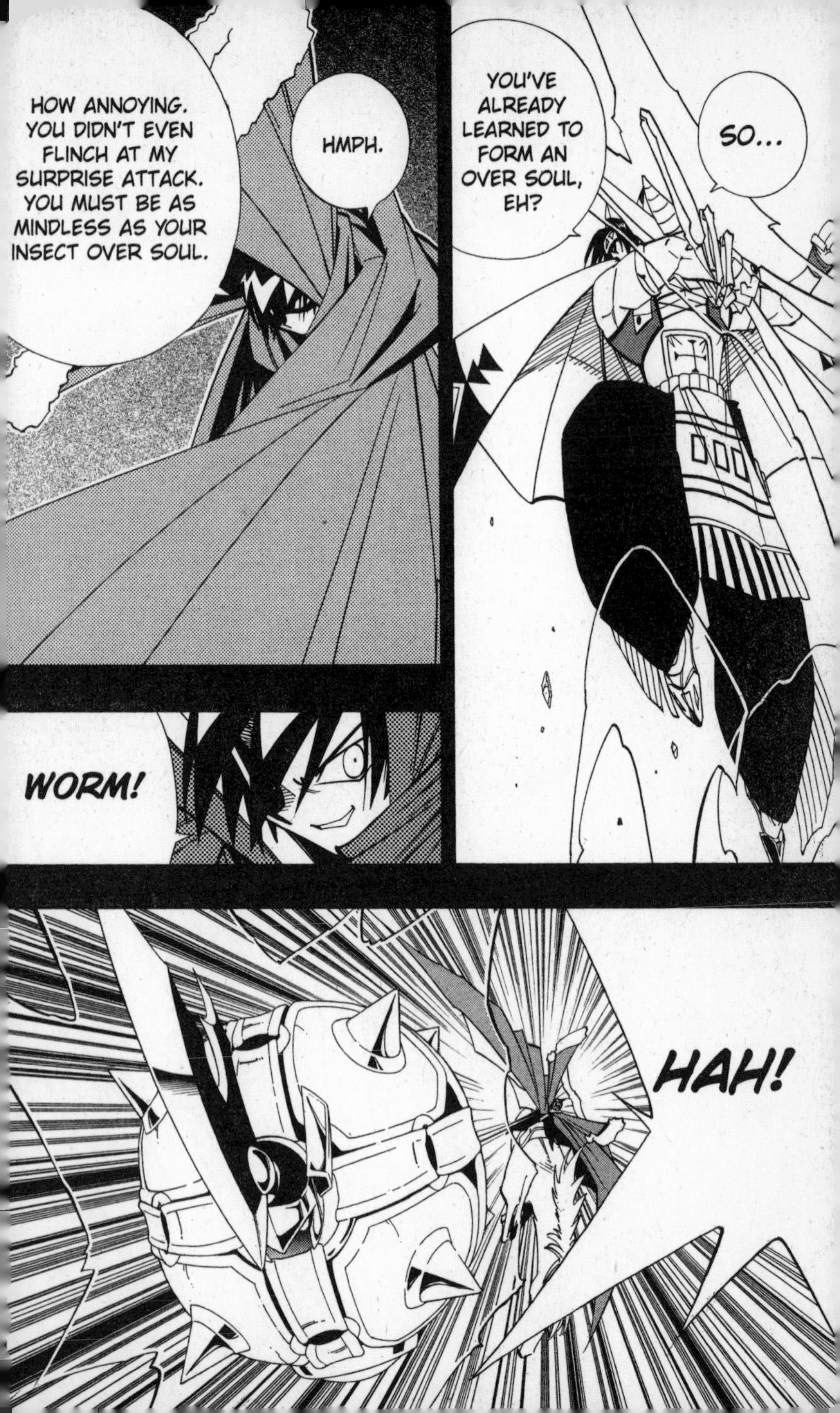
SO...
YOU'VE ALREADY LEARNED TO FORM AN OVER SOUL, EH?
HMPH.
HOW ANNOYING. YOU DIDN'T EVEN FLINCH AT MY SURPRISE ATTACK. YOU MUST BE AS MINDLESS AS YOUR INSECT OVER SOUL.
WORM!
HAH!

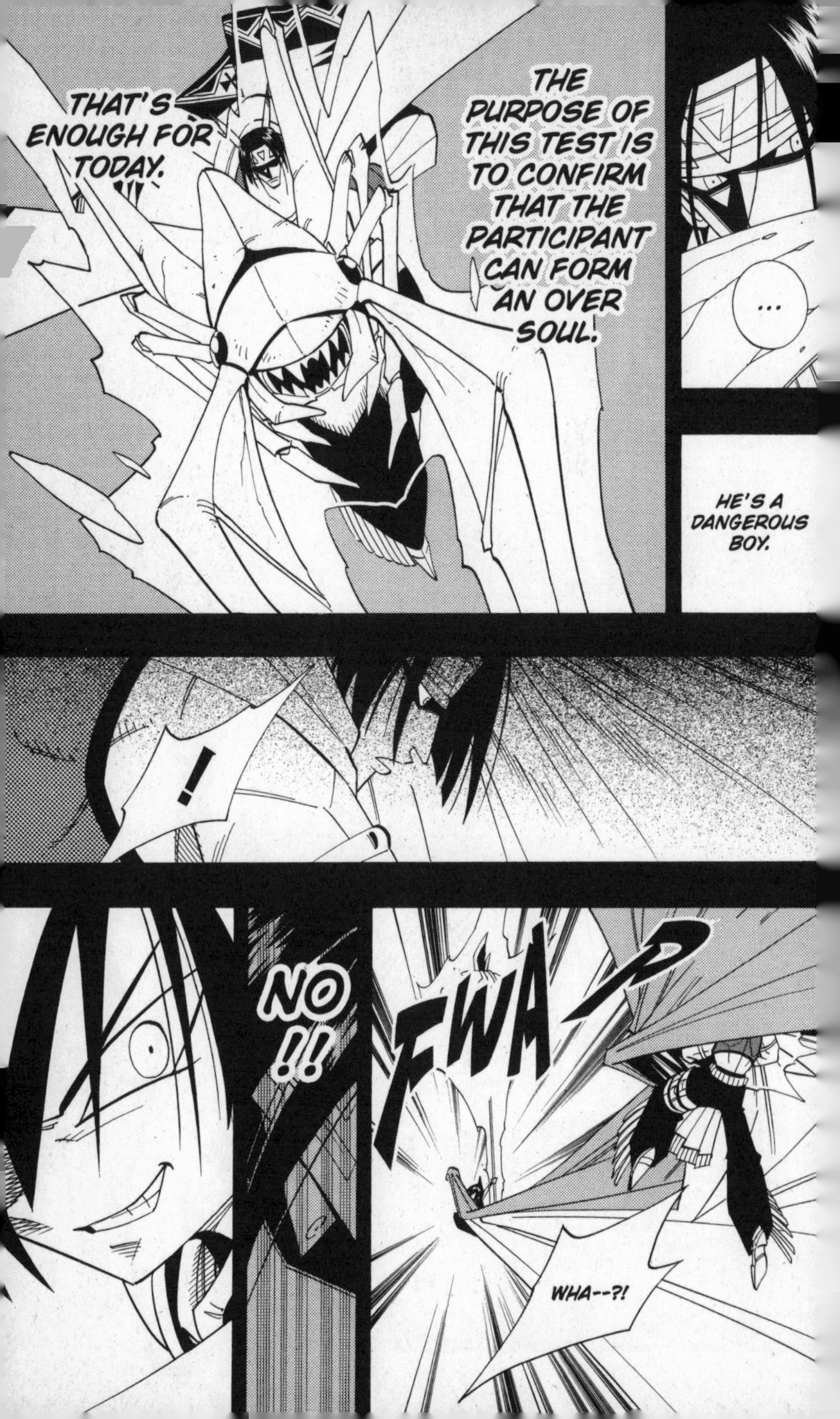
...
HE'S A DANGEROUS BOY.
THE PURPOSE OF THIS TEST IS TO CONFIRM THAT THE PARTICIPANT CAN FORM AN OVER SOUL.
THAT'S ENOUGH FOR TODAY.
!
FWAP
WHA--?!
NO !!

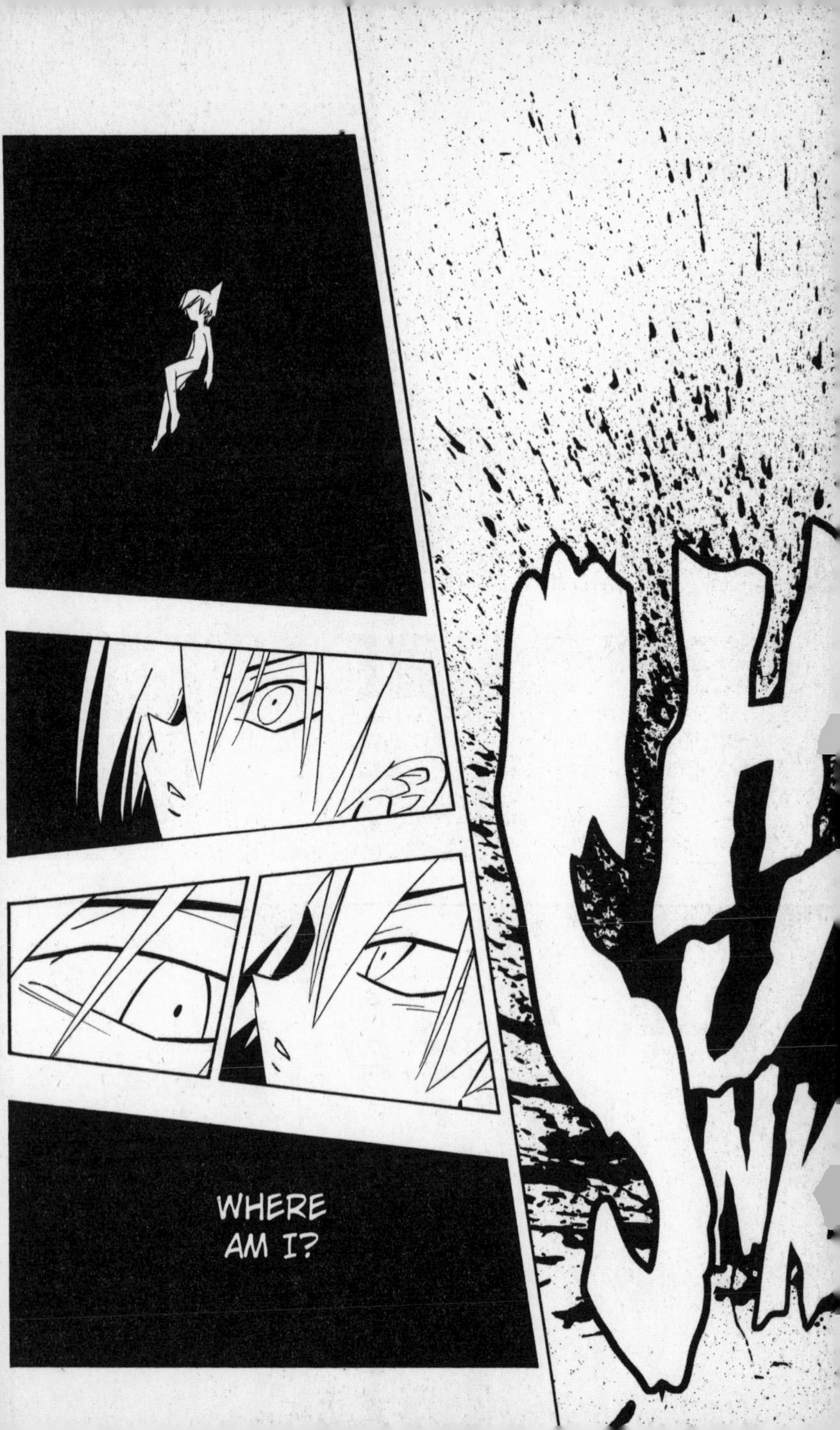
WHERE AM I?

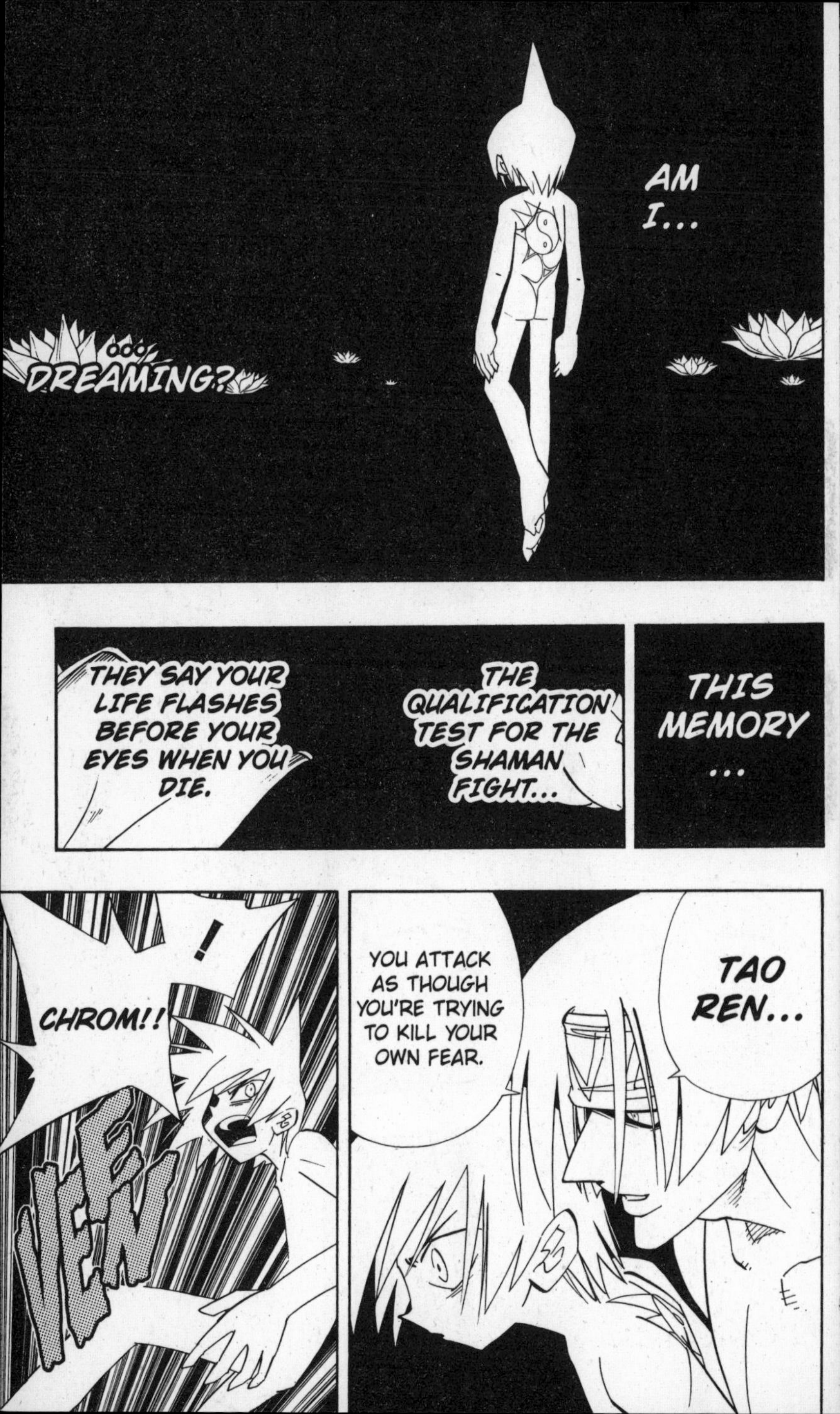
AM I...
...DREAMING?
THIS MEMORY ...
THE QUALIFICATION TEST FOR THE SHAMAN FIGHT...
THEY SAY YOUR LIFE FLASHES BEFORE YOUR EYES WHEN YOU DIE.
TAO REN...
YOU ATTACK AS THOUGH YOU'RE TRYING TO KILL YOUR OWN FEAR.
!
CHROM!!

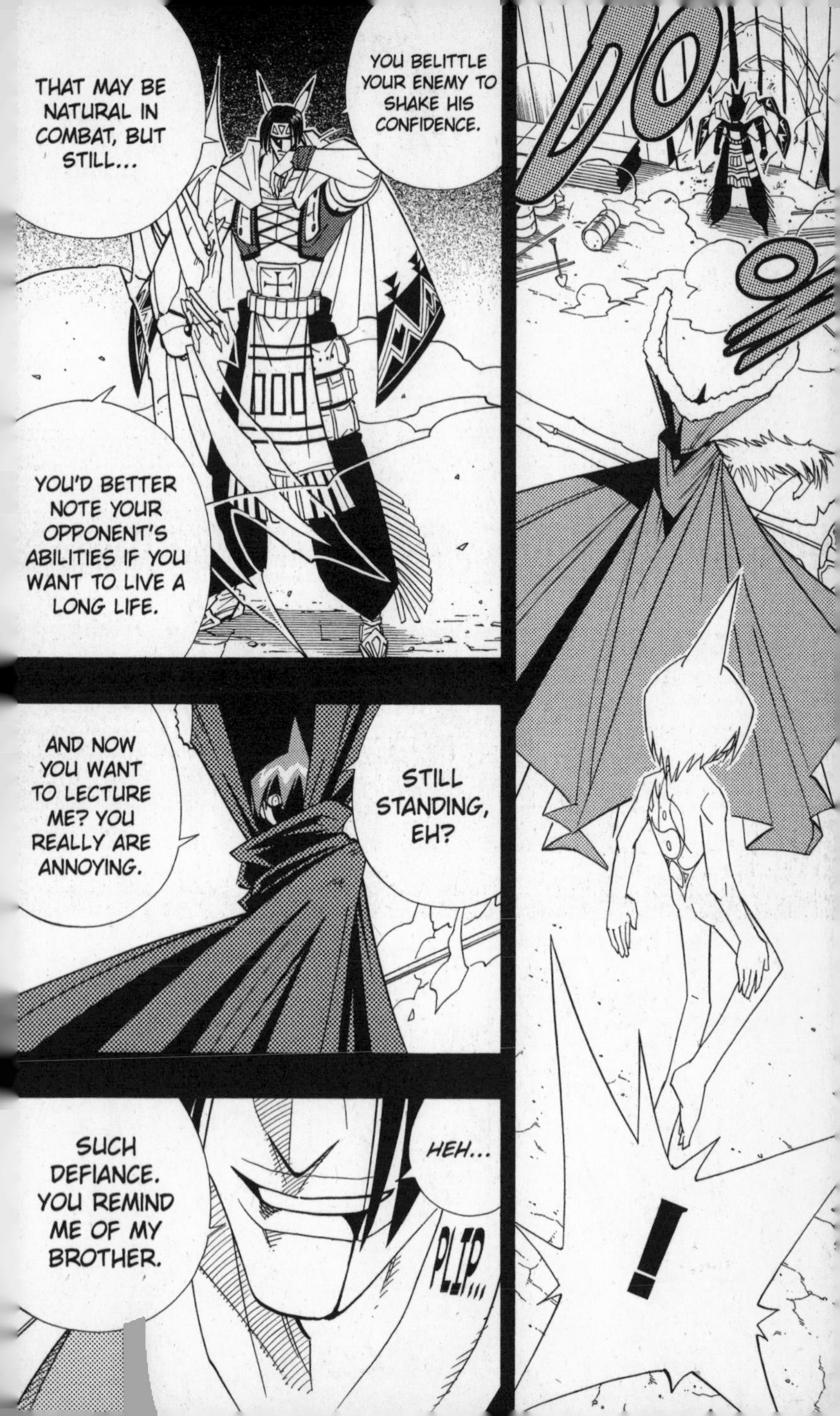
!
YOU BELITTLE YOUR ENEMY TO SHAKE HIS CONFIDENCE.
THAT MAY BE NATURAL IN COMBAT, BUT STILL...
YOU'D BETTER NOTE YOUR OPPONENT'S ABILITIES IF YOU WANT TO LIVE A LONG LIFE.
STILL STANDING, EH?
AND NOW YOU WANT TO LECTURE ME? YOU REALLY ARE ANNOYING.
HEH...
PLIP...
SUCH DEFIANCE. YOU REMIND ME OF MY BROTHER.

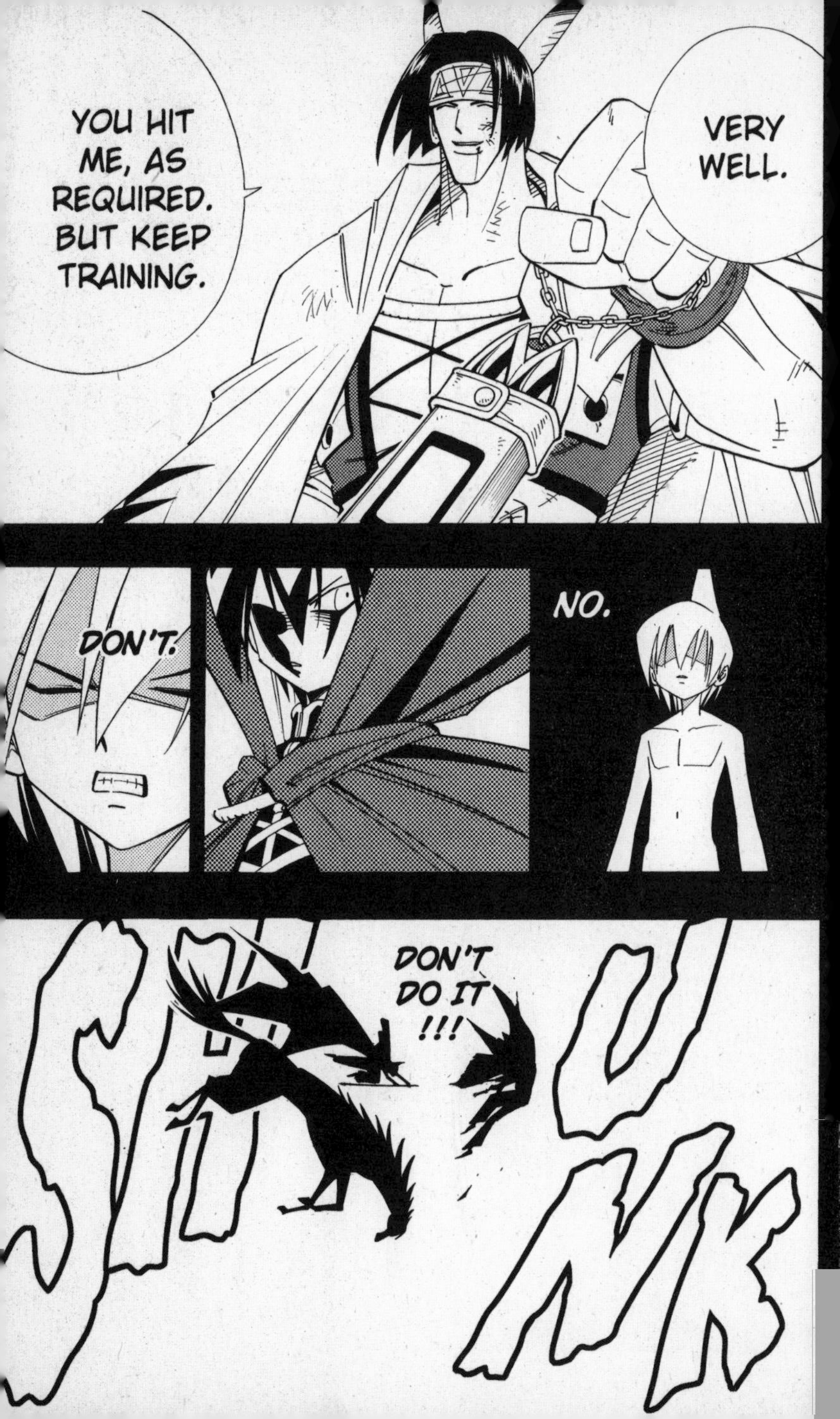
VERY WELL.
YOU HIT ME, AS REQUIRED. BUT KEEP TRAINING.
NO.
DON'T.
DON'T DO IT !!!
SHUNK

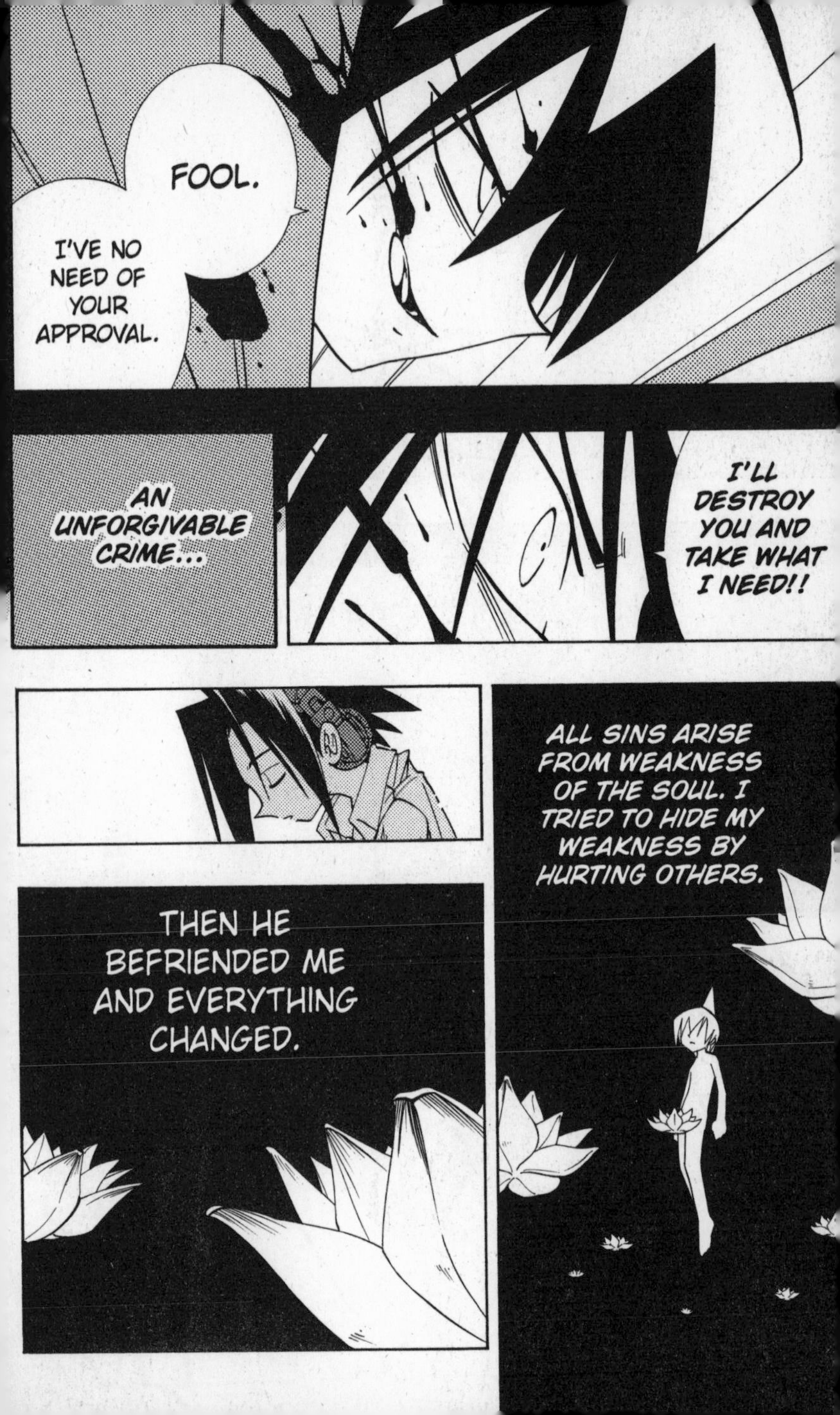
FOOL.
I'VE NO NEED OF YOUR APPROVAL.
I'LL DESTROY YOU AND TAKE WHAT I NEED!!
AN UNFORGIVABLE CRIME...
ALL SINS ARISE FROM WEAKNESS OF THE SOUL. I TRIED TO HIDE MY WEAKNESS BY HURTING OTHERS.
THEN HE BEFRIENDED ME AND EVERYTHING CHANGED.

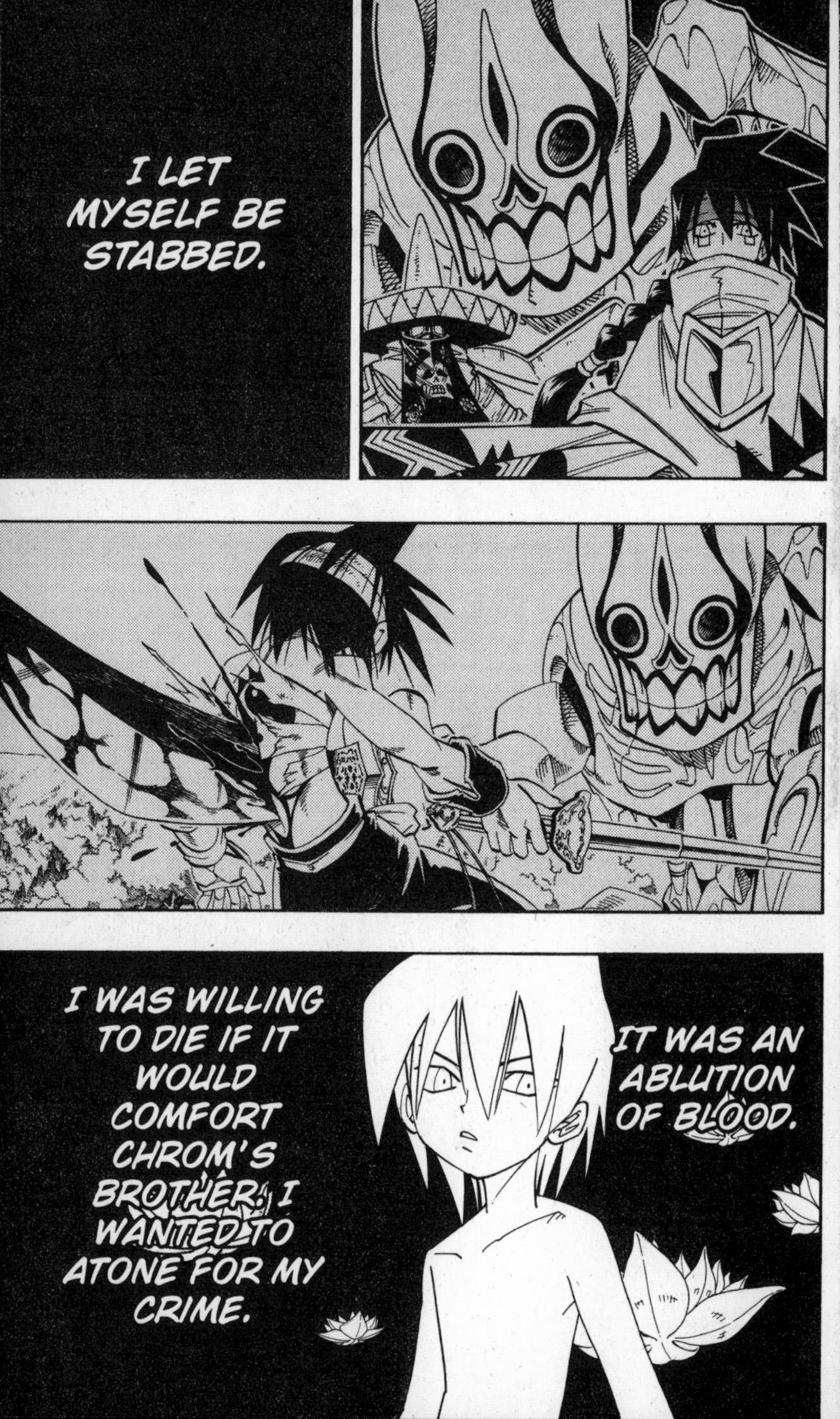
I LET MYSELF BE STABBED.
IT WAS AN ABLUTION OF BLOOD.
I WAS WILLING TO DIE IF IT WOULD COMFORT CHROM'S BROTHER. I WANTED TO ATONE FOR MY CRIME.

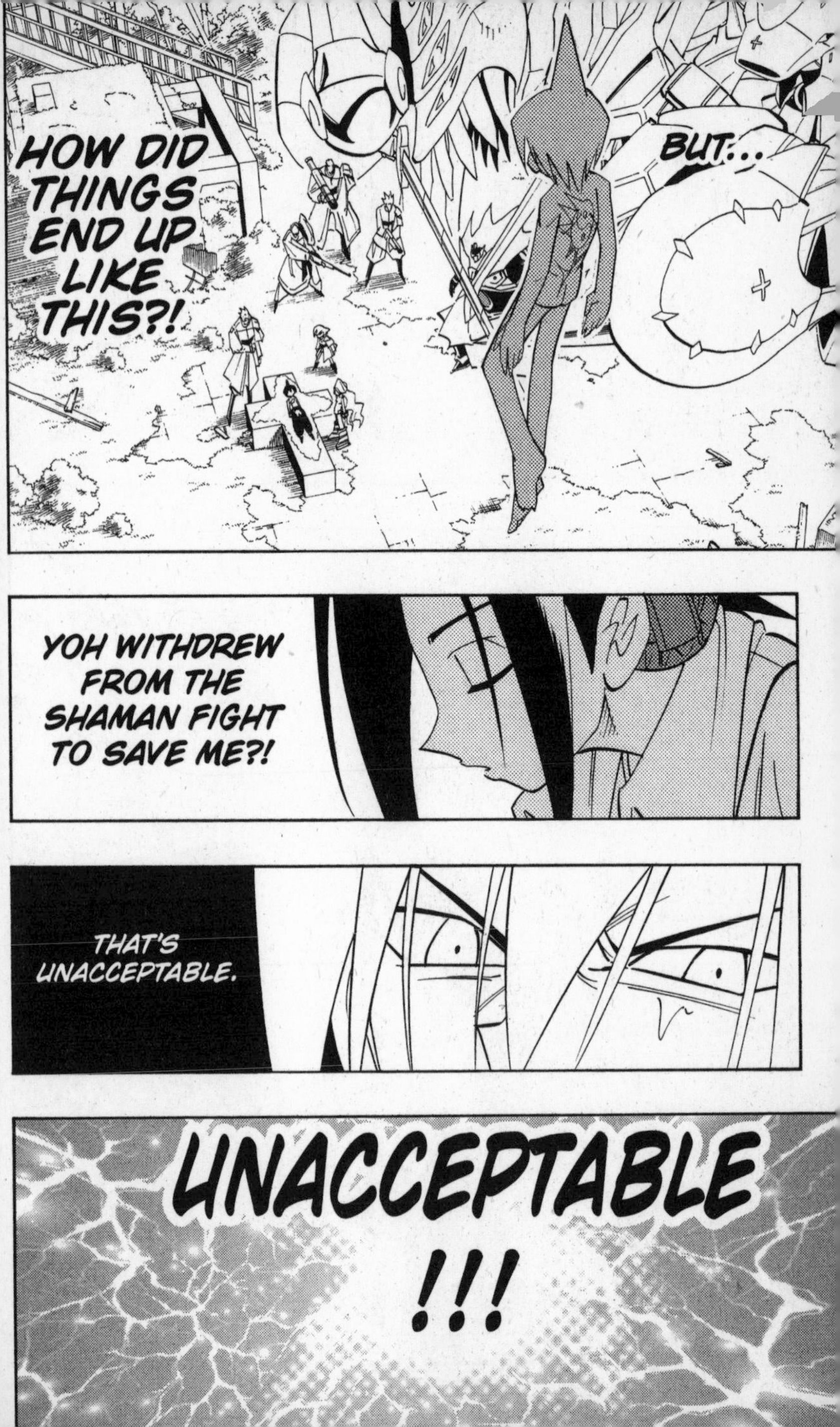
BUT...
HOW DID THINGS END UP LIKE THIS?!
YOH WITHDREW FROM THE SHAMAN FIGHT TO SAVE ME?!
THAT'S UNACCEPTABLE.
UNACCEPTABLE !!!

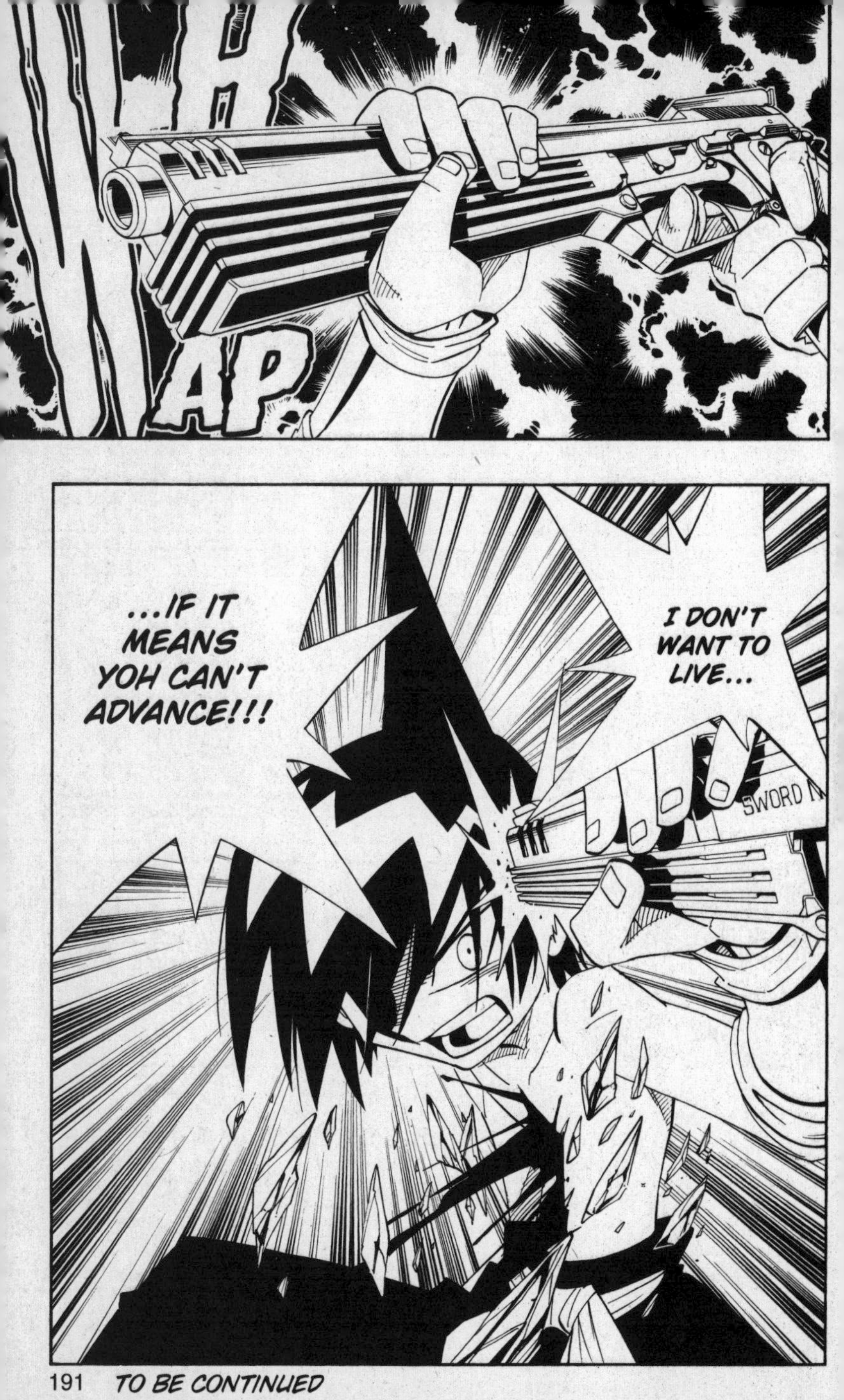
AP
I DON'T WANT TO LIVE...
...IF IT MEANS YOH CAN'T ADVANCE!!!
SWORD

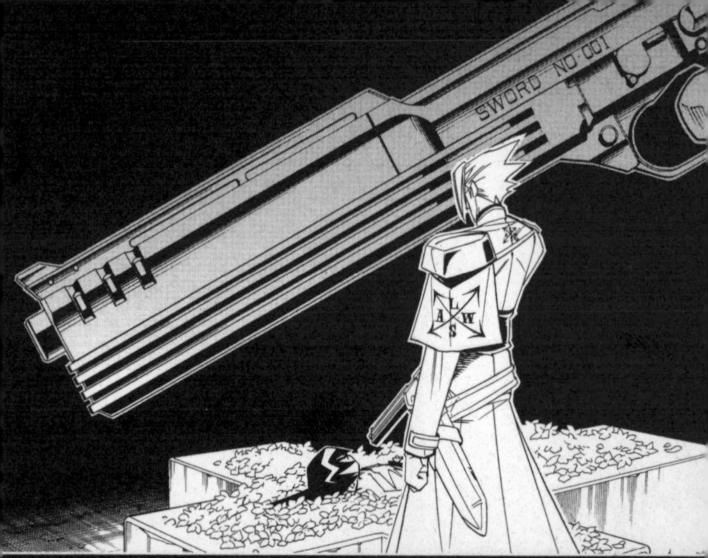
SWORD NO·001

IN THE NEXT VOLUME...

Lady Jeanne prepares to perform the ritual that will revive Ren. But will the rest of the X-LAWS let Ren live once he's revived? Meanwhile, Horohoro stumbles onto a cluster of Hao's thugs who are using their might to overpower the Icemen! Will Horohoro have what it takes to stop them?

AVAILABLE MARCH 2009!